VIRGINIA WOOLF
& THE PROBLEM OF THE SUBJECT

VIRGINIA WOOLF
& THE PROBLEM OF THE SUBJECT

Feminine Writing in the Major Novels

MAKIKO MINOW·PINKNEY

Edinburgh University Press

First published by The Harvester Press Limited
© Makiko Minow-Pinkney, 1987

© Makiko Minow-Pinkney, 2010

Edinburgh University Press Ltd
22 George Square, Edinburgh

www.euppublishing.com

Typeset in Garamond 11/12pt
by Quality Phototypesetting Ltd, Bristol, and
printed and bound in Great Britain by
CPI Antony Rowe, Chippenham and Eastbourne

A CIP record for this book is available from the British Library

ISBN 978 0 7486 4194 9 (paperback)

The right of Makiko Minow-Pinkney
to be identified as author of this work
has been asserted in accordance with
the Copyright, Designs and Patents Act 1988.

For my parents

Contents

Preface

Central to my analysis of Woolf's work are five novels: *Jacob's Room, Mrs. Dalloway, To the Lighthouse, Orlando* and *The Waves*. These are written in pursuit of her modernist project but, as I shall argue below, her modernism was at the same time a feminist subversion of conventions. Woolf's fiction has, surprisingly, been relatively underemphasised in the recent intense revival of interest in her work. Directed towards the centenary in 1982, the revival has at its centre a 'family' industry which includes Quentin Bell's biography, and publication of Woolf's innumerable letters and diaries and of other previously unpublished material. This extensive new access to Woolf's personal life has generated a psychoanalytical criticism that focuses on her actual mental illness rather than the possibility of new readings of her texts—a neglect which this book hopes to remedy. The linkage of psychoanalysis and Woolf is of course not an arbitrary one. The Hogarth Press has been Freud's English publisher since 1921, and we can sense the great impact of Freudian psychoanalysis in Woolf's references to 'our psychoanalytical age' (*CE*, 2:142). In a review called 'Freudian Fiction' she criticised the particular use the novelist J.D. Beresford had made of Freudian theory: 'It simplifies rather than complicates, detracts rather than enriches' (*CW*, 154). I shall seek to heed this caveat in the studies that follow.

The second major impulse behind the recent Woolf revival is contemporary feminism. Feminist assessments of Woolf's aesthetics (Elaine Showalter, Sidney Janet Kaplan) have often been on the whole negative, continuous with the Marxist or *Scrutiny* critiques of the 1930s: Woolf as sheltered, hypersensitive invalid lady, unable to cope with a harsh 'reality'. But a major shift in evaluation has been initiated by American feminists around Jane Marcus, who aims to retrieve the radical political dimension of Woolf's writing.[1] This has been a deeply valuable project, but precisely because these writers are so eager to dispel the old image of ethereal aestheticism, they tend to eschew full-scale dealings with Woolf's formal experimentation in the series of novels from *Jacob's Room* to *The Waves*. What is needed now, however, is to radicalise the reading of these texts and of the aesthetic behind them, and I have sought to bring the resources of contemporary critical theory to bear upon them, stressing those aspects of theory which seem to me most germane and illuminating for each particular novel. Far from being a flight from social commitment into an arcane modernism, Woolf's experimental novels can, I shall argue, best be seen as a feminist subversion of the deepest formal principles—of the very definitions of narrative, writing, the subject—of a patriarchal social order.

I could not have embarked upon the project that this book represents without the generous encouragement, at an earlier stage of my postgraduate career, of Professor Kyoichi Ono. I would like to thank Dr. John Rignall for his valuable supervision and kind support during the long and sometimes troubled years of my research. Takayuki Tatsumi supplied me with helpful materials from America; Gillian Beer and Bernard Bergonzi offered useful suggestions when examining the thesis of which this book is a later form; Dianne Chisholm also offered helpful comments. I owe a longstanding debt to my female friends teaching at various levels in the Japanese education system. Thank you to Tony, for cycling into the gale; and the dedication to this book records my deepest gratitude of all.

Abbreviations

(All works are published by the Hogarth Press.
The date of first publication is given in brackets)

BA *Between the Acts* (1941), London, 1965
CE *Collected Essays*, 4 volumes, edited by Leonard Woolf, London, 1966-7
CW *Contemporary Writers*, edited by Jean Guiguet, London, 1965
H   *Virginia Woolf: The Waves, the Two Holograph Drafts*, transcribed and edited by J. W. Graham, London, 1976
HH *A Haunted House and Other Stories* (1944), London, 1962
JR *Jacob's Room* (1922), London, 1980
L   *The Letters of Virginia Woolf*, 6 volumes, edited by Nigel Nicolson and Joanne Trautmann, London, 1975-80
MB *Moments of Being: Unpublished Autobiographical Writings*, edited by Jeanne Schulkind (1976), London, 1978
MD *Mrs. Dalloway* (1925), London, 1980
O   *Orlando: A Biography* (1928), London, 1978
QB *Virginia Woolf: A Biography*, by Quentin Bell, 2 volumes, London, 1972
RO *A Room of One's Own* (1929), London, 1967
TG *Three Guineas* (1938), London, 1968
TL *To the Lighthouse* (1927), London, 1977
VO *The Voyage Out* (1915), London, 1965
W   *The Waves* (1931), London, 1976
WD *A Writer's Diary*, edited by Leonard Woolf (1953), London, 1969
Y   *The Years* (1937), London, 1965

Acknowledgements

The author and publishers wish to thank the Virginia Woolf's Literary Estate, the Hogarth Press and Harcourt Brace Jovanovich, Inc., who have kindly given permission to reproduce extracts from Virginia Woolf's writings.

CHAPTER 1

Feminism and Modernism in Woolf

Virginia Woolf's essay 'Modern Novels', which under its later title became famous as a manifesto of literary modernism,[1] was not a sudden revolutionary argument with no wider literary context. By the time of its publication in the *Times Literary Supplement* in April 1919, four volumes of Dorothy Richardson's *Pilgrimage* had been published (Woolf reviewed the fourth, *The Tunnel*, in February 1919) and James Joyce's *Ulysses* had appeared in instalments in *The Little Review*. In the same periodical, one year before Woolf's 'Modern Novels', May Sinclair had published a full assessment of Richardson's novels, using, probably for the first time in a literary context, the term 'stream-of-consciousness'; it is known that Woolf made notes from this for her own essay.[2] In *Some Contemporary Novelists (Women)* in 1920, R. Brimley Johnson discussed an emerging trend among female novelists: ' [She] has abandoned the old realism. . . . She is seeking, with passionate determination, for that reality which is behind the material, the things that matter, spiritual things, ultimate Truth. And here she finds man an outsider, wilfully blind, purposely indifferent'.[3] It is not clear if Johnson had read Woolf's 'Modern Novels', but clearly his account of this 'New Realism', which searches for truth behind the veil of masculine materialism and of which Richardson is the foremost practitioner, shows a strong affinity with Woolf's own demand for a new literature. But for Woolf herself at this stage, this new literary vision pertains to a generation; it is not gender-specific. She periodises literary history by the reign of monarchs—spiritual Georgians against materialistic Edwardians—not by the difference between sexes.

The literary transformations around 1920 have been connected

1

by Elaine Showalter to the rise of 'a female aesthetic' which 'reversed the orthodox argument that women have limited experience by defining reality as subjective': 'Novels written by early twentieth-century women were anti-male, both in the sense that they attacked ''male'' technology, law, and politics, and that they belittle masculine morality'.[4] Certainly Dorothy Richardson emphatically defined her aesthetic as feminine in the 1938 foreword to *Pilgrimage*: 'attempting to produce a feminine equivalent of the current masculine realism'.[5] For Richardson, this feminine realism is superior in that it can reach a deeper reality because of the intuitive, pluralistic nature of female consciousness.

It is clear that Woolf's own early declarations of literary identity repress a potential feminist awareness and universalise the issue into the Oedipal polemic of the generations. And it was true, after all, that many male writers (Joyce, Eliot, Strachey, Forster, Lawrence) were committed to literary projects more or less related to female 'New Realism'. Woolf sees a danger across this whole range of modernism which is, however, significantly exacerbated for the woman writer. If one rejects the dessicated objectivism of realist conventions, there looms the trap of the 'egotistical self; which ruins Joyce and Richardson'; 'becoming as in Joyce and Richardson, narrowing and restricting' (*WD*, 23). Together with this 'cramp and confinement of personality' (*CE*, 2:159), the subjectivistic concentration on self tends to produce what Woolf terms 'self-consciousness'—the sudden literary lapse from the concrete enactments of experience to shrill social protest. All outsiders, the oppressed, the marginal, are vulnerable to this vice. American writers, women, working men, negroes or anyone 'who for some other reason is conscious of disability' tends to violate the organic textures of the literary work (2:144). The pressures on women are particularly acute, however, vitiating aspects of the work even of Charlotte Brontë and George Eliot, let alone innumerable lesser women writers. If the male writer suffers self-consciousness as an aspect of the general experience of modernity and its dissolution of tradition, then clearly the woman writer's sense of the injustice of women's position, with its temptations of bitterness, denunciation, resentment, reinforces the danger.

Woolf's second dissatisfaction with the modernist text concerns its fragmentation. In the review of Richardson she applauds her literary technique, which attains 'a sense of reality far greater than that produced by the ordinary means', yet also complains of the lack of 'some unity, significance, or design' which 'we should perceive in the helter-skelter of flying fragments'. She demands that 'the flying helter-skelter resolve itself by degrees into a perceptible whole' (*CW*, 121). From this point of view, the distortions produced by social self-consciousness are just one aspect of the more general chaotic dispersal of the modernist work. By contrast, the two desiderata of impersonality and synthesis/totality constitute what Woolf terms 'poetry', as here defined by her symbolist modernism.

In 1929, when Woolf for the first time fully discusses women and fiction, she hopes that improvements in the economical and educational conditions of women will encourage 'the greater impersonality of women's lives' and result in 'poetry' in women's fiction: 'It will lead them to be less absorbed in facts. . . . They will look beyond the personal and political relationships to the wider questions which the poet tries to solve—of our destiny and the meaning of life' (*CE*, 2:147). In 'The Art of Fiction' she speculates on the possibility of the novel becoming a 'work of art', aspiring beyond its traditionally mimetic relationship—that of 'a parasite'—to life. In 'The Narrow Bridge of Art' (1927) she suggests an 'unnamed variety of the novel' which will be poetry but not written in verse, dramatic and yet not a play (it will be actualised as *The Waves*). She emphasises that it will 'stand further back from life' (*CE*, 2:224-5). Her insistence on abolishing the sociological realism of an Arnold Bennett is consistent with her earlier challenges to Edwardianism, but the concept of 'poetry' marks a further theoretical break. For in the earlier essays Woolf still invoked 'reality', 'trueness to life'. 'Without life nothing else is worthwhile' (2:105): there is no disagreement on this in both camps, and this was indeed the whole point of Brimley Johnson's label, 'New Realism'. Similarly, even while arguing that the kind of characters that are real to her are radically different from those which Bennett finds convincing, Woolf had conceded to him the necessity of characters as vital components of a novel. But she now moves further away from realism, sociological or New, and desires that fiction become poetry, no longer representing but rather presenting or constructing reality. Writing about literary modernism, David Lodge notes 'a general tendency to develop . . . from a metonymic (realistic) to a metaphoric (symbolist or mythopoeic) representation of experience. Virginia Woolf exemplifies this tendency very clearly.'[6] Woolf's manifesto declarations and her actual literary practice from *Jacob's Room* to *The Waves* show her pursuit of a symbolist modernism, which aims to create meaningful pattern by imposing artistic form on the supposed chaos of the phenomenal world. While thus establishing her avant-garde identity, Woolf represses an incipient feminism that had, however, been in evidence in both her earliest novels, *The Voyage Out* and *Night and Day,* in which young heroines break away from conservative Victorianism in search of a new vision. This is also true of the short story 'A Society', which is a prototype of *A Room of One's Own* and *Three Guineas.* In this light, it is interesting that Woolf published her first major feminist essay 'Women and Fiction' and its extended version *A Room of One's Own* in 1929 when her fame was highest after the successive publication of her series of major novels and when she was contemplating a play-poem, *The Waves,* the final embodiment of her symbolist ideal.

A Room of One's Own (and 'Women and Fiction') is a rewriting of 'Modern Fiction', presenting what was once a generational issue in terms of gender difference. Earlier, Woolf expressed the dissatisfaction of younger writers with literary conventions that denature their own vision. Now she explicitly identifies the 'arbiters of that convention' as men:

> as they have established an order of values in life, so too, since fiction is largely based on life, these values prevail there also to a great extent.
> It is probable, however, that both in life and in art the values of a woman are not the values of a man. Thus, when a woman comes to write a novel, she will find that she is perpetually wishing to alter the established values—to make serious what appears insignificant to a man, and trivial what is to him important. (*CE*, 2:145-6)

But 'in the midst of that purely patriarchal society' (*RO,* 112), the critic of the opposite (male) sex sees in this alteration of the current scale of values 'not merely a difference of view, but a view that is weak, or trivial, or sentimental, because it differs from his own' (*CE,* 2:146). A further difficulty for women is the inadequacy of the language of novelistic texture as well as narrative structure. Woolf advocates that the woman writer alter the current 'man's sentence', which is 'unsuited for a woman's use' (*RO,* 115), 'until

4

she writes one that takes the natural shape of her thought without crushing or distorting it' (*CE*, 2:145). At the level of macro-structure, women need to reshape a literary form which 'has been made by men out of their own needs for their uses' and to provide 'some new vehicle' (*RO*, 116).

Yet even in her earlier writings Woolf begins to attribute the 'Georgian' literary revolt to the difference of the specifically female writer. Already in 1918 she noted in a review of Johnson's *The Women Novelists* that from the difference of view between man and woman 'spring not only marked differences of plot and incident, but infinite differences in selection, method and style' (*CW*, 27). Reviewing *The Tunnel*, she points to Richardson's 'genuine conviction of the discrepancy between what she has to say and the form provided by tradition for her to say it in' (*CW*, 120). Richardson herself had argued that the discrepancy derives from sexual difference: 'a woman is at a disadvantage—because they speak different languages. . . . she must . . . stammeringly, speak his'.[7] Woolf also points to this discrepancy, quoting Miriam Henderson's objection to writing a book with 'mannish cleverness', 'like a man' (*CW*, 120). 'The spasmodic, the obscure, the fragmentary' attempt of the modernists to break down the 'sleek, smooth novels' and 'portentous and ridiculous biographies' of the older generation is based on 'the difference of view, the difference of standard' as a woman (*CE*, 1:336, 204). The modernist revolt attempts to rupture both the oppressive ideology of sameness of Victorian patriarchy and the superficiality of the Edwardians who failed to question it. This revolt represents the assertion of a radical alternative to what contemporary feminists regard as a phallocentric society and culture. For women this conflict with oppressive conventions is naturally the crucial issue for their own sex, though the conflict was actually shared by both men and women. For Woolf, the feminist and modernist aesthetics converge, at least initially, in this attempt to challenge phallocentricism.

But around 1920 Woolf predominantly urges only the modernist case, as if she represses the feminist version, 'resist[ing] the temptation to anger' (*CE*, 2:144) for, as she repeatedly contends, sexual self-consciousness and bitterness denature one's writing. Not that she was by any means free of anger. Arnold Bennett's *Our Women* (1920) and its attendant publicity led her to consider 'making up a paper upon Women, as a counterblast to Mr Bennett's adverse views' (*WD*, 28-9). This paper has not survived, if it was ever begun, but her indignation was finally discharged through correspondence with a columnist in the *New Statesman* (Desmond MacCarthy) who endorsed Bennett's argument that 'intellectually and creatively man is the superior of woman', and that 'no amount of education and liberty of action will sensibly alter' that fact. In her letters Woolf refutes this essentialist argument and protests that women's lack of artistic and intellectual achievement is culturally determined, the result of 'some external restraint upon their powers'. This contention foreshadows the arguments in *A Room of One's Own*. Genius is not a singular, solitary birth; it requires a long tradition and favourable external conditions (education, freedom of action). In her version of T.S. Eliot's 'Tradition and the Individual Talent', 'you will not get a big Newton until you have produced a considerable number of lesser Newtons'. She demands that women 'should differ from men without fear and express their difference openly',[8] but the Bennetts and MacCarthys impede this possibility. Bennett's anti-feminism may thus have given a sharper edge to Woolf's hostility to his literary values.

Woolf expressed difference openly, however, only as that of a new generation. The temptation to anger, the pressure of fear, were still too great. Her own literary position was still too insecure for her to assert woman's difference and be treated seriously in literary debate. Even when, in 1929, she can to a certain extent express her feminist protest openly, she adopts a strategy of humour and satire, defending herself with 'fiction' and 'lies' rather than 'facts' and 'truth' (*RO*, 7). Facts are completely ruled by men, there are none left for women; Shakespeare's sister can only be retrieved in fiction, for she is a completely 'lost' existence in history. Galsworthy, already a victim in 'Modern Fiction', is taken up in *A Room of One's Own* and his works criticised for their pure maleness: 'It is not only that they celebrate male virtues, enforce male values and describe the world of men; it is that the emotion with which these books are permeated is to a woman incomprehensible' (*RO*, 153).

With her earliest literary adversaries now redefined as masculinist, Woolf also distances herself from her former allies, who are now seen as representatives of the dominant male culture. In 'The Leaning Tower' (1940) she describes the writers whose best books were written between 1910 and 1925 as tower-dwellers. The 'representative names' include Forster, Strachey, Eliot, Huxley. All these writers (D.H. Lawrence is the major exception) have been raised 'above the mass of people', they stand 'upon a tower raised above the rest of us' and founded on their middle-class birth and expensive education at the public schools and ancient universities (*CE*, 2:168-9). This is also true, she points out, of the groups which wrote between 1925 and 1939, but the tower of this last generation is precarious, about to topple. If Woolf situates herself in 'the mass of people', 'the rest of us', she clearly views the fact of her middle-class birth as a less radical determinant than exclusion from the (male) educational process. Dissociating herself from previous allies, she writes: 'are we not commoners, outsiders?' Alluding to a resonant image from *A Room of One's Own,* where the heroine upsets a Beadle by trespassing on the turf of an Oxbridge college, she recommends trespass, transgression: 'Let us trespass at once. Literature is no one's private ground . . . . Let us trespass freely and fearlessly and find our own way for ourselves' (2:181). She looks forward to the next, post-war generation when all towers will have disappeared, affording the possibility of a literature of outsiders, commoners.

It is perhaps more than mere accident that in her initial contention with Bennett, Woolf symbolised 'the spirit we live by, life itself'—the vision the novelist must capture—as 'Mrs Brown', an insignificant elderly woman. The voice of this woman, 'protesting that she was different', has been silenced or ignored in the novels of Bennett, Galsworthy and Wells: 'They have looked . . . at factories, at Utopias, even at the decoration and upholstery of the carriage; but never at her'. Discussing a passage from Bennett's *Hilda Lessways,* Woolf complains: 'we cannot hear her mother's voice, or Hilda's voice' (*CE*, 1:330). To make the woman's voice heard, one might be led 'to destroy the very foundation and rules of literary society . . . . Grammar is violated; syntax disintegrated' (334). In *A Room of One's Own* she contends that 'for the whole of that extremely complex force of femininity' to be expressed, 'the resources of the English language would be much put to the stretch, and whole flights of words would need to wing their way illegitimately into existence' (*RO*, 131). Having declared that 'the Edwardian tools are the wrong ones for us to use', her own untiring fictional experiments are a pursuit of the woman's voice, altering current novelistic structure and texture 'until she writes [a sentence] that takes the natural shape of her thought without crushing or distorting it' (*CE*, 1:332, 2:145). This, she writes in 1920, is 'a task that must be accomplished before there is freedom or achievement', referring to the frustration of Bathsheba in *Far from the Madding Crowd*, who says that she has 'the feelings of a woman' but only 'the language of men'.[9]

For Woolf, then, aesthetic innovation and feminist conviction are deeply interlinked, and her notion of *androgyny* mediates between the two. Inasmuch as Woolf's feminism is underemphasised, though still latently present, in her early modernist manifestos, her concept of androgyny can be seen as an attempt to theorise after the fact vital new insights to which she had already broken through in literary practice. In discussing Dorothy Richardson's *Revolving Lights*, Woolf applauds its sentence as 'the psychological sentence of the feminine gender', and her description could be applied to her own writing: 'of a more elastic fibre than the old, capable of stretching to the extreme, of suspending the frailest particles, of enveloping the vaguest shapes'. 'It is a woman's sentence, but only in the sense that it is used to describe a woman's mind by a writer who is neither proud nor afraid of anything that she may discover in the psychology of her sex' (*CW*, 124-5). However, while she advocates a specifically feminine sentence, Woolf elsewhere warns that 'it is fatal for anyone who writes to think of their sex. It is fatal to be a man or woman pure and simple'. She therefore defines the ideal state of the creative mind as 'androgynous': 'one must be woman-manly or man-womanly' (*RO*, 156-7). The logic which holds together these two seemingly contradictory arguments—a writer must be androgynous, sexually unconscious: a woman writer must find or forge the woman's sentence—is the principle of *difference* as opposed to the logic of identity. The forgetting of one's sex does not erase difference, for 'that curious sexual quality . . . comes only when sex is unconscious of itself' (*RO*, 140). And after all the concept of androgyny is possible only on the basis of the existence of two distinct genders. Against an Enlightenment universalism which defines humanity as disembodied Reason and reduces sexual difference to a merely phenomenal form, Woolf argues: 'if two sexes are quite inadequate, considering the vastness and variety of the world, how should we manage with one only? Ought not education to bring out and fortify the differences rather than the similarities? For we have too much likeness as it is' (*RO*, 132). Androgyny is the rejection of sameness. It aims to cultivate difference on an individual level, in the teeth of a cultural impulse to reduce the two sexes into something which is seemingly neither, but in actuality male.

Yet as Stephen Heath notes in *The Sexual Fix*, this argument is a double-edged weapon. Optimally, 'it can function . . . as the beginning of an alternative representation, as an insistence against the one position, the fixed sexual order, man and woman', but on the other hand, 'it can return constantly as a confirmation of that fixity, a strategy in which differences . . . are neutralised into the given system of identity, the two halves—masculine and feminine—adding up to the same old *one*'. Bisexuality can thus become an ideological trap, as happens, according to Heath, in the cases of Freud and D.H. Lawrence. For them, 'the basis of that polarity [man/woman] . . . is the man, the phallus, the phallic organisation of the sexual'. So bisexuality, as plurality opened up in the individual, is in fact 'reduced in the very beginning . . . to the system of the one-phallic-identity'.[10]

'It is fatal to be a man or woman pure and simple'. This is no mere figure of speech, since writing founded on such monolithic positions 'is doomed to death', 'it ceases to be fertilised' (*RO*, 157). Meaning, it is here implied, can be produced only in the play of difference. Julia Kristeva makes a similar point when she writes of 'sexual difference, not as a fixed opposition (''man''/''woman''), but as a process of differentiation' to which 'the truly great ''literary'' achievements bear witness'. She continues: 'All speaking subjects have within themselves a certain bisexuality which is precisely the possibility to explore all the sources of signification, that which posits a meaning as well as that which multiplies, pulverises, and finally revives it'.[11] Woolf does, to be sure, refer to 'the unity of the mind', 'a natural fusion'. But this is not a single unitary state but rather a 'wholeness' composed of heterogeneity. For the mind 'seems to have no single state of being . . . . It can think back through its fathers or through its mothers' (*RO*, 146-7). The homogeneous unity of the mind is, to Woolf, only a fiction maintainable by 'repression'. Mary Jacobus rightly interprets Woolf's androgyny as 'a simultaneous enactment of desire and repression by which the split is closed with an essentially utopian vision of undivided consciousness. The repressive male/female opposition which ''interferes with the unity of the mind'' gives way to a mind paradoxically conceived of not as one, but as heterogeneous, open to the play of difference'.[12] The rejection of homogeneity and the realisation of this paradoxically heterogeneous harmony is Woolf's aim in elaborating the utopian concept of androgyny. It is not, at any rate, a Hegelian *Aufhebung* of opposed terms.

The assertion of the specificity of the feminine in language becomes important in this context of the defence of difference against the existing order of a discourse of sameness organised around a single standard, the man or, in psychoanalytic terms, the phallus. In the male text Woolf finds the 'straight dark bar . . . ''I'' ' casting a domineering phallic shadow across the page and obliterating all else' (*RO*, 150). Hence Woolf explains the 'I' of her own discourse in *A Room of One's Own* as 'only a convenient term for somebody who has no real being', and 'Mary' or many 'Marys' (8). It is in this sense that Woolf can, without self-contradiction, urge the need for a specifically feminine sentence at the same time as she advocates an ideal of androgyny for the writer's mind. Woman is privileged—or rather forced—to attain an androgynous position and to reveal the fictionality of the dominant male ideology of the same by deconstructing masculine discourse. For woman is situated at once outside and inside the dominant order. In spite of her difference she too is necessarily submitted to phallocentricity in order to gain access to what Lacan calls the symbolic, to language and culture. The woman's mind 'can think back through its fathers or through its mothers'. She 'is often surprised by a sudden splitting off of consciousness . . . when from being the natural inheritor of that civilisation, she becomes, on the contrary, outside of it, alien and critical. Clearly the mind is always altering its focus, and bringing the world into different perspectives' (*RO*, 146). Woman is androgynous because of this internal 'split' in her consciousness. Woolf's position is close to that of the French feminist theorist Hélène Cixous, who also defines woman's position as 'neither outside nor in' and privileged for its 'bisexuality'. 'Now it happens that, at present, for historico-cultural reasons, it is women who are opening up to and benefitting from this vatic bisexuality which doesn't annul differences but stirs them up, pursues them, increases their number. In a certain way, "woman is bisexual": man . . . being poised to keep glorious phallic monosexuality in view'.[13]

What, then, is the difference between men and women? In particular, what is a feminine writing? Stephen Heath points out the dangers of the argument in favour of 'difference', which can with alarming ease merge into familiar reactionary positions:

> a tourniquet operates, in which the real necessity to claim difference binds back, and precisely from the difference claimed, into the renewal of the same, a reflection of the place assigned, assigned as difference. Patriarchy, men in its order, has never said anything but that women are—the woman is—different: they are *not men*, the difference maintained supports the status quo, the difference derived, derived ideologically, from nature, the appeal to the biological, 'undeniable'.

It is therefore crucial to break away from any such essentialist definition of difference, which 'is always itself a form of social representation, within a particular structure of assumption and argument'.[14] Woolf takes scrupulous care not to fall into essentialism. At the beginning of *A Room of One's Own* she wards off the problem: 'I have shirked the duty of coming to a conclusion upon [the question of] the true nature of women' (*RO*, 6). Elsewhere she argues: 'But what is "herself"? . . . what is a woman? I assure you, I don't know; I do not believe that you know; I do not believe that anybody can know until she has expressed herself in all the arts and professions open to human skill'. Woman is a project, not a given; femininity is a representation and cultural construction, not an eternal essence. Women are so radically various—their 'rooms differ so completely' (*RO*, 131)—that all Woolf can say she has discovered is that 'a woman . . . is not a man'.[15] Discussing Brimley Johnson's book *The Women Novelists*, she agrees with him that 'a woman's writing is always feminine' and continues: 'the only difficulty lies in defining what we mean by feminine. He shows his wisdom not only by advancing a great many suggestions, but also by accepting the fact . . . that women are apt to differ'. The attempt at definition makes a circular argument around the term 'difference', since it cannot make any reference outside it; feminine difference is defined only by the tautology of 'difference'. 'The essential difference' between novels by men and women 'lies in the fact that each sex describes itself' rather than in 'the obvious and enormous difference of experience'

11

(*CW*, 26). Here again the difference does not get referred back to experience outside representation, but rather depends, in circular fashion, on the very representation of difference itself. The crucial task is to free the feminine from the essentialist 'difference', which is itself the construction of a representation within a particular ideology, and to understand it as a problem produced in representation.

In the light of this, Elaine Showalter's well-known critique of Woolfian androgyny may be reconsidered. In *A Literature of Their Own* Showalter argues that Woolf's androgyny 'represents an escape from the confrontation with femaleness or maleness', and that her famous definition of life as a luminous halo or semi-transparent envelope is 'another metaphor of uterine withdrawal and containment'. The false transcendence of 'sexual identity' or, in Showalter's phrase, 'the flight into androgyny' entails 'evasions of reality' and of 'the female experience', and results in Woolf's 'progressive technical inability to accommodate the facts and crises of day-to-day experience, even when she wanted to do so'.[16] Showalter's stress on 'confrontation', 'sexual identity', 'experience', posits a unified subject which is the sole agent of its own development set over against the environment. But if, as structuralism has argued, the human subject is born into a pre-existing network of sign-systems and constituted in and by them, then 'identity', either social or sexual, cannot be taken as a self-evident starting point. There is no simple confrontation of human subject and world. Nor are we justified in a naïve belief in authentic experience, which is always already implicated in the surrounding structures. Experience never comes into being without representation, as Woolf was well aware in *A Room of One's Own* where she appeals to the order of fiction rather than facts, lies rather than truth, in her attempt to construct a female perspective. Showalter's term 'confrontation' (in this case of woman and man, woman and a patriarchal society) offers as indubitable starting-point a subject-object polarity that is, in fact, already reified and abstract. The feminist text must call into question the very identities which support this pattern of binary opposition. The concept of androgyny then becomes radical, opening up the fixed unity into a multiplicity, joy, play of heterogeneity, a fertile difference.

In her account of subjectivity and self, Showalter is very near to Lukács' famous denunciations of modernism, as is indicated by her reference to his formulations in her critique of Woolf. In *The Meaning of Comtemporary Realism* Lukács notoriously attacks modernist literature, defining it as an 'attenuation of reality and dissolution of personality': 'Man is reduced to a sequence of unrelated experiential fragments'.[17] He sees this 'modernist schizophrenia' as leading to passive impotence in the face of capitalist industrialisation, and for Showalter, analogously, Woolf's description of 'consciousness as passive receptivity' is, in one sense, 'an extension of her view of women's female social role: receptivity to the point of self-destruction'.[18] The human being is deprived of active subjectivity in dialectical relationship with world history. Though Lukács does not specifically mention Woolf, her work might well be one of the targets of his attack, where it might figure as an instance of the dissolution of the self into which modernism is presumed to have collapsed.

The psychoanalysis of Jacques Lacan, influenced as it has been by structuralism, offers a radically new view of the problem of subjectivity and questions the Lukácsian notion of the autonomous self confronting the outer world. For Lacan there is no natural, unitary subject, no *Cogito*. His notion of the 'mirror-stage' maintains that the baby, lacking the ability to coordinate movements of the body and thus experiencing fragmentation, comes to discover unity by a mirror-like identification with the image of another. Only by this misrecognition of itself as a whole in identification with the image of the other can the child constitute the self. This one-to-one identification, which subordinates the child to its image, to its mother, to others, is alienating, and this fundamental gap opened between the subject and its own self—in which, indeed, the infant discovers his self—can never be bridged. Questioning the integrity of the 'I', Lacan reveals that the fragmentation which Lukács interprets as the pathology of modernism is a universal fact of the human subject. Misrecognition *(méconnaissance)* constitutes the ego; autonomy is illusion, fiction. 'It is in the other that the subject first lives and registers himself'.[19]

If the assumption of the autonomous subject and fixed identity has been problematised by structuralism and psychoanalysis, then 'reality', the very ground of Lukács' realist aesthetics, has also been put into question. The work of semioticians like Roland Barthes maintains that the 'reality' to which realism appeals is an ideological construction, as Woolf had herself argued in 'Mr.

13

Bennett and Mrs. Brown': 'If you say to the public with sufficient conviction: ''All women have tails, and all men humps'', it will actually learn to see women with tails and men with humps' (*CE*, 1:332). The formal characteristics of the realist novel —narrativity, plot, character—are also radically put into question, in both semiotic theory and modernist literary practice. Woolf 'insubstantises' reality 'wilfully' and dismisses the criticism that she cannot create characters: 'It's only the old argument that character is dissipated into shreds now; the old post-Dostoievsky argument' (*WD*, 57).

Gillian Beer has pointed out the neglect of Woolf's 'narrative politics' in Elaine Showalter's critique. Against Showalter's impatient claim that Woolf withdraws from the facts and crises of everyday experience, Beer argues: 'If Virginia Woolf moves away from facts and crises it is because she denies the claim of such ordering to be all-inclusive'.[20] Within the arena of feminist criticism, a polemic analogous to the realism-modernism debate in Marxism (Lukács versus Brecht) is thus fought out. Either one demands that the novel possess a new realist *content,* so that a new consciousness and a will to transformation may arise; or one rejects the very form of realism as simply an impediment. I want to argue that the two trends—feminist aesthetic and modernist aesthetic—are, at least in Woolf's case, the two faces of a single project. Since for her modernism and feminism constitute a single awareness and concern, her declaration of an urgent need for new fictional modes is a protest against Lacan's symbolic order. According to Lacan, this order of discursive and symbolic action operates with the phallus as the privileged signifier. It fixes difference along the axis of having or not having the phallus, and thereby refers to a condition outside which makes significance possible. This symbolic order, to which the human being has to submit in order to become a speaking subject, is acquired as the child abandons the diadic, Imaginary mother-child relationship through the acceptance of a third term, the Name-of-the-Father. This is accomplished through the resolution of the castration complex, in which the child confronts the existence of the phallus and the possibility of losing it, and accepts the father's 'no' to its desire for the mother's body.[21] Since the symbolic order is constructed on the privileging of the phallus, any alternative form or language will have to be non-phallocentric.

The convergence between modernism and feminism can be expressed in Lacanian terms. Modernism may be seen as an attempt to reintroduce the repressed Imaginary into a symbolic order identified with an oppressive Victorianism by modern writers. The Imaginary is the realm of the immediate dual relationship of child and mother in the pre-Oedipal phase; it precedes the emergence of the distinct self. But the child must break from its fusion with the maternal body through the Name-of-the-Father into a mediate relationship, i.e., the symbolic. In this theoretical scheme the revolt of the Imaginary is an attempt to retrieve the maternal. Such a model has been outlined by Hélène Cixous, who criticises the privileged place accorded the phallus in Lacanian accounts of language and sexual difference, as well as his valorisation of the symbolic. She defends a mode of writing that inscribes the feminine: 'Writing in the feminine is passing on what is cut out by the Symbolic, the voice of the mother, passing on what is most archaic. The most archaic force that touches a body is one that enters by the ear and reaches the most intimate point'.[22] In *Virginia Woolf and the Androgynous Vision* Nancy Topping Bazin explains Woolf's concept of reality in terms of a 'manic-depressive' psychology. Partly because Woolf associates mania with her mother and depression with her father, Bazin argues that the terms manic/depressive merge into the opposition between feminine and masculine. Woolf's aim is to achieve a balance between these two forces, symbolised as the 'androgynous mind'. But Bazin's paradigm of depressive/father and manic/mother should be seen as a universal problem for a human subject which is produced in the confrontation of the Imaginary with the symbolic, rather than as Woolf's personal family tragedy, and should thus be considered in the wider context of modernism and feminism. Similarly, the relation between these two terms should not be seen as confined to female writers in general for, as Stephen Heath has suggested, 'modern writing has been precisely bound up with the question of female language, feminine discourse'. For in modernist writing, with its dislocations of syntax, its displacement of positions, the question of feminine discourse emerges 'as a challenge to the fixity of identity, as a challenge to the "male" and "female" which are the very terms—the places—of that identity, as a challenge to the very principle of sexual identity, the whole fix of "sexuality"'.[23]

If 'feminine' writing is an attempt to inscribe positions against or alternative to those of the dominant male order, then the possibility of such writing does not exclusively correspond to biological gender. From the feminist perspective, however, it cannot perhaps be finally separated from a specifically feminine content, from its inscription by a biological woman. Male writers may have used a sentence similar to Dorothy Richardson's, 'but there is a difference', Woolf argues: 'Miss Richardson has fashioned her sentence consciously' in order to 'descend to the depths and investigate the crannies of Miriam Henderson's consciousness' (*CW*, 124). In any attempt to adumbrate the qualities of a feminine discourse one tends, perhaps inescapably, to appeal to an analogy with women's physical characteristics, bodily experiences, sexual behaviour or even with conventional images of 'femaleness' offered by the existing order. Woolf talks about a need for the book 'to be adapted to the body' (*RO*, 117), and employs terms like 'elastic', 'frailest', 'enveloping' in her description of Richardson's 'sentence of the feminine gender' (*CW*, 124). May Sinclair notes interminability as a characteristic of Richardson's sentence; Gillian Beer remarks Woolf's deliberate 'avoidance of narrative climax', 'arousal without climax' in *The Waves;* the French feminist theorists who have done most to develop the concept of feminine writing also refer to its 'liquid flow', 'endlessness' or a writing 'in white ink [milk]'.[24] Yet there is once again a danger that this writing will end up merely reproducing the 'embedded assumptions about male and female characters', for Gillian Beer shrewdly notes that Arnold Bennett's description of George Eliot's writing as 'feminine'—'in its lack of restraint, its wordiness, and the utter absence of feeling for form that characterises it'—coincides precisely with recent feminist declarations, except that the value judgements are reversed.[25] Yet the valorisation of the 'feminine' remains meaningful precisely as a strategy of reversal, as a challenge to conventional norms of writing.

Recent French writers seek to address the problem of feminine discourse at a deeper, more structural level than that feminine language which feminists have always attacked as the very locus of sexism on the socio-linguistic level. Working in the ambit of post-structuralism and neo-Freudian psychoanalysis (whether for or against Lacan), these theorists construe language, the symbolic order, representation itself as made possible by the repression of 'woman'. Both Freudian and Lacanian psychoanalysis can only define woman as non-man, as absence, lack, excess, the blind spot. These feminist writers start from psychoanalysis, but simultaneously go beyond it in deconstructing binary oppositions of presence/absence organised around the phallus as the Signifier (what Cixous terms 'hierarchised oppositions'): full presence-masculine-active-positive-coherent (superior), absence-feminine-passive-negative-incoherent (inferior). They offer a theoretical understanding of femininity as the term which has been repressed into marginality and silence by the order of representation, this constituting the very condition for the functioning of the symbolic order. Exposing the logocentrism of Western culture as patriarchal in its very formation, they advocate feminine writing as the space where that repressed term—woman's desire, *jouissance, la mère qui jouit*—speaks, as voicing this muted Other.

The difficulty is, then, how this feminine language is possible, if the repression of the feminine is the very condition of the human subject's speech; or how the refusal of language and phallocentricity is possible without a collapse into silence or even psychosis. Julia Kristeva's theory of the subject as a subject in process/on trial, and of poetic language, offers a new understanding of the dynamics of the repressed term—the maternal or the pre-Oedipal—in its relations to the repressive forces, and helps to resolve the difficulty. Kristeva is dissatisfied with linguistic theories whose self-assigned object is strictly 'formal' and which can only conceptualise the subject as a 'transcendental ego' and thereby exclude any 'externality'. She proposes a dialectical notion of language as a 'signifying process' which has two modalities: semiotic and symbolic. She offers a new concept of subjectivity, which is seen as a constant process of the dialectic between these two heterogeneous modalities. To distinguish it from the traditional concept of the unitary fixed subject, she calls her own notion a 'subject in process/on trial' (*sujet en procès*). The Kristevan symbolic, like Lacan's own, is founded on repression, on the 'splitting' of the subject into conscious and unconscious, signifier and signified. It is the realm of signification and law, the sum and locus of human society. The other modality, the semiotic—which will be a central concept in my study of Woolf's novels—'logically and chronologically precedes the establishment of the symbolic and its subject'.[26] It is the complex of bodily drives,

17

linked to the pre-Oedipal primary processes which displace and condense both energies and their inscription—predominantly the oral and anal impulses, incorporation and aggressive rejection. Discrete quantities of energy move through the body of a 'subject' that is in fact not yet constituted as such. Under the constraints of biological growth and social and familial structures, they are gradually, provisionally fixed into different semiotic materials—sound, movement, colour, shape. This constant flow of drives articulates what Kristeva terms, in a borrowing from Plato's *Timaeus,* the *chora:* 'an essentially mobile and extremely provisional articulation constituted by movements and their ephemeral stases'. The *chora* is 'analogous only to vocal or kinetic rhythm', it 'has no thesis and no position' (*RPL,* 25-6). Without unity or identity, this rhythmic space is nevertheless subject to 'a regulating process' different from that of the symbolic law, and thus constitutes a basis for signification. We can imagine the semiotic *chora* 'in the cry, the sounds, the gesture of the baby'. In adult discourse, 'the semiotic functions as rhythm, prosody, word game, the no-sense of sense, laughter'.[27] Thus the semiotic is distinguished from signification, which is 'a realm of positions'.

Positionality, by which signification becomes possible, requires the identification of the subject and its distinction from objects. The subject must separate from and through his image, from and through his objects. Kristeva calls this 'break' which produces the positing of signification, the *thetic phase.* This thetic subject governs the whole tradition of Occidental thought and is the basis of its rationalism. Kristeva sees its clearest expression in the 'transcendental ego' of Husserl:

> The thetic permits the constitution of the symbolic with its vertical stratification (referent, signified, signifier) and all the subsequent modalities of logico-semantic articulation. The thetic originates in the 'mirror stage' and is completed, through the phallic stage, by the reactivation of the Oedipus complex in puberty; no signifying practice can be without it. Though absolutely necessary, the thetic is not exclusive: the semiotic, which also precedes it, constantly tears it open, and this transgression brings about all the various transformations of the signifying practice that are called 'creation'. (*RPL,* 62)

The thetic phase 'marks the threshold between the semiotic and the symbolic' (48). As 'the precondition for such a heterogeneity', it allows the dialectic between these two realms (63). This is the crux of Kristeva's theory of *signifiance* as 'heterogeneous practice'. It is an 'unlimited and unbounded generating process', an 'unceasing operation of the drives toward, in and through language; toward, in and through the exchange system and its protagonists—the subject and his institutions'. It involves 'neither anarchic, fragmented foundation nor schizophrenic blockage'; it is rather 'a structuring and de-structuring *practice,* a passage to the outer *boundaries* of the subject and society' (17). For though Kristeva clearly valorises the irruption of the semiotic, she also stresses the necessity of the thetic.

In poetic practice the breach of the semiotic is necessarily relative. A text requires 'a completion', 'a kind of totalisation of semiotic mobility', in order to hold together as a text: 'This completion constitutes a synthesis that requires the thesis of language in order to come about, and the semiotic pulverises it only to make it a new device' (51). This is what distinguishes a text as signifying practice from neurotic or psychotic discourse. The 'valorisations of presymbolic semiotic stases, not only require the ensured maintenance of this signification but also serve signification, even when they dislocate it' (65). Kristeva focuses particularly on poetry because it is situated directly over the schism between the symbolic and semiotic practices and impulses. Poetic language, she argues, 'reintroduces through the symbolic that which works on, moves through, and threatens it'—the semiotic (81). She champions avant-garde texts (Artaud, Mallarmé, Lautréamont, Joyce) which demonstrate a destruction of the unified thetic subject through the articulation of the semiotic. Such texts, shattering positionality, unleash a profound force of rupture or 'negativity' that might, just possibly, constitute a terrain where a new kind of subject and discourse could be engendered. Without transforming the subject, Kristeva argues, there will be no revolution on the socio-symbolic level either. Only 'the production of a different kind of subject' can bring about 'new social relations' (105). Hence she regards the literary text as 'a practice that could be compared to political revolution': 'the explosions set off by any practice-process within the social field and the strictly linguistic field are logically (if not chronologically) contemporaneous, and respond to the same principle of unstoppable breakthrough; they differ only in their field of application' (104). For her the works of avant-garde modernism are revolutionary, playing a role in the subversion and transformation of capitalist society.

However, this link between textual and political practice remains problematic in Kristeva, and is the point where her work has been most stringently criticised. Allon White remarks:

> The space between the formal textual innovations which she describes and the radical political practice (feminism) to which she subscribes is never satisfactorily filled, since the destruction of syntactic order and pronominal stability in a poetic discourse, even when it can be appropriated for political use is, always and only, a negative politics, an evanescent disruption, incapable of identifying its own political agent (masculine or feminine).

For White, then, Kristeva's 'psycho-anarchic aesthetics' replaces the repressive phallocentric logos by a 'politically impotent', 'drifting', 'dispersed' subject, which will be dangerously vulnerable to the force of social history.[28] Yet, on the other hand, Kristeva is criticised by other feminists for her valorisation of the symbolic as a necessary resource and her rebarbatively theoretical discourse. The fact that these criticisms come from both sides suggests that they abstractly single out what is, in her theory itself, a necessary dialectic between anarchic destruction and repressive mastering of these desires and impulses—neither of which must be reduced to the other. She precisely distinguishes her own work from the 'psycho-anarchism' of writers like Laing and Cooper, Deleuze and Guattari who fetishise the moment of de-structuration and a-signification. 'Schizophrenic flow' exists, she argues, 'only through language, appropriating and displacing the signifier to practice *within* it the heterogeneous generating of the "desiring machine"' (17). Such one-sided theorists reduce away the *dialectical* practice of heterogeneity.

A more consequent political critique has been made by Toril Moi, who notes the absence of any materialist analysis of social relations in Kristeva's key concept of 'marginality'. This notion, Moi objects, 'lumps together all kinds of marginal and oppositional groups as potentially subversive of the social order'. But Kristeva ignores the paradox of the social position of women and the working class, who are both central *and* marginal in relation to the processes of production and reproduction; it is precisely this paradox which makes these oppressed groups potentially revolutionary. But the intelligentsia—avant-garde or not—may well be truly peripheral and have no crucial function in the economic order. Moi concludes: 'Kristeva's grossly exaggerated confidence in the political importance of the *avant-garde* is based on her misrecognition of the difference between its political and economic position and that of women or the working class'.[29]

Within feminism itself, Kristeva has denied any essentialist definition of woman and feminine writing, taking to task her coevals who are somewhat ambivalent on this point. Irigaray's use of woman's auto-eroticism, her sexual organs being composed of 'two lips which embrace continually', provides a series of bodily metaphors that come perilously close to biological essentialism. Cixous also maintains woman's closeness to the body, defends the characteristics of the writing of women who speak with the body, yet in the face of this biologistic tendency she names James Joyce and Jean Genet as well as Colette and Marguerite Duras as exceptional writers who successfully articulate a feminine discourse.[30] Kristeva disrupts a 'romantic' belief in feminine identity and sees such literary practices as the mere inverse of phallocratism: for all their revolutionary rhetoric, they only reinstate the site of women's oppression and confinement. For Kristeva, femininity is a psychical position, not an essence, an archaic phase of experience that remains available as a possibility rather than a substantive identity specific to women. 'In "woman", I see something that cannot be represented, something that is not said, something above and beyond nomenclatures and ideologies. There are certain "men" who are familiar with this phenomenon; it is what some modern texts never stop signifying'.[31] The archaic psychical site of the semiotic is not feminine, for it is situated in the pre-Oedipal phase, i.e., before sexual difference appears. Though the semiotic *chora,* as pre-Oedipal, is linked to the mother in contrast to the symbolic which is governed by the Law-of-the-Father, yet the pre-Oedipal mother contains, for the baby, both masculinity and femininity.

According to Kristeva, the little girl in her psycho-sexual development within Western monotheistic societies faces a stark choice: either mother-identification or father-identification. 'In the first case, the pre-Oedipal phases (oral and anal eroticism) are intensified', and as a heterosexual woman she attains to 'vaginal *jouissance*'. In the second case, the daughter gains access to the symbolic at the expense of the pre-Oedipal phase and the vagina, 'wip[ing] out the last traces of the body of the mother'. The girl's different mode of entry into the Oedipal phase puts woman into a more complex position than the man's, both precarious and privileged. Kristeva argues:

> the daughter is handed the keys to the symbolic order when she identifies with her father: only there is she recognised not in herself but against her rival, the vaginal, *jouissante* mother. Thus, at the price of censuring herself as a woman, she will be able to bring to triumph her henceforth sublimated sadistic attacks on the mother whom she has repressed and with whom she will never cease to fight, either . . . by identifying with her, or . . . by pursuing her as erotic object.[32]

In other words, woman cannot but be androgynous. Even if she identifies herself with the mother in the position of the repressed and marginal, she must have a certain identification with the father in order to sustain a place in the symbolic order and avoid psychosis. On the other hand, if she identifies herself with the father, denying the woman in herself, she is none the less biologically female: the father-identification remains precarious, stands always in need of defence. Here arises the tragic difficulty for women artists who try to situate their work over the interplay of the symbolic and the semiotic. For the male, the reactivation of the pre-Oedipal phase as the semiotic ruptures the symbolic causes laughter and pleasure. But for the woman, 'the rush of these nonsensical, periphrastic, maternal rhythms in her speech, far from soothing her, far from making her laugh, destroys the symbolic armour: makes her ecstatic, nostalgic, or mad . . . . A woman has nothing to laugh about when the paternal order falls'. However, because of this precarious, double position, woman is also in a sense privileged, in touch with the possibility of a utopian existence which lives at once desire and repression, summons *jouissance* and yet has voice in the socio-symbolic order. 'It is not certain that anyone here and now is capable of it', Kristeva laments, but if anyone is, it will be 'a woman perhaps . . .'.[33]

Woolf, too, talks of the 'split' in the woman's consciousness, which can 'think back through its fathers or through its mothers', and defines women as 'trespassers' who emerge from the margin to which they are allocated, transgressing the boundaries that delimit inside from outside (*RO*, 146). She insists that 'poetry ought to have a mother as well as a father', that a great literary mind must be 'androgynous' (155). Her argument, clearly, has an affinity—which this book will explore at length—with Kristeva's theory of poetic language: poetry is poised over the tension between thetic and semiotic practices. Woolf is, indeed, one of the few women writers occasionally mentioned by Kristeva, who is notoriously dismissive of the works of women. She deals with Woolf briefly in one short chapter of *About Chinese Women* and also in 'Oscillation between power and denial'. Woolf's writing is seen as an example of a woman's discourse in which language is 'seen from a foreign land', 'from the point of view of an asymbolic, spasmodic body', but, Kristeva demurs, she does not go so far as to 'dissect language as Joyce does'.[34] It is in the light of this admittedly qualified endorsement that I seek, where appropriate, to demonstrate in detail the value of Kristeva's theoretical exposition of Woolf's literary practice in the chapters that follow.

CHAPTER 2

Jacob's Room

When Woolf condemns the Edwardian novelists, arguing that 'for us those conventions are ruin, those tools are death', her protest is not simply against the style of one specific literary generation (*CE*, 1:330). Probing her discontent, one encounters a more fundamental dissatisfaction with representation or, in Lacanian terms, with the symbolic order and its intrinsic phallocentricity. In this sense, as I argued above, Woolf's critique of Edwardian realism is ultimately a feminist protest as well. The famous 'series of gig-lamps symmetrically arranged' is an image of the ordered life of the 'thetic' subject. In opposing this, Woolf evokes the excluded psychic dimension—not the rigidly coherent but rather the 'varying', 'unknown', 'uncircumscribed', that which shows 'aberration or complexity' in the unformed haze of its 'luminous halo, a semi-transparent envelope' (2:106). As pre-given structure, the symbolic order necessarily alienates the incommensurable dimension of existential reality. Chiding the Edwardians for their literary inability to grasp, 'whether we call it life or spirit, truth or reality, this, the essential thing' (2:105), she deplores their complacent blindness to the very possibility of such a truth or final signified, that which Lacan calls the Real and which can never finally be caught in language. The desire for truth produces only an endless chain of signs, yet literature refuses to abandon its quest for a final adequation of language and the real. For as Roland Barthes argues: 'apropos of knowledge, literature is categorically realist, in that it never has anything but the real as its object of desire; and I shall say now . . . that literature is quite stubbornly unrealistic; it considers sane its desire for the impossible'.[1] Woolf criticises Edwardian 'realism' in the name of this more radical 'real'.

In *The Voyage Out* Terence's desire to 'write a novel about Silence' incarnates this contradiction (*VO*, 262). He seeks to write a *novel* because the desire for a final truth is not abandoned, but a novel about *silence* because language necessarily defers that truth indefinitely. Woolf's short story title, 'An Unwritten Novel' (1920), also encapsulates the impossible desire for a full representation that escapes the duplicities of language, that would not, in Jacques Derrida's terms, surrender presence to 'difference'. In another early sketch, 'Monday or Tuesday', the heron or narrative consciousness passes in the sky, 'desiring truth, awaiting it, laboriously distilling a few words, for ever desiring' (*HH*, 12). Woolf's fiction is driven forwards by this desire for a meaning that would at last halt the frustrating play of signs. The quest takes as its starting-point the signs which fill the world, but the endeavour to read them correctly and grasp truth only fabricates more signifiers. This deferring (*différance*) of truth sustains the discourse of the stories. 'The Mark on the Wall' (1917) is the very first example of Woolf's distinctive modernist writing. It records the attempt to decipher a sign (the mark) on white paper (the wall), which turns out at last to be a snail. Yet even if one finds out what the mark really is, the narrator writes early in the story, 'what should I gain?—Knowledge? Matter for further speculation?' (46).

'An Unwritten Novel' also involves a curious sign—the woman opposite on the train—inviting the narrator to decipher it: 'I read her message, deciphered her secret, reading it beneath her gaze' (16). Yet truth is elusive and the final revelation postponed. This deferring provokes the play of the narrator's imagination and thus constitutes the very ground of her discourse: 'Have I read you right? But the human face—the human face at the top of the fullest sheet of print holds more, withholds more'. In Lacanian psychoanalysis, the human gaze is crucial in the 'mirror relation', in which the Imaginary object bolsters the subject in an illusory self-identity by reflecting back an image that is at once itself and another, and this proves to be the germinating moment in the writing of a story. The narrator of 'An Unwritten Novel' is trapped into this illusory identification with the object by a woman's eyes.

While all other passengers 'forbade intercourse', the woman 'gazed into my eyes as if searching any sediment of courage at the depths of them'. The story records a process of increasing identification with the woman's acts: 'she had communicated, shared her secret, passed her poison' (15-16). Only from this Imaginary perspective could the narrator start writing the woman's story, but once it is established, she has to shield her eyes from the other's gaze to continue this illusory identification. Subject and object are now interchangeable: 'who was saying that eggs were cheap? You or I?' (21). Intermediate hindrances become transparent and the meaning of the object shines forth naturally. An ideal state of self-presence is achieved: 'when the self speaks to the self, who is speaking?' (24). However, it is all illusion. When the woman opens her eyes again, the narrator discovers that they do not after all reciprocate in the Imaginary: 'Now, eyes open, she looks out; and in the human eye—how d'you define it?—there's a break—a division—so that when you've grasped the stem the butterfly's off' (20). The collapse of the Imaginary is not simply the destruction of the other, since self and other are mutually dependent. Identity splinters with the failure of the specular relationship: 'my world's done for! What do I stand on? What do I know? . . . Who am I?' (26). As its title suggests, 'An Unwritten Novel' dramatises the problem of writing, the impossibility of closing the gap between the subject who writes and the object written about.

In January 1920 Woolf writes in her diary: 'some idea of a new form for a new novel. Suppose one thing should open out of another—as in *An Unwritten Novel*—only not for 10 pages but 200 or so . . . *Mark on the Wall, K.G.* and *Unwritten Novel* taking hands and dancing in unity' (*WD*, 23). This new novel becomes *Jacob's Room,* the first experimental novel written after her 1919 aesthetic manifesto, which it attempts to implement. After completing it, she wrote: 'There's no doubt in my mind that I have found out how to begin (at 40) to say something in my own voice' (*WD*, 47). Fundamentally an extension of the experimental short stories, the novel's major concern is a sign which remains elusive and enigmatic. The impossibility of reaching a final truth precipitates a suspicion of signification itself, and dissolves the complacent signifier-signified equivalence of Edwardian realism.

The labour expended by Wells, Bennett and Galsworthy to prove 'the solidity, the likeness to life' is not merely wasteful, but rather 'labour misplaced to the extent of obscuring and blotting out the light of the conception' (*CE*, 2:106). In opposition to them, Woolf announces her ambition towards a new novel in the diary entry already partially quoted above: 'no scaffolding; scarcely a brick to be seen; all crepuscular, but the heart, the passion, humour, everything as bright as fire in the mist' (*WD*, 23). This ambition is not simply the formal concern of *Jacob's Room* but also its theme. Woolf's polemic against stultifying Edwardian realism is directly enacted in Jacob's exasperation with the Cambridge tutor, Mr. Plumer. He despises a luncheon party dominated by 'Shaw and Wells and the serious sixpenny weeklies!' and wishes to 'restore his sense of freedom' (*JR*, 33). The world of the older generation is a gross material 'scaffolding' or 'brick', which smothers the flame of the free spirit—'places of discipline against a red and yellow flame'. Jacob shares his author's literary defiance: 'there will be no form in the world unless Jacob makes one for himself' (34). If the subject of the novel is 'What is Jacob?', it is also the impossibility of articulating, let alone successfully fulfilling this concern in the available literary forms. In 'Modern Fiction' Woolf defends the 'spiritual' James Joyce against Edwardian 'materialism':

> he is concerned at all costs to reveal the flickerings of that innermost flame which flashes its messages through the brain, and in order to preserve it he disregards with complete courage whatever seems to him adventitious, whether it be probability, or coherence, or any other of these signposts which for generations have served to support the imagination of a reader. (*CE*, 2:107)

These are of course as much Woolf's own concerns as Joyce's, for in *Jacob's Room* she too abandons probability, coherence, signposts, in order to let the hero's youthful 'flame' burn as it really is. David Lodge has characterised the experimentalism of this novel as a 'technique of radical and stylish deletion'. This is, he argues, 'the operation by which metonymic devices are produced', for 'structurally *Jacob's Room* belongs in the metonymic category': 'Its experimentalism is all performed on the chain of combination—the chain of contiguous events that is Jacob's life—and consists mainly in cutting away huge sections of this chain and viewing the remainder from odd angles and perspectives'.[2] The text moves from one event to another, one scene to another, from one character's speculation on Jacob to another's impression of him. It accumulates people, objects, hints around Jacob, but the centre itself remains curiously vacant—'the silent young man', 'how little he said' (*JR*, 58, 116). Nor does the text offer us a phenomenology of the protagonist's mind. We are informed that 'he lacked self-consciousness' (69), and the stress on his 'unconsciousness' is recurrent. Jacob is a lacuna in the consciousness of the text, an absent centre, a fissure in the novel round which the other characters gravitate. This technique of 'deletion' to create a central lacuna in the novel is Woolf's specific against Edwardian realism. She denounces Bennett as 'the worst culprit'. In his novels, 'there is not so much as a draught between the frames of the windows, or a crack in the boards. And yet—if life should refuse to live there?' (*CE*, 2:104). His immaculate construction drives life from the text, as if only chinks, cracks and crevices let through the air that sustains its flame. At one point, *Jacob's Room* reports the opinion that 'character-drawing is a frivolous fireside art, a matter of pins and needles, exquisite outlines enclosing vacancy, flourishes, and mere scrawls' (*JR*, 154-5). If it is so, then vacancy had better be left undisguised, for one will anyway endow Jacob with 'all sorts of qualities he had not at all' (72). Aware of the formidable problems of epistemology and signification, the novel refuses to define an 'essence' of Jacob. If one tries to do so, 'there remains over something which can never be conveyed to a second person save by Jacob himself. Moreover, part of this is not Jacob but Richard Bonamy—the room; the market carts; the hour; the very moment of history' (71). The best the novel can do is to move around Jacob in metonymic fashion, collecting odds and ends from his environment—hence *Jacob's Room* rather than, say, *Jacob Flanders*.

Over the doorway of Jacob's eighteenth-century rooms 'a rose, or a ram's skull, is carved in the wood' (69, 176). This curious indeterminacy is not just another contribution to the book's characteristic 'effect of haziness' which, as Hermione Lee points out, arises 'largely from the syntactic qualities of the writing'. In fact, even an astute practical critic like Lee represses this peculiar ambiguity, reducing it simply to 'his London rooms with the ram's skull over the door'.[3] From a mere descriptive viewpoint, it is difficult to see how two such different objects could be confused with each other. We may therefore interpret the phrase as a trace of the novel's reflexive meditations on the nature of the fictional process itself. The ram's or sheep's skull is a key image associated with Jacob from the beginning. 'The sheep's jaw with the yellow teeth' is offered as an image of the intense reality of Jacob's being, in contrast to the stifling world of the Plumers (34). As a boy, Jacob had picked up a sheep's skull on the beach, as if the novel sought to infuse the breath of life into it. A skull that might be transfigured into a 'luminous halo' may be seen as an emblem of the novel's aspiration to totalise a series of glimpses and hints into a triumphant revelation of the essence of Jacob's being.

The hesitation between 'ram's skull or rose' points to a central polarity in Woolf's aesthetic: the opposition of allegory and symbol. The question at stake in *Jacob's Room* is whether the novel can transform the scattering of inert objects in, say, Jacob's empty room at Cambridge into an organic unity, a skull into a rose or symbol. Paul de Man, in his campaign against the Romantic fetishisation of the symbol, argues that it is the product of the organic notion of literary form, in which life and form are identical—an effect valued by Coleridge as 'translucence'. 'The material substantiality dissolves and becomes a mere reflection of a more original unity that does not exist in the material world'. If the symbol is 'an expression of unity between the representative and the semantic function of language', as ideality shines through a reduced materiality, allegory appears, in contrast, mechanical and uncouth. In the allegorical form the original meaning is devoid of substance. In contrast to the symbol, in which the yoking of being and signification is based on 'the organic coherence of the synecdoche', in allegory 'it is a pure decision of the mind'. Or in Frank Lentricchia's terms: 'symbol is ontologically full while allegory is thin at best, and at worst ''unsubstantial'' . . . only an illusion of being'.[4]

I have cited David Lodge's argument that Woolf exemplifies a general modernist tendency to develop from metonymic (realist) to metaphoric representations of experience. But though she certainly belongs to this symbolist heritage of Anglo-American modernism, seeing her age as fragmented and in need of poetic 'synthesis' or redemption, Woolf also has a clear-sighted awareness that the symbolist dream of organic unity is no longer easily attainable; truth and sign have fallen asunder. By a significant ambiguity—ram's skull or rose—the novel suggests that a distance has opened between Woolf's aspirations to totality and what the text actually shows. The novel early on inscribes a dour awareness of the impossibility of the symbol, with the sign now radically dissevered from the origin. As Jacob picks up the sheep's skull on the beach, his brother Archer calls him: 'The voice had an extraordinary sadness. Pure from all body, pure from all passion, going out into the world, solitary, unanswered, breaking against rocks—so it sounded' (7). Symbolism is only possible in the context of what Jacques Derrida terms 'phonocentricism', which postulates the 'absolute proximity of voice and being, of voice and the meaning of being, of voice and the ideality of meaning'.[5] For this belief is the founding myth of the symbol, which redeems the materiality of language from within. Archer's cry is a utopian image of language, whose possibility is, however, immediately denied by the fact that it is unanswered, hence its 'extraordinary sadness'. This cry for Jacob is repeated by Bonamy at the end of the novel; in this case, too, it receives no answer. The novel deconstructs phonocentricism in practice despite its own deep nostalgia for a transcendental source of meaning.

The novel is obsessed with the problem of the sign's radical separation from the origin and with the problem of speech and writing, for this latter opposition is another version of the duality of symbol and allegory. Symbolism is possible only in the context of a phonocentricism that subdues the materiality of the sign to a surge of spirit, while writing may be taken as an allegory of allegory itself, since it draws scattered material fragments into endless, unmotivated formations of meaning. Such concerns are best focused when the question of the letter is broached: 'Let us consider letters . . .'. What is at stake is not just the problem of epistles but of signs in general, of writing itself: 'to see one's own envelope on another's table is to realise how soon deeds sever and become alien. Then at last the power of the mind to quit the body is manifest, and perhaps we fear or hate or wish annihilated this phantom of ourselves, lying on the table'. Writing is the death of the origin; letters are 'speech attempted', 'venerable', 'brave', 'forlorn, and lost'. But sending one's voice itself by telephone is no more successful: 'Can I never know, share, be certain'? (91-2). The phonocentric myth is deconstructed even by such everyday experiences, and the nature of language as 'proto-writing', as a system of differences prior to the division between speech and writing, is revealed. Once cut off from the origin—and this is necessary for signification to function—writing possesses an alarming freedom of its own and becomes untrustworthy. Moreover, in addition to this inherent duplicity of language, the writer may not even aim to convey truth. Mrs. Flanders never writes to her son the jealously Oedipal messages she most wants to. Nor does Jacob write what matters to him: 'that letter-writing is practised mendaciously nowadays, particularly by young men travelling in foreign parts, seems likely enough' (124). Inherently or contingently, letters are false, as are all written texts.

The same theme is emphasised with names and epitaphs. Though proper names should have a privileged relation to original truth, they fail to grasp it or are actually deceitful. The connection between the name and its bearer is dubious and arbitrary. Betty Flanders chose the epitaph 'Merchant of this city' for her husband's tombstone, though there is no reason why he should be called so: 'he had only sat behind an office window for three months, and before that had broken horses . . .' (14). More ironically, the prostitute Florinda was given her name 'by a painter who had wished it to signify that the flower of her maidenhood was still unplucked' (76). The confidante, Mother Stuart, meaningfully points out that Stuart is the name of a royal house, 'but what that signified, and what her business was, no one knew' (76). Another example of the lack of necessity linking name and bearer is the villa of the Cambridge don, Plumer. It is dubbed 'Waverley', but in the most inconsequential way: 'not that Mr. Plumer admired Scott or would have chosen any name at all, but names are useful when you have to entertain undergraduates' (31). How, moreover, will one arrive at truth, however inquisitive one might be, if one does not get the name right in the first place, like Mrs. Papworth—'Mr. Sanders was there again; Flanders she meant' (100). In the act of naming language reveals the arbitrariness on which its referential function is based. By foregrounding the ironic ineptitude or even sheer effacement of names *Jacob's Room* puts any belief in original truth into radical doubt.

Already distanced from the origin, the sign is only distanced further by any effort to return it to its source. Two months after his departure for Greece, Jacob's face is replaced in Fanny Elmer's mind by another sign, the statue of Ulysses:

> Sustained entirely upon picture post cards for the past two months, Fanny's idea of Jacob was more statuesque, noble, and eyeless than ever. To reinforce her vision she had taken to visiting the British Museum, where, keeping her eyes downcast until she was alongside of the battered Ulysses, she opened them and got a fresh shock of Jacob's presence, enough to last her half a day. (170)

Since Ulysses is celebrated in Homer for his cunning, resourcefulness and deceit, we may interpret him here as a figure for the untrustworthiness of language itself. The quest for hidden meaning results only in the endless replacement of one signifier by another, 'but something is always impelling one to hum vibrating, like the hawk moth, at the mouth of the cavern of mystery' (72). A cavern may be penetrated, but the image of the moth suggests that to do so may be self-destructive. Both the quester and the object are moths, a double image Woolf uses in 'An Unwritten Novel': 'Have I read you right? . . . the moth that hangs in the evening over the yellow flower . . . I won't raise my hand. Hang still, then, quiver, life, soul, spirit' (*HH*, 20). Jacob himself is an enthusiastic moth-hunter, and the novel ominously associates this pursuit with death. On the night when he catches a rare species, 'a tree had fallen . . . a sort of death in the forest' (*JR*, 21, 30).

In its nostalgia for a Utopia of the full sign, Western thought has traditionally accorded a special position to ancient Greece. It is thus not surprising that Greek culture is a persisting enthusiasm of Jacob's and that he travels to Greece to experience it first-hand in the course of the novel: 'we are the only people in the world who know what the Greeks meant' (75). He is compared to the statue of Ulysses, and even the sheep or ram's skull associated with him links him to classical Greece. For the wood-carved ram's skull over the door is an eighteenth-century motif revived from classical Greek and Roman sculpture by Robert Adam.[6] Sharing Jacob's enthusiasm, Woolf in her essay 'On Not Knowing Greek' (1925) expounds the conventional Western idea of Greece as the utopian origin. 'The stable, the permanent, the original human being is to be found there'—thus she praises Sophocles (*CE*, 1:4). She acclaims the 'symbolic power' of Aeschylus, which lets the essence of meaning shine through his metaphors. 'The meaning is just on the far side of language. It is the meaning which in moments of astonishing excitement and stress we perceive in our minds without words'. She emphasises that Greek drama is meant to be listened to, not read.

> For none of these dramatists had the licence which belongs to the novelist, and, in some degree, to all writers of printed books, of modelling their meaning with an infinity of slight touches which can only be properly applied by reading quietly, carefully, and sometimes two or three times over. Every sentence had to explode on striking the ear, however slowly and beautifully the words might then descend, and however enigmatic might their final purport be. No splendour or richness of metaphor could have saved the *Agamemnon* if either images or allusions of the subtlest or most decorative had got between us and the naked cry. (1:8)

Not only in drama but in all areas of life, people judged 'by ear', 'sitting out-of-doors at the play or listening to argument in the market-place'. They were therefore 'far less apt than we are to break off sentences and appreciate them apart from the context' (1:10).

Woolf's praise of Greece is permeated by Derrida's 'phonocentricism'. The 'general force' of Aeschylus, the Sophoclean 'type of the original man or woman', the meaning which 'we perceive in our minds without words'—all these exemplify what Derrida views as the Western inheritance from Greek philosophy: 'the feelings of the mind, expressing things naturally, constitute a sort of universal language which can then efface itself'. The qualities of Greek style—'to speak plainly yet fittingly without blurring the outline or clouding the depths' (1:11)—are derived, in Woolf's speculations, from the warm climate which allows an outdoor existence in a small, organic community where 'everyone knows everyone else'. Her conception is similar to the 'authentic' community Derrida discusses: 'a community of speech where all the members are within earshot', where mutual relationships are aural and unmediated, unlike the fragmentary social relations of modern society, which pass through the detour of the written document. (Hence the novel's ambivalence towards letters and phone-calls, those unsatisfactory but indispensable substitutes for a true community). In Derrida's mythical community, language is speech rather than writing, and 'because the voice, the producer of *the first symbols,* has a relationship of essential and immediate proximity with the mind', the signifier and the signified do not yet know disparity.[7] This authentic community is now irretrievably lost. Even the Greek language survives only in the 'fallen' mode of writing: 'We cannot hear it', Woolf laments (1:11). To show how far we are from the 'whole fling' of the Greek original, she instances Shelley taking twenty-one words of English to translate thirteen words of Greek.

Woolf contends that there is one unmistakable characteristic of Greek literature: it is an *impersonal* literature, free from self-consciousness. This point bears upon *Jacob's Room,* for, as I have noted, unconsciousness is a key element of the (non-)characterisation of Jacob. Unselfconscious and classically distinguished in appearance, Jacob is clearly associated with Greek art (Ulysses). Such impersonality derives from the happy unity of meaning and being, idea and form. Jacob is no more afflicted by T.S. Eliot's 'dissociation of sensibility' than Greek art itself. Indeed, Eliot's related concept of the 'objective correlative' is not irrelevant here. Mowbray Allen has suggested that its origin might be traced back to Pater and beyond him to the Hegelian idea of Greek art: 'perfect harmony between the idea and its external manifestation, constitutes the second form of art—the Classic Form . . . a perfect harmony between the idea as spiritual individuality, and the form as sensuous and corporeal reality'.[8] The 'objective correlative' aspires towards this perfect match of inner and outer. It is 'a set of objects, a situation, a chain of events which shall be the formula of that *particular* emotion; such that when the external facts, which must terminate in sensory experience, are given, the emotion is immediately evoked'.[9] Poetic symbolism involves such a belief in 'a special unarbitrary mode of language', in which the signifier or body or sensuous form is made luminous by the spirit within.[10] It is then no surprise that the symbolist Eliot diagnoses Woolf's collection of short stories, *Monday or Tuesday,* in precisely these terms:

> the secret of the charm of Mrs. Woolf's shorter pieces is the immense disparity between the object and the train of feeling which it has set in motion. Mrs. Woolf gives you the minutest datum, and leads you on to

explore, quite consciously, the sequence of images and feelings which float away from it. The result is something which makes Walter Pater appear an unsophisticated rationalist, and the writing is often remarkable. The book is one of the most curious and interesting examples of a process of dissociation which in that direction, it would seem, cannot be exceeded.[11]

These experimental short stories are, indeed, in scandalous opposition to the canons of Eliot's aesthetic in exploiting the 'dissociation' of object and feeling; *Jacob's Room*, as an extension of them, would also earn Eliot's critique. Both thematically and formally, the novel demonstrates a 'postlapsarian' awareness of a catastrophic unhinging of being and meaning, of form and idea, and is tormented by its urgent need to decipher signs from which God has withdrawn. It is Jacob himself who is cast as this absent God, leaving only shards, shreds and signs for us to ponder over. The narrator's celebration of Jacob expresses nostalgia for the lost origin, hence that unidentified 'overpowering sorrow' (*JR*, 47) which underpins the elegiac tone of the novel throughout.

Jacob incarnates a 'Greek' plenitude of meaning that the novel simultaneously knows to be unattainable. His lack of self-consciousness pertains to him at least as much as an *empty* sign as a desirably full one. When the novel first offers a detailed description of his room at Cambridge, it is empty: 'listless is the air in an empty room, just swelling the curtain; the flowers in the jar shift. One fibre in the wicker arm-chair creaks, though no one sits there' (37), and these very lines are repeated after Jacob's death at the end of the novel. The faint movement of air gives a brief, illusory effect of his spirit animating the room, but only in the end emphasises its vacancy the more poignantly—thus the novel acknowledges Jacob as an empty sign. If this is so, then the answer to the hesitation between 'rose' and 'ram's skull' seems to incline towards allegory rather than symbol. The innumerable objects that gather round the empty centre stubbornly refuse to be synthesised into an organic whole. Despite the novel's symbolist nostalgia for the phonocentric ideal—a voice purged of materiality—it remains ineradicably allegorical. Objects, people, activities accumulate until 'the observer is choked with observations' (67). Too many objects present themselves, provocatively or tantalisingly, as signs to be read, 'so many things to look at' (79).

Each had his past shut in him like the leaves of a book . . . and his friends

35

could only read the title, James Spalding or Charles Budgeon, and the passengers going the opposite way could read nothing at all—save 'a man with a red moustache', 'a young man in grey smoking a pipe'. (63)

Every face, every shop, bedroom window, public-house, and dark square is a picture feverishly turned—in search of what? It is the same with books. What do we seek through millions of pages? (96)

The world becomes text, alluring one towards a final meaning with its profusion of emblems, but instead of offering a moment of totalisation, it overloads, even overwhelms the observer with more and more signifiers.

Walter Benjamin, as one of the critics who attempts to redeem allegory from its Romantic denigration, notes of the Baroque *Trauerspiel:* 'Seventeenth-century allegory, obsessed as it is by emblem and hieroglyph, is a profoundly visual form; but what swims into visibility is nothing less than the materiality of the letter itself'. [12] In the light of this comment, one might consider the short story, 'The Lady in the Looking-Glass' (1929), which focuses some of the issues raised by *Jacob's Room*. It attempts to decipher an enigmatic sign, Isabella ('reticent', like Jacob), in her room while the house is empty. In the looking-glass, objects cease 'to breathe and lie still in the trance of immortality' and become signs, while in the real world, the faint noise of the outside air—'the voice of the transient'—comes and goes 'like human breath' (*HH*, 87). The convolvulus, letters, traces, the 'spindly and hieroglyphic' legs of the furniture consitute a sprawling mesh of signs, opaque and material, which we can designate *écriture.* But the narrative desires to capture Isabella's 'profounder state of being . . . the state that is to the mind what breathing is to the body' (90). The dualism breathing/body, voice/writing structures the story, and the narrator seeks a phonocentric truth free of the clogging materiality of body or language. Isabella is compared to 'the fantastic and the tremulous convolvulus', but the narrative condemns its own simile as 'worse than idle and superficial': 'they are cruel even, for they come like the convolvulus itself trembling between one's eyes and the truth' (87). The paradox of figurative language is that despite its effort to violently 'turn' (trope) literal meaning in order to hew close to the object, it displays an autonomous life beneath which the object is submerged. This fear of figurality lies deep within the

36

traditional empiricism of English culture, and is common both to Woolf and to one of her severest critics, F.R. Leavis. In *Revaluation* Leavis denounces Shelley's poetry for its surplus of signification, for the

> general tendency of the images to forget the status of the metaphor or simile that introduced them and to assume an autonomy and a right to propagate, so that we lose in confused generations and perspectives the perception or thought that was the ostensible *raison d'être* of imagery . . . a recognised essential trait of Shelley's: his weak grasp upon the actual. [13]

Refusing a humbly referential function, Shelley's metaphors foreground only themselves. They enact the kind of 'dissociation' between object and feeling that Eliot identified in Woolf's work. The desire for transparent reference is the other side of Woolf's demand for speech rather than writing, breathing essence rather than the inspissation of the bodily phenomenon. For both Leavis and the narrator of the story, the signifier is tolerable only at the moment of its self-effacement before the signified: 'There must be truth; there must be a wall' (*HH*, 87).

At last Isabella herself appears. Under the pressure of the interpreter's desire to 'fasten her down there', the sign opens itself to indeterminacy and polyvalence (89). Her expression is 'mocking or tender, brilliant or dull', and one is left only with the 'indeterminate outline' of her face. But the story seems to have its moment of revelation in which the elusive sign is finally seized, as Isabella renders herself a sign in the tableau of reflections in the mirror:

> At once the looking-glass began to pour over her a light that seemed to fix her; that seemed like some acid to bite off the unessential and superficial and to leave only the truth . . . Everything dropped from her—clouds, dress, basket, diamond—all that one had called the creeper and convolvulus. (91-2)

But just as one expects to encounter 'the hard wall beneath' the creepers and hieroglyphs, 'the woman herself', 'there was nothing. Isabella was perfectly empty' (92). The sign conceals nothing; there neither was once an origin, nor ever will be a final meaning, behind it. The signifier precedes the signified. One cannot reach

37

back to an 'essence' of Isabella from the 'traces' of her found in the letters in her room (88), for meaning does not precede its trace, but is always part of a system of traces. There is, Derrida argues, no pure presence, for presence is only a 'synthesis of traces'.[14] Derrida interrogates the hierarchy which has subjugated writing to speech, and exposes the *mauvaise foi* of speech as the self-presence of meaning. Writing is not the secondary trace of a pre-existing truth, nor an innocent recording technique. Rather than being superfluous to meaning, the 'trace' or 'proto-writing' is the very condition of signification. As Isabella stands 'veined and lined', there are only traces—creepers and tendrils with no supporting wall. Nostalgia for a transcendental source of meaning is disappointed by the figurality of language, 'like the convolvulus itself trembling between one's eyes and the truth'. Isabella 'suggested the fantastic and the tremulous convolvulus rather than the upright aster, the starched zinnia, or her own burning roses alight like lamps on the straight posts of their rose trees' (87). Here, as with the rose and ram's skull of *Jacob's Room,* two possibilities are presented: the 'allegorical' convolvulus, whose tangled lines baffle a gaze that seeks truth, and Walter Benjamin's 'auratic' object,[15] the lamplike rose, a symbol in which the essence of being shines as a luminous halo. Isabella is finally a convolvulus rather than a burning rose, and so too is Jacob. Though Woolf's texts aspire to the symbol, they also inscribe a recognition that such triumphs of transcendental meaning may no longer be possible in a fallen world. This 'fall', I shall suggest, is related by the novel to the First World War.

It is well known that Woolf located the change of 'human character' 'in or about December, 1910' (*CE,* 1:320). Her reasons for assigning that date (King Edward's death in May, the first Post-Impressionist exhibition) are qualified by her jesting tone, the excessive precision; epochs do not arrive so punctually. Apart from December 1910, she often names the First World War as a turning point involving radical social change.[16] In *A Room of One's Own* the sight of a tailless cat triggers this awareness. At luncheon parties before the war, the narrator claims, people were 'accompanied by a sort of humming noise, not articulate, but musical, exciting, which changed the value of the words themselves' (*RO,* 19). She contrasts 'the difficulty of modern poetry' with the naive energies of Victorian verse. Tennyson and

Christina Rossetti, like the Romantics for Matthew Arnold, do not know enough, but Woolf is here more inclined to lament their lost vigour and 'abandonment' than to praise the moderns for their ironic sophistication. 'Shall we lay the blame on the war? When the guns fired in August 1914, did the faces of men and women show so plain in each other's eyes that romance was killed?' (23). Whether this is a desolating loss of belief or rather an awakening into maturity from the 'illusion' or *mauvaise foi* of the Victorians, it is clear that in this postlapsarian age, when the transcendental signified has withdrawn, symbolism is not possible. It is no longer an unproblematic task to totalise the complex experiences of modernity. Allegory becomes, in Fredric Jameson's words, 'the privileged mode of our own life in time, a clumsy deciphering of meaning from moment to moment, the painful attempt to restore a continuity to heterogeneous, disconnected instants'.[17] Hence *Jacob's Room* moves from moment to moment, object to object, in metonymic fashion as it seeks to decipher the emblems it encounters.

I have used the image of a theological 'fall' in discussing *Jacob's Room,* for it is the catastrophic advent of the First World War which pitches English culture out of Edwardian innocence into the embittered 'experience' of the 1920s. This theological metaphor is also crucial to the symbolist aesthetic, since the symbol is a postlapsarian fragment of a unity of being that was once continuously available in the mythic organic community. Symbolist history is preoccupied with locating the precise moment of this fall from grace—the Renaissance for Yeats, the English Civil War for Eliot—and Woolf applies this paradigm to her own experience of contemporary history. But the historical 'fall' is a punctual event that brings to consciousness what has, in fact, always existed or, more strictly, in this particular case, what has *never* existed—the plenitude of the sign.

The war destroys Jacob, as it does the possibility of symbol. But though he is its victim, a youthful life wasted in the elders' war, the relation between him and the war is in fact more complex than this. Jacques Derrida's deconstruction of the 'theological' model of history is helpful in analysing this relation. For Derrida, there is no moment of pure presence which then succumbs to a disastrous Fall because presence is 'always already' inhabited by difference. 'Evil' or 'experience' does not come from outside to overthrow a defenceless innocence; 'innocence' is always contaminated by its opposite principle from the start. When Saussure complains that writing, which should be a secondary technique for recording speech, is insidiously denaturing pronunciation itself, Derrida retorts that 'the ''usurpation'' of which Saussure speaks, the violence by which writing would substitute itself for its own origin . . . such a reversal of power cannot be an accidental aberration. Usurpation necessarily refers us to a profound possibility of essence'.[18] *Jacob's Room* itself hesitates between a theological and 'Derridean' view of history: '''Jacob'', wrote Mrs. Flanders, with the red light on her page, ''is hard at work after his delightful journey . . .'' ''The Kaiser'', the far-away voice remarked in Whitehall, ''received me in audience''' (*JR*, 173). The juxtaposition first dramatises the incommensurability of private and public life. It implies that the former is the helpless victim of the latter's large-scale machinations. The passage is thus a grim dramatic irony, where the audience is allowed a fuller glimpse of the imminent catastrophe than Mrs. Flanders. Yet in the light of the text's ambivalence over Jacob, we may also sense Derrida's 'profound possibility of essence'. The novel ironises its own irony, raises its initial irony to the second degree. The initially shocking gap between public and private blurs and narrows to the point where Jacob and the Kaiser do not seem so different after all; both are representatives of a blind and destructive patriarchy.

The novel at various points notes Jacob's complicity with this destructive male power. In *Three Guineas* Woolf explicitly connects Fascist war-mongering to a male aggressiveness which has been nurtured by a long tradition of education and come to be regarded as innate. This is an association that *Jacob's Room*, far less emphatically, also suggests. When the boy Jacob is hunting for moths late at night, 'the tree had fallen':

There had been a volley of pistol-shots suddenly in the depths of the wood. And his mother had taken him for a burglar when he came home late . . . . The tree had fallen, though it was a windless night, and the lantern, stood upon the ground, had lit up the still green leaves and the dead beech leaves. It was a dry place. A toad was there. And the red underwing had circled round the light and flashed and gone. The red underwing had never come back, though Jacob had waited . . . !' 'How you frightened me!' she had cried. She thought something dreadful had happened. (21-2)

The incident remains mysterious, its aftertaste only a vague ominousness. Only retrospectively can it be seen as foreboding Jacob's tragic end. Mrs. Flanders's lamentation—'the only one of her sons who never obeyed her'—hints that Jacob's death is the result of his evading maternal solicitude. From the beginning of the novel he is 'tiresome', 'naughty', 'a handful', 'obstinate', towards his mother (5-9). This childish intractability merges into Jacob's general revolt against the parental generation, as in the cases of Mr. Plumer or a Professor Bulteel of Leeds—revolts that are 'insolent' yet endorsed by the narrator as 'perfectly right'. Yet there is an ambivalence here. Two issues—Jacob's revolt against the whole older generation, and his departure from the mother's space into the man's world—are shown in conjunction, but are in fact not reducible to each other. Jacob is presented simultaneously as an idealist rebel who stands up against the despicable world of the elders, and yet also as an adherent of the masculinity which is the very founding principle of that world. This ambivalence afflicts *Jacob's Room* throughout and points towards the fundamental problem of the novel.

The moth Jacob hunted escapes, and given the general symbolic value of the moth in Woolf—'life, soul, spirit' (*HH*, 20)—this midnight hunt clearly suggests a violent intrusion into privacy. The strange group of images associated with the falling tree reappears later in the description of King's College Chapel, Cambridge, and links the university display of masculine virtue with the ominous destruction of life. The narrator praises the light of Cambridge, projected out by the human intellect into an otherwise dark, formless chaos. The sky here seems 'lighter, thinner, more sparkling than the sky elsewhere' (*JR*, 29-30). In the procession of young men, 'how airily the gowns blow out, as though nothing dense or corporeal were within'. Cambridge is the locus of phonocentricism, where a spiritual voice or light triumphantly shines forth, subduing materiality. But that this can only be achieved by some unnaturally rigid control of the will is implied by the petrified 'sculptured faces' that sustain this 'certainty, authority controlled by piety'. This strenuous triumph of the human will over Nature is further instanced by the stained glass of the Chapel.

Neither snow nor greenery, winter nor summer, has power over the old stained glass. As the sides of a lantern protect the flame so that it burns steady even in the wildest night—burns steady and gravely illumines the tree-trunks—so inside the Chapel all was orderly. Gravely sounded the voices; wisely the organ replied, as if buttressing human faith with the assent of the elements. (30)

In this sanctuary of learning human power heroically subdues the hazardous flux of Nature, leaving 'all very orderly'. Here, then, emerges a polarity characteristic of Woolf's work: on the one hand human will and reason, an ordered civilisation; on the other, Nature, darkness, chaos. A globe of light pure of contaminating materiality confronts the fertile yet threatening world of Darwinian evolution and flux; this is another version of the opposition symbol/allegory. Land and sea become major images for each term of the polarity. Viewed from the ceaselessly undulating sea, the Cornish coast wears 'an extraordinary look of calm, of sunny peace, as if wisdom and piety had descended upon the dwellers there' (47). Timothy Durrant, navigating his yacht, serves as an image of heroic Man on a solitary journey through the universe, bearing onwards the light of civilisation. For Woolf, this formidable responsibility is specifically associated with the male. It receives its most memorable embodiment in Mr. Ramsay in *To the Lighthouse,* where the sea is on the whole a menacing 'fluidity' contrasted with 'inside the room' where exist 'order and dry land' (*TL,* 152-2). But, as I shall argue in my discussion of *Mrs. Dalloway,* the sea also has a more benign, equally traditional value as the 'maternal' ocean, the primitive matrix of the world.

In the face of the 'trampling energy' of the night wind, the subtleties of individual difference and the niceties of everyday social decorum are equally irrelevant. 'All faces—Greek, Levantine, Turkish, English—would have looked much the same in that darkness'. Yet despite the formidable power of the flux, the will affirms itself: 'At length the columns and the Temples whiten, yellow, turn rose; and the Pyramids and St. Peter's arise, and at last sluggish St. Paul's looms up'. In the end, indeed, the night wind and the 'sea coldly, greenly, swaying outside' become almost imperceptible to the citizen immersed in the routines of 'the day's meaning' (*JR,* 161). For the light of civilisation has long since 'dried the melancholy mediaeval mists; drained the swamp and stood glass and stone upon it' (163). None the less, these impressive achievements will at last become mere pieces of broken bone to be rummaged through by the archaeologist of the future. Who, the narrator asks, 'save the nerve-worn and sleepless, or thinkers standing . . . on some crag above the multitude, see things thus in skeleton outline, bare of flesh? In Surbiton the skeleton is wrapped in flesh' (162). The novel's recurrent imagery of skulls and bones serves as a stark reminder of the grim, inescapable flux and decay of Darwinian Nature. Darwinism retains for *Jacob's Room* all the traumatic force it had for the Victorians themselves. 'Perhaps . . . we do not believe enough. Our fathers at any rate had something to demolish', and Jacob still believes enough to pit political commitment against the nihilistic 'dark waters which lap us about' (173). But the dark waters are such a radical nullification of the socio-symbolic human world that both novel and hero are pessimistic about this political project: 'what use are fine speeches and Parliament, once you surrender an inch to the black waters?' (138). This loss of belief, whether or not it was illusion in the first place, leaves the moderns powerless. Of the death of 'romance' in *A Room of One's Own,* the narrator asks: 'Why, if it was an illusion, not praise the catastrophe, whatever it was, that destroyed illusion and put truth in its place?' (*RO,* 23). But she none the less covets the passion which illusion could generate, and which alone can sustain the globe of civilising light, the symbol, in defiance of the engulfing flux. If error is, as Nietzsche argues, necessary rather than contingent, life-sustaining rather than a dangerous confusion, then the narrator is well justified in asking 'which was truth and which was illusion . . .?' (23-4).

Woolf's attitude to the contending forces of natural flux and the light of humanity is ambivalent. Nature, to be sure, is fearful, hostile, impenetrable by human reason. A lantern put under a tree attracts every insect in the forest: 'they amble round the lantern and blindly tap as if for admittance . . . something senseless inspires them' (*JR,* 30). Nature is irreducible to human purposes, whereas the human world is a zone of security under the governance of reason.[19] But such valuations can also be reversed. For the reasonable order imposed by the human will on Nature can be seen as a force which damages, even destroys, life in the necessary process of providing security. The lantern in the forest in one sense is under threat, in another itself brusquely violates the dark, seething fertility of the natural world: 'a terrifying volley of pistol-shots rings out . . . a tree has fallen' (30). The aspiration towards disembodied 'light' in King's College Chapel also atrophies the spontaneous energies of life by its constricting use of the will. Such restraint is the governing principle of society in general, of 'the strokes which oar the world forward', of

> men as smoothly sculptured as the impassive policeman at Ludgate Circus. But you will observe that far from being padded to rotundity his face is stiff from force of will, and lean from the effort of keeping it so. When his right arm rises, all the force in his veins flows straight from shoulder to finger-tips; not an ounce is diverted into sudden impulses, sentimental regrets, wire-drawn distinctions. The buses punctually stop. (155)

The callous inhumanity of the social force that subdues men to such actions is best attested in the description of a naval engagement which immediately precedes the policeman's 'force of will'. The battle ships ray out and the master gunner, with superb accuracy, fires: 'With equal nonchalance a dozen young men in the prime of life descend with composed faces into the depths of the sea; and there impassively (though with perfect mastery of machinery) suffocate uncomplainingly together' (155). The militarist suppression of natural emotion reduces the young men to the sub-human status of 'tin soldiers', 'fragments of broken match-stick'. There is a certain pathos in such phrases and yet a sense that, in themselves consenting to this dehumanisation, these youths have forfeited a right to our full sympathy when they at last become victims of the violence such dehumanisation had always implicitly entailed.

The forces which such men fear as dangerous, and suppress in order to sustain civilisation, include 'sudden impulses, sentimental regrets, wire-drawn distinctions'. These categories might be conventionally regarded as 'feminine', and certainly are so regarded by the novel, as for instance in Mrs. Flanders who, though she is a mature woman of fifty with three sons, remains 'impulsive at heart' (90). Inquiry into human character, into 'deeps of feeling', is marginalised by 'the men in clubs and Cabinets' to the fireside or drawing-room, female spaces where such women's chatter can be tolerated as a mere 'matter of pins and needles' (153-5). For if even 'an ounce' of the force of male will were 'diverted' by sensation or feeling, the whole imposing social edifice would, in principle if not in immediate practice, be jeopardised.

44

The 'sculptured faces' of these men in turn recall Jacob. Ulysses was Fanny's substitute for him, and Florinda declares, 'You're like one of those statues' (79). Jacob's masculinist rejection of feminine diversions is revealed by his musings in King's College Chapel. He feels that women should be banished: 'If the mind wanders it is because several hat shops and cupboards upon cupboards of coloured dresses are displayed upon rush-bottomed chairs. Though heads and bodies may be devout enough, one has a sense of individuals—some like blue, others brown; some feathers, others pansies' (30-1). Again, then, women seduce into errancy that 'force of will' that should flow with the unilateral rigidity of the policeman's gestures. Colourful individuals in contrast to the white-robed choristers, they disrupt, by their irreducible sensuousness, the men's aspirations to a realm of pure spirit. More insultingly, Jacob compares women to dogs, for 'a dog destroys the service completely', and associates them with incontinent natural impulse: 'wander[ing] down the aisle, looking, lifting a paw and approaching a pillar with a purpose that makes the blood run cold with horror'. Faced with an impossible ideal of devout concentration, Jacob's mind has not unnaturally begun to wander, but he projects the blame for his own lapses onto the women present at the service. However 'devout, distinguished, and vouched for' by their husbands' spirituality and learning, they are irredeemably tied to the body—'as ugly as sin', reflects Jacob. His reference to 'sin' recalls my account of the 'fall' of the sign. On the evidence, Jacob seems likely to ascribe to women responsibility for this 'fall', which has reduced the sign to an allegorical status in which its materiality tempts one away from the rigours of pure spirit. Later in Greece which, as I argued above, is the utopian origin of phonocentricism, Jacob is again annoyed by women who 'spoil things' by their disorderliness.

For women themselves, however, matters are otherwise. For them, the 'fall' has happened in the very beginning; the sign is 'always ready' material. The impossible asceticism of the male project to exclude materiality (the woman) as disruption has precipitated the calamity of war. The war in turn has shattered the male illusion, and led to the subjective acknowledgement of a fallen state that, objectively, had 'always already' been the case. *A Room of One's Own* declares that the war 'was a shock (to women in particular with their illusions about education, and so on) . . . the faces of our rulers in the light of the shell-fire. So ugly they looked—German, English, French—so stupid' (RO, 23). As evidence of the bankruptcy of the very principle of masculine culture, the war was a liberating experience for women, however painful. 'The Mark on the Wall' meditates on social change: 'the masculine point of view' has become since the war 'half a phantom to many men and women, and soon, one may hope, will be laughed into the dustbin . . . leaving us all with an intoxicating sense of illegitimate freedom'. After the disappearance of all masculinist constraints there might arise a utopian world which would have dispensed with the technicians of the inhumane will: 'a world without professors or specialists or house-keepers with the profiles of policemen' (HH, 44-6).

Unleashed by the First World War, this critique of the dominant masculine ideology is latently present in *Jacob's Room* itself. A proto-feminist hostility emerges at innumerable moments in the novel and yet never becomes a fully focused theme. The marginal objections remain dissociated from each other, never cohere into a global critique. The novel sides with the feminine characteristics that men implacably suppress; 'who shall deny that this blankness of mind, when combined with profusion, mother wit, old wives' tales, haphazard ways, moments of astonishing daring, humour, and sentimentality—who shall deny that in these respects every woman is nicer than any man?' (*JR*, 9). This passage describes Mrs. Flanders who suffers a moment of scatter-brained forgetfulness, the nuisance of which she dissolves in humour. For the novel, this lack of concentration is the condition of an almost overflowing mental abundance, which contrasts favourably with the rigid impassivity of the traffic policeman at Ludgate Circus. But if Mrs. Flanders's 'polyphonic' mind makes her less 'practical' than the narrowly utilitarian policeman, she is also *more* practical in the sense of being closer to the down-to-earth necessities of human living than he is. What she has temporarily forgotten is 'the meat!', the humble but necessary flesh which the lofty responsibility of the male guardians of civilisation causes them to lose sight of. Later as she writes a rejection of Mr. Floyd's proposal she suddenly wonders, 'Did I forget about the cheese?' (19). The female mind operates simultaneously on various levels, as in the more famous juxtaposition of Mrs. Ramsay's epiphanic revelation and the *Boeuf en Daube* in *To the Lighthouse*, which I discuss below. Such juxtapositions subvert a 'male' standard of literary relevance, in the way that Woolf elsewhere more programmatically recommends. They exemplify 'the difference between the man's and the woman's view of what constitutes the importance of any subject' (*CW*, 27). They demonstrate, as had Imagism in contemporary poetry,[20] that life does not necessarily exist 'more fully in what is commonly thought big than in what is commonly thought small' (*CE*, 2:107). Not that, for the woman, the 'small' necessarily excludes the 'big' as, for the male, the big tends to do to the small. The 'base' materiality of the cheese does not prevent Mrs. Flanders from rising to the occasion created by the grander issues of love and matrimony. Predictably 'inconsequent', her letter is none the less 'such a motherly, respectful . . . regretful letter' that Floyd treasures it for years (*JR*, 19).

It is not so far from the narrator's comment that 'every woman is nicer than any man' to Mrs. Norman's sudden alarm—'men are dangerous'—as Jacob enters her compartment on the train. (28). But the novel hints at a female response to this potential danger. Contemplating her old cat Topaz (a keepsake from Mr. Floyd), Mrs. Flanders 'smiled, thinking how she had had him gelded, and how she did not like red hair in men' (20). As if the initial gelding were not enough, she reflects that Topaz 'one of these days would have to be killed'. The derivation of the cat from Floyd suggests that violence directed at it is simultaneously directed at him as male. This suggestion is strengthened by the remarkable proliferation of maimed men in the novel. Mr. Curnow 'lost an eye' in a gunpowder explosion; old Jevons is dead and buried, 'with one eye gone' (100); Betty Flanders' admirer, Captain Barfoot, is lame and lacks 'two fingers on the left hand' (23). Such injuries are often the result of military service, but are also informed by Mrs. Flanders' smile at the gelded cat, which testifies to a latent desire to castrate. The lost eyes are a Freudian equivalent of castration as well as testimony to military honour, and Mrs Flanders' fondness for Barfoot may relate to his being safely 'lame'.

The novel is deeply ambivalent towards the male world, which is both repressive and apparently indispensable. Though Barfoot is lame, he is the strenuous representative of civilisation, a lone hero 'on the Bridge at night' who inspires women with the feeling that 'Here is law. Here is order. Therefore we must cherish this man' (26). There is 'something rigid about him', as there was in the

47

Ludgate policeman. The novel's critique of Barfoot's values emerges in displaced form in the smothered rebelliousness of Mrs. Jarvis, who resents the rigid division of sexual roles. 'Yet I have a soul . . . and it's the man's stupidity that's the cause of this, and the storm's my storm as well as his' (26). 'Too good for such a quiet place', the discontented Mrs. Jarvis can find no outlet for her energy and talent. In this she is representative of the novel's women generally, who live frustrated in conditions of social and often geographical marginalisation. The Captain's invalid wife is 'civilisation's prisoner', confined to a bath-chair on the esplanade at Scarborough (23). Mrs. Pascoe lives in a lonely cottage on the Cornish cliff-edge, dreaming absorbedly of sophisticated high society in London. Mrs. Durrant has access to that London world, but this hardly guarantees her satisfaction. 'Enunciating strident politics with Sir Somebody', she is impressively 'phallic' in style— 'aquiline', 'hard as iron' and 'imperious' (56, 153-4). But she is in the end excluded from the decision-making centres of Whitehall where 'the course of history' is 'manfully determined' (172). None the less, she reveals an impressive astuteness: 'Poor Jacob . . . . They're going to make you act in their play' (60). As Paul Fussell notes in *The Great War and Modern Memory,* her phrase resonates beyond the amateur theatricals of its local context to that 'unthought-of kind of amateur theatre, where Jacob will be destroyed'.[21] The most poignant of these frustrated women is Clara Durrant, powerless, overshadowed by her mother, 'a virgin chained to a rock' (122).

In contrast to these impotently peripheral women, Jacob and his friends are destined from the start to be the bearers of the dominant culture, and this remains true despite their youthful revolt and coltishness. 'Himself the inheritor', Jacob is in Cambridge to receive the 'gift' accumulated by 'generations of learned men'. Not surprisingly, therefore, he looks 'satisfied; indeed masterly' (43). And the *Room* of the novel's title is precisely the 'Room of One's Own' which the women addressed in the later feminist tract so disablingly lack. Though Jacob represents the vitalistic forces of life in contrast to the oppressive social world of the Plumers—all Shaw, Wells and serious weeklies—he himself enacts a repressive blindness in relation to the women of the novel. He and Bonamy 'never noticed' the latter's charwoman, despite her 'motherly' care of them, and Jacob is culpably insensitive to Fanny's 'sentiment and sensation' or Clara's 'deeps of feeling' (153). This groundswell of female suffering articulates a deep-seated critique of Jacob as representative upper middle-class young man. The First World War was then for Woolf a terrible proof of the fundamental wrong-headedness, even bloody-mindedness, of this masculine ideology, exposing the dangerous imbalance of its expulsion of the feminine. Her critique of Edwardian realism was always in principle, if not at once in practice, a critical exposure of male ideology, for this period would come to seem to her the culmination of 'the masculine point of view' (*HH*, 44), as in 'The Mark on the Wall'. But her dissatisfaction with particular forms merges into a dissatisfaction with form as such, with the very principle of narrative fiction or even with language itself, which is necessarily 'phallogocentric' and therefore falls under Woolf's suspicion. [22]

The novel protests the phallogocentricism of writing at its very beginning, in the account of Mrs. Flanders' letter-writing. It testifies to the peculiar difficulties a woman faces when she tries to write—lack of a private space within the home, family demands, pressures, disruptions that render the style of her writing scrappy and inconsequent. The novel both deplores women's lack of access to the material conditions that enable male writing *and* valorises their stylistic inelegance as a more richly pluralistic mode of writing than its male counterpart. But the text does not remain on the empirical level of household interruptions. More radically, Mrs. Flanders' letter seems to exemplify the novel's own project for a new mode of writing. The letter she pens on the beach retains all the contingent, even material circumstances which belong to the time of its writing: the blot of ink where her pen momentarily sticks, as well as her tear stains. It overturns male canons of objectivity, impersonality and relevance—all of which protect the ideality of meaning from the material body of the signifier. This accidental materiality does not simply spoil the neat appearance of the letter but erodes even its syntax. 'Slowly welling from the point of her gold nib, pale blue ink dissolved the full stop' (*JR*, 5), and the falling tears worsen the blot. She continues writing, 'ignoring the full stop'. Like the letter, later described as 'in pale profusion, dried by the flame, for the blotting-paper's worn to holes and the nib cleft and clotted', her writing does not achieve any sharp definition or precision of meaning. Its content includes 'the cloudy future flocks' of chickens, and even her vigorous son becomes 'Jacob in the blur of her outline' (90). Describing this letter, the novel's own prose enacts its very qualities, as Hermione Lee has shown. Both point of view and point in time fluctuate. Syntactic ambiguities and 'the haziness of some of the images' oddly juxtaposed, produces 'the blur of outline'. Such characteristic ambiguities produce 'all at once the sense of several, habitual scenes in Mrs. Flanders' life'.[23]

This rejection of one-dimensional syntax and shapely narrative progression loosens the ligatures of Kristeva's 'thetic subject', which is the locus of choice, judgement, integration. The thetic is, in more Woolfian terms, a 'policeman' of the subject. It keeps the self straight on 'the continuity of our ways' and saves it from being cast out of society into 'chasms' (95). To escape this rigidly linear control is in one sense liberating, in another a dangerous approach to chaos. Writing is by nature linear; one *must* judge and select, abandoning a 'polymorphous perversity' of the signifier. In *Jacob's Room* the narrator laments the impossibility of totality. 'To prevent us from being submerged by chaos, nature and society between them have arranged a system of classification . . . stalls, boxes, amphitheatre, gallery'. Hence 'one has to choose one's seat', but to do so deprives one of the possibility of other views: 'Never was there a harsher necessity! or one which entails greater pain, more certain disaster; for wherever I seat myself, I die in exile' (67-8). Thus the text juxtaposes innumerable objects, characters, offering as many glimpses and perspectives on them as possible, though it simultaneously knows that totality is impossible. Though it prefers the wayward impulses of women to the control of an impassive police, it also acknowledges the necessity of the 'judging' policeman. Without the Dionysiac 'drums and trumpets—the ecstasy and hubbub of the soul', life is an oppressive suffocation (112); but without some measure of restraint it is a lethal chaos. The novel thus agrees with Roland Barthes that 'the text needs its shadow: this shadow is *a bit* of ideology, *a bit* of representation, *a bit* of subject',[24] or in Kristeva's terms acknowledges the need of a *dialectic* of semiotic impulses and thetic control. This dialectic is figured in a powerful metaphorical passage:

> What can be more violent than the fling of boughs in a gale, the tree yeilding itself all up the trunk, to the very tip of the branch, streaming and shuddering the way the wind blows, yet never flying in dishevelment away?

The corn squirms and abases itself as if preparing to tug itself free from the roots, and yet is tied down.

Why, from the very windows, even in the dusk, you see a swelling run through the street, an aspiration, as with arms outstretched, eyes desiring, mouths agape. And then we peaceably subside. For if the exaltation lasted we should be blown like foam into the air. The stars would shine through us. We should go down the gale in salt drops—as sometimes happens. (119)

Semiotic subversions must at last be held in place by a thetic *rappel-à-l'ordre*.

Not only Mrs. Flanders' letters but those of the women in the novel generally contain irrelevances to the ideality of meaning. Florinda's letters also often have tear stains; Mother Stuart scents her pages to attain 'a flavour which the English language fails to provide' (92). While women's letters are soiled or defaced by misspelling or erratic language, Jacob's letters come predictably much closer in both style and subject to the phallogocentric ideal: 'long letters about art, morality, and politics' (92). The epistolary contrast between men and women persists throughout the novel: men are lucid, logical, orderly, singleminded; women lack concentration, are erratic, abundant, polyphonic. Even the intellectual Miss Umphelby, Cambridge lecturer in classics, conforms to this pattern. As she saunters along the Backs, she wanders mentally off into irrelevance: 'if I met him [Virgil], what should I wear?' (40). She falls away from male standards, but the male scholars themselves only adhere to them in a deeply compromised way. In the great Virgilian scholar Cowan, there is a fundamental falsity; Virgil would be shocked at his own image 'in his snug little mirror'. The ideal light of erudition, which ought to be seen 'far out at sea over the tumbling waves', finds itself mired in the smug complacencies and petty wordly concerns of the scholars: 'such is the fabric through which the light must shine, if shine it can' (40).

Similar contrasts are registered in another sanctuary of learning—the British Museum. As in King's College Chapel, women disturb the male either by 'overbalancing' their books or by trampling across all categories of human knowledge like Miss Marchmont. She seeks to prove her theory that 'colour is sound', and in her system politics and art—'Mr. Asquith's Irish policy and

Shakespeare'—merge seamlessly together, in what seems to be a brilliant anticipation of Kristeva's 'revolution in poetic language'. But she appears to the destructively analytic Frazer merely another example of 'abhorred vagueness' (104-5). Dingy and dishevelled, their rooms 'not very clean', these female readers pursue scholarship despite economic hardship. Julia Hedge bitterly notes the contrast with Jacob: 'what has he got to do except copy out poetry?', while she is disturbed by her feminist indignation against the museum into the self-consciousness that *A Room of One's Own* deplores. 'One leaf of poetry was pressed flat against another leaf, one burnished letter laid smooth against another in a density of meaning, a conglomeration of loveliness' (106). Whether it is the narrow probing focus of the male mind or the more diverse erratic play of the female that can best attain a 'loveliness' of meaning buried in the millions of pages stored in the museum is not clear. If the troubled or whimsical minds of Julia and Miss Marchmont seem hardly up to the task, the novel's stress on 'density' and 'conglomeration' seems equally to rebuff the penetrating searchlight of the male intellect, suggesting an inert materiality that even it cannot penetrate.

If the novel in these various marginal ways calls into question the phallogocentric ideology, it none the less faces the embarrassing problem that its own hero is a man. In this light, Jacob's encounter as a boy with the sheep's skull may be interpreted as the discovery of his own male sexuality. He finds the skull as he flees distraught from the lovers he had encountered: 'stretched entirely rigid, side by side, their faces very red, an enormous man and woman'. 'Not far from the lovers lay the old sheep's skull without its jaw', and thus the association of the skull and sexuality is forged. Mrs. Flanders angrily demands that Jacob abandon it, and chooses this moment to tell of Mr. Curnow's loss of an eye in an explosion, 'aware all the time in the depths of her mind of some buried discomfort'. This monitory tale serves as a threat of castration whereby the mother tries to force her son to abandon the sexuality he has just assumed. Suddenly alarmed by her 'responsibility' and 'danger', she anxiously reflects that her sons have no father, 'no man to help with the perambulator' (7-9). The skull, the lost eye, the mother's premonition of danger, also point to Jacob's death in the war. But the 'sexual' and proleptic functions of the skull are not incompatible. It is precisely Jacob's maleness that 'kills' him in a

war that is the inevitable consequence of an inhumane masculine
ideology.

Because its hero is a man to whom in part the novel desires to pay
homage, its feminist critique remains scattered and half-
suppressed. In the 1920s Woolf regarded the male Georgian
writers as allies in her anti-Edwardian crusade, but, as I noted in the
previous chapter, she dissociated herself from them in 'The
Leaning Tower' in 1940. This shift of allegiance is also enacted in
the novel. For in the first instance Jacob detests his own age, 'Mr.
Masefield . . . Mr. Bennett. Stuff them into the flame of Marlowe
and burn them to cinders' (105). But as the feminist Julia Hedge
remarks, Jacob also 'looked a little regal and pompous'. His
antagonism to the older generation is in the end a mere Oedipal
contention and not a Woolfian difference of view—thus 'Julia
Hedge disliked him naturally enough' (106). Jacob's complicity
with a world he detests had also been signalled earlier in the novel.
He is moved to sharp indignation by the intolerable Plumers. 'He
was impressionable', the narrator notes, 'but the word is
contradicted by the composure with which he hollowed his hand to
screen a match. He was a young man of substance' (34). The
'contradiction' registered here is the ambivalence I have tried to
focus throughout this chapter, but in the course of the text it
resolves itself into an increasing acknowledgement of Jacob's
maleness. 'For he had grown to be a man' (138), a fact all the
women in the novel have come to terms with, some gloomily, some
desperately. Hence the narrator's anxiety that 'a difference of sex'
and age may prevent her understanding 'what was in his mind'
proves more deeply significant than it initially appeared (93), and
points to the 'impossibility', the unresolved tensions, of Jacob as
hero of the book. His emptiness at one level reveals the nature of the
sign, and at another derives from the tension between male
protagonist and proto-feminist novel, which means that Jacob as
character cannot in any full sense be fleshed out. The absent centre
that Jacob is—ram's skull rather than rose—exposes
simultaneously the hollow illusions both of logocentricism and of
masculine cultural values.

CHAPTER 3

Mrs. Dalloway

Jacob's Room, then, is more of a 'ram's skull' than a 'rose', and Woolf noted anxiously that people would view it as 'a disconnected rhapsody' (*WD,* 46). She would now have to progress beyond it, but without simply negating its achievement. In *Mrs. Dalloway* she comes close to the view of life recommended in 'Modern Fiction': 'not a series of gig-lamps symmetrically arranged' but a 'luminous halo' (*CE,* 2:106). While writing the novel she had discussed the problems of her work in correspondence with Jacques Raverat. Himself a painter, Raverat discussed with her the dilemmas posed by the essentially linear nature of writing. He proposed an anti-linear account of the effect of a word, which is like casting a pebble into a pond: 'There are splashes in the outer air in every direction, and under the surface waves that follow one another into dark and forgotten corners'. This phenomenon, he argued, can only be represented by some graphic expedient such as placing the word in the middle of the page and surrounding it radially with associated ideas. Woolf replied that it was precisely to this that she aspired, 'to catch and consolidate and consummate . . . those splashes of yours'.[1]

I wish to consider the novelistic techniques which enabled Woolf to claim that she had exorcised the spell which Middleton Murry and others said she had laid herself under with *Jacob's Room* (*WD,* 68). The disjointed fragmentation of that novel is transcended in *Mrs. Dalloway* by the systematic use of 'represented speech' (free indirect speech) which generates an effect of subjective haziness—a 'semi-transparent envelope'—across the whole text.[2] The so-called 'stream of consciousness' or 'indirect interior monologue' based on represented speech allows the novelist's discourse to move from a character's interior world to the exterior world (or vice versa) in a homogeneous medium, which produces a continuous indeterminacy. The subject of any apparently seamless passage is constantly shifting:

> Remember my party, remember my party, said Peter Walsh as he stepped down the street, speaking to himself rhythmically, in time with the flow of the sound, the direct downright sound of Big Ben striking the half-hour. (The leaden circles dissolved in the air). Oh these parties, he thought; Clarissa's parties. Why does she give these parties? he thought. Not that he blamed her or this effigy of a man in a tail-coat with a carnation in his button-hole coming towards him. Only one person in the world could be as he was, in love. And there he was, this fortunate man, himself, reflected in the plate-glass window of a motor-car manufacturer in Victoria Street. All India lay behind him; plains, mountains; epidemics of cholera; a district twice as big as Ireland; decisions he had come to alone—he, Peter Walsh; who was now really for the first time in his life in love. Clarissa had grown hard, he thought; and a trifle sentimental into the bargain, he suspected, looking at the great motor cars capable of doing—how many miles on how many gallons? For he had a turn for mechanics; had invented a plough in his district, had ordered wheel-barrows from England, but the coolies wouldn't use them, all of which Clarissa knew nothing whatever about. (*MD*, 54-5)

The paragraph opens with Peter echoing Clarissa's cry and proceeds in conventional narrative style (not entirely straightforwardly, however—Peter projects on to Big Ben qualities he believes himself to possess, 'direct, downright'). After the parenthetic refrain describing Big Ben, Peter's interior monologue is presented, in this case in 'direct speech' without quotation marks: 'Why does she give these parties, he thought . . .'. But his thoughts and perceptions are now presented in the third-person past tense ('represented speech'). However, at certain moments it becomes unclear whether this is interior monologue or narrative description. 'Looking at the great motor cars capable of doing . . .' might be a simple description of an action, but 'how many miles on how many gallons?' confirms that it is a transcription of Peter's perceptions. Nor is one sure whose logic is represented by the immediately following 'For . . .', a connective used recurrently throughout the book. The sentence is ambivalently poised between a straightforward statement about Peter and the contents of his consciousness, though as it proceeds it becomes more and more like his own monologue.

Another important formal development in *Mrs. Dalloway* is what Woolf terms the 'tunnelling process'—'by which I tell the past by instalments, as I have need of it' (*WD*, 61). During the course of the day Clarissa, Peter and Sally all delve into their common past, their youthful days at Bourton. The tense system of these scenes from the past is inconsistent. Since the characters' present is given, in traditional narrative style, in the past tense, their past should presumably be in the pluperfect, but this is not the case. After recalling a painful encounter with Clarissa at Bourton, Peter protests, 'No, no, no! He was not in love with her any more!' (*MD*, 85). The discourse returns to his present, but the tense remains the same as that used in the remembered scene; from a formal point of view, past and present are indistinguishable. In fact, within Peter's memory-image, though it is initially clear that the scene occurred in the past ('She came into a room; she stood . . .'), matters become gradually ambiguous; present and past are fused. In the last few lines the Clarissa resurrected from the past is no longer merely the young girl at Bourton but the latter-day Clarissa as well.

The text presents itself as a homogeneous unity in the conventional narrative guise of third-person past tense, but is in fact radically heterogeneous. Subjects of sentences are continually shifting, and writing is made 'porous' by the tunnelling process. One is suddenly pitched into a 'cave' of the past, for Woolf records her 'discovery: how I dig out beautiful caves behind my characters' (*WD*, 60). An early paragraph of the novel epitomises these characteristics:

What a lark! What a plunge! For so it had always seemed to her when, with a little squeak of the hinges, which she could hear now, she had burst open the French windows and plunged at Bourton into the open air. How fresh, how calm, stiller than this of course, the air was in the early morning; like the flap of a wave; the kiss of a wave; chill and sharp and yet (for a girl of eighteen as she then was) solemn, feeling as she did, standing there at the open window, that something awful was about to happen; looking at the flowers, at the trees with the smoke winding off them and the rooks rising, falling; standing and looking until Peter Walsh said, 'Musing among the vegetables?'—was that it? (*MD*, 5)

The 'hinges' of Woolf's transitions don't usually 'squeak' as noticeably as here. One technical means of oiling them is the conjunction 'for', which as in the above passage often connects slightly different planes of discourse in a very loose, characteristically 'half-logical' way.[3] A profuse use of present participles, another characteristic of Woolf's writing, loosens the binding function of syntax. Its effect is to attenuate human energy: contrast 'she looked at the flowers' with 'looking at the flowers', where activity is reduced to contemplative stasis. The present participles begin as supplements to a main clause, but generate an autonomous energy; they meander lyrically on until disrupted by Peter's brusque comment. Transformed into a present-participle phrase, an action composed of subject-verb becomes an adverbial or adjectival phrase, and as a result the sentence gives a sense of the simultaneity of several acts and states. Thus writing can to a certain extent go beyond its essential linearity. Woolf diagnosed this effect, somewhat anxiously, in her diary: 'It is a disgrace that I . . . write sloppily, using nothing but present participles. I find them very useful in the last lap of *Mrs D*' (*WD*, 66).

A further fine example of her transcendence of narrative linearity is the scene in Regent's Park with its aleatory method of composition. As one character strolls beside another who had till then been the focus of narrative attention, so the 'fickle' narrative abandons its object to follow the newcomer. A sense of the co-existing currents and eddies in the park is thereby created. In its nimble manoeuvring between individuals and groups, the narrative in Regent's Park is behaving like a hostess at a party, and this is no accident. Parks and parties are privileged symbols for Woolf because they are protected enclaves outside the normal run of social life. They are places of a libidinal indulgence that must be repressed elsewhere, mini-utopias of the senses. Every time Clarissa gives a party she has a 'feeling of being something not herself, and that everyone was unreal in one way: much more real in another'. 'Unreal' because detached from everyday occupations but 'more real' because in touch with libidinal energies the social ego represses. Hence 'it was possible to say things you couldn't say anyhow else . . . to go much deeper' (*MD*, 187-8). Bourton, with its spacious grounds and continuous social gatherings, derives its resonance in the novel from being both park and party at once.

In his famous discussion of *To the Lighthouse* in *Mimesis*, Erich

Auerbach asks 'who is speaking in this paragraph?'. He sees its narrator as 'spirits between heaven and earth, nameless spirits capable of penetrating the depths of the human soul . . . but not of attaining clarity as to what is in process there, with the result that what they report has a doubtful ring'.[4] This unidentifiable narrative voice is achieved by 'represented speech' suspending the location of the subject between character and author. This ambiguous 'between-ness' produces at once an intimate internalised tone and a certain indirectness; we are so near to, yet somehow distant from, the process of the character's mind. The reader's sense of distance is confused in a mode of writing 'all crepuscular . . . as bright as fire in the mist' (*WD*, 23). 'Who is speaking?' asks Auerbach, and in the case of the conjunction 'for' one might well ask 'who is reasoning?'. Or again: 'It was quite different here from Westminster, she thought, getting off at Chancery Lane. It was so serious; it was so busy. In short, she would like to have a profession. She would become a doctor, a farmer . . .' (*MD*, 150-1). With the phrase 'in short', one senses a narrative voice which judges and sums up for the reader, but the discourse glides quickly back into the flow of Elizabeth's consciousness. Whenever we try to pinpoint the locus of the subject, we get lost in a discursive mist. Consider Holmes' visit to Septimus: 'When the damned fool came again, Septimus refused to see him. Did he indeed? said Dr. Holmes, smiling agreeably. Really he had to give that charming little lady, Mrs. Smith, a friendly push before he could get past her into her husband's bedroom' (102). 'The damned fool' is of course Septimus' language, though the whole sentence is straightforward narrative. 'Charming little lady' is Holmes' phrase, but 'smiling agreeably' and 'a friendly push' are neither simply an objective narrative account nor straightforwardly Holmes' own point of view. 'Agreeable' and 'friendly' are corroded by Septimus' 'damned fool', which is backed up by the context of the whole passage; they acquire an ironic edge which satirises Holmes' self-complacency. The narrative voice is fractured, wavering, multiple, closer to Auerbach's 'spirits' in the plural than to J. Hillis Miller's 'omniscient narrator'.[5] In terms of feminist theory, what Woolf's writing effects is a denial of the unified subject which supports all discourse and is necessarily 'masculine', since the symbolic order is established with the phallus as its fundamental signifier. The narrative consciousness in her writing, if indeed there is one, has stopped judging, interpreting, explaining; it has no single identity or position. It is not, in Kristeva's terms, a 'thetic' subject. Or if that is strictly impossible, since the symbolic is sustained by the thetic subject, at least the latter's control is minimised and the other modality of signifying practice—the semiotic realm—is granted as much autonomy as possible.

The extent to which Woolf is playing with the conventions of novelistic interpretation is revealed as the aeroplane flies over London forming letters of smoke, presumably as an advertisement. 'Only for a moment did they [the letters] lie still; then they moved and melted and were rubbed out up in the sky, and the aeroplane shot further away and again, in a fresh space of sky, began writing a K, and E, a Y perhaps?' (23-4). For this 'key' to all mythologies is doubtless the transcendental signifier or solution to the hermeneutic riddle of the novel. Woolf tantalises us with its possibility only to withdraw it at once. As narrator, she refuses an 'authoritarian' relation to her own novel. Rejecting the thetic self of keys and master-codes, Woolf once declared: 'when I write I'm merely a sensibility' (*WD*, 48). This practice of writing as an asocial 'sensibility' aroused much hostile criticism in the 1930s, especially from *Scrutiny*. Its argument that her work is mere subjectivism to be rejected by the mature adult with a responsible life in society is summed up in Leavis' article of 1942.[6] But a more positive assessment of Woolf must rather emphasise that her writing makes the fixed 'I' or K-E-Y recede. It loosens the ligatures of the unifying subject so as to produce a style whose characteristics are simultaneity and fluidity. Yet she never destroys the thetic 'I' completely, which is after all impossible as long as one wants to remain within language (and sane). Nor does she ever go as near to shattering language as James Joyce. Her work is not a drastic demolition but a subtle and elegant infraction of syntactic laws in order to undermine the protocols of writing. It loosens the relations of subject and object (which the thetic subject sustains) by present-participles or intrusive phrases between subject and predicate, or by breaking up noun-verb or subject-object relations into a mere listing of nouns, and thus disrupting the logical relations which language produces for a human subject by its syntactic order. 'Looseness' is a term that indicates for Woolf that her writing is going well: 'I feel as if I had loosened the bonds, pretty completely and could pour everything in. If so—good'. Or again, 'the diary writing has greatly helped my style; loosened the ligatures' (*WD*, 62, 69).

In Kristevan terms, Woolf's texts disperse the transcendental unified subject that underpins male rationality and narrative, and open new possibilities for subjective activity. Her writing subverts this positionality and tries to adumbrate the area anterior to the logical, judging, naming subjectivity, to bring in the semiotic as the domain of rhythm, sounds, intonation, colour and shape. In her writing rhythm is always very conspicuously at work. Moreover, colours often come into the foreground, detached from their objects, as in such curious intense sketches as 'Blue and Green' and 'Kew Gardens':

> Yellow and black, pink and snow white, shapes of all these colours, men, women, and children were spotted for a second upon the horizon, and then, seeing the breadth of yellow that lay upon the grass, they wavered and sought shade beneath the trees, dissolving like drops of water in the yellow and green atmosphere, staining it faintly with red and blue. (*HH*, 39)

Woolf was criticised by her contemporaries for her failure to create 'characters', but clearly she seeks a state of human being prior to its consolidation into personality. Her work thus undercuts

> the masculine point of view which governs our lives, which sets the standard, which established Whitaker's Table of Precedency, which has become, I suppose, since the war, half a phantom to many men and women, which soon, one may hope, will be laughed into the dustbin where the phantoms go, the mahogany sideboards and the Landseer prints, God and Devils, Hell and so forth, leaving us all with an intoxicating sense of illegitimate freedom (*HH*, 44)

It is only 'reality' or 'character' as defined by this deeply compromised perspective that Woolf is 'unable' to create. 'I dare say it's true, however, that I don't have that ''reality'' gift. I insubstantiate, wilfully to some extent, distrusting reality—its cheapness. But to get further. Have I the power of conveying the true reality?' (*WD*, 57). The 'true reality' is reality for women; but Woolf is nervous of the censorship and condemnation of men. Julia Kristeva writes: 'In women's writing, language seems to be seen from a foreign land . . . . Estranged from language, women are visionaries, dancers who suffer as they speak'.[7] In a foreign land, one is naturally more cautious about infractions of the law because of the danger of expulsion. So Woolf would never go to extremes as Joyce did, and throughout her career kept a conventional form of narrative writing in the third-person past tense, for 'writing must be formal. The art must be respected' (*WD*, 69). Her literary affirmation of 'true reality' remains well protected by an apparent formality as it subtly undermines the fixed positionality of the subject in language. Her natural descriptions often emit a lateral message about the process of the novel's own construction, as in this self-reflexive description of a London cloudscape.

> Fixed though they seem to be at their posts, at rest in perfect unanimity, nothing could be fresher, freer, more sensitive superficially than the snow-white or gold-kindled surface; to change, to go, to dismantle the solemn assemblage was immediately possible; and in spite of the grave fixity, the accumulated robustness and solidity, now they struck light to the earth, now darkness. (*MD*, 153).

In a similar way, the apparently ordered 'assemblage' of Woolf's own prose may be dismantled in a flash by some disorientating slippage of narrative voice or some 'tunnelling' and mining of the present by the past.

By disrupting linearity and achieving simultaneity, she modifies the status of the subject. For the unified self is only one stage of a 'subject in process/on trial' (as Auerbach seems to have realised instinctively in his reference to 'what is in process' in the depths of the Woolfian 'soul'). The true subject is not a linear 'series of gig-lamps symmetrically arranged', but is evoked by the more spatial image of 'a luminous halo'. Though the phrase 'from the beginning of consciousness to the end' implies some kind of temporality, yet the image of 'envelope' does not really coincide with the concept of linear continuity. In this image of 'this varying, this unknown and uncircumscribed spirit' with its 'aberration' and 'complexity', Woolf offers us a subject which has no simple unity, no clear boundary between itself and other. The 'envelope' is 'semi-transparent' and therefore not a clear-cut distinction between spirit and world. Woolf's idea of self denies homogeneity: 'she [Nature] let creep instincts and desires which are utterly at variance with his [man's] main being, so that we are streaked, variegated, all of a mixture' (*CE,* 4:161).

In writing *Mrs. Dalloway* Woolf aspires to be 'only a sensibility', 'not having to draw upon the scattered parts of one's character' (*WD,* 48), and this is the mode of being the novel itself presents. Phyllis Rose calls it 'the most schizophrenic of English novels'.[8] There is a parallel between the mode of subjectivity that constitutes the stylistic principle of the book, and the state of being of Clarissa and the other characters. Only by a conscious 'assembling' of her scattered parts into one centre can the heroine attain a social identity as Clarissa Dalloway: 'collecting the whole of her at one point (as she looked into the glass) . . . . That was her self—pointed; dart-like; definite. That was her self when some effort, some call on her to be herself, drew the parts together' (*MD,* 42). It is not only in her youth that she believed in 'a transcendental theory' that 'the unseen part of us, which spreads wide', might survive. Now as she walks through London she feels herself part of the trees at home, of the house, of people she had never met: 'being laid out like a mist between the people she knew best, who lifted her on their branches as she had seen the trees lift the mist, but it spread ever so far, her life, herself' (11-12). Whether walking through London, alone in her attic, or retiring in the middle of the party into privacy, Clarissa is mostly presented in a state of being where she does not need to 'draw the parts together'. In this context it is interesting to note how obsessive she is about shoes and gloves: 'old Uncle William used to say a lady is known by her shoes and her gloves . . . . Gloves and shoes; she had a passion for gloves' (13-4). It is as if without this minute 'passionate' attention the extremities of the body cannot be trusted not to fly asunder, acting out the physical dissociation their owner so often experiences!

Clarissa would not say of anyone that 'they were this or were that'. To her, identity is not true; it is impossible for her to be one thing and not the other. 'She felt very young; at the same time unspeakably aged. She sliced like a knife through anything; at the same time was outside, looking on' (10). In a state of constant assemblage and dissolving, 'she would not say of Peter, she would not say of herself, I am this, I am that' (11). 'On the ebb and flow of things', her dispersed parts momentarily fuse with objects she passes as she walks, and she becomes rhythm, sound, colour, shape. Even the sense of the body as a whole disappears: 'this body she wore . . . with all its capacities, seemed nothing—nothing at all. She had the oddest sense of being herself invisible; unseen; unknown' (13). In this state of being, she recalls the dirge sung over the apparently dead Imogen in *Cymbeline:* 'Fear no more the heat o' the sun/ Nor the furious winter's rages'. With the self 'dead', freed from ego-identity, there is no longer death: 'here, there, she survived, Peter survived, lived in each other, she being part, she was positive, of the trees at home' (11). Later, sitting down to mend her silk dress, the focused 'centre' or 'diamond' (42) of her consciousness dissolves and she becomes one with the physical rhythm of her manual occupation. 'So on a summer's day waves collect, overbalance, and fall; collect and fall; and the whole world seems to be saying ''that is all'' more and more ponderously, until even the heart in the body which lies on the beach says too, that is all' (44-5). The ego gone, there is only body, movement, colours, sound, pulsing rhythms: 'the body alone listens to the passing bee; the wave breaking; the dog barking, far away barking and barking'.

What is true of Clarissa applies to most of the characters. Septimus naturally experiences a similar state of mind, for his ego has collapsed into psychosis. He no longer retains Clarissa's power to 'collect the whole of her at one point'. He experiences his body as 'connected by millions of fibres' with the leaves of trees (26); everything becomes quickening colour and sounds, rising and falling rhythms. The sea imagery which evoked Clarissa's experience while mending the dress recurs:

> Septimus Warren Smith lying on the sofa in the sitting-room; watching the watery gold glow and fade with the astonishing sensibility of some live creature on the roses, on the wallpaper. Outside the trees dragged their leaves like nets through the depths of the air; the sound of water was in the room, and through the waves came the voices of birds singing. Every power poured its treasures on his head, and his hand lay there on the back of the sofa, as he had seen his hand lie when he was bathing, floating, on the top of the waves, while far away on shore he heard dogs barking and barking far away. Fear no more, says the heart in the body; fear no more. (153-4)

This recurrent sea imagery figures some great semiotic *chora* traversed by natural pulses, rhythms and currents in which one can lapse out into a state of libidinal bliss. But having asserted the utopian value of the semiotic, the novel then tries to recontain the sensory energies it has released. It does so by what the Russian Formalists term a 'motivation of the device', naturalising and thus 'taming' the semiotic impulses it has unleashed. It does so in two ways. First, by locating the events of the novel shortly after the First World War: 'For it was the middle of June. The war was over' (6). After this great disruption of national life, the simplest routines and objects have a vivid novelty they would otherwise lack. The disruptive intensity of the novel's sensory perceptions are rationalised as the simple expression of relief at national survival. Secondly, semiotic intensities are naturalised by being implicitly presented as the effects of a summer heat wave. Under this heat and pressure, sensory impressions become surcharged, almost surreal, as in the 'Kew Gardens' passage I cited above. Mrs. Dalloway's utopian impulse to celebrate the semiotic as an end in itself is constrained by a need for naturalistic motivation, just as Woolf mines the laws of writing from *within* rather than brazenly flouting them like James Joyce.

One cannot go on living with the self in abeyance, for this is the dividing line between sanity and madness. Though she enjoys the other mode of being, Clarissa also 'assembles that diamond shape, that single person' or 'thetic' subject. But she sees this ego as essentially possessive and domineering, and her decision not to marry Peter Walsh is her rejection of masculine egotism, 'for in marriage a little licence, a little independence there must be between people living together day in day out' (10). Peter's continuous fondling of his pocket-knife is an assertion of this masculinity, though it ironically points to his insecurity in the role (his attraction for women is that he is 'not altogether manly')(172). Though the masculine ego has constituted civilisation as rational, at the same time it leads humanity to the destruction of world war by its rapacious aggression, as I argued in the previous chapter. Throughout the novel the impact of the First World War is recalled, 'tears and sorrows', 'a miracle thinking of the War', and Septimus is its major victim as a case of the 'deferred effects of shell shock' (201). The novel thus expresses the spiritual bankruptcy to which pure masculinity leads humanity. Septimus 'developed manliness' in the war (95-6), the effect Mr. Brewer desired for him when he advised football; but the emotional turbulence which Septimus has had to repress in doing so has destroyed his being. He is 'a border case' (93), who has tried to internalise the self-definitions of a domineering capitalist and imperialist society but who is annihilated as its victim and scapegoat. In its depiction of his fate at the hands of society, the novel fulfils Woolf's intention 'to criticise the social system, and to show it at work, at its most intense'(*WD*, 57).

The incarnation of the imperialist spirit is Sir William Bradshaw, who champions society with his perfect 'sense of proportion' and will 'for dominion' (110, 112). 'Sir William not only prospered himself but made England prosper, secluded her lunatics, forebade childbirth, penalised despair, made it impossible for the unfit to propagate their views until they, too, shared his sense of proportion' (110). The connection between the social prosperity that 'proportion' fosters and imperialist colonisation is more explicit in the case of its sister goddess, 'Conversion'. She is even now engaged

> in the heat and sands of India, the mud and swamp of Africa, the purlieus of London, wherever, in short, the climate or the devil tempts men to fall from the true belief, which is her own—is even now engaged in dashing down shrines, smashing idols, and setting up in their place her own stern countenance. (110-11)

'Conversion' does not only operate on the international political level. It is also another name for a male egotism which feasts on the wills of women, adoring its own features stamped on the face of them. Lady Bradshaw is its victim, and Woolf's tone is accordingly less severe toward her: 'Fifteen years ago she had gone under . . . the slow sinking, water-logged, of her will into his' (111).

The novel's treatment of the mysterious car in which greatness (the Queen or Prime Minister?) passes through London satirises the whole machinery of British Empire. There are merely 'rumours', 'nobody knew whose face had been seen', and yet this is enough to send men, if need be, 'to the cannon's mouth, as their ancestors had done before them' (17, 21). But the novel can find few supporters of such a satirical stance among its own characters. Peter Walsh regards himself as an outcast and seems to turn a critical eye on the tediousness of high society; he had been a 'Socialist, in some sense a failure' (56). Yet at deeper levels of personal commitment he responds fervently to the imperialist order. He admires the boys' military marching, for they symbolise 'duty, gratitude, fidelity, love of England': 'it's strange, he thought, what a sentiment I have about that, disliking India, and empire, and army as he did' (61-2). Exceptional in having an element of 'unmanliness', he cannot after all escape a sentimental admiration of patriarchal civilisation: 'the show was really very tolerable' (62). Being fundamentally on the side of Sir William Bradshaw, he could not understand the agony of Septimus (as Clarissa does). He sees the ambulance which carries away Septimus after his suicide, but checks his imagination and empathy with the victim in the spirit of Bradshaw's sense of proportion: 'Ah, but thinking became morbid, sentimental . . .' (166). Despite his illusion that 'he had escaped! was utterly free', Walsh is deeply complicit with nationalism. Yet his criticism of Clarissa on the same issue will none the less stand. She too is the very converse of satirical. She has an 'absurd and faithful passion' for the royal family, 'since her own people were courtiers once', and her party too is partly a gesture of reverent service to this myth (7).

However, she harbours deep within her a total rejection of the masculine ego which constitutes this society. This secret space within the self is symbolised by her attic, to which she ascends 'like a nun withdrawing, or a child exploring a tower' (35). These two images convey the ambivalence of the attic, which is at once a place of deathly renunciation and also a locus of excited new life and discovery. A related ambivalence characterises Woolf's entire treatment of this episode. Clarissa's spiritual trauma is a result of Lady Bruton not inviting her to a lunch party with Richard. The effect is out of all proportion to the cause, and a note of satire is introduced, as if this scene were so sensitively significant to Woolf that it could not be introduced without a protective outworks of irony. Its centrality to the novel is signalled none the less. As Clarissa mounts the stairs, it is 'as if she had left a party . . . had shut the door and gone out and stood alone, a single figure against the appalling night'. She 'leaves' her party before she had ever given it, and the attic episode is thus more spiritual focal point than satirical interlude. In the attic Clarissa discards social pretensions: 'women must put off their rich apparel. At mid-day they must disrobe' (35). She doffs her yellow feathered hat in a symbolic gesture. For earlier when learning from Hugh Whitbread of his wife's 'internal ailment' Clarissa had felt 'very sisterly and oddly conscious at the same time of her hat' (8). A spontaneous movement of female solidarity is undercut by her awareness of herself as sexual object of the male gaze, and in laying aside the hat she renounces her coquettish self-consciousness in a return to 'sisterliness'. It is as if the sheets of the attic bed, which are 'clean, tight stretched in a broad white band', symbolise Clarissa's intact hymen. For this attic is the space where she rejects all men, even Richard who is the 'most disinterested' among the politicians: 'she could not dispel a virginity preserved through childbirth which clung to her like a sheet'; 'through some contraction of this cold spirit, she had failed him. And then in Constantinople, and again and again' (36). The sexual implications of her withdrawal to the attic are complex. It is naturalistically motivated by the fact of her having a bad heart, but then both Clarissa and Richard exploit this biological datum to their own ends. 'Richard insisted, after her illness, that she must sleep undisturbed' (35). He adopts the Bradshaw approach, invoking the 'disinterested' authority of medical science to impose constraints on female desire. But Clarissa trumps this manoeuvre: 'really she preferred to read of the retreat from Moscow. He knew it', and the final curt sentence carries a stinging humiliation for her husband. This antagonism is repeated a little later. When Richard goes to bed, he 'as often as not, dropped his hot-water bottle and swore! How she laughed!' (37). This is not just an affectionate chuckle at a spouse's clumsiness. In its excess it has an edge of malice, as if Clarissa were mocking the feeble substitute (hot-water bottle) for the female bodily warmth she is denying him. The image of Napoleonic retreat through snow symbolises Clarissa's 'contraction of this cold spirit'. Yet unlike the retreat from Moscow her withdrawal does not come nearer to any southern source of warmth. She retreats further and further into the attic: 'Narrower and narrower would her bed be' (35).

Feminist theorists argue that the fact that the baby girl's first love-object is a body of her own sex, the mother's, constitutes the basis of woman's narcissistic disposition. It will be difficult for a woman's later relations with men to overcome her original loss of the mother's body. In one sense, narcissism simply marginalises women, reducing them in the male view to the trivia of dress and appearance, to personal vanity. But carried to an extreme, it becomes threatening to men, opening the dangerous prospect of women attaining mutual sexual satisfaction without any need of the male sex. Peter Walsh, who seeks 'compassion, comprehension, absolution' in womanhood, is constantly confronted by Clarissa's total rejection: 'this coldness, this woodenness, something very profound in her . . . an impenetrability' (68). The most vivid image of this is their encounter as she sits mending her dress. There is a mythic resonance as a long-absent Ulysses returns to claim a Penelope whose busy weaving has kept away false suitors. But the scene is more complex than this; there is a compacting of mythic roles. Peter is both Ulysses (newly returned) and false suitor (her true husband, Richard, is away), and Clarissa emphasises his latter role by continuing busily to sew. However, nor is Richard altogether the true possessor. Clarissa often thinks of the extreme joy she might have had if she had married Peter: 'this gaiety would have been mine all day' (52). She thus in a sense rejects both of them. When she hears Walsh at the door 'she made to hide her dress, like a virgin protecting chastity', and a subdued note of sexual violation pervades the scene: '"And what's all this?" he said, tilting his pen-knife towards her green dress' (45-6). Her sewing up of the dress becomes the restitching into wholeness of a hymen which Walsh constantly threatens to tear.

Because her libido folds narcissistically in upon itself, Clarissa ultimately rejects all relationships. Aware of this cold spirit, she feels 'I am alone for ever' (53), at the same time acclaiming the importance of 'privacy of the soul'. The dialectic within Clarissa between this cold contracting of the self and the schizophrenic dispersal I discussed earlier is obliquely recognised by the novel in its suggestive remark about the negligible figure of Mr. Bowley as he waits at Buckingham Palace: 'Little Mr. Bowley . . . was sealed with wax over the deeper sources of life, but could be unsealed suddenly, inappropriately, sentimentally, by this sort of thing' (23). These two impulses are also conveyed in the lines from *Cymbeline:* 'Fear no more the heat o' the sun/Nor the furious winter's rages'. It is the psychic 'heat o' the sun' which melts the sealing wax and unleashes the experience of dissociation. Clarissa's attic is clearly an allusion to that which contains Bertha Mason in *Jane Eyre,* but Woolf has reversed the values traditionally associated with the 'madwoman in the attic'. Whereas Bertha's attic is a place of tropical heat and sexuality, of latent physical violence, Clarissa's has the chill atmosphere of a mortuary.

Yet Clarissa can occasionally overcome the 'contraction of this cold spirit' in her relations with women. She yields to 'the charm of a woman, not a girl' (namely, the mother), and this experience is explicitly sexual:[9]

> It was a sudden revelation, a tinge like a blush which one tried to check and then, as it spread, one yielded to its expansion, and rushed to the farthest verge and there quivered and felt the world come closer, swollen with some astonishing significance, some pressure of rapture, which split its thin skin and gushed and poured with an extraordinary alleviation over the cracks and sores. Then, for that moment, she had seen an illumination; a match burning in a crocus; an inner meaning almost expressed. But the close withdrew; the hard softened. (36)

The culmination of these experiences with women, 'the most exquisite moment of her whole life', is the kiss with Sally Seton (40). Clarissa acclaims this love with Sally for its 'purity' and 'integrity', which are impossible in a relationship with a man, which always becomes domination by the latter. Bonds with men, especially their culmination in marriage, are a menace to the freedom of women. They constitute a kind of delayed repetition of the girl's transition from an active mother-attachment to mere mother-identification, which securely fixes her as a castrated being in patriarchal society.[10] Marriage breaks up the bond between women to prevent them from uniting in a republic of women. Hence 'a sense of being in league together, a presentiment of something that was bound to part them (they spoke of marriage always as a catastrophe), which led to this chivalry, this protected feeling' (39).

The old woman opposite Clarissa's window is a mirror image of herself in her attic, a symbol of both independence and isolation in patriarchal society. With 'a room of her own', she lives up to the demands of Woolf's major feminist tract. 'It was fascinating, with people still laughing and shouting in the drawing-room, to watch that old woman, quite quietly, going to bed alone' (204). This mirror image endows Clarissa with the strength to resist the colonisation of herself by 'the contagion of the world's slow stain',[11] from the 'incessant parties . . . blunting the edge of her mind' (87). The characters are continually criticising each other, but the novel implies that there may exist a strong bond between women in spite of differences and hostility:

> her inquiry, 'How's Clarissa?' was well known by women infallibly to be a signal from a well-wisher, from an almost silent companion, whose

utterances (half a dozen perhaps in the course of a lifetime) signified recognition of some feminine comradeship which went beneath masculine lunch parties and united Lady Bruton and Mrs. Dalloway, who seldom met, and appeared when they did indifferent and even hostile, in a singular bond. (117)

There is a bond even between such profoundly different types as Clarissa and Miss Kilman. The relationship has a fierce intensity unparalleled in any of her dealings with men:'she hated her: she loved her' (192).

The problem for woman is to assert a female specificity as difference and to open up a space for this difference in the masculine structure of society. This is not to be achieved simply by the assertion of women's comradeship; it involves, rather, the question of the subject. Having remained close to the maternal body in spite of its enforced repression, the girl or woman inscribes herself naturally within the semiotic, in touch with what Kristeva terms the 'spasmodic force' of the repressed. Her task is then to affirm this force, to find the practices appropriate to it, but this is not a matter of its defining a separate, substantive symbolic of its own. It will rather at best be enacted as a moment *inherent* in the rejection of the process of the ruptures, of the rhythmic breaks. Kristeva writes: 'Insofar as she has a specificity of her own, a woman finds it in asociality, in the violation of communal conventions, in a sort of a-symbolic singularity'.[12] Menaced equally by the paternal paranoia and the mother's schizophrenia, the daughter must maintain herself in a difficult equilibrium between the two.

Women must somehow keep a hold on the symbolic, and thus as if in reinforcement of the mirror phase—the threshold of the formation of the unitary ego—Clarissa needs her own reflection: 'the delicate pink face of the woman . . . of Clarissa Dalloway; of herself' (42). She 'assembles' the self 'when some effort, some call on her self' constrains her, and then becomes conscious of the lack of 'something central which permeated' (36). This lack is the maternal body which she must repress to become a subject in the symbolic. Because of this denial of the maternal and her own body, 'there was an emptiness about the heart of life; an attic room' to which she austerely withdraws 'like a nun' (35). Sally, who more fully owns her body, is quick to detect this absence in Clarissa: 'But—did Peter understand?—she lacked something' (207). The novel stresses this withdrawal from the body in several ways. Clarissa had 'grown very white since her illness'. She is the mere ghost of a woman, cut away by physical infirmity from the energies of bodily life. There is, moreover, 'a touch of the bird about her, of the jay, blue-green, light, vivacious.' (6). Such energy as she retains is light and ethereal, more spiritual than physical. And, finally, she is in her fifties, cut off by the fact of menopause from the fertile biological processes of ovulation and menstruation.

The most positive representation of the body in the novel is the younger Sally Seton, who 'forgot her sponge, and ran along the passage naked' (38). Sally's fascination for Clarissa is 'a sort of abandonment', that is, her different relationship to her own body. Sally teaches Clarissa about sex, speaks of sexual matters in front of men, shocks others by running along the passage naked. She confidently asserts herself as a woman, 'as if she could say anything, do anything' (37). Not that her feminist boldness goes altogether unpunished. Hugh Whitbread's kiss is an act of sexual violence, the rape on a miniature scale of a woman who has dared argue that her sex should have the vote. But to our and Clarissa's disappointment the apparently fearless Sally has married a capitalist millionaire and now has five sons. Maternity is the only female identity which is valorised by patriarchy. Only as a mother is a woman allowed to have her sexuality as difference, to own her body and social place. The novel's arch-rebel becomes a sober conformist, 'Lady Rossiter'.

Repressing the body, Clarissa is given a place in the symbolic order constructed around the Name-of-the-Father:

> this body, with all its capacities, seemed nothing—nothing at all. She had the oddest sense of being herself invisible; unseen; unknown; there being no more marrying, no more having of children now, but only this astonishing and rather solemn progress with the rest of them, up Bond Street, this being Mrs. Dalloway; not even Clarissa any more; this being Mrs. Richard Dalloway. (13)

'Not even Clarissa': once subdued to the laws of the father, a woman is next handed over to another man, the husband, as commodity in the structure of patriarchal exchange relations. Throughout the novel Clarissa's mother is curiously repressed, though her father is always prominent in her memories. Only once, at the party, does a guest exclaim that Clarissa looks that night 'so like her mother': 'And really Clarissa's eyes filled with tears', but this brief 'return' of her mother is instantly cancelled by her duty as hostess of patriarchy (193). This repression of the mother is also a denial of the maternal in herself, 'unmaternal as she was' (209). Women have to be the daughters of their fathers, not their mothers. Childbirth can no more rupture her hymen outwards than the phallus could inwards; she retains 'a virginity preserved through childbirth' (36). She cannot move from girlhood to full womanhood, and is constantly defensive about her own maternity. Even Walsh notices the over-emphasis with which she declares 'Here is my Elizabeth' (53), and later concludes that the daughter probably does not get on with her mother. Seeing Clarissa, Walsh notes that women 'attach themselves to places; and their fathers—a woman's always proud of her father' (62). In 'Mrs. Dalloway in Bond Street' Clarissa recalls 'A happy childhood—and it was not to his daughters only that Justin Parry had seemed a fine fellow'.[13] Breaking away from the mother, Clarissa accepts the role prescribed by the paternal law, becoming 'the perfect hostess' (9). And this repudiation of the mother is repeated in Elizabeth; Sally could 'feel it by the way Elizabeth went to her father' (213).

The pain of severance from the maternal generates in the subject for the rest of its life a desire for its overcoming, but the risk of fusing with the mother is shown in Peter's dream in Regent's Park. He falls asleep beside an elderly nurse who 'resumed her knitting' as he began snoring. Here is a female knitter more reassuring than the formidable Clarissa-Penelope. Peter's dream of the solitary traveller evokes some ultimate principle of womanliness which will 'shower down from her magnificent hands, compassion, comprehension, absolution' (64). Walsh had found himself repelled by the 'coldness' and 'impenetrability' of Clarissa, and therefore thinks 'rather let me walk straight on to this great figure, who will, with a toss of her head, mount me on her streamers and let me blow to nothingness with the rest' (64). Fusion with the maternal is thus an instant dispersal of the human subject. But the passage is deeply ambivalent because the novel recognises that Peter is invoking an ideology of femininity in order to avoid contact with the *real* woman. Hence it speaks of 'the visions which ceaselessly float up, pace beside, put their faces in front of, the actual thing', and hence the satirical tone, as when the Sirens are 'lolloping away on the green sea waves'. Yet even this ideological stereotype of the feminine does answer to certain deep-seated needs of the subject, and the sea imagery relates to those more utopian visions of the sea as a great pulsing semiotic *chora* which I discussed earlier.

The voice of the 'battered woman' singing opposite the tube station is precisely the voice of the mother, issuing from 'a mere hole in the earth' (91). The woman or mother is always a void, a hole in discourse—as the unconscious, the unrepresentable: 'so rude a mouth, a mere hole in the earth, muddy too, matted with root fibres and tangled grasses', an image irresistibly suggesting the female genitals. This singing voice 'bubbles up without direction, vigour, beginning or end' and 'with an absence of all human meaning into ee um fah um so/foo swee too eem oo' (90). A mere rhythmic babble of phonemes, this 'old bubbling, burbling song' of the pre-symbolic becomes something like the very energy behind evolution. It has endured 'through all ages—when the pavement was grass, when it was swamp, through the age of tusk and mammoth'. The ancient woman offers an alternative, 'feminist' view of evolution to set against the patriarchal social Darwinism of Sir William Bradshaw, whereby only the fittest or those with a 'sense of proportion' survive.

Just as the broken syllables of the old woman's song escape the lexical and syntactic grids of the symbolic order, so she has no place within society but wanders freely as a tramp. Clarissa, in contrast, is 'a perfect hostess'. But this complicity with patriarchy arouses an intense hostility in Miss Kilman, who has been 'cheated' by the male social order (136). Kilman is a 'phallic woman', who identifies with the Father, denying her femaleness and 'becoming' a man herself.[14] Hence Clarissa can only conceive of Kilman's hated existence as a phallic scraping of delicate interior membranes: 'It rasped her, though, to have stirring about in her this brutal monster . . . had the power to make her feel scraped, hurt in her spine; gave her physical pain' (15). Kilman does not 'dress to please', and hates Clarissa's feminine delicacy and fashionableness—'the most worthless of all classes' (136). But because of her inferior class-position, Kilman has had to adopt the most aggressive masculine values to secure a niche for herself. She is dominated by the male spirit of 'conversion' and even her love for Elizabeth becomes a rapacious desire for possession. In attempting to conform to the mores of male society, Kilman has had to repress the maternal and the body, just as Clarissa did.

'It was the flesh that she must control' (141). She must subjugate 'her unlovable body', and desperately resorts to religion, 'for the light in the Abbey was bodiless' (147). It is her superabundant physicality—'her largeness, robustness and power'—that strikes people, taking the form of a powerful *smell* about which the novel remains coy. At tea, Elizabeth reflects that 'it was rather stuffy in here' and when she gets out finds 'the fresh air so delicious' (145-9). Earlier Clarissa thinks of Kilman 'mewed in a stuffy bedroom' (14), and when she reflects that 'year in year out she wore that coat; she perspired; she was never in the room five minutes without making you feel her superiority', this final noun is not quite what we had been expecting! It is precisely the effort to repress the body that turns it sour and rancid, for Kilman's disgusting odour is in stark contrast to the healthy smell of Richard Dalloway: 'when he came into the room he smelt of stables' (208). The heavy stress on Kilman's perspiration reveals her as a principle of heat in contrast to Clarissa as the principle of ice and austerity, and this may lend another meaning to Clarissa's desire to 'fear no more the heat o' the sun'.

'With all this luxury going on, what hope was there for a better state of things? Instead of lying on a sofa . . . she should have been in a factory' (137). Kilman's denunciation of Clarissa is perfectly justified, and Peter similarly criticises her indolent life-style. By making Kilman so distastefully aggressive, however, the novel encourages us to discount her attack on Clarissa's complicity with the patriarchy, the contradiction that she depends on an imperialistic society to afford the material conditions for the possibility of values—'the privacy of the soul' (140)—which that society at the same time negates. This is the very contradiction that Raymond Williams has noted of Bloomsbury in general: that the Bloomsbury intellectuals were culturally superior to and contemptuous of the bourgeoisie to whom they were mere administrative functionaries.[15] Clarissa's distant attitude to Sally's husband as self-made capitalist further attests this distaste for the bourgeoisie, as does the novel's hostility to Sir William Bradshaw as a member of the ideological thought-police of the capitalist order. Bradshaw in turn is suspicious, even aggressive towards 'cultivated people' (108). This contradiction in Clarissa cannot be evaded: her stoical, almost existential anguish and her creative energy in organising the party, on the one hand; her role as snobbish and superficial hostess of high society, on the other. This was Woolf's worry too: 'the doubtful point is, I think, the character of Mrs. Dalloway. It may be too stiff, too glittering and tinsely' (*WD*, 61). But because of the 'heavy, ugly, commonplace' nature of the accuser, Woolf can make her heroine's defence more convincing than it could otherwise have been.

But though Clarissa and Miss Kilman are starkly opposed, the novel does none the less propose a mediation of their antagonistic qualities in Lady Bruton, whom Clarissa in a sense envies. Like Kilman, Lady Bruton is a physically powerful, emphatically phallic woman. She is 'a strong martial woman' with a 'ramrod bearing' who 'could have worn the helmet and shot the arrow', thus contrasting with the physical slightness of Clarissa (*MD*, 198). But like Clarissa, Lady Bruton belongs to the upper echelons of society and, unlike Miss Kilman, she has little intellect: 'Debarred by her sex, and some truancy, too, of the logical faculty (she found it impossible to write a letter to the *Times*)' (198). 'Derived from the eighteenth century', she belongs decisively to the past. As an aristocrat, it is appropriate that the positive values associated with the body should attach to her, since the aristocracy as a class is defined by its blood and breeding. These values have migrated downwards socially, attaching themselves to the lower classes represented by Kilman and becoming negative and dystopian in the process. It is Kilman's fusion of mind and body that makes her, politically, so dangerous in the novel, for she incarnates two of the most potent middle-class images of social subversion. On the one hand, she is a menacing utopianist who constructs cerebral schemes for the total renovation of society. Hence her enthusiasm for post-revolutionary Russia, which places her in the Jacobin tradition first denounced in the name of piecemeal, 'organic' reform by Edmund Burke. Sally and Clarissa were enthusiastic over William Morris in their teens—'they meant to found a society to abolish private property' (38)—and such youthful infatuations, the novel implies, display an innocent idealism. Kilman falls out of favour because she has poor enough taste still to be adhering to socialist principles in her forties. But she is not only abstract revolutionary, but also represents the middle-class fear of the lower orders as 'mob', as a pre-rational body clamouring for gratification, violently overturning social constraints. Hence the novel's stress on Kilman's voracity: her wolfing down of eclairs, her desire for the sensory pleasures she has been deprived of. But in uniting these two images of revolution, she is also rendered powerless. Mind and body tug in opposite directions, and the overall effect is to leave Kilman static and impotent in the middle. Thus Clarissa finally defeats her because the 'abducted' Elizabeth returns to the family.

> Love and religion! thought Clarissa, going back into the drawing-room, tingling all over . . . The cruellest things in the world, she thought, seeing them clumsy, hot, domineering, hypocritical, eavesdropping, jealous, infinitely cruel and unscrupulous, dressed in mackintosh coat, on the landing; love and religion. Had she ever tried to convert anyone herself? Did she not wish everybody merely to be themselves? And she watched out of the window the old lady opposite climbing upstairs . . . . There was something solemn in it—but love and religion would destroy that, whatever it was, the privacy of the soul. The odious Kilman would destroy it. (139-40)

In these terms Clarissa defends herself over caring more for her roses than the Armenians: 'Hunted out of existence, maimed, frozen, the victims of cruelty and injustice . . . no, she could feel nothing for the Albanians, or was it the Armenians? but she loved her roses (didn't that help the Armenians?)' (133). She asserts this in contrast to Kilman who 'would do anything for the Russians', 'starve[s] herself for the Austrians', but 'in private inflicted positive torture, so insensitive was she, dressed in a green mackintosh coat' (14). Though Clarissa's argument is little more than a caricature, her point is that callousness of feeling causes oppression, and that it is therefore useless to react to injustice with the very kind of insensitivity which brought it into being in the first place. She rejects politics as incompetent; most areas of life 'can't be dealt with, she felt positive, by Acts of Parliament' (6). However, a world groaning under injustice can hardly wait for a total change of the political system brought about simply by loving roses. Mrs. Dalloway is such a 'pure' revolutionary that she ends up being reactionary. Though she feels the need for wholesale social transformation, she suspects the practical means of change (political action) as themselves bearing the dominative values of the system they are attacking. To attempt to transform society is, for Clarissa, to be complicit with its worst values. Even socialism is no more than a disguise for the tyrannical spirit of 'conversion'. It 'walks penitentially disguised as brotherly love through factories and parliaments; offers help, but desires power' (111). This view is a further consequence of the Romantic suspicion of abstract political thought, and its effect is to leave Clarissa in a state of total political quiescence.

But the novel does not ignore the contradiction in Clarissa's views about society. Returning from her expedition to the florist, she reflects:

> how moments like this are buds on the tree of life . . . but all the more, she thought, taking up the pad, one must repay in daily life to servants, yes, to dogs and canaries, above all to Richard her husband, who was the foundation of it . . . one must pay back from this secret deposit of exquisite moments (33)

But her guilty exquisite moments are ironised by being shaken the very next instant by the news that Lady Bruton had asked Richard to lunch without her. Earlier in the novel Mrs. Dempster had already been used to satirise Clarissa's arguments about 'roses'. For Mrs. Dempster, life has been bitter, she has given to it 'roses; figure; her feet too': 'Roses, she thought sardonically. All trash, m'dear. For . . . life had been no mere matter of roses' (31).

Septimus is another victim of patriarchy, its 'scapegoat' (29). He had left home as a boy 'because of his mother; she lied' (93-4), and educated himself in public libraries. His growth is a process of breaking away from the Mother and assimilation to the locus of the Father. He works within capitalism, for a firm of auctioneers, valuers and estate agents, and finally goes to war in which he 'developed manliness'. But in this final stage of his cultivation of 'masculinity' Septimus has broken down: 'in the War itself he had failed' (106). His obsession that 'one must be scientific' represents the imperative towards rationality of the patriarchal civilisation. But he at last finds that 'he could reason; he could read . . . he could add up his bill', but he could not feel: 'his brain was perfect; it must be the fault of the world then—that he could not feel' (98).

Like Clarissa and Kilman, Septimus cannot come to terms with the body. 'His body was macerated until only the nerve fibres were left. It was spread like a veil upon a rock' (76). He invokes a Shakespearean loathing of 'the sordidity of the mouth and the belly', and rejects his wife's wish to have a son: 'the business of copulation was filth to him before the end' (98-9). But the refusal to procreate is also a refusal of the symbolic order. Septimus refuses to take the final step into patriarchy by becoming a father himself. His sense of being alone and helpless—'exposed on this bleak eminence, stretched out' (159-60)—is analogous to the fear of the infant bereft of the mother. He wishes to retrieve the maternal, which the Name-of-the-Father forbids. Its bitterly resented prohibition is represented in the novel by Holmes and Bradshaw: 'What right has Bradshaw to say ''must'' to me?' (162). With the breakdown of the symbolic and the return of the repressed, Septimus loses the capacity for communication. He talks to himself, hears voices which do not exist, hears birds speak in Greek. Communication as the exchange of signs is made possible only within the symbolic order, through the split in the subject which is established by the intervention of the phallus in the unity with the mother. In Septimus' madness, the division between signifier and signified is no longer clear. Words and things are confused, imagination and reality no longer distinguishable. 'And the leaves being connected by millions of fibres with his own body, there on the seat, fanned it up and down; when the branch stretched he, too, made that statement' (26). 'He was not Septimus now' (27): he can no longer sustain a stable self, and body, world, word fuse, intersect and traverse each other. Inner meaning seems about to emerge from the world at any moment. The word is no longer an empty sign but an absolute reality through which truth shines with no dividing bar between signifier and signified: 'The word ''time'' split its husk; poured its riches over him . . .' (78). Septimus had always been interested in poetry and now, released from the constraints of the symbolic order, he emerges as a paradigm of the symbolist poet. For him, 'Nature signified by some laughing hint . . . her determination to show . . . always beautifully, and standing up close to breathe through her hollowed hands Shakespeare's words, her meaning' (154). When he escapes the 'forcing' of souls by a human nature that he conceives as 'the repulsive brute, with the blood-red nostrils':

> to watch a leaf quivering in the rush of air was an exquisite joy. Up in the sky swallows swooping, swerving, flinging themselves in and out, round and round, yet always with perfect control as if elastics held them;

and the flies rising and falling; and the sun spotting now this leaf, now that, in mockery, dazzling it with soft gold in pure good temper; and now and again some chime (it might be a motor horn) tinkling divinely on the grass stalks—all of this, calm and reasonable as it was, made out of ordinary things as it was, was the truth now; beauty was everywhere. (77-8)

In this state Septimus enjoys colours, rhythms, sounds with extreme intensity as the thetic subject is dissolved into the semiotic *chora* it had formerly so severely repressed.

However, the society which the Name-of-the-Father upholds does not leave one alone. It drives a wedge between subject and the maternal body, signifier and signified. Clarissa understands Septimus' suicide as 'defiance. Death was an attempt to communicate, people feeling the impossibility of reaching the centre which, mystically, evades them; closeness drew apart; rapture faded; one was alone. There was an embrace in death' (202). In psychoanalytic terms, the 'embrace' which Septimus aims at in death may be regarded as an embrace with the Mother. It is impossible to reach the 'centre', since the subject is split in its very constitution. It is this embrace which Clarissa seems to experience for a moment with women: *jouissance*[16] which 'gushed and poured with an extraordinary alleviation over the cracks and sores' when she saw 'an inner meaning almost expressed' (36).

What is crucial is not how Clarissa deciphers Septimus' suicide, but *that* she deciphers it, that a relation is established between the two figures. If Septimus does indeed 'embrace' the Mother in death, it is because he now in a sense *has* a 'mother' who acknowledges him: 'She felt somehow very like him' (204). The novel is deeply marked by the images of the absent son and the grieving mother, and in this respect is a development of the closing pages of *Jacob's Room.* Early on Clarissa thinks of Mrs. Foxcroft 'eating her heart out because that nice boy was killed and now the old Manor House must go to a cousin; or Lady Bexborough who opened a bazaar, they said, with the telegram in her hand, John, her favourite, killed' (7), Clarissa's thoughts revert several times to Lady Bexborough, for news of her son's death intrudes as brutally into her bazaar as news of Septimus' does into Clarissa's party. The figures of bereaved mother and absent son also haunt Peter Walsh's dreams: 'an elderly woman who seems . . . to seek over the desert, a lost son; to search for a rider destroyed; to be the figure of the mother whose sons have been killed in the battles of the world' (65). When Clarissa 'understands' Septimus' suicide she momentarily assumes the guise of this archetypal bereaved mother.

Though Septimus perished under the pressure of a patriarchal society, Clarissa 'had escaped' by submitting herself to the Law and obtaining protection:

> there was the terror; the overwhelming incapacity, one's parents giving it into one's hands, this life, to be lived to the end, to be walked with serenely; there was in the depths of her heart an awful fear. Even now, quite often if Richard had not been there reading the *Times* . . . she must have perished. She had escaped. But that young man had killed himself. (203)

She concedes her compromises, 'her disgrace . . . She had schemed; she had pilfered . . . She had wanted success' (203). In contrast, the old woman in the house opposite affirms the imperishable existence of the soul, which entirely escapes the social world. She represents a woman's space, a room of one's own, independent of male-dominated society. By means of this mirror image of her self—'the old lady stared straight at her!' (204)—Clarissa can secure this female space in herself.

Clarissa survives despite or perhaps because of her contradictions; Septimus vicariously represents the risk of a total rejection of patriarchal law, and perishes. He is both the absent son, united with the mother only in the Pyrrhic moment of death, and a surrogate for Clarissa, committing suicide on her behalf. In Woolf's original plan Clarissa was herself to die.[17] The invention of Septimus is thus a defensive 'splitting', whereby Clarissa's most dangerous impulses are projected into another figure who can die for her; to this extent, she and he are one composite character. The internal split in Clarissa which worried Woolf—existential anguish versus social superficiality—reveals that the problem of woman opens on to the problems of subjectivity and of writing. How is it possible to recognise and valorise the position of woman as difference? There are two obvious ways open to feminists. One may deny the difference in order to be admitted as subject in the symbolic order, becoming a token man. Or one may refuse the symbolic altogether, and risk being even more marginalised than before or, worse, expelled as mad from society. These alternatives are in a sense represented by Kilman and Septimus; Clarissa must negotiate a precarious balance between them. Either way, a woman is grievously at risk. Clarissa sees her sister Sylvia, 'on the verge of life, the most gifted of them', killed by a falling tree—'all Justin Parry's fault' (87). The Father kills the most gifted girl by means of the Phallus (tree). No wonder then that Clarissa 'always had the feeling that it was very, very dangerous to live even one day' (11). Hence her strategy of wariness: 'her notion being that the Gods, who never lost a chance of hurting, thwarting and spoiling human lives, were seriously put out if, all the same, you behaved like a lady' (87), and we can rewrite 'gods' here as 'men'. To behave 'like a lady', as patriarchy's 'perfect hostess', is thus a cautious programme for survival.

To avoid total submission to the Law of the Father, gaining a place in the symbolic at the price of negating women's difference, but also to avoid expulsion from the symbolic into complete silence: one can only oscillate between these two positions, living a tension which must not be fully resolved in either direction. A woman must reject the frozen identity of the subject but not relinquish subject-hood altogether. This dialectic between stasis and rupture is precisely what the novel's style achieves. Of it, as of the cloudscape, 'Fixed though they seemed at their posts . . . nothing could be fresher, freer, more sensitive . . . to change, to go, to dismantle the solemn assemblage was immediately possible' (153). Clarissa often experiences the moment of suspense between stasis and rupture: 'How fresh, how calm, stiller than this of course, the air was in the early morning . . . and yet . . . solemn, feeling as she did, standing there at the open window, that something awful was about to happen' (5). And this momentary pause in the dialectic is memorably repeated in Septimus:

> I went under the sea. I have been dead, and yet am now alive, but let me rest still, . . . as, before waking, the voices of birds and the sound of wheels chime and chatter in a queer harmony, grow louder and louder, and the sleeper feels himself drawing to the shores of life, so he felt himself drawing towards life, the sun growing hotter, cries sounding louder, something tremendous about to happen. (77)

This suspense and adventure of the subject are often evoked in terms of sea imagery: 'an exquisite suspense, such as might stay a diver before plunging while the sea darkens and brightens beneath him, and the waves which threaten to break . . .' (34-5). It is a pause or poise or indeterminacy between life and death.[18] Clarissa's heart hesitates between life and death in 'a particular hush, or solemnity; an indescribable pause; a suspense . . . before Big Ben strikes' (6). Big Ben in a sense represents the Father (Peter had earlier identified with its 'direct downright' sound). Tolling the hours, it dissects the continuum of life and imposes a structure. *Mrs. Dalloway* was, indeed, titled *The Hours* in the early stages of Woolf's writing (*WD*, 57-62). 'Shredding and slicing, dividing and subdividing, the clocks of Harley Street nibbled at the June day, counselled submission, upheld authority, and pointed out in chorus the supreme advantages of a sense of proportion' (*MD*, 113). Time also introduces death by its measuring out of life, which itself, as sheer semiotic energy, does not know it. Time is alien to the polymorphous mode of being: 'she feared time itself . . . how little the margin that remained was capable any longer of stretching, of absorbing, as in the youthful years, the colours, salts, tones of existence' (34). Representing patriarchal law, aligned with the William Bradshaws of the world, Big Ben subjugates even the most recalcitrant subjects to the social order: the old lady 'was forced, so Clarissa imagined, by that sound, to move, to go' (140). As lawgiver, it forces the imperative 'must' on the human subject. As Clarissa lets the hours impose a structure on her life, she collects the dispersed parts of her self into a social entity: 'The clock was striking . . . . But she must go back. She must assemble' (204-5). Her life is continual dispersion and reassembly. The subject is neither 'this' nor 'that'. Its true 'site' is the very dialectic between dissemination and reconstruction: the melting away of the shell of the self by the sun's heat and the freezing of it again into a hard crust by the thetic winter of Big Ben. 'Fear no more the heat o' the sun/Nor the furious winter's rages'.

In *Anti-Oedipus* Deleuze and Guattari provocatively claim: 'A schizophrenic out for a walk is a better model than a neurotic lying on the analyst's couch'.[19] Clarissa is a decentred subject of flows and part-objects, like Septimus, but she is also the cool, composed hostess of the evening party. Her contradictoriness and internal divisions denote the difficult problem of women's writing itself, since her subjectivity is at the same time the mode of the subject in the writing of the novel. How can a woman give voice to the place of women and reject masculine discourse without being marginalised into madness and silence? If language and the symbolic order are essentially masculine, this is only possible through the repression of the woman. Even the 'martial' Lady Bruton, who talks about politics like a man, has no power of language and logicality. Women have to constitute themselves as split subjects to enter the symbolic and play a man's game. So Woolf never radically destroys the laws of syntax. She lets grammar dissect and regulate the flow of the subject's desire, and keeps the conventional narrative form of third person and past tense. Within this apparent conformism, however, her writing tries to give voice to the specificity of a female subject who is outside any principle of identity-to-self, which can identify with multiple scenes without fully integrating herself into them.

CHAPTER 4

To the Lighthouse

When Roger Fry inquired what 'symbolic meaning' the arrival of the characters might have, Woolf replied:

> I meant *nothing* by *The Lighthouse.* One has to have a central line down the middle of the book to hold the design together. I saw that all sorts of feelings would accrue to this, but I refused to think them out, & trusted that people would make it the deposit for their own emotions—which they have done, one thinking it means one thing another another. I can't manage Symbolism except in this vague, generalised way. Whether its [*sic*] right or wrong I don't know; but directly I'm told what a thing means, it becomes hateful to me. (*QB*, 2:129)

Evoking a motif of the quest, the novel's title makes the lighthouse a hermeneutic provocation, goading the reader into a sense of tantalising but never quite delivered significance. In its elusiveness, the lighthouse becomes a second-order symbol, a symbol of Symbolism itself, of the belief that art can redeem into order the chaotic flux of perception. For the novel illustrates modernism's 'general tendency to develop . . . from a metonymic (realistic) to a metaphoric (symbolist or mythopoeic) representation of experience'.[1] The lighthouse concentrates the issue of symbolism, but does not exhaust it; symbols, and meditations on symbols, are scattered throughout the text.

I argued above that though *Jacob's Room* aspires to the 'rose' or symbol, it remains aware of its actual failure to achieve more than the 'ram's skull' of allegory. On the face of it, *To the Lighthouse* seems more successful in its pursuit of symbolism. Mrs. Ramsay's privileged moments are miniature symbols, unifying 'unrelated passions', making 'of the moment something permanent' (*TL*,

230, 249). Lily too partakes in the symbolic vision, witnessing the Ramsays' ascent from contingent ordinariness to universal 'symbols of marriage' (115). As artist, she seeks to charge the everyday with a wealth of meaning and wonder, 'to be on a level with ordinary experience, to feel simply that's a chair, that's a table, and yet at the same time, It's a miracle, it's an ecstasy' (309-10). Her fidelity to 'ordinary experience' aligns her initially with Mr. Ramsay's philosophical empiricism, yet she will not rest there, seeking also a numinous glow that will redeem the object. She feels that Mrs. Ramsay's achievements remain in the mind 'like a work of art', and both mothering and painting have the same symbolic goal: 'in another sphere Lily herself tried to make of the moment something permanent' (249). Lily's picture is a figure for the text itself, since both painter and novelist seek that 'central line down the middle' which will solder their artefacts together. Lily ponders 'how to connect this mass on the right hand with that on the left' (86), how to find some mediation between the rigidly closed terms of a binary opposition. The central line which accomplishes this may itself be seen as symbolising the Lighthouse. But the question to be asked of the novel is whether it fully succeeds in its 'official' symbolist project. Gillian Beer argues that *To the Lighthouse* is a 'post-symbolist novel' in that 'symbolism is both used and persistently brought into question',[2] and there does indeed seem to be a discrepancy between declaration and achievement—an ambivalence for which Mrs. Ramsay provides a helpful image early in the text. Putting the children to bed, she tactfully manages to make Cam believe that the boar's skull (another version of the ram's skull of *Jacob's Room*) does not exist and that only the bird's nest in the beautiful valley does, while simultaneously convincing James that the skull is still there. This is a self-reflexive image of the novel, which itself employs such contradictory logic.

Stylistically, *To the Lighthouse* brings to full maturity the techniques of *Mrs. Dalloway* in its use of stream-of-consciousness and also in the greater density of metaphor and simile in the local texture of its writing. This triumph of metaphor is itself a *thematic* concern of the book, for it is possible to read the polarity of Mr. and Mrs. Ramsay as an opposition between literal meaning and metaphoricity. The rigorous propositional discourse of the philosopher is contrasted with the symbolic language of art.

Boasting of 'his own accuracy of judgement', Ramsay refuses to tamper with facts, never altering 'a disagreeable word to suit the pleasure or convenience of any mortal being' (13). Mrs. Ramsay, on the other hand, as an artist whose raw materials are emotions, distorts and exaggerates as necessary according to the human context of her discourse. Since Plato's expulsion of poetry from his Republic, philosophy has distanced itself from literature, denigrating it for the deceitful or dangerous potential of its fictions. If Mrs. Ramsay mentions 'something about "waves mountains high"', the rigorous rationalist Charles Tansley answers, 'yes . . . it was a little rough' (18). As a British empiricist, Mr. Ramsay represents a double chastening of philosophy. To its inaugural expulsion of literature, he adds a deep-grained suspicion of far-fetched metaphysical speculation. He represents, as it were, the very philosophy of philosophy, its most stringent self-discipline.

The opposition of philosophy and fiction emerges at the very start of the novel in the contention over the trip to the Lighthouse. 'Yes, of course, if it's fine tomorrow', says Mrs. Ramsay, filling her son with an intense joy which, however, is cut short by her husband: 'But . . . it won't be fine' (12). Enraged by the 'extraordinary irrationality' of his wife, Ramsay regards her remark to James as a mere story of some 'fabled land'; she 'in effect, told lies' (53-4). But the very intensity of his reaction here suggests already, as I shall argue at length below, that he is not the impersonal arbiter he takes himself to be. When attacked by her husband in the name of his uncompromising Reason or Logos, Mrs. Ramsay defends herself in the name of 'people's feelings' (54). At this moment she is aligned with the values of art against philosophy, since she is 'keeping her head as much in the same position as possible' for the sake of Lily's painting. Moreover, she dreams of her future delight if her son should 'turn out a great artist' (52). Soon after, Ramsay returns to tease James, tickling his bare calf with a stick: 'James will have to write *his* dissertation one of these days' (53). Flaunting the power of the phallus ('sprig'), the father mocks his son's incompetence and warns him that he must one day resemble his father, thus threatening to end the relationship with the mother. Mrs. Ramsay has been knitting a 'reddish-brown stocking' for the sick little boy on the Lighthouse, but since James yearns to be the boy on the Lighthouse, she is in a sense knitting it for him. Designed to protect her son's bare leg against the paternal sprig, the stocking's real purpose is displaced into kindliness towards the Lighthouse boy, so that the depth of Mrs. Ramsay's resistance to her husband may be muted. But the stocking is not only defensive. It will also be a counter-phallus, in the spirit of Roland Barthes' remarks on 'the symbolism of the braid': 'Freud, considering the origin of weaving, saw it as the labour of a woman braiding her pubic hairs to form the absent penis'.[3] James inhabits a classical Oedipal triangle as philosophy and art, reality and fiction, struggle over and for him.

But though philosophy tries to purge literature in the name of the transparency of language to truth, it soon discovers that its relation to its 'discredited' counterpart is less secure than it thought. Ramsay may regard his wife as an impediment to his nobler aims, but in fact he 'depended' on her continual demands for sympathy: 'to be taken within the circle of life, warmed and soothed, to have his senses restored to him, his barrenness made fertile' (62). Yielding to his demands, Mrs. Ramsay practises on him the very mode of rhetoric he had denounced when she satisfied James with it. Ramsay, 'filled with her words, like a child who drops off satisfied', offers no acerbic rejoinders now (64). In a brief subversive impulse which she tries at once to suppress, Mrs. Ramsay is able 'to feel finer than her husband', to admit that she is not 'entirely sure, when she spoke to him [i.e. flattered him], of the truth of what she said'. She projects on to an anonymous general subject her own central but inadmissable perception: 'people said he depended on her' (65). The novel both controls and releases this feminist subversiveness through the figure of Charles Tansley. By divorcing the most disagreeable aspects of 'Ramsayism' from the hero and projecting them on to his disciple, the text reduces the ambivalence of Mr. Ramsay himself and makes easier the idealisation of him in which it occasionally indulges. At the same time, the hostility that is properly a response to Ramsay can be more readily expressed towards the meaner figure of his acolyte. Though still in displaced forms, Mrs. Ramsay can become positively castrating towards him. Walking into town with Tansley, she observes a 'one-armed man' sticking up a circus poster: 'his left arm had been cut off in a reaping machine two years ago' (23). It seems to me to be the thought of the amputated limb rather than the circus itself which 'filled her with childlike exultation and made her forget her pity' in a sudden access of castrating rebellion against her usual sympathetic role. When vexed later by Tansley, Mrs. Ramsay turns the pages of the store's list in search of 'the picture of a rake or a mowing-machine' (29). She follows a chain of associations—mowing, reaping-machine, amputated arm—in another subdued threat of castration.

The relationship of the Ramsays enacts a Derridean deconstruction of the usual hierarchy philosophy/literature. Philosophy constitutes itself in relation to the Logos

> by identifying as its Other a fictional and rhetorical mode of discourse, and the demonstration, carried out for example in some of Nietzsche's texts, that philosophy too is a rhetorical structure, based on fictions generated by tropes, leads one to posit what one might call an archi- or proto-literature which would be the common condition of both literature and philosophy. Philosophy cannot escape the rhetorical, the literary, the linguistic.[4]

As a version of philosophy versus literature, the polarity of man and woman in *To the Lighthouse* is governed by the theological metaphor of the Fall. The initial terms are seduced out of their native realm of pure spirit into the fallen world of materiality, body or signifier: 'Of course Ramsay had dished himself by marrying a beautiful woman and having eight children' (141). Women are simultaneously elegant trinkets to have about the home and immovable leaden weights that shackle the free play of the male mind. For Ramsay, his wife and child are 'trifles so slight compared with the august theme just now before him', yet 'he would have written better books if he had not married' (73, 110). Women are a danger both quantitative and qualitative. They take up one's time, making one's books shorter: 'if he had been alone dinner would have been almost over now; he would have been free to work', complains William Banks (138). But, more radically, they infiltrate the very substance of one's thinking, not just truncating one's books but making them qualitatively worse. Women menace philosophy from both the outside and the inside, and have all the ambivalence of the Derridean 'supplement'. The superfluous, women and children, that which philosophy seeks to purge itself of, soaks into the very core of its being.

Ramsay condenses into a single figure two illustrious literary predecessors, Casaubon and Lydgate from *Middlemarch*. Like the former, he is a dried-up aging academic, a man no longer capable of living up to his former promise. Like the latter, he regards himself as ruined in his intellectual career by marriage to a trivial wife. Mr. Ramsay is much concerned with 'subject and object' (40), and it is a split between these two faces of reality that is at issue here, since he is objectively a Casaubon but subjectively a Lydgate. A similar split characterises the relation between his philosophy and life. As an empiricist, he regards the subject as a *tabula rasa,* humbly awaiting the outer world to imprint its messages upon it. Personally, however, he is a moral *idealist.* His ego swells to absorb into itself every aspect of its world, imperiously shaping objects to its subjective needs. My comparison with *Middlemarch* is prompted by the novel's own curious reference to the book. In a discussion of Eliot, Minta is 'really frightened, for she had left the third volume of *Middlemarch* in the train and she never knew what happened in the end' (153). *To the Lighthouse* chops up *Middlemarch* as the reaping-machine had earlier lopped off the bill-sticker's arm. A Bloomian 'anxiety of influence' is at work here, as the novel 'castrates' a commanding precursor on its own theme of the intellectual husband. *Middlemarch* must be silenced because we might compare Mrs. Ramsay as well as her husband to her Eliotic predecessors. For if she is certainly not the idealistic Dorothea, she can only be the structural equivalent of the repulsive Rosamund Vincy, representing in more benign form the social banalities of the latter. But this is not an identification *To the Lighthouse* cares to pursue.

Both Mr. and Mrs. Ramsay see each other as an inadequate Nature that needs the support of themselves as Culture. Ramsay's clumsy physical gestures remind his wife of 'the great sea lion at the Zoo tumbling backwards after swallowing his fish and walloping off' (55). Ramsay in turn sees her as a deficient Nature, lovably defenceless. She and James are 'children picking up shells, divinely innocent and occupied with little trifles . . . . They needed his protection; he gave it them' (56-7). But Ramsay is a child too, as far as his wife is concerned. He may see himself as a Promethean quester, but she comforts him 'as a nurse carrying a light across a dark room assures a fractious child' (63). To impute to anyone the status of a child is to express loving protectiveness, but also to reify one's relations with them. Adults-as-children are locked in an eternal stasis of the personality; the protective love one extends to them is regressive. To see the other as child is also a technique for avoiding blame and friction, for his or her petulance then becomes a simple expression of Nature, rather than a tension within a real and developing relationship. In a relation with a not yet fully developed subject, one can be master. Mrs. Ramsay wishes 'always to have had a baby'; 'she was happiest carrying one in her arms. Then people might say she was tyrannical, domineering, masterful, if they chose; she did not mind' (94).

In seeing each other as children, both husband and wife project their own lack on to the other sex. In this novel it is not only the woman who suffers a lack that puts her in need of protection. Mrs. Ramsay pities 'men always as if they lacked something—but women never, as if they had something' (133). This shifting of the locus of lack enters and confuses the sexual imagery of the text. On the one hand, Mrs. Ramsay's responsiveness to Ramsay's demands for sympathy opens a warm female interior into which the male, as 'beak of brass', plunges himself. As John Mepham notes, the sexual theme 'is also present in a series of words which function simultaneously in several of these strands of metaphor (''pulse'', ''throb'', ''erect'', ''aglow'', ''she bade him take his ease there, go in and out, enjoy himself'')'.[5] But her response is not only receptive, she is not only an empiricist *tabula rasa*. 'Animated and alive', she also 'pours erect into the air a rain of energy, a column of spray' (61-2). 'There throbbed through her, like a pulse in a spring which has expanded to its full width and now ceases gently to beat, the rapture of successful creation' (64). Different aspects of the male sexual act are split apart and attributed to characters of the opposite sex. Ramsay retains only its physically penetrative side, that aspect which, when isolated, can be seen as a brute violence forcing its way into the delicate membranes of the female. The more 'positive' side of the male sexuality, the ejaculation of fertilising seed deep within the female, is projected on to Mrs. Ramsay. In this divorce between 'form' and 'content', Ramsay retains only the physical husk of the act, while his wife appropriates its inner procreative kernel. Hers is the deeper activity of the teeming energy of the semen as opposed to the merely 'histrionic' activity of the physical mechanism that deposits it. Freud argues that it is improper to identify femininity with passivity, masculinity with activity. For him the opposition active/passive characterises the infantile anal phase, whereas masculine/feminine is the logic of adult sexuality; to confuse the two is 'the error of superimposition'.[6] Active and passive are the qualities of biological drives, not genders. If *To the Lighthouse* consents to some degree to Mrs. Ramsay's 'passive' role of ministering angel in the house to her 'active' intellectual husband, of subsidiary nurse to his primary speculations, it also suggests a simultaneous counter-logic. The 'passive' role turns out to display a *truer* activity than the 'active', and the 'subsidiary' is revealed as essential to that 'primary' function to which it had initially seemed a mere external crutch. Ramsay's self-serving opposi- tions—between philosophy and fiction, men and women—are, to cite Derrida, 'a violent hierarchy' and not 'the peaceful co- existence of a *vis-à-vis*'.[7] Yet the text dismantles these hierarchies to the point where the excluded term becomes the inner truth of its opposite, where people at last acknowledge that 'he depended on her' (65).

Mr. Ramsay is both phallus and child, Mrs. Ramsay both open womb and phallus. Though this ambivalence characterises their relation in general, it is brought to a sharp focus in the Oedipal crisis of their son James. The father is a disturbing intruder into the Imaginary 'perfect simplicity and good sense of his relations with his mother' (61). Mrs. Ramsay is thus phallic because the pre- Oedipal child has not yet discovered her 'castration'. Since James has not yet accepted his submission to the father, he sees Ramsay as in part just another demanding child, lacking something which the mother, as whole, can fill with her 'phallus'. Yet he also does experience the mother's lack, in two ways. He wants to be the phallus *for* her, filling her lack along the lines of Freud's equation faeces-penis-child: James 'stood stiff between her knees' (63). He also experiences her lack as her powerlessness to resist the insistent penetrations of the father, 'the beak of brass, the arid scimitar of his father, the egotistical man' (63). Inasmuch as his mother desires this penetration, she also implicitly desires her son's impotence, rejecting him as *ersatz* phallus for the father's real one. A substitute is only important as long as you do not have the real thing, and James will finally be abandoned: 'she had gone away and left him there, impotent' (287). James ultimately accepts his symbolic castration and the Law of the Father. He abandons the desire to be the phallus for the mother and waits to become like his father, 'having' the phallus himself.[8] During the boat trip he completes the paternal identification, becoming himself 'the lawgiver' to Cam (260).

Binary oppositions and hierarchies in this novel are ceaselessly undone. Philosophy condemns fiction, but does not escape a persistent fictionality of its own. Ramsay denounces his wife for the rhetorical nature of her language—its distortions of fact, its virtual lies—and this rhetoricity has a twofold nature. She uses tropes rather than a supposedly 'transparent' language that would let truth shine unimpededly through. But her discourse is also rhetorical in that it is attuned to specific situations, taking its predominant colouring from the present needs of its interlocutors rather than aspiring to impersonal objectivity. The irony of Ramsay's denunciation of his wife is that he himself is equally 'guilty' of this practice. He is far from the strict adherent to referentiality that he imagines himself to be; Lily is alarmed by the 'touch . . . of exaggeration' in his face (241). If his wife angers him so much, it is not simply that her fictionality grates on his nerves as the converse of his own convictions. It is rather that she might compel him to face up to the secret truth of his own discourse. She is both the binary opposite of philosophy and a dangerous revelation of its own procedures. Ramsay sees her as his contrary, divided from him by the sharp line between truth and fiction. But there is in fact a continuum between husband and wife, the latter revealing, as Nietzsche had argued, that truth is just a metaphor or fiction whose fictionality we have forgotten. At crucial moments in the text the polarity truth/fiction is suddenly reversed. All her husband's 'phrase-making was a game', reflects Mrs. Ramsay: 'it annoyed her, this phrase-making, and she said to him, in a matter-of-fact way, that it was a perfectly lovely evening' (110). Ramsay is contradiction incarnate: a philosophical empiricist who is an emotional idealist, a remorseless enemy of fiction who indulges in incessant self-pitying fables. Though he demands objectivity, he will not even allow literature the kind of universality it might justly claim. Instead of reading literary texts as statements about human nature in general, he manipulates them to his own subjective purposes. Orchestrating an 'impure rhapsody', he cannot renounce the 'delicious emotion' aroused by the poetry he recites (44). As a literary reader, he is guilty of that very 'affective fallacy' for which he criticises his wife. Ramsay wildly exaggerates and distorts as a reader of verse, seeming to believe that by an 'explosion' (316) of literariness in this special realm he can purge his thought of rhetorical elements that might otherwise contaminate his philosophy.

Mrs. Ramsay is both wanderer in the 'fabled land' and stubbornly 'matter-of-fact', a contradiction inherent in the stereotypical image of women. At one level, woman represents the *body,* that substratum of materiality without which her husband's abstract creations could not exist but which also threatens to 'dish' them. Woman's own evident physicality—the facts of menstruation, of childbearing—and her down-to-earth role in child care qualify her for this identification with the body or matter. Yet, at another level, she is also the *irrational,* her everyday intellectual caprices being only a short distance from psychosis and insanity. While her husband's speculations involve a self-discipline of mutual entailment (from P to Q to R, in Ramsay's terms), hers are unconstrained, excessive. Female biology is simultaneously the opposite of the male intellect and the ground for intellect's dangerous liberation into fancy or madness. Matter-of-fact and fable-making at the same time, woman is denigrated by the men in the text on both grounds alternately, while she is valorised over them by the novel for the same contradictory reasons. Mrs. Ramsay thus represents both an excess and a lack of speech. Tansley sees women as doing 'nothing but talk, talk, talk', yet she reflects that Mr. Ramsay 'found talking so much easier than she did. He could say things—she never could' (134, 190). Similarly, when she does talk, her language is both charged with subjectivity and yet strangely void of it. It is full of her caringness as social unifier, yet strikes its hearers as curiously elusive. She is metaphorically described as 'tablets bearing the sacred inscriptions, which if one could spell them out would teach one everything, but they would never be offered openly, never made public' (82). Her openness to Ramsay's 'arid scimitar' is counterbalanced by her opacity as sign to everyone in the book. Her discourse admits subjectivity (kindliness) at one level only to conceal it tantalisingly at another. It is the exact opposite of her husband's, which claims to be an impersonal vessel of facts but is actually charged with his manipulative emotions. Like *Jacob's Room,* then, *To the Lighthouse* is also a project to decipher the enigmatic 'sign' of its protagonist.

Both Mr. and Mrs. Ramsay have their own specific mode of truth. The former cannot reach Z, 'if thought ran like an alphabet from A to Z' (184-5). The alphabet here is a metaphor for the linearity of Ramsay's thought, but also a figure for the necessary figurality of philosophy itself. It is not incapacity that prompts Woolf to use this way of representing his thought, as if she were simply unable to render his researches in the highly specific way George Eliot evokes Lydgate's. Her point is rather that philosophy is originarily figurative, organised around certain master-tropes. The figure of the alphabet is thus not just an illustrative analogy, which is how philosophy would like to see its own metaphors. Ramsay's linearity also implies a view of the nature of time: each step being generated by its predecessor, both philosophy and time are rigidly consequential. The possibility of tomorrow's trip to the Lighthouse is totally determined by a present configuration of factors—clouds, wind, air-pressure. This discipline of linearity becomes a harsher ascesis in his relation to the objects of his thought. Lily sees his work as a meditation on 'a scrubbed kitchen table': 'this seeing of angular essences, this reducing of lovely evenings, with all their flamingo clouds and blue and silver to a white deal four-legged table' (40-1). This scrubbed table epitomises his anti-rhetorical discourse: 'something bare, hard, not ornamental . . . uncompromisingly plain' (240-1). With 'no colour to it', his language refuses the colours of rhetoric. But his fidelity to the unadorned object is paradoxical. His essences 'reduce' the very objects they should render up, bleeding them dry of all specificity and in a sense cancelling them out.

Mrs. Ramsay has her own mode of access to truth, as when she sits alone knitting: 'Losing personality, one lost the fret, the hurry, the stir; and there rose to her lips always some exclamation of triumph over life when things came together in this peace, this rest, this eternity' (100). Ramsay reduces, but his wife synthesises as experiences 'come together' in her moments of vision. Such privileged moments seem anti-social; they contrast with what she temporarily sees as the mere fret of socialising. Yet they do share the unifying structure of her great moments of social achievement. Inside or outside her community, Mrs. Ramsay always achieves 'a summoning together' (100). Ramsay's meditations on 'subject and object and the nature of reality' (48), here give way to an indifferentiation of the subjective and objective. His wife sits 'with her work in her hands until she became the thing she looked at—that light for example'. She feels 'they [things] expressed one; felt they became one; felt they knew one; in a sense were one'. The female subject can reach out to its world in this way because it was never a unified sealed self in the first place. A division in that subject facilitates its responsiveness to objects. Auto-affection—one part of the subject lovingly touching another—can be projected outwards. Merging with her objects, Mrs. Ramsay 'felt an irrational tenderness thus (she looked at that long steady light) as for oneself': 'she praised herself in praising the light'. Aspects of the subject reach towards each other in a sexual embrace—'a bride to meet her lover'—that ends in orgasm. The lighthouse is 'stroking with its silver fingers some sealed vessel in her brain whose bursting would flood her with delight', and this delicate digital caressing of surfaces seems far preferable to Ramsay's arid phallic penetrations. In a series of provocative essays, Luce Irigaray has related this division in the female subject to the structure of the female sexual organs: '*She is neither one nor two.* She cannot, strictly speaking, be determined either as one person or as two', for 'a woman ''touches herself'' constantly without anyone being able to forbid her to do so, for her sex is composed of two lips which embrace continually. Thus within herself she is already two—but not divisible into ones—who stimulate each other'.[9] *To the Lighthouse* adds a nuance to this account. Woman's necessary self-caress has become numb through familiarity. Her auto-affection must make a detour outside itself into objects, swerving from the subject but only to the smallest extent that is compatible with its orgasmic return in a full, 'defamiliarised' self-embrace. But as a necessary mediation, the Lighthouse becomes an object of fear, 'the steady light, the pitiless, the remorseless, which was so much her, yet so little her' (101-3). Auto-affection must pass through the Lighthouse on its way back to itself, but also risks being trapped in it, the temporary mediation becoming a prison. In the subject's need for the object to complete the circular journey back to itself, it falls into the object's power; the Lighthouse 'had her at its beck and call'. Irigaray's work is a helpful starting-point, but not fully adequate to these complexities.

Mrs. Ramsay's dinner party is another privileged moment, a triumph of 'merging and flowing and creating'. She here glimpses something 'immune from change [which] shines out . . . in the face of the flowing, the fleeting' (163). Her achievement is symbolically crystallised in the poem recited at the end of dinner. Like her own discourse, its words are both bafflingly opaque signifiers and yet full with the subject's desire: 'she did not know what they meant', yet they 'seemed to be spoken by her own voice, outside herself, saying . . . what had been in her mind'. Similarly, the words are both anonymous, as if 'they had come into existence of themselves', but also the collective self-expression of the dinner party, 'their own voice speaking'. In this utopian linguistic moment, the disquieting features of writing—its anonymity, its opacity—are both acknowledged and surpassed in the Hegelian sublation. We approach what Derrida terms 'the absolute proximity of voice and being . . . of voice and the ideality of meaning'.[10] In the privileged moments there is a stress on a certain transcendence of materiality. Sitting at the window, she feels 'all the being and the doing . . . evaporated' (99). Later, in the security of the dinner party, she casts off solidity: 'she hovered like a hawk suspended; like a flag floated in an element of joy' (162). But such access to the self-presence of meaning is ephemeral: with her foot on the threshold, she knows that it had become 'already the past' (173). Mrs. Ramsay is both more 'solid' than her husband, closer to the day-to-day routines of domestic life, and more 'immaterial' than he is, since even into his boldest speculations he takes nagging self-centred doubts about his own fame. She, on the other hand, is capable of a proper transcendence of the personal, shedding all attachments to become 'a wedge-shaped core of darkness' (99). Mrs. Ramsay outdoes her spouse in both directions, and this is appropriate, since she represents fictionality or literature against his philosophy. Literature is more material than philosophical discourse, because it offers a sensuous 'body' while the latter aspires to the grey universality of the concept. Yet it outdoes philosophy on the latter ground too. The very concretion of the literary text allows it to concentrate a wealth and play of ideal meaning far above philosophy's stricter joining of single signifieds to unambiguous signifiers.

We can pursue these contrasts into the couple's own reading of texts. When Mrs. Ramsay returns to the room after dinner, impelled by 'something I have come to get . . . without knowing quite what it was', the words of the poem arise spontaneously in her mind. Language precedes the subject's intentionality, and Mrs. Ramsay's response is indeed to the purely signifying rather than signified aspects of these words, 'washing from side to side of her mind rhythmically'. She begins reading 'at random', not asserting control of the matter but surrendering to it in a happy mood of serendipity, and again 'she only knew this is white, or this is red. She did not know at first what the words meant at all' (183-4). In contrast to the stress on her transcendence at dinner, it is now materiality that is foregrounded, her relish for the sumptuousness of the signifier without immediate regard for its content. Language is experienced here at the level of the Kristevan semiotic, as sheer rhythm, intonation, sound and colour. Mr. Ramsay, however, remains masterfully in control of the text, 'weighing, considering, putting this with that as she read' (182). Though the novel at one point maintains that he 'forgot himself completely' as he reads, it in fact demonstrates that he is incapable of doing any such thing. His secret motive for starting Scott's novel is to assess his prospects with futurity: 'if young men did not care for this [Scott], naturally they did not care for him either' (186). The exact analytic play of mind as he weighs and judges is in fact in the service of his monstrous ego. As usual, *To the Lighthouse* is more explicit in its denunciations of the stooge Tansley: 'he wanted to assert himself . . . that was what his criticism of poor Sir Walter, or perhaps it was Jane Austen, amounted to. "I – I – I"' (165).

The highlight of 'The Window' is Mrs. Ramsay's reading of the sonnet: 'All the odds and ends of the day stuck to this magnet; her mind felt swept, felt clean. And then there it was, suddenly entire shaped in her hands, beautiful and reasonable, clear and complete, the essence sucked out of life and held rounded here—the sonnet' (186-7). The danger of a Woolf heroine is that she may seem to be a glorified but finally frivolous bourgeois housewife, and Mrs. Ramsay must be given a nobility of her own that will redeem the drabber aspects of domesticity and outdo the genuine if limited idealism of her husband. Fiction never rests quite easily under philosophy's charge that it is unserious, and seeks to gain the upper hand over its accuser on the latter's own terms. This is achieved by the sonnet, which captures an 'essence' of its own in contrast to the 'angular essences' of Ramsay's thought. 'Sucked out of life' might seem to relate this to the reductive violence of philosophical analysis, but this is in fact not so. There is a benign 'sucking', that, say, of the child which relieves its mother of a reserve with which she would otherwise be painfully over-full, as well as the vampiric sucking of Ramsay's 'beak of brass'. Poetry reaches essences without sacrificing phenomena. The sonnet is 'beautiful and reasonable', achieving a sensuous perfection of form as well as the universality of the concept. It reconciles all the oppositions around which 'The Window' has been organised; it fuses form and content, the *dulce* and the *utile*. It is a symbol in its own right, but also a figure for Mrs. Ramsay's earlier moments of symbolic vision, alone and at the dinner party. Having the best of both worlds, the symbol appropriates for literature the best qualities of philosophy without importing with them its defects. Mrs. Ramsay closes this section of the novel 'smiling. For she had triumphed again' (191).

Even in 'The Window', when Mrs. Ramsay goes 'a sort of disintegration set in' (173), and this disintegration is fully realised in the second section, 'Time Passes'. This section represents a fall from grace, from the idyllic, 'organic' time of its predecessor to the painful 'postlapsarian' visit to the summer house. The salvation of the symbolic moment gives way to a clumsy deciphering of meaning from moment to moment. I argued in my second chapter that Woolf locates the historical moment of the fall from Symbolism as the First World War, an event encompassed in the ten-year period covered by 'Time Passes'. But in this novel there is an interplay between the war and Mrs. Ramsay's death. Both events are perfunctorily noted in parentheses, both are in some sense the loss of the possibility of totalising meaning. Her death precedes the war and in a sense is not unrelated to it. With the loss of the harmonising principle of femininity, the aggressive male ego bursts out on an international scale into militarism and violence. In *Three Guineas* Woolf more fully elaborates this connection between the loss of a certain kind of femininity and the likelihood of war.[11] But since Mrs. Ramsay also represents the old Victorian order, the war is in a sense the cause of her death—the death less of a single woman than of a civilisation. This dialectical relation between the personal and political is sustained in the central image of the decaying summer house. The house represents the body of the mother, Mrs. Ramsay, in ways to which the psychoanalysis of Melanie Klein has alerted us and which I shall explore below. But it is also the figure of an entire social order, taking its place alongside such literary houses as Mansfield Park or Howard's End.

'Time Passes' offers only a glimpse of the fuller symbolic perceptions of its predecessor. For a moment 'divine goodness had parted the curtain and displayed behind it, single, distinct, the hare erect; the wave falling; the boat rocking'. Yet even this is a redeemed Nature without a perceiving subject. Mrs. Ramsay is no longer included as a key term in the symbolic equation, and the curtain of materiality falls again (*TL,* 198-9). There remains only a lingering sense of a possible transcendence behind objects. The beneficent exchanges between self and Nature—'how beauty outside mirrored beauty within'—are no longer possible when, from the very depths of Nature, there arises the trace of war's carnage: 'a purplish stain upon the bland surface of the sea as if something had boiled and bled, invisibly, beneath' (207). In one sense, 'the mirror was broken', and a brutalised Nature no longer reflects civilisation back to itself; but in another it now gives a truer reflection, since that brutality was always already latent in civilisation. Nature is Culture's opposite, as the Scottish climate takes its slow, destructive toll of the house. But at another level it is in touch with a profound destructiveness of Culture's own. What is literally destroying the house is rain, rats and wind, but what is figuratively destroying it is the First World War. The mirror is twisted into a double layer by this contradiction: 'the mirror itself was but the surface glassiness when the nobler powers sleep beneath' (208). I take 'nobler powers' to be a bitter irony. If the symbolist vision is a myth, what 'sleeps beneath' is the lurking bloodiness of world war, which is both the negation of civilisation and its highest reach (in technology, in the planned mobilisation of whole societies). At its utmost limit civilisation seems to be indistinguishable from barbarism. 'Did Nature supplement what men advanced?' asks the novel anguishedly (207), and the answer is both yes and no. 'Supplement' here must be given the weight of its Derridean ambivalence—'progress as the possibility of perversion', 'both humanity's good fortune and the origin of its perversion'.[12] Reflecting culture back upon itself in the symbolistic mirror, Nature completes it, yet it risks showing it a natural violence that may strike an answering chord in culture itself.

Just as Nature mirrors Culture, woman mirrors man, reflecting an image that bolsters him in his self-identity. In *A Room of One's Own* Woolf remarks that 'women have served all these centuries as looking-glasses possessing the magic and delicious power of reflecting the figure of man at twice its natural size' (*RO,* 35). Woman, like Nature, should also ideally supplement what man had advanced. Mrs. Ramsay is a mirror for her husband and family, securing their self-identity by reflecting back a coherent image of the subject. Luce Irigaray argues, like Woolf, that the female mirror 'is entrusted by the (masculine) ''subject'' with the task of reflecting and redoubling himself. The role of ''femininity'' is prescribed moreover by this masculine specula(risa)tion and corresponds only slightly to women's desire, which is recuperated only secretly, in hiding, and in a disturbing and unpardonable manner'.[13] As a Victorian angel in the house, Mrs. Ramsay attempts to conform to this role and is considered historically obsolete by a younger female generation which 'sport[s] with infidel ideas . . . of a life different from hers . . . not always taking care of some man or other' (*TL*, 16). Yet however pious she may be, no 'angel in the house' can fully sustain her role. There always remains a margin of excess female desire, jostling against the limits society imposes on it. Mrs. Ramsay feels guilt at a sense of being 'finer than her husband' (65), extreme discomfort at not being sure that he is as academically gifted as she has just assured him he is. Desire may be defused by displacement (Tansley) or by the substitute gratifications of literature, as when Mrs. Ramsay reads the tale of the Fisherman's Wife to James: 'For my wife, good Ilsabil, Wills not as I'd have her will' (90). Or there may be socially allowable modes of female self-assertion, as in Mrs. Ramsay's penchant for matchmaking. On occasion she even has something of the subversiveness of a Miss Kilman, and is also accused by another woman of 'robbing her of her daughter's affections', of 'wishing to dominate' (92).

'No image . . . comes readily to hand bringing the night to order and making the world reflect the compass of the soul' (199). With this breakdown of the mirror, the formerly excluded Otherness at last emerges. The images of natural fecundity, the 'rain of energy', which once attached to Mrs. Ramsay are now writ large in the natural world, where they become brutal and promiscuous: 'winds and waves disported themselves like the amorphous bulks of leviathans whose brows are pierced by no light of reason, and mounted one on top of another, and lunged and plunged in the darkness or the daylight (for night and day, month and year ran shapelessly together) in idiot games'(208-9). Evolution runs in reverse in this section, as Nature resists teleological progress. The Ramsays' house figures in miniature their leisured Victorian order, and is eroded by a slow but persistent and ultimately near-devastating assault. Women and Nature are in many ways linked in this novel, and Nature's assault on the house may be seen as enacting the dangerous liberation of Mrs. Ramsay's subterranean desire. At the same time, as I suggested, the house stands for Mrs. Ramsay herself, just as school buildings, as Melanie Klein has demonstrated, may represent the body of the mother for the pupil. Feelings and activities in relation to the building (entering, defacing, breaking) are then charged with psychoanalytic meaning.[14] Nature in part releases a subversive female fecundity, but also enacts a male sexual assault on a building that represents Mrs. Ramsay as woman rather than Victorian. Moonlight 'gliding gently as if it laid its caress' ominously becomes 'the trifling airs, nibbling, the clammy breaths, fumbling' till at last 'a thistle thrust itself between the tiles in the larder' (212-3), a penetrative gesture that recalls Ramsay's arid beak-thrusts into his wife.

'What power could now prevent the fertility, the insensibility of nature?' (213). The answer is Mrs. McNab who at first sustains, at last redeems, the house. 'The voice of witlessness', she is more Nature than Culture, a fact attested to by her difficulty in walking. She and Mrs. Bast 'lurched', 'their legs ached', she 'hauled herself upstairs and rolled from room to room' (202, 215). Claude Lévi-Strauss has a helpful remark in his discussion of Oedipus, whose name means 'swollen-foot': 'in mythology it is a universal characteristic of men born from the Earth that at the moment they emerge from the depth they either cannot walk or they walk clumsily'.[15] Mrs. McNab is thus a chthonic being in touch with telluric powers. In contrast to her husband, Mrs. Ramsay represents Nature, but in contrast with McNab she is associated with an effete bourgeois culture against the more robust face of Nature itself. Strong class feelings are evoked here. McNab 'mumbles out the old music hall song' (203), becoming one of those racy lower-class entertainers like Marie Lloyd to whom both Woolf and T.S. Eliot liked to condescend.[16] Early in the novel Mrs. Ramsay pays a charity visit to some poor women in town. Two hundred pages later the shards and shreds of her social world are put back into order by just such women, and this is another example of the novel's deconstructive strategies. The excluded term turns out to be the inner truth of its dispossessor. The relation of the Ramsays to the McNabs and Basts reveals the irony of Hegel's master-slave dialectic, where the master ultimately becomes more enslaved than the wretches who serve him. The mirror that is Mrs. Ramsay is broken, but McNab too has an interest in mirrors. 'With her sidelong leer', she 'stood and gaped in the glass'; she 'twist[s] her face grinning in the glass' (203). Later, in a perhaps provocative gesture, she 'stood arms akimbo in front of the looking-glass' (209). This persistent irreverence suggests her rejection of the reflecting and magnifying of the male ego which is Mrs. Ramsay's role in life. Though class superiority leads to a female scorn for McNab, there is another, proto-feminist impulse at work here. She is envied for her liberation from a stultifying feminine role—hence the crazy energy that attaches to her despite her physical deformities. Male work is 'spiritualised' in *To the Lighthouse* by being represented as Ramsay's speculations, female work is brutalised in McNab. Mrs. Ramsay offers a median position at once desirable and false. A woman's work may be the organising of dinner parties, and the novel is justly appreciative of the values that may be achieved there. But there is another possibility. A woman might equally work in the *public* sphere, earning the five hundred pounds that would let her maintain a room of her own. Whether Mrs. Ramsay is the final synthesis of spirit and labour, or whether there might be some other female possibility that she obscures—these are questions for Lily Briscoe.

In the third section, 'The Lighthouse', Lily probes deeply into the lost vision of 'completeness' and 'wholeness' associated with Mrs. Ramsay (295). Gayatri Spivak has argued that '*To the Lighthouse* can be read as a project to catch the essence of Mrs. Ramsay', and thus as another work on the theme I traced above in 'An Unwritten Novel' and *Jacob's Room*. For Spivak, the structure of the book is a grammatical allegory: 'Subject (Mrs. Ramsay)—copula—Predicate (painting)'.[17] Lily's picture carries the symbolic meaning of realising Mrs. Ramsay's essence. This is a matter of the process rather than content of creation, for Lily's act of painting duplicates the social 'summoning together' of the older woman (100); it will 'assemble outwardly the scattered parts of the vision within' (204). But the harmonising process operates in different 'directions' in each case. Whereas Mrs. Ramsay must bring outward units (guests) into some inner, spiritual community, Lily must bring inner units (ideas, feelings, forms) into a coherent outer objectification.

Both women share a certain disjunction of inner and outer. At one level Lily pursues her intense meditations over Mrs. Ramsay's death, while at another she wonders whether she shouldn't 'fetch another cup of coffee'. Such banal outward preoccupations threaten to ironise her deeper concern, reducing it to a mere 'catchword . . . caught up from some book' (225). Mrs. Ramsay had lived the same split between metaphysical thought and the insistent trivia of life. The most famous instance occurs during her visionary perceptions at dinner: 'It partook, she felt, carefully helping Mr. Bankes to a specially tender piece, of eternity' (163). The reader is forced to enact the disjunction as conventional expectations—tender piece of . . . meat—receive a defamiliarising shock. Nor, once this initial shock has been negotiated, will the phrase settle comfortably into a single meaning. Does this juxtaposing of incommensurables ironise the symbolic vision, or does it rather, as in Eliot's definition of Metaphysical wit, yoke heterogeneous ideas by violence together in the flash and fusion of the conceit? Both possibilities seem alternately valid, and the disjunction is perhaps mediated by the structure of the *meal,* which both satisfies basic biological needs and is a cultural and signifying occasion, affirming shared semiotic systems (codes of etiquette). Animality and civilisation, fact and value, are joined together in the shared meal.

Eliot had seen Woolf's writing as 'one of the most curious and interesting examples of a process of dissociation' (see Chapter 2). Yet for Woolf the moment of dissociation or fall is the First World War, an event which Mrs. Ramsay's own disjunction between 'meat' and 'eternity' precedes. Mrs. Ramsay is, moreover, a representative of solid Victorian values and not a dissociated modernist. The 'discrepancy' she experiences—'that was what she was thinking, this was what she was doing' (130)—is a matter of gender rather than history, of being a woman in *any* society rather than being a member of this one at this moment. Women's intellectual capacities are in constant tension with the mundane round of the domestic world they maintain. Mrs. Ramsay must contemplate the mentality of great men while inspecting 'whether those were fresh mole-hills on the bank' (112). But though this disjunction between female being and doing is transhistorical, it also has its historical modifications and is exacerbated in the modern age. Mrs. Ramsay's division is between the physical and the mental, and is a situation not without compensations. It offers the possibility of an inner refuge even within oppression, because thoughts can range widely while the body is mechanically occupied.[18] In Lily's case, however, this split is internalised. This leaves her body free, and it is possible to be a painter rather than a housewife. But it is now a facet of woman's own nature that is trapped in meniality, and this is an oppression more intimately enslaving than the physical conformism of Mrs. Ramsay. In *A Room of One's Own* Woolf points out that, deprived of her own retreat, woman must always write or think in the midst of the distractions and pressures of daily life. In *Jacob's Room* Betty Flanders was the image of this dilemma, writing her letters in a chaos of children and housework. To live through this disjunction between inner and outer, aspiration and brute fact, is painful, but this tension may be more fructifying than the male exclusiveness that simply abolishes one of the two terms. Woolf's own writing—with its various points of view, its different levels of living, thinking, acting, gesture, in a single sentence, its numerous interjections and digressions within a single syntactic unit—all this enacts a commitment to the heterogeneity of female experience. In 'Modern Fiction' she advises her reader: 'Examine for a moment an ordinary mind on an ordinary day. The mind receives a myriad impressions—trivial, fantastic, evanescent, or engraved with the sharpness of steel. From all sides they come, an incessant shower of innumerable atoms' (*CE*, 2:106). The irony of this in relation to *To the Lighthouse* is that Mr. Ramsay's empiricist philosophy, with the mind as passive recipient of external sensation, turns out to be Mrs. Ramsay's daily experience at the centre of a bustling household of guests, servants and children.

Lily's task is to catch Mrs. Ramsay's essence by completing her picture, but she refuses the male reductivism of 'angular essences'. Whereas Ramsay penetrates his wife as 'beak of brass' or 'arid scimitar', Lily follows what Irigaray terms a strategy of 'the fluid' as against the masculine economy of 'the solid'.[19] 'What device for becoming, like waters poured into one jar, inextricably the same, one with the object one adored? Could the body achieve it, or the mind, subtly mingling in the intricate passages of the brain? or the heart?' Demanding 'intimacy itself', Lily desires 'nothing that could be written in any language known to men' (*TL*, 82-3). In its linearity, such (male) language has something in common with phallic penetration as a mode of knowledge; it enters the object at a single point and from a single perspective. In contrast, Lily dreams of multi-perspectivism and simultaneity. Against the male gaze, so icily focused that it cannot grasp the trivial or evanescent, she demands 'fifty pairs of eyes to see with' (303); it is 'not knowledge but unity that she desired' (83). Penetration must give way to gentle envelopment. The former burrows at a single point in order to infiltrate the core of its object, while the latter surrounds so caressingly that the object rather becomes *its* inner core. 'One wanted most some secret sense, fine as air, with which to steal through keyholes and surround her where she sat knitting, talking, sitting silent in the window alone; which took to itself and treasured up like the air which held the smoke of the steamer, her thoughts, her imaginations, her desires' (303-4). Envelopment is a mode of total contact that paradoxically leaves the loved object its autonomy, whereas male penetration makes a localised incision but claims absolute possession. Lily seeks a love that is 'distilled and filtered; love that never attempted to clutch its object' (77). Irigaray further elaborates this distinction: 'Nearness . . . is not foreign to woman, a nearness so close that any identification of one or the other, and therefore any form of property, is impossible. Woman enjoys a closeness with the other that is so near she cannot possess it, any more than she can possess herself'.[20]

This strategy of 'fluidity' is also that adopted by the author, whereby she seeks to achieve those female 'infinite differences in selection, method and style' (*CW*, 27) from 'masculine' writing. Her ideal strategy of writing is well epitomised in the movements of Mrs. Ramsay's mind at the dinner party. She feels that she can see the others' thoughts and feelings 'without effort like a light stealing under water so that its ripples and the reeds in it and the minnows balancing themselves, and the sudden silent trout are all lit up hanging, trembling' (165). Here, as in Lily's own multi-perspectivism, a different strategy for knowing the object is adumbrated, and Woolf too tries to 'go round' the characters, 'unveiling . . . their thoughts and feelings' (165). In 1926, while writing *To the Lighthouse,* she felt she had achieved this: 'It is proved, I think, that what I have to say is to be said in this manner', 'I have made my method perfect' (*WD*, 99, 102). Her main literary device to this end, as I pointed out above, is 'free indirect speech', which produces a fluid, unstable status for the locus of the subject of the sentence. The author can situate herself somewhere between narrative omniscience and the character's own consciousness, or move smoothly from one character's thought to another's within a single sentence. 'She hovered like a hawk suspended; like a flag floated in an element of joy which filled every nerve of her body fully and sweetly, not noisily, solemnly rather' (*TL*, 162). The metaphors here can no longer be identified as emanating either from the author's or Mrs. Ramsay's point of view; they are indistinguishably fused: '. . . for it arose, she thought . . .'; it is Mrs. Ramsay's own thinking, but too elaborate for a direct transcription of her consciousness. The strategy is never a clutching or violent penetrating but a 'stealing under water'. For 'when you've grasped the stem the butterfly's off'. 'I won't raise my hand', Woolf writes, 'Hang still, then, quiver, life, soul, spirit . . . I, too, on my flower' (*HH*, 20). If one aspires, like Mrs. Ramsay, to hold 'the whole . . . together', one must respect the alterity of the object despite the infinite nearness one aims at. Hence the 'doubtful ring', the continual indeterminacy, which Auerbach pointed to in his seminal discussion of Woolf's narrative viewpoint in *Mimesis*. [21]

Male love in the novel is violent but fascinating, a conjunction of impulses that points to the masochism instilled in women by centuries of subordination. To Lily, Paul Rayley's love has a fierce phallic power that would be her destruction; it is 'the most barbaric of human passions' (*TL*, 159). As a 'bully with a crowbar', Paul is another version of Ramsay's 'brass beak', and such penetratingness is experienced by Lily as a threat to the integrity of her being, of which her physical virginity is both emblem and shield. Just as Mrs. Dalloway tucks away the dress she is mending from Walsh's pen-knife, 'like a virgin protecting chastity, respecting privacy' (*MD*, 45), so too does Lily draw her skirts closer round her ankles to ward off Ramsay's demand for female submission (*TL*, 236). Just as Clarissa feels compunction over her frigidity, so does Lily have a sense of guilt over her coldness to Ramsay, which reveals how deeply she has internalised her culture's hostile valuations of spinsterdom. She regards herself as a 'miserable sinner', 'not a woman, but a peevish, ill-tempered, dried-up old maid presumably' (234). 'Presumably' marks her distance from the self-accusation even as she makes it. She is 'not a woman' in the sense that she will not succumb to the role demanded of women in her society, but since there is no available social language for the role she aspires to, she must define herself in the very terms of her enemies. Prue Ramsay is the novel's most graphic image of a surrendered virginity. Her state just before marriage is projected out on to the spring, which 'like a virgin fierce in her chastity, scornful in her purity, was laid out on fields wide-eyed and watchful and entirely careless of what was done' (204). Later we learn, in a casual parenthesis, that Prue has died during some illness connected with childbirth. Virginity is not a sufficient guarantee of its own survival; it must mute its 'fierceness' and cultivate more subtle tactics. Prue's death warns that Mrs. Ramsay's role as generator of life is not *immediately* available to the next generation. If it is to be sustained, it can only be so by indirection. After Mrs. Ramsay's death, sexual penetration threatens death to her successors.

Lily's defence against this phallic threat is her painting: 'it had flashed upon her that she would move the tree to the middle, and need never marry anybody' (271). Her profession as painter affords her this 'enormous exaltation', allowing her to evade penetration by in a sense taking her place among the penetrators themselves. Torn though she is between her own stance and the conventional values she has internalised, Lily at last breaks painfully beyond the socially given definitions of femininity. Though at one level she responds strongly to female self-sacrifice—'the most supreme bliss of which human nature was capable'—she also dryly admits that 'the reason of it escaped her' (233). Not admitting vaginal *jouissance,* she cannot imitate them; in her view, 'there is nothing more tedious, puerile, and inhumane than love' (160).

Though Lily attempts to catch the essence of Mrs. Ramsay in her painting, she has a persistent fear that artistic representation will freeze the flow of life, leaving her with a Ramsayan angular essence. Recent feminist theory throws light on this fear by suggesting that representation is only possible at the expense of the body—both one's own body ('the inadequate name of some uncommanded diversity of drives and contradictions')—and the body of the mother.[22] To enter the symbolic order involves abandoning the maternal body and repressing polymorphous desires. Before she exchanges 'the fluidity of life for the concentration of painting', Lily suffers 'a few moments of nakedness' as if she were 'an unborn soul, a soul reft of body, hesitating on some windy pinnacle and exposed without protection' (245). Lily's soul is bodiless in a double sense. It is 'reft of body', in that it has been torn away from the maternal into the order of representation, yet it is also 'unborn', hovering on the verge of incarnation in the physical work and substance of the painting itself. Jane Gallop argues that 'the conflict is always between body . . . and Power, between body and Law, between body and Phallus, even between body and Body. The second term in each pair is a finished, fixed representation. The first that which falls short of representation'.[23] But the body has a relatively greater role in painting than in writing. Urged by 'a curious physical sensation', Lily draws her first stroke on the canvas, and she sustains her painting by ' a dancing, rhythmical movement' (244). This rhythmic ebb and flow, like tone and colour, constitutes a key element of the Kristevan semiotic, that shifting configuration of somatic impulses which is more archaic than language. Painting is a network of conventions of representation, but its physicality gives it an unusual closeness to the body. As sticky viscous substance, oil paint may carry psychoanalytical impulses connected to the bodily secretions of infantile experience. Presenting themselves within the signifying activity, rhythm and its related semiotic impulses can alone traverse the gulf between (maternal) body and representation. 'With some rhythm which was dictated . . . by what she saw', Lily successfully reconciles fluidity with concentration: 'while her hand quivered with life, this rhythm was strong enough to bear her along with it on its current' (246).

Unlike her author, Lily need not struggle directly with the order of language in her pursuit of representation. Yet even so Tansley's mocking words ring in her mind: 'women can't paint, can't write' (247). Substituting a sign for the immediacy of a reality, language distances that which it was supposed to make present: 'how could one express in words these emotions of the body? express that emptiness there? . . . It was one's body feeling, not one's mind' (274-5). Lily fears Reason's imposition of categories on its unformed raw material. 'What she wished to get hold of was that very jar on the nerves, the thing itself before it has been made anything' (297). In this distrust of language she differs from Mrs. Ramsay herself. The latter's trust in fiction and tropes was sustained by the solid Victorian routine she inhabited, but such social props have failed Lily, having been destroyed by the First World War. The social guarantees of language are no longer to be trusted, and only one's own immediate experience can prevent the dispersal of language into insincere rhetoric. This linguistic *rappel-à-l'ordre* was the experience of a whole younger generation. Enticed into war by rousing patriotic rhetoric, it had encountered the brutal realities of trench-warfare. After this disjunction of signifier and signified, rhetoric is discredited by its association with the *dulce et decorum* of the older generation. Hence T.E. Hulme's Imagist desire to 'hand over sensations bodily',[24] a phrase which could serve to describe Lily's own artistic ambition.

Mrs. Ramsay proves difficult for Lily to handle artistically: 'Beauty . . . came too readily, came too completely. It stilled life—froze it'(273). An excess at the level of the signifier may be as damaging as Ramsay's reduction of objects into 'angular essences'. To relish the 'sumptuousness' of the signifier is not the opposite of the hermeneutic reduction to a lean and hungry essence, but rather an alternative manifestation of tactlessness on the interpreter's part. Surfaces are valued by Woolf, and Ramsay is wrong to neglect them, but still more valuable is the moment when they at last seem to yield up an inner depth. Truth is an *unveiling,* as when 'divine goodness had parted the curtain' briefly in 'Time Passes'. As a painter, Lily has an acute eye for sensuous detail, yet she also fears that such vivid physical surfaces might be 'like curves and arabesques flourishing round a centre of complete emptiness', and yearns for the moment when 'beauty would roll itself up' (275-7). Curtains can be drawn or, more actively, truth may press rupturingly through them. Lily imagines that if Mr. Carmichael had spoken, 'a little tear would have rent the surface of the pool. And then? Something would emerge. A hand would be shoved up, a blade would be flashed' (276). This blade is not, as it were, Peter Walsh's pen-knife; it is held by a *woman,* the Lady of the Lake of Arthurian legend, who would here be Mrs. Ramsay. Later Lily reflects that when the surfaces of daily life are in abeyance she feels 'something emerge. Life was most vivid then' (294). The Lady of the Lake's blade can be read in terms of the 'maternal phallus'. Mrs. Ramsay is seen as the ultimate source of order by Lily; she is indeed the object of the latter's transference. 'In Lacanian terms, the silent interlocutor . . . is the subject presumed to know, the object of transference, the phallic Mother, in command of the mysterious processes of life, death, meaning and identity'.[25] Lily depends on Mrs. Ramsay, for 'she knew knowledge and wisdom were stored in Mrs. Ramsay's heart' (83). I have already noted aspects of the phallic imagery that attach to Mrs. Ramsay, who pities men 'always as if they lacked something' (133), that is, it is she who possesses the phallus. Hence 'the astonishing power that Mrs. Ramsay had over one. Do this, she said, and one did it' (271). It is perhaps Julia Kristeva who has most valuably emphasised the difficulties posed by this recognition of the mother's 'phallus': 'that every subject poses him/herself in relation to the phallus has been understood. But that the phallus is the mother: it is said, but here we are all *arrêtés* . . . by this ''truth''' .26 When Lily reflects that Mrs. Ramsay 'was irresistible. Always she got her own way in the end', she feels a deep grudge against this formidable phallic power (157). But, according to Jacques Lacan, the phallus 'can play its role only when veiled'.27 Hence Mrs. Ramsay must be veiled beneath the 'cover of beauty', to which she adds a tantalising gift for silence: 'she was reserved. Nobody knew exactly what had happened to her' (300). Provoking gossip and speculation—'what was there behind it?'—she acquires all the more significance by her twinned beauty and unforthcomingness. She becomes the Lacanian 'subject presumed to know', in command of the mysterious processes of life and identity, and 'directly she went a sort of disintegration set in' (173).

Though death seems to be a defeat for her, consigning the values she represents to the past, it in fact in a sense turns out to be the subtlest of her triumphs. After the successful dinner party Mrs. Ramsay reflects on Paul and Minta whom she had matched: 'They would . . . come back to this night . . . wound about in their hearts, however long they lived she would be woven' (175). She reflects triumphantly that the entire scene will be revived again in their lives. A relevant parallel—with gender transposed—can be drawn with Freud's myth of the murder of the primal father in *Totem and Taboo*. Reserving all the women for himself, the father is killed by the jealous sons, but he in fact turns out to be stronger dead than alive. Feeling guilt as well as liberation in his death, the brothers internalise the dead father, granting him a reign more thorough than the actual man could have achieved. Mrs. Ramsay herself has a dim premonition that, as a sort of primal mother, she too will be internalised by her survivors. Most of the characters in the novel experience enough impulses of irritation or hostility towards Mrs. Ramsay alive to lay the groundwork for a sense of guilt once she is dead. There is a notable absence of mourning for her, as if Ramsay's histrionics had left everyone else in a state of emotional numbness. 'What did she feel?' Lily wonders on her first morning at the summer house, 'Nothing, nothing . . .' (225). Indeed, if she feels anything it is anger, blaming Mrs. Ramsay for a sudden death that leaves her confused and unable to paint.[28]

Mrs. Ramsay is Lily's vicarious mother, determined to drive this difficult 'daughter' into her own feminine role. She is the 'Angel in the House' whom Lily must kill so that she can establish her own identity as a new woman, professional, unmarried, independent. In 1931 Woolf argued that killing the Angel in the House was essential for a woman to become a writer. Woolf summarises the angelic credo: 'Be sympathetic; be tender; flatter; deceive; use all the arts and wiles of our sex. Never let anybody guess that you have a mind of your own' (*CE*, 2:285). This might stand as Mrs. Ramsay's own manifesto. She flatters and deceives her husband, 'disliked anything that reminded her that she had been seen sitting thinking' (*TL*, 108). In her 1931 paper on the Angel, Woolf pleads 'self-defence. Had I not killed her she would have killed me' (*CE*, 2:286). Lily must make a similarly 'murderous' self-assertion. Mrs. Ramsay 'cared not a fig for her painting', declares that 'she must . . . they all must marry' (*TL*, 80), and only Lily's hard-won confidence in her art allows her to affirm her spinsterhood and at last 'stand up to Mrs. Ramsay' (271). Painting on the lawn, Lily rejects Ramsay's demand for sympathy, refusing the conventionally feminine role. At the dinner she was forced by Mrs. Ramsay to 'renounce' self-expression for 'the hundred and fiftieth time', but now instead of floating 'off instantly upon some wave of sympathetic expansion . . . she remained stuck' (143, 234). However, the degree of her psychic autonomy should not be overestimated. Like Freud's mythical father, Mrs. Ramsay exercises a fuller sway in death than in life. Lily sees her rejection of the role of Angel in the House as involving *self*-murder: 'not a woman, but a peevish, ill-tempered, dried-up old maid presumably'. 'Presumably', as I have suggested, denotes distance, but Lily can sustain it only intermittently. 'Not a woman', she confuses her own femaleness with a socially produced 'femininity', but this is in the first place a confusion and then imposition that her culture insists upon. Her society can only interpret affirmations of female difference outside its code of the feminine as madness, invisibility, non-existence. Earlier, Lily had pleaded for 'her own exemption from the universal law' of reproduction: 'she liked to be herself; she was not made for that' (81). Again there is an elision of terms—between a need to reproduce which is 'universal' in the sense that the race will otherwise expire, and the socially specific definitions of how that need shall be structured. Though the content (childbirth) is constant, the form is always historically produced. Lily emphatically rejects the form, which is the ideology of the Angel in the House, but so deep is her cultural conditioning that she cannot distinguish the content from it. She abjures motherhood as well as angelism, which reveals how deeply the act of rebellion is constrained by the very society it seeks to transcend.

The first part of *To the Lighthouse* valorises Mrs. Ramsay over her husband, but the final section articulates the need for the 'daughter' to reject the mother (as far as she is able) without, however, merely returning to a position undifferentiated from that of the father himself. The daughter is always in danger of being engulfed by the mother. There is 'a structural weakness in the distinction between a girl and her mother', notes Jane Gallop in *Feminism and Psychoanalysis:* 'woman needs language, the paternal, the symbolic order, to protect herself from the lack of distinction from the mother'.[29] The 'astonishing power that Mrs. Ramsay had over one' may be sheer paralysis and must be resisted. In this necessity there perhaps lies a further ambivalence of the First World War. It is a tragic loss of full meaning, yet it also overthrows the intimidating parents, affording a possibility of freedom. Paul and Minta's marriage is a failure in Mrs. Ramsay's terms, yet it has none the less entered a new interesting phase: 'we can over-ride her wishes, improve away her limited, old-fashioned ideas' (269). 'Triumphing' over Mrs. Ramsay as she had over her husband, Lily reflects: 'It has all gone against your wishes. They're happy like that; I'm happy like this. Life has changed completely' (269).[30]

Woman needs the symbolic order to protect herself from a potential lack of differentiation from the mother. But this patriarchal order also commands her to be *like* her mother. Children of both sexes must turn away from their first, maternal love-object, but the boy turns away only 'provisionally', since his adult love-object will be one of the same sex. The girl, however, must turn from the mother to the father. This overcoming of the Oedipus complex in identification with the role of the parent of the same sex is enacted by James and Cam in the boat trip to the

Lighthouse. After his long Oedipal hatred of Ramsay, James finally realises that 'they alone knew each other', and he begins to regard himself as inheritor to the Father: '''We are driving before a gale—we must sink'', he began saying to himself, half aloud exactly as his father said it' (312). In reward, he is recognised by the father when Ramsay praises his steering. Cam is initially tempted to yield to the Father's speech by accepting his naming of the dog for her. 'No one attracted her more' than Mr. Ramsay, and she puts herself in the place of the mother and is caught in the speech of the Father: 'she murmured, dreamily, half asleep, how we perished, each alone' (293). Yet this episode has a curious disjunction of form and content. It enacts the oldest of stories—resolution of the Oedipal complex—in a highly atypical situation—a boat sailing from the Hebrides to the Lighthouse. Society's most familiar, indeed formative, gesture is projected out to its frontiers. The implication is that this resolution is only possible in these unique circumstances, in what now seems an unusual 'laboratory' experiment in human emotions. Cam and James reproduce the Ramsayan roles in the next generation, but they are isolated figures, while the 'mainland' belongs to Lily and her painting.

The first adventure of Woolf's professional life was to kill the Angel in the House, but the second has yet to be achieved: 'telling the truth about my own experiences as a body' (*CE*, 2:228). She doubts whether any woman has solved this yet, but the full reason is deeper than the contingent fact of the social censorship she points to. Since the symbolic order is constituted by the repression of the somatic, to 'express' the body is to transgress the limits of representation. Lily's near-impossible desire to articulate 'these emotions of the body' (*TL*, 274) risks subverting the symbolic and precipitating madness or even death. In the event, she only just stays on *this* side of the boundary: 'Heaven be praised . . . . She had not obviously taken leave of her senses. No one had seen her step off her strip of board into the waters of annihilation'(278). Her problem is to connect left and right, to 'achieve that razor edge of balance between two opposite forces; Mr. Ramsay and the picture' (296). Her difficulty is located in the infinitesimal distance 'from conception to work', where 'demons' lurk (34). Without the symbolic order—representation, identification with the father—then the 'conception' or inner picture, which is also the body, will be forever muted, yet the former is at the same time the very force that represses the latter. Ramsay must be one element in the razor-edge 'balance', yet every time he comes near 'ruin approached; chaos approached' (229). Lily's aesthetic ideal serves as a self-reflexive statement of the novel's own aspiration: 'Beautiful and bright it should be on the surface, feathery and evanescent . . . but beneath the fabric must be clamped together with bolts of iron' (264). This is clearly a version of the simultaneously solid and free-floating clouds of *Mrs. Dalloway*. Lily is in the double-bind of needing the Law of the Father to distance herself from the (unrepresentable) mother, yet finding that the symbolic endlessly defers the unmediated *jouissance* she also desires, that 'very jar on the nerves, the thing itself before it has been made anything'. To this degree, Lily is in accord with Ramsay. Whereas she hopes to catch the bodily intuition before it is caught in the toils of signification, he aims to press signification to its limit where it yields the philosophical 'thing in itself'. Both may in this respect be contrasted with Mrs. Ramsay. Accepting the necessary materiality of language, she knows 'the inadequacy of human relation-ships, that the most perfect was flawed', always impeded by signification (66). She accepts that the human subject is involuntarily caught up in 'lies' and 'exaggeration': 'she never could say what she felt' (190).

In her desperation Lily turns to Mr. Carmichael. He alone in the novel is indifferent to Mrs. Ramsay's power; since he lacks nothing, she can get no purchase upon him. 'Mrs. Ramsay would ask him . . . wouldn't he like a coat, a rug, a newspaper? No, he wanted nothing' (299-300). 'Always content and dignified', Carmichael may be regarded as enviably in posssession of the phallus (150). He does not suffer that 'splitting' of the subject which is the condition of entry into the symbolic order; he is 'gorged with existence' or presence (274). Inscrutably wise, he is associated with the glimpsed possibility of ultimate meaning: 'had Mr. Carmichael spoken, a little tear would have rent the surface of the pool . . . . Something would emerge' (276). As an artist, he has an affinity both with Lily, who moves the canvas 'close enough for his protection' from Ramsay (229), and with Mrs. Ramsay (briefly at dinner, 'looking together had united them')—(151). He presides over both the landing at the lighthouse and the completion of Lily's painting, and his presence suggests the unsatisfactoriness of the novel's offered resolution. The text invests him with much pomp and circumstance: he is an 'old pagan God' with a trident, a Druidic bard with a 'long white robe' improvised out of a table napkin (319, 172). Yet apart from chanting the poem at dinner he never speaks; moreover, his consciousness is never rendered from the inside. I suggest that this is because he embodies an impossibility, representing both the endless deferral involved in the practice of art *and* the present, full possession of the phallus. Each one of these aspects cancels the other, yet the novel insists Carmichael has both. It therefore gives him an inflated external grandeur to compensate for its inability to flesh out his inner life. He is a blank or absence in the text. He marks the site of a desirable but contradictory resolution to the tug-of-war between body and representation.

Lily at last completes her picture: 'as if she saw it clear for a second, she drew a line there, in the centre' (320). Left and right sides, Mr. and Mrs. Ramsay, the symbolic and somatic, are joined *and* divided in a single stroke, and the crucial question is which way the stress falls here. Just before drawing the line, Lily looks at the steps and confirms that 'they were empty'. Yet 'somebody' —'whoever it was stayed still inside'—casts a shadow over the steps exactly as Mrs. Ramsay would have done. Lily's vision attains a definite signified (Mrs. Ramsay) which is the effect of the indeterminate signifier, the anonymous shadow. In general, a shadow is the trace of a presence which precedes it, but in Lily's epiphany, presence or vision is secondary to the trace itself. This is the very principle of the symbolic order, and I propose to read Lily's line as an allegorical statement of the Saussurean algorithm $[\frac{S}{s}]$, which for Lacan denotes the unsurpassable separation of the subject of conscious discourse from the unconscious. Despite the general euphoria of its last pages, the novel quietly retains certain key qualifications of Lily's vision—'*as if* she saw it clear'. The dream of identity between left and right, body and symbolic order persists, but the inescapable fact of their alienation is also acknowledged. Lily's final line is as ambivalent as the Phallus itself, which is both disjunction and copula at once. Anika Lemaire argues that the phallus is 'a copula—a hyphen—in the evanescence of its erection—the signifier par excellence of the impossible identity'.[31] The novel cannot end on full presence, but must note its passing: 'I have had my vision'. This is in one sense loss, but also a sort of liberation, bleak but real, for the vision is Lily's bond to Mrs. Ramsay. It is tragically brief but also a debt settled. Mrs. Ramsay is

115

now fixed in the representation, and Lily can now perhaps cast off her fixation and move on.

Lily's line is also a Lighthouse, which in turn is 'a central line down the middle of the book to hold the design together'. Lily's line and the Lighthouse coincide in a way reminiscent of Mrs. Ramsay's own projections of auto-affection earlier in the book. But a 'division of labour' has now set in. Whereas Mrs. Ramsay's auto-affection passed through the Lighthouse on its circular journey back to itself, Mr. Ramsay must physically go to the Lighthouse, while Lily draws the line which coincides with it. The structure of symbolism is thus now broken. Lily's line represents an unsurpassable bar between lived experience and the symbolic order, which always objectively exists but comes to subjective consciousness as the result of a historical 'fall' from the plenitude of the Ramsays to the dearth suffered by the post-war generation. It is the necessary condition of the subject as such, and reacts back to interrogate the symbolic visions of the first half of the novel. The book's ambivalent attitude to this bar or gap is finally grounded in the daughter's fraught relation to the mother. Mrs. Ramsay's death is the bleak loss of the possibility of total meaning, yet it also reveals an arbitrariness in the sign which reduces even her impressive symbols into fictional constructs with no compelling authority over the next generation.

CHAPTER 5

Orlando

Orlando has been perhaps the most neglected of Woolf's novels among her critics. Quentin Bell's judgement is representative: 'I think she saw well enough that *Orlando* was not ''important'' among her works' (*QB*, 2:138), and Woolf herself disparagingly described it as 'a joke', 'farce', 'a writer's holiday', 'an escapade' (*WD*, 105, 117-8, 124). She thus reinforces the case of all those subsequent critics who have seen the novel as mere 'intrusion' or 'interruption' of her supposedly more mainstream serious poetic novels. Yet we should not confound a 'joke' with mere insignificance, even if the author herself invites us to do so, for Freud has demonstrated in *Jokes and their Relation to the Unconscious* that in the jest and the relief gained from it there resides the truth of the unconscious. The intensity of Woolf's 'will-to-joke' suggests some significant psychic impulse: '*Orlando* was the outcome of a perfectly definite, indeed overmastering impulse. I want fun. I want fantasy. I want (this was serious) to give things their caricature value .... The vein is deep in me—at least sparkling, urgent' (*WD*, 136). Two impulses are inscribed in this diary entry: surface (fun, play) and depth (urgent, overmastering), and they interbreed in strange ways. In the light of a 'serious' drive towards 'caricature' we can no longer accept the firm binary opposition which allows critics to deprecate *Orlando* as 'unserious'. Conventionally, we assume that seriousness is primary and that play or joke is derivative, just as (a related case) we assume that literal meaning precedes its 'transfer' in the metaphor. Yet Woolf's comments on *Orlando* constantly overturn this assumption, affirming instead the primacy of play. Though she started the novel as a joke, she involuntarily became serious. Hence

117

her worries: 'begun on 8th October, as a joke; and now rather too long for my liking. It may fall between stools, be too long for a joke, and too frivolous for a serious book' (*WD*, 124). The constant repetition of 'jokiness' in the diary alerts us to forces operating here that are stronger than our usual, attenuated notion of 'play' will admit. Compare a disturbing earlier entry: 'How extraordinarily unwilled by me but potent in its own right . . . *Orlando* was! as if it shoved everything aside to come into existence' (120).

The diary also offers an explanation for this 'overmastering impulse' to have a joke. Recording for the first time an idea for some literary project of the fantastic—'fantasy', 'sapphism', 'satire'—she notes: 'I feel the need of an escapade after these serious poetic experimental books whose form is always so closely considered' (105). This account dovetails with her categorisation of 'the Satirists and Fantastics' between 'The Psychologists' and 'The Poets' in the essay 'Phases of Fiction', written contemporaneously with *Orlando*. In it, too, she argues for 'a craving for relief' from psychologically orientated literature:

> The mind feels like a sponge saturated full with sympathy and understanding; it needs to dry itself, to contract upon something hard. Satire and the sense that the satirist gives us that he has the world well within his grasp, so that it is at the mercy of his pen, precisely fulfil our needs. (*CE*, 2:89)

Satire is valued for its power to master reality. Writers of satire and the fantastic work in 'freedom' in their 'changed attitudes to reality', over which they have the upper hand. They do not labour 'under the oppression of omniscience' like the psychologists, and this gives the reader too a sense of freedom (*CE*, 2:89-91). Maria DiBattista is the only critic who gives adequate recognition to Woolf's overmastering impulse and argues that such play is never simply gratuitous: 'Both the urgency and seriousness of caricature as a species of Woolf's comic, playful expression in *Orlando* spring from an aggressive impulse directed against all she perceives as threatening to the integrity and freedom of the self'.[1] In order to give a full asssessment of *Orlando*, it is necessary to probe into the particular constraints against which Woolf's fantasy protests and from which it is generated, for in Rosemary Jackson's account of the genre, fantasy attempts 'to compensate for a lack resulting from cultural constraints: it is a literature of desire'.[2] The desire in this case is so radical that it was immediately repressed by the author herself as a 'joke', and has subsequently been dismissed (i.e. repressed) by critics as non-essential.

Woolf's first rudimentary idea for a fantasy was 'The Jessamy Brides' about 'two women, poor, solitary at the top of a house'; 'satire and wildness' hinting at 'sapphism'. Seven months later, this scheme becomes *Orlando:* 'Vita; only with a change about from one sex to another' (*WD*, 105, 116). Literary fantasy is thus from the beginning twined with the themes of woman and sexuality. In this period Woolf was active in writing on feminist issues, and the most substantial fruit of that concern was *A Room of One's Own,* based on lectures she gave at Cambridge immediately after the publication of *Orlando.* Since she was stepping into her father's footsteps (he had been tutor at Trinity College), she may be seen as acting out that change of sex that *Orlando* had thematised, and at Cambridge too she was 'playful' where solemnity was more likely to have been expected.

As I suggested in my first chapter, Woolf faces a tension between feminism and the aesthetic ideology of Symbolist modernism. For the Symbolist work of art, ideas or statements are taboo; a poem must not mean but be. Critics may have overestimated the role of idealist modernism in Woolf, ignoring the counteracting political motifs, yet it is none the less true that she remains to a degree trapped within the modernist categories. Anything like a 'direct' expression of feminist anger, she contends, distorts the art-work. In *A Room of One's Own* she points to an 'awkward break' in *Jane Eyre,* which she identifies more generally in 'Women and Fiction' as a characteristic of nineteenth-century women novelists:

> That is an awkward break . . . . The continuity is disturbed . . . the woman who wrote those pages had more genius in her than Jane Austen; but if one reads them over and marks that jerk in them, one sees that she will never get her genius expressed whole and entire. Her books will be deformed and twisted. She will write in a rage where she should write calmly. She will write foolishly where she should write wisely. She will write of herself where she should write of her characters. She is at war with her lot. (*RO*, 104)

Female anger or ambition as a woman are the last thing Woolf wants to betray; hence the oblique approach and playful style in both *Orlando* and *A Room of One's Own*. Elaine Showalter rightly points out the technical similarities of these books: 'repetition, exaggeration, parody, whimsy, and multiple viewpoint'.[3] Woolf's playfulness, then, does not mean secondariness or unseriousness, but is a necessary detachment and disguise, a deliberate narrative politics by which she can express what she otherwise prohibits herself—that which the straightforward style cannot articulate within its legitimate confines. Playfulness begins as a stratagem, but ultimately attains a more radical value and subsumes 'seriousness', which then becomes a subordinate moment within it.

The most radical fantastic elements in *Orlando* are Orlando's immense life span and the sex-change in the middle of the book with Orlando's subsequent androgynous character. According to Jackson, fantasy 'takes metaphorical constructions literally'.[4] Orlando lives more than three hundred years and at the end of the book is still only thirty-six, but the reader may 'reverse' the course of fantasy, reading it as a metaphor for the tradition and ancestry that make the individual's existence possible. However, the fantasy of sex-change and androgyny offers more resistance to naturalisation, as is shown by the fact that critics of Woolf's notion of androgyny cannot reinterpret it in a more acceptable light but have to confront and challenge it directly. Elaine Showalter, most famously, has denounced Woolf's 'flight' into androgyny: 'Androgyny was the myth that helped her evade confrontation with her own painful femaleness and enabled her to choke and repress her anger and ambition'. Showalter argues, contrary to Woolf's view that anger and protest are flaws in art, that the woman writer should immerse herself in 'the individual experience, with all its restriction of sex and anger and fear and chaos':

> A thorough understanding of what it means, in every respect, to be a woman, could lead the artist to an understanding of what it means to be a man. This revelation would not be realised in any mystical way; it would result from daring to face and express what is unique, even if unpleasant, or taboo, or destructive, in one's own experience, and thus it would speak to the secret heart in all people.[5]

Though she criticises Woolf's androgynous artist for 'mystically transcend[ing] sex', Showalter's alternative is as mystical as

Woolf's. Her last sentence perhaps already betrays the simplistic sentimentality of her argument. The stridency of the revolt Showalter calls for entails the risk that the patriarchy might simply eliminate women's 'anger and fear and chaos' as insanity, illogicality, disorder. Women need a more subtly resourceful strategy to let their indignation take effect; their relation to the dominant culture must be oblique. 'At once within this culture and outside it', as Mary Jacobus remarks, 'the woman writer experiences not only exclusion, but an internal split'. This intricate mode of working at once inside and outside culture 'challeng[es] its terms while necessarily working within them'. It is this acrobatic feat of continually crossing the boundary of the dominant culture in pleasurable satire and fantasy that Woolf chose for *Orlando* and *A Room of One's Own*. Jacobus suggests that women reread Woolfian 'androgyny' in the light of this difficult challenge to transgress the very ground one must also necessarily work within: 'a simultaneous enactment of desire and repression by which the split is closed with an essentially utopian vision of undivided consciousness'.[6] The ideal androgynous mind does not—*pace* Showalter—flee into asexuality and eunuchism, but is rather 'a constant alternation' between the inside and the beyond of culture and the sign. In Kristeva's words, 'an impossible dialectic: a permanent alternation: never the one without the other'.[7]

Critics such as DiBattista have suggested a certain continuity between *To the Lighthouse* and *Orlando*. Lily's discovery of her 'mother' and making peace with her 'father' are seen as anticipating the resolution of the dualism of male/female (aggressive/self-sacrificing, rational/emotional) which *Orlando* bodies forth literally in its sex-change. Yet Orlando's androgynous disposition does not in fact emphasise the fusion of opposites. This is made startlingly clear by the fact that Nancy Topping Bazin's *Virginia Woolf and the Androgynous Vision* largely ignores *Orlando*, which offers no foothold to an argument that sees the androgynous vision as a mystical union of manic (female) and depressive (male) views of the world. She interprets Woolf's androgyny simply as 'a certain equilibrium between the masculine and the feminine visions'.[8] The fact that androgyny is broached again in *Orlando* suggests that any supposed resolution in *To the Lighthouse* is less definitive than has been assumed.

At a key point in *Orlando*, Orlando and Shelmerdine suddenly cry, '''You're a woman, Shel!'' . . . ''You're a man, Orlando!''', and the narrator stresses: 'Never was there such a scene of protestation and demonstration as then took place since the world began' (*O*, 227). The change of sex is a defining moment for the fantasy of *Orlando* in that it shows the nature of fantasy itself, which I take to be the transgression of boundaries as a play with the limit, as a play of difference. Rosemary Jackson points out that the fantastic narrative does not operate metaphorically to produce a synthesising image or symbol; it rather remains on the surface. In it, one object, instead of standing for another, literally becomes that other, slides through the boundary into the other 'in a permanent flux and instability'.[9] This superficiality and metonymical displacement is certainly the contrary of the metaphorical depth which Woolf usually aimed at. In *Orlando* she had purposely avoided 'difficulty': 'I did not try to explore . . . . I never got down to my depths'; she intended to write 'all over hastily' (*WD*, 136, 120). Jacques Lacan writes: 'what do we have in metonymy other than the power to bypass the obstacles of social censure? This form . . . lends itself to the truth under oppression'.[10] The oppressed truth in *Orlando* is the very notion of androgyny itself. Specially 'unthinkable', it cannot be treated in Woolf's usual metaphorical manner; it verges too much on the comically ribald to allow an earnest attempt to embody it in poetic symbol. It can only be expressed metonymically by 'a change about from one sex to another' (*WD*, 116); a man or woman slides into a woman or man as 'farce' (hence comic 'drag'). Androgyny in *Orlando* is not a resolution of oppositions, but the throwing of both sexes into a metonymic confusion of genders.

As a kind of textual 'foreplay' to the radical transgression of the sexual dividing line, many other instances of transgression occur. Orlando's sudden love for Sasha emerges prior to the division of gender: when he first sees her he does not know whether the figure is a 'boy's or woman's'. Accordingly, his metaphors for Sasha—'whatever the name or sex'—are a pell-mell of categories: 'Images, metaphors of the most extreme and extravagant twined and twisted in his mind. He called her a melon, a pineapple, an olive tree, an emerald, and a fox in the snow'. As a man, he automatically categorises this desirable object as woman in a synaesthetic confusion: 'he did not know whether he had heard her, tasted her, seen her, or all three together' (*O*, 36-7). Sasha represents otherness to him; she is a foreign woman with whom he cannot communicate except in French, which is a foreign tongue for both. 'There was something hidden' in her, for her true origin is unknown: 'something rank in her, something coarse flavoured, something peasant born?' (50). Hence all English 'words failed him. He wanted another landscape, and another tongue' (45). He is drawn to and beyond the uttermost limits of himself; embraces are only possible (and thus also impossible) if the other is indeed the other, on the other side of the boundary of self. Orlando had almost despaired when he for a moment thought that Sasha was 'of his own sex': 'all embraces were out of the question' (37). Metamorphosis on a small scale has already happened, for 'the change in Orlando himself was extraordinary' (40).

Urged by Sasha's complaint that 'it was like being in a cage', Orlando takes her beyond the confines of the English court. 'The couple was often seen to slip under the silken rope, which railed off the Royal enclosure from the public part of the river and to disappear among the crowd of common people' (42). Ignoring social boundaries, they seek a passionate embrace in the farthest reaches of the frozen Thames. This fevered pursuit of a mysterious foreign woman, which overthrows court decorum and demarcations, is appropriately situated in an exceptional moment of time produced by the sudden and unprecedented Great Frost. The routine business of life comes to a standstill, and instead London enjoys 'a carnival of the utmost brilliancy' (34). We can link this carnival to Jackson's account of the phenomenon (which relies on Mikhail Bakhtin): 'Carnival was a temporary condition, a ritualised suspension of everyday law and order'.[11] In the carnivalistic situation, free contact between the ranks is permitted and sexual taboos are broken. Sasha is so uncategorisable in terms of Orlando's social world that she is wholly ambiguous. He cannot decide whether his sight of her 'in the arms of a common seaman' is fact or imagination. During this suspension of common sense and order, his own sexuality is at last liberated, and Woolf's writing here achieves its maximum sexual intensity, more so even than in the evocations of sexual rapture in *Mrs. Dalloway.*

The ice which 'did not melt with their heat' (43) eventually thaws just before Orlando's planned elopement with Sasha. The freezing of the river suspends law and order, and liberates 'a whole gay city' on the ice (58). But for life to continue, the flow of social time must resume, the carnivalistic suspension of history be overcome: suddenly unfrozen, the river becomes 'a race of turbulent yellow waters'. Thus Orlando cannot after all transgress the limits of the court to embrace Sasha. He remains behind as she flees to Russia, and with its consummation thwarted, desire for otherness turns into revulsion: 'he hurled at the faithless woman all the insults that have ever been the lot of her sex. Faithless, mutable, fickle' (61). To understand her, Orlando has to wait until he himself can cross the gulf of gender into this other side.

Exiled from court to country, Orlando first undergoes a trance-like seven days' sleep which represses his part in the passionate carnival world; he wakes 'to have an imperfect recollection of his past life' (63). After an uneventful century on his estate the same pattern of transgression (slipping out of the silken rope), carnival and flood is repeated, leading to Orlando's most radical transgression of all. What compels him to take the first step outside his confinement is an amorous incident with the Archduchess Harriet. He flees the Duchess, but with an intensity of revulsion that is beyond what her limited advances to him can explain. It seems rather that he projects out on to her his *own* sexuality, from which he then recoils. He can escape the woman, but not those aspects of his own self which he invests in her. In fleeing the Archduchess, he flees aspects of his masculinity which he now denounces as disgusting (they had earlier repelled Sasha), and in this limited sense his metamorphosis into a woman is already prefigured at the end of Chapter 2.

The fantastic transgression of the boundary of sex actually takes place in surroundings of radical otherness—the Eastern world of Constantinople, a novelistic choice which perhaps relates to that discourse of Otherness that Edward Said terms 'Orientalism'. Escape from the silken ropes is again effected. Between his diplomatic duties Orlando 'would pass out of his own gates . . . . Then he would mingle with the crowd on the Galata Bridge' (114). The great celebration for conferring the Dukedom on Orlando is again a special time in which quotidian business is temporarily suspended, to the point where the Turks expect a miracle. The English feel 'considerable uneasiness' that the imperialist hegemony and 'the superiority of the British' may be subverted. Though the agitation at the party is quelled, Orlando that night marries a gypsy woman, as is later revealed by a document left in the room. Subversion takes place first on a personal rather than political level, in a marriage that violates imperialist canons of social and racial decorum. But as it approaches its most radical dissolution of limits in androgyny, the text shows an embarrassed reluctance to proceed; Orlando falls into a trance again. In the world around him, political transgression is achieved, and in a 'terrible and bloody insurrection', the 'Turks rose against the Sultan' (122). The moment of the fantastic—reversal of sex—and political revolution do not quite coincide, but none the less sustain an essential relation to each other.

Despite textual delays and resistances, naturalised by the editorial inconvenience of burnt holes in the document, when Orlando wakes, 'he was a woman' (126), a sentence as ungrammatical as the transformation it records is bizarre. After a gap of five asterisks, as if the only way to show the division of sex were this hiatus, the novel describes its androgyne, though still referring to 'him': 'his form combined in one the strength of a man and a woman's grace'. Whereas his previous trance repressed carnivalistic transgression, this trance *is* transgressive, dissolving the limits of gender. The change from man to woman is a castration, but 'seemed to have been accomplished painlessly and completely'. Physical form alone alters: 'in every other respect, Orlando remained precisely as he had been. The change of sex, though it altered their future, did nothing whatever to alter their identity. Their faces remained, as their portraits prove, practically the same' (126-7). Even memory of the past remains intact, and Orlando only recognises his/her new sexual identity through the image in the mirror.

The biographer's statements about unaltered identity do not necessarily deny the difference between the sexes, but do deny biologism. Orlando's biological change does not of itself entail a change of personality. Since he has not yet begun to live as a woman in a specific context, he 'remains precisely as he has been'. But 'it alters their future', because his sexuality will be constructed from now on in socio-cultural context. The novel dismisses 'biologists and psychologists' who will discuss the hero's sexuality endlessly and futilely, implying that sexuality is constructed, not given in nature (127-8). In its latter half Orlando is constituted as a woman, and since sexuality is not 'natural', his/her gender becomes a legal matter for the courts to decide. As Stephen Heath argues:

the individual subject is not constructed from sexuality, sexuality is constructed in the history of the subject, with difference a function of that construction not its cause, a function which is not necessarily single (on the contrary) and which, *a fortiori*, is not necessarily the holding of the difference to anatomical difference (phallic singularity). Production, construction in the history of the subject, sexuality engages also from the beginning, *and thereby*, the social relations of production, classes, sexes.[12]

In the face of this mysterious change of sex, many people's reaction, from the 'naturalist' point of view, is to try to prove '(1) that Orlando had always been a woman, (2) that Orlando is at this moment a man' (127). Curiously, these two contradictory positions are in a sense both true. Having lived as a man, Orlando at this moment remains one; s/he will have to learn to be a woman through the years to come. Yet as a man, he had never been particularly virile. After the transformation, his housekeeper confides that 'it was no surprise to her (here she nodded her head very knowingly)' (155).

After the change of sex, the erstwhile Ambassador becomes a gypsy in the mountains, as Woolf joins a long literary tradition that associates gypsies with anarchic liberation and energy. Unselfconscious about 'her' new sexuality, she remains as ambiguous as Turkish coats and trousers—'worn indifferently by either sex'—and does not yet need to behave according to a rigid code of manners as a woman. Gypsy society constitutes another version of carnival, in which 'the gypsy women, except in one or two important particulars, differ very little from the gypsy men' (140). As a public figure, Orlando had been a comical mix of the two publicly active men of *Mrs. Dalloway:* Hugh Whitbread with his devotion to empty official routine, and Peter Walsh as practical colonial administrator. But s/he now abandons any 'important part in the public life of his country' (110), and revels in the relaxed, sensuous life of the present moment. His/her new-found views accord with the philosophy of the gypsies, who despise formal styles of behaviour, and all power and rank. This makes them attractively rebellious, but never a political menace. They are a counter-culture rather than an oppositional one, regarding the very effort to organise in resistance to the dominant culture as a capitulation to its modes. Joining them is a way for Orlando (and the novel) to avoid taking an attitude to the Turkish revolutionaries.

Orlando's new viewpoint accords with the feminist stance that the author assumes elsewhere. Even while the hero himself was a committed politician, the biographer's attitude was obliquely satiric and similar to that adopted in *A Room of One's Own.* Orlando formulates anti-bureaucratic attitudes through gypsy life, yet gradually this view is connected specifically with her femaleness. She perceives that though 'the man looks the world full in the face, as if it were made for his uses', 'the woman takes a sidelong glance at it, full of subtlety, even of suspicion' (171); this is the 'sudden splitting off of consciousness' discussed in *A Room of One's Own (RO,* 93). On ship to England, Orlando fully realises her disinheritance as a woman: 'all I can do, once I set foot on English soil, is to pour out tea and ask my lords how they like it' (*O,* 144). But as new experience inducts her into the female role, initial resentment turns into quiescence. Like all other Woolfian female heroines, she at last happily gives up politics for a spiritually richer inner life.

> Better is it . . . to be clothed with poverty and ignorance, which are the dark garments of the female sex; better to leave the rule and discipline of the world to others; better to be quit of martial ambition, the love of power, and all the other manly desires if so one can more fully enjoy the most exalted raptures known to the human spirit. (146)

Even here, however, Orlando is not identifying spirituality with some innate 'femininity'. She sees clearly that it is forced upon women by men who 'dress up like a Guy Fawkes and parade the streets, so that women may praise you' and 'deny a woman teaching lest she may laugh at you' (144). She decides to use such 'dark garments' to enjoy the exalted raptures of 'contemplation, solitude, love'. The reader is likely to respond here with an irony Orlando herself does not feel, since contemplation, solitude and love are not the exclusive prerogative of women; Orlando as man had indulged in all of them. The biographer therefore underlines the danger of accepting the produced definition of one's sex and 'the extreme folly—than which none is more distressing in women or man either—of being proud of her sex' (146). This kind of valorisation of either sex would tend to fix the social construction as innate, naturally given.

This points to a difficulty in Woolf's feminism. She rejects the privatised role of women in her society, but her notions of any possible public roles are also conditioned by that society. She cannot see any public commitment other than the empty vacuities of the Hugh Whitbreads, and views the externals of British politics—its antiquarian pomp and ritual—as the beginning and end of it. Missing the raw exercise of power behind all that, she tends merely to despise rather than hate politics: 'prancing down Whitehall on a war-horse' and 'sentencing a man to death' are to be denounced almost without distinction (146). Another problem is that Woolf highly values the qualities fostered in the oppressed sub-culture (solidarity, sensibility, etc.), and her feelings about liberation are always ambivalent because she feels these qualities will be lost in the process. *Three Guineas* struggles with but never finally resolves this tension in her feminism: a demand for liberation, a desire to preserve difference.

By having a character become a woman at the age of thirty, Woolf can bring a critical adult consciousness to bear on the feminisation usually undergone by a female child. Fantasy lets her write a *Bildungsroman* with an already mature protagonist. The incident which best reveals that sex is not a nature but a social product occurs as soon as Orlando returns to England. Her sex together with other issues of property and paternity comes under legal deliberation. 'Thus it was in a highly ambiguous condition, uncertain whether she was alive or dead, man or woman, Duke or nonentity' (153). Thus 'sex becomes a legal fiction, like paternity and property rights', as DiBattista argues, confirming Terry Eagleton's contention that 'the ''private'' is always a juridically demarcated space, produced by the very public structures it is thought to delimit'. DiBattista also notes the feminist satire in the 'equation' quoted above: 'To be alive is to be a man is to be a titled aristocrat. To be dead is to be a woman is to be a social nonentity'.[13] After some hundred years' deliberation, the lawsuits are settled; Palmerston announces that Orlando's sex is 'beyond the shadow of a doubt . . . female' (229). This arbitrary proclamation is undercut by the fact that Orlando and her lover have just discovered 'You're a woman, Shel!', 'You're a man, Orlando!' (227), and by the reader's knowledge of Orlando's androgynous life in the eighteenth century. The court admits Orlando's womanhood and property rights only at the expense of 'her' marriage with Rosina

Pepita and its offspring (three sons); moreover, the judgement does not admit female descendants hereafter. Thus Orlando's femaleness is provisionally accepted only to eliminate a worse social threat to property (gypsy origins), and womanhood is anyway finally expelled from the pedigree to secure patriarchal 'rights'.

Living as a woman in a society structured by the division of sexes, Orlando cannot help being constituted as 'woman' along the lines of this division: 'what was said a short time ago about there being no change in Orlando the man and Orlando the woman, was ceasing to be altogether true'. 'More modest, as women are, of her brains . . . more vain, as women are, of her person', Orlando the woman now prompts the biographer to remark that 'a certain change was visible . . . even in her face'. Speculating on the cause and effect of these changes, the text proposes the 'philosophical' theory that 'clothes change our view of the world and the world's view of us'. 'Vain trifles' clothes may be, yet the effect of having skirts around her legs has already been shown to have an impact in the development of Orlando's new womanhood. Reversing the presumed relationship of priority between humanity and its signifying systems in good structuralist fashion, the narrator argues: 'it is clothes that wear us and not we them'. However, the text offers another theory to which 'on the whole, we incline': 'the difference between the sexes is, happily, one of great profundity. Clothes are but a symbol of something hid deep beneath. It was a change in Orlando herself that dictated her choice of a woman's dress and of a woman's sex'. The previous case now seems reversed, as some feminine 'essence' is given priority over female social existence, yet if we take the 'change in Orlando herself' to be her physical change of sex, the sentence becomes circular, its first and last phrases coinciding with each other. It is then the word and fact of 'change' itself that loses its obviousness, as the text elaborates: 'perhaps in this she was only expressing rather more openly than usual . . . something that happens to most people without being thus plainly expressed' (170-1). The nature of the change is never specified or clarified. For since, as I argue below, Woolf believes that the difference between the sexes cannot be defined in terms of biological or immanent essences, then 'change' from one sex to the other cannot be specified either.

Orlando enacts 'a vacillation from one sex to the other' and changes behaviour and clothes accordingly; this is not a once and for all change to a fixed essence of femininity or masculinity. 'Different though the sexes are, they intermix'. We face 'a dilemma': the difference between the sexes does not simply coincide with biological gender-difference, for 'often it is only the clothes that keep the male or female likeness, while underneath the sex is the very opposite of what it is above' (171-2). Thus she negates the previous essentialist argument on clothes and sexual difference. But intermixture does not mean fusion into homogeneous unity, for the difference between the sexes remains 'one of great profundity'. Yet this difference in turn cannot any longer be confounded with biological determination. Profound yet intermixing, such 'difference' becomes as difficult a term as 'change' itself. As I noted in my first chapter, Woolf often emphasises sexual 'difference' in her essays, while at the same time carefully avoiding any essentialist definition of it. Difference between the sexes exists only in relation to each other and to the representation of it. It is a matter of where the dividing line is, and its location varies historically and socially. Any definition only has meaning in relation to a specific socio-historical context, since there is no innate bond between signifier and signified. Woolfian androgyny is analogous to Saussure's definition of language. Just as language is a system of differences without 'positive' terms, so is gender a system of differences without any immanent essences. Thus androgyny opens up new possibilities in the fixed division of gender. 'She was man; she was woman . . . . It was a most bewildering and whirligig state to be in' (145). This 'whirligig' is Woolf's attempt to solve that dilemma for feminism that Julia Kristeva has most sharply posed: how to achieve the 'masculine, paternal' identification which supports time and symbol, in order to have one's voice heard in politics and history, but simultaneously to preserve otherness, to summon 'this timeless "truth"'—formless, neither true nor false, echo of our *jouissance,* of our madness, of our pregnancies—into the order of speech and social symbolism'.

Orlando attempts to realise precisely the 'impossible dialectic' Kristeva evokes: 'a constant alternation between time and its "truth", identity and its loss . . . never the one without the other'.[14] Such sexual oscillation is not unique to Orlando, for 'in every human being a vacillation from one sex to the other takes place' (171). The novel generalises the phenomenon of heterogeneity; Orlando is just more honest and open than most people to 'this mixture in her of man and woman, one being uppermost and then the other' (172). Changing 'frequently from one set of clothes to another' and living both sexes, Orlando 'reaped a twofold harvest . . . the pleasures of life were increased and its experiences multiplied' (199-200). Reading 'in a China robe of ambiguous gender', engaged in the economic management of the estate, receiving aristocratic proposals of marriage, fighting duels and serving as a naval captain, Orlando alternates between time and truth, history and the timeless, at once active participant in society and the muted object of male desire. S/he slides from woman to man, from man to woman, as easily as she changes clothes, metamorphosing in a permanent flux. The author does not present androgyny as a Hegelian synthesis of man and woman; Orlando lives alternation not resolution.

In a sense, this points to the limits of our thinking within patriarchal societies in which sexual differences are so implacably structured that they do not even allow a utopian imagination of a new sexuality. However much 'whirligig' Orlando experiences, sexual differences persist almost stereotypically. Orlando's manliness involves nonchalance about clothes, impatience with household matters, bold and reckless activity. Her womanly disposition involves lack of male formality and desire for power, 'tears on slight provocation', weakness in mathematics. Androgyny itself is 'non-conceptual' and unrealistic, but its components are presented in terms of naturalistic stereotypes. Non-naturalism—the fantastic—typically arises from the continual shifting between such naturalistic components. The fantastic is not simply irrational: 'it exists in a parasitical or symbiotic relation to the real'. In order to put the category of the 'real' into question, the fantastic needs realistic forms, at least initially. Through such forms it speaks all that is unsaid and unsayable in the positivist narrative. Fantasy exists in the shifting of the 'real' and 'imaginary'; it is the systematic inscription of 'hesitation' between them. No metaphor can condense into a single image this constant transgression of sexual boundaries; it can only be presented in metonymical displacement, a sliding of one form into another.[15] Hence Woolf's choice of the genre, of 'externality' over poetic depth (*WD*, 118), for this novel of androgyny was a right and necessary one.

The representation of androgyny as continual displacement of boundaries broaches the theme of disguise, with which the text is obsessed from the start. Orlando is proclaimed 'he' in the book's first sentence, but already 'the fashion of the time did something to disguise it' (15). As the biographer reflects later, clothes alone define as male or female the individual person in whom, in fact, a vacillation between sexes constantly takes place. Clothes attempt to 'fix' the aberrant sexuality, as Palmerston's legal decision does later. The text often describes ambiguous clothes which shake people's automatic sartorial identification of gender. When Sasha first appears, 'the loose tunic and trousers of the Russian fashion served to disguise the sex' (36). Such incidental concealment of sex becomes a more conscious manipulation of disguise in the Archduke; he finally reveals himself as a man, leaving 'a heap of clothes . . . in the fender' (162). Orlando is equally given to disguise. On the first night of her adventures she 'flung off all disguise and admitted herself a woman' in the street woman's room (197). 'Disguise' is a play with the boundary between seeming and being, blurring their sharp distinction and opening up a space of heterogeneity within unitary being. The recurrent disguises are another enactment of the impossible concept of androgyny, a literal realisation of the heterogeneity of sexuality by metonymical movement, though now on a naturalist level. In the end 'disguise' is no longer necessary: even without it Orlando recognises a woman in Shel, Shel a man in Orlando. They reject an apparent unitariness of sex that is only held in place by clothes as signifying systems.

Orlando's search for 'male' nocturnal adventure reflects partly her fidelity to her own turn of sexual disposition, but also dissatisfaction with the male friendship and love she has experienced as a woman, whether with the Archduke, 'London society' or the literary wits. Subtly or bluntly, she is excluded from society. Dumb and disillusioned mediator to the wits, 'Orlando poured out tea for them all', in bitter fulfilment of her earlier prediction (191). Rambling through the night disguised as a man, however, she strikes up a friendship with the street women. As when slipping out of the 'silken ropes' of the Royal enclosure with Sasha or in Constantinople as Ambassador, Orlando adds another to her/his series of social transgressions. If Orlando were in the usual sense a man, a relationship with a whore would not be transgressive at all, but rather an accepted act of sexual exploitation. But though they are socially functional, the prostitutes and their unwanted offspring are driven into the margins of society, just as Orlando's sons by the Spanish dancer were pronounced illegitimate. Orlando's friendship with these outcasts is a socially transgressive act, yet since many of them are illegitimate daughters of earls or even of the king, they are in a bitterly ironical sense her equals. She is elected a member of 'the society of their own' (198), a phrase which glances back to the short story 'A Society' and points a parallel with *A Room of One's Own* and *Three Guineas*, which advocates 'the Society of Outsiders'. 'A woman must have money and a room of her own if she is to write fiction' (*RO*, 6), but a prostitute too needs a room of her own. Orlando has a mansion with 365 bedrooms, but the prostitutes too have their own space, albeit in the margins of the social. They differ in degree, not kind, from other women; their exclusion exposes the blatant truth of that 'marginalisation' to which every woman is in fact subjected. Woolf also argues that literary 'masterpieces are not single and solitary births . . . the experience of the mass is behind the single voice' (*RO*, 98). But women are deprived of this necessary sense of community. In fiction, they 'are shown in their relations to men', never allowed to exist in their own right or in relation to other women (124). This one-sided picture is both cause and effect of the actual plight of women in society. The lack of material conditions deprives women of the freedom necessary for forming their own community, and at the same time the absence of any representations of women's mutual relationships undermines their belief in their practical relations with other women. Woolf in *Orlando* tries to fill this representational gap through the utopian imagining of friendship between Orlando as duchess and the street women. The ground of this bond is that both aristocrat and whores are free from the bourgeois values of thrift and prudence. This episode tries to flesh out *A Room of One's Own*'s imaginary sentence—'Chloe liked Olivia' (123)—which has never yet been written. It aims to overcome fiction's failure to depict female words and gestures 'when women are alone, unlit by the capricious and coloured light of the other sex' (127).

Orlando gives expression not only to friendship but also to love between women. Even after Orlando has become a woman, it remains women that she loves, 'through the culpable laggardry of the human frame to adapt itself to convention' (*O*, 147). Thus the text 'exculpates' the then shocking issue of lesbianism by the fantastic device of Orlando's sex-change. After this cunning naturalisation, the author asserts that the hero(ine)'s former love for Sasha has not changed. On the contrary, 'if the consciousness of being of the same sex had any effect at all, it was to quicken and deepen those feelings which she had had as a man'. Indeed, this love is now purified of the epistemological distortions of gender division: 'this affection gained in beauty what it lost in falsity . . . . At last, she cried, she knew Sasha as she was' (147). This utopian love rebuts men's belief '''that women are incapable of any feeling of affection for their own sex and hold each other in the greatest aversion''' (199). Women's existence has not yet been recognised in its entirety and as difference; in literature women are only 'shown in their relation to men'. Therefore without men, women do not exist. Hence in *Orlando* Mr. S.W.'s arrogant claim that '''when they lack the stimulus of the other sex, women can find nothing to say to each other. When they are alone, they do not talk, they scratch''' (199). Orlando's earlier conversational difficulties with the Archduke sufficiently ridicule the banalities to which women are reduced by men. To defy male arrogance, the text shows Orlando and Nell in a state of extreme merriment and ease, and the biographer dismisses the male beliefs by proclaiming, 'Orlando professed great enjoyment in the society of her own sex' (199).

Yet women's desire does not get into the order of representation. Women are 'always careful to see that the doors are shut and that not a word of it gets into print' (198). So too Freud had asked, 'What does a woman want?', and Lacan complains that 'ever since the time we've been begging them, begging them on bended knee to try to tell us about it [*jouissance*], well, not a word! We've never managed to get anything out of them'.[16] Women cannot articulate their desire, since the symbolic order is constituted precisely by its repression. The very question, 'what does a woman want?', denies the existence of women's desire. *Orlando* elaborates: 'All they desire, we were about to say when the gentleman took the very words out of our mouths. Women have no desires, says this gentleman, coming into Nell's parlour' (198-9). The repression of all that women are identified with—the unconscious, dreams, the body, psychosis, desire, the Imaginary—constitutes the symbolic order, and in this sense women can be said not to exist.[17] Already in 1919 Woolf showed her insight into this problem in an essay on George Eliot. Discussing Eliot's heroines, Woolf reaches far into the predicament women face: 'The ancient consciousness of women, charged with suffering and sensibility, and for so many ages dumb, seems in them to have brimmed and overflowed and uttered a demand for something—they scarcely know what—for something that is perhaps incompatible with the facts of human existence' (*CE*, 1:204). Inevitably, therefore, when Orlando, Nell and other women try to speak of what they desire their words are snatched away by the man, repressed and denied.

The spirit of the nineteenth century proves extremely antipathetic to Orlando. 'Aware of her defeat', her career here reaches its nadir (*O*, 220). As an age of odious sentimentality, domesticity and rigid convention, the century proves deeply antagonistic to the ideal of androgyny. Though Fredric Jameson has occasionally used Orlando as the image of an unchanging, transcendent personality passing through the centuries, social and historical factors are in fact fully admitted as constitutive for the human subject in the novel.[18] Such continuity as Orlando does maintain is solely bolstered by her country house—'the house, the gardens are precisely as they were' (214)—and is not a matter of a personal 'essence' at all. The Victorian period, despite Orlando's hostility to it, necessarily reshapes her as its product. The determination of consciousness by the social infrastructure also entails the determination of the individual by his or her signifying systems. Orlando proves unable to master her own writing. As she gathers together her reflections on 'the eternity of all things', she is interrupted by her servants 'as if to rebuke it', and then prevented by ' a blot' made by her pen and ink. Subsequently, the pen takes matters into its own hands 'to her astonishment and alarm', and produces 'the most insipid verse she had ever read in her life' (215). Her past androgynous experiences are steadily effaced until she becomes 'the very image of appealing womanhood': 'Her words formed themselves, her hands clasped themselves, involuntarily, just as her pen had written of its own accord. It was not Orlando who spoke, but the spirit of the age' (222). The novel confirms its earlier structuralist speculation that it is clothes that wear us rather than we who wear them.

The only freedom left to Orlando is to erase her involuntary production by spilling ink over it, a gesture of pure negativity. Author and protagonist both concede the latter's 'defeat' in an age in which there no longer seem to be sources of solidarity in alternative or oppositional cultures. There are no Victorian equivalents of the Turkish gypsies or the eighteenth-century prostitutes. It is impossible for a woman to be independent in an age when 'everyone is mated' and 'the new discovery' prevails: 'each man and each woman has another allotted to it for life, whom it supports, by whom it is supported, till death them do part' (221). Deprived of the freedom that had been the necessary condition of her literary production, Orlando reaches her nadir. She walks on the moor, collecting wild birds' feathers. She is driven to the very margins of society, as were such Victorian authoresses as Emily Brontë, whom Woolf names in her preface as among the 'friends' who assisted her in writing the novel. Orlando is now almost on the point of stepping out of society and history into timelessness: 'She quickened her pace; she ran; she tripped .... Her ankle was broken'. Crippled, she lies content on the ground, for as I argued in the previous chapter, lameness is a sign of intimate connection with the earth, and Orlando accordingly finds her 'mate' in the moor: 'I am nature's bride' (223). She reveals herself as a being who cannot be completely circumscribed within the social. Her temporary lameness is the sign of her fleeing from patriarchal control, but also prevents her from fully escaping it. The crinoline which impedes her free movements is not enough after all; she has to be more thoroughly deprived of freedom to the point where she can be 'rescued' by a man. Breaking her ankle is in a sense the 'death' of the woman as independent being. When Shelmerdine, as romance prince, appears to rescue her, she cries: 'I'm dead, sir!' (225), and at last receives a legitimate place in Victorian society.

The function of the marriage to Shelmerdine is to accommodate Orlando to the 'spirit of her age', at least on the surface. The novel must let the marriage temper Orlando to Victorianism, while at the same time distinguishing it from the loveless contemporary couplings the book denigrates. Thus Orlando likes her husband (which is perhaps not unrelated to the fact that he's always away!), maintains friendships outside marriage, still preserves her creative desires. For in a sense the purpose of this marriage is to enable Orlando to write her poem: 'the transaction between a writer and the spirit of the age is one of an infinite delicacy, and upon a nice arrangement between the two the whole fortune of his works depends'. What Woolf regards as the 'happy position' is that in which one need neither fight nor submit to one's age, and Orlando now achieves this precarious balance: 'Now, therefore, she could write, and write she did' (239-40). In her essays too, Woolf is no less adamant that conflict with the spirit of the age can produce only a literary 'monster' (214). 'Consciousness of self, of race, of sex, of civilisation', she writes in 'American Fiction', 'have nothing to do with art' (*CE*, 2:113). This is not, however, to deny the vital impact of sexual, social and racial conditions, for she expressly affirms the power of these determinations on literary production in *A Room of One's Own* and 'Women's Fiction', and no less so in *Orlando* by making the intervention of the spirit of the age explicit. But passion such as resentment, unhappiness, anger, whose intensity cannot be objectified into the impersonal forms of art, 'introduces a distortion and is frequently the cause of weakness' (*CE*, 2:144). Marriage with Shelmerdine saves Orlando from disabling self-consciousness in an age so antipathetic to her that it threatens to provoke bitter resentment.

Orlando's marriage also seeks to realise the androgynous ideal in the only form which is now permissible. It is a necessary compromise now that her eighteenth-century androgyny is repressed by a more rigid conventionality. But this utopian 'androgynous' marriage none the less remains one of the less convincing parts of the book, since it is after all a social facade; it is more a device to maintain appearances than a radical exploration of the issues. But in addition to its utopian dimension, sketching the possibilities of androgyny—'''You're a woman, Shel!'' she cried . . . ''You're a man, Orlando!'' he cried' (*O*, 227)—the marriage also has its ideological aspect. It is in this relationship that Orlando arrives at last at a conviction of 'rare and unexpected delight': '''I am a woman'', she thought, ''a real woman, at last''' (228). Moreover, it is at this point that she is legally pronounced a woman. What convinces Orlando of her womanliness is a feeling of maternal protectiveness incited by the odd vision of Shelmerdine as a 'boy . . . sucking peppermints' (227) during his passionate struggle against the waves. Here Woolf seems to be betraying some intractable personal limitation, a kind of feminist 'bad conscience', about what real womanhood is. For Woolf, her mother Julia Stephen and her sister Vanessa are always the model of complete womanliness. Mature, motherly, abundant, protective, practical, they embody precisely those qualities which Woolf feels she lacks. She describes Vita too in this vein: 'there is her maturity and full breastedness . . . her motherhood . . . her being in short (what I have never been) a real woman'. Woolf's difficult sense of her own inadequacies as a 'real woman' have been canvassed in Phyllis Rose's *A Woman of Letters*.[19]

Just before the birth of the son—an event which is abruptly presented and seems irrelevant in context—the narrator presents Orlando in ecstasy, and thus implicitly endorses the Kristevan view that a child is the 'sole evidence, for the symbolic order, of *jouissance*'.[20] Shelmerdine is away off Cape Horn, but he is none the less the source of Orlando's ecstasy. This sudden spasm, prompted by 'a toy boat on the Serpentine' which she relates to his ship, completely nullifies the values which society upholds: usefulness, practicality, logic, in short, the symbolic order itself.

> 'A toy boat, a toy boat, a toy boat', she repeated, thus enforcing upon her self the fact that it is not . . . eight-hour bills nor covenants nor factory acts that matter; it's something useless, sudden, violent . . . a splash; like those hyacinths (she was passing a fine bed of them); free from taint, dependence, soilure of humanity or care for one's kind; something rash, ridiculous, like my hyacinth, husband I mean, Bonthrop: that's what it is—a toy boat on the Serpentine, ecstasy—it's ecstasy that matters. (258-9)

Risking life itself, ecstasy casts away the articles and covenants of society, and the writing itself enacts the sudden, ridiculous 'spirts' and 'splashes' it speaks of. A casual circumstance (the hyacinths she happens to pass) becomes an integral part of the vision: 'She did not care in the least what nonsense it might make, or what dislocation it might inflict on the narrative'. The image of the boy sucking peppermints prompted a maternal protectiveness, but the image of the boy on the boat or the 'toy boat' shifts from loving gentleness to a more violent *jouissance* which threatens to subvert the repressive paternal order. Orlando's ecstasy on the banks of the Serpentine can be compared to Clarissa Dalloway's experience of intense joy while walking in London. Just as Clarissa prefers roses to Armenians, so too does Orlando's enthusiasm for the toy boat risk triviality, and yet is more subversive than initially it seems. It aligns her with Septimus against Bradshaw and his 'sense of proportion'. In *Orlando* too this polarisation is represented. The scholarly protocols of Nick Greene's article had plunged her into the depths of despair, but 'the toy boat had raised her to the heights of joy'. The heavy traffic keeps Orlando 'standing there, repeating ecstasy, ecstasy, or a toy boat on the Serpentine, while the wealth and power of England sat . . . in four-in-hand, victoria and barouche landau' (259). Orlando regards these portly figures as unwieldy 'leviathans' who cannot accommodate 'stress, change and activity'. In this sense, her love for Shelmerdine, who is 'rash', 'ridiculous' and invariably sails 'uselessly', is already antithetical to the values of Victorian capitalism, which repress the non-utilitarian and non-productive. If this feeling of Orlando's were intensified, then we should emerge into Septimus' disgust with humanity. If this vision moves from conventional maternal love to *jouissance,* then the fact of Orlando's own childbirth tends rather in the opposite direction, from challenge to convention. Though the child constitutes the sole evidence, for the symbolic order, of *jouissance* and pregnancy, it is also, ironically, the means whereby the woman will receive a place and function in the symbolic at the cost of *jouissance* itself.

The text shows as much embarrassment as it did at the moment of the sex-change in confronting Orlando's desire and its fulfilment, which at last however cannot be denied. The biographer wishes 'to mitigate, to veil, to cover, to conceal, to shroud this undeniable event'. Seeking to articulate this unrepresentable 'natural desire' and its fulfilment, the text resorts to the intervention of the music of the barrel-organs: 'allow it, with all its gasps and groans, to fill this page with sound' (263). In Kristevan terms, semiotic elements—sound, rhythm, melody—disrupt the symbolic (the written page). For Kristeva writes, the 'semiotisation of the symbolic . . . represents the flow of jouissance into language'.[21] Orlando too has tried to ignore desire and its consequence, her pregnancy, because this is the Victorian age of damp, of 'undistinguished fecundity' (208). 'The sexes drew further and further apart . . . . Evasions and concealments were sedulously practised on both sides' (207). The British Empire is constructed under male domination, denying women's desire, their *jouissance.* Women's minds now flow in the narrow channels of 'modesty and shame'. The crinoline symbolises the age: heavy and drab, it 'impeded' women's movements. Its function is to conceal the 'deplorable' fact of pregnancy, 'the fact that she was about to bear a child? to bear fifteen or twenty children indeed, so that most of a modest woman's life was spent, after all, in denying what, on one day at least of every year, was made obvious' (212). The music of the barrel-organ rescues the narrator from the linear narrative progression which biographical responsibilities impose. She lets herself be carried away by the music on 'the most clumsy, the most erratic' 'little boat' of 'thought'. Freed from formality, the text becomes increasingly whimsical in tone—'what is this place? . . . Well, Kew will do'—and intimate: 'Do you recognise . . .? Oh yes, it is Kew! So here we are at Kew, and I will show you today . . .' (263). The writing glides with free and irrelevant 'hops and skips' in enjoyment of its 'holiday' or 'escapade', just as *Orlando* was intended as an escapade for its author herself. Since any content will suffice—'Well, Kew will do'—language does not exist here purely for the sake of the signified. The sentences are formed and urged on by rhyme—'flinging a cloak under . . . an oak'—and the biographer modulates into a more characteristically Woolfian style. The narrator does not conceal the privilege of the semiotic—'as the rhyme requires'—indeed she rather emphasises her playful nonchalance concerning the signified; 'Wait! Wait! The kingfisher comes; the kingfisher comes not', and it hardly matters which. The linear passage of time is also loosened. The mind is freed from that irrevocable succession of present moments which Clarissa experienced listening to Big Ben and which Orlando suffers as the oppression of the present. Present and past mingle. To walk through the flowers in Kew Gardens is 'to be thinking of bulbs, hairy and red, thrust into the earth in October; flowering now' (264). Generative erotic images emerge in the narrative before 'denial [is] impossible; the fact that she was about to bear a child' (212). This respite is in fact less a means of evasion than the only way to approach desire and *jouissance*. To walk in Kew is 'to be dreaming of more than can rightly be said' (264), for these semiotic 'dreams' beyond representation embrace all that is outside the symbolic order.

Freed from thetic control, the mind brims over: 'it slops like this all over the saucer', it takes 'silly hops and skips' in 'the most erratic' way. It also recalls a blazing 'fire in a field against minarets near Constantinople'. Whether this is the biographer's memory or the author's or Orlando's remains indeterminate. The actual scenery, dreams, past and present, memory, intermingle to the point where it no longer matters whose dreams or memories they are. 'Hail natural desire! Hail happiness!': desire and *jouissance* now clearly challenge the dominance of the symbolic order, and threaten the symbolic chain or what Kristeva terms 'the well-oiled order of communication (and, thus, society)'.[22]

> Hail! . . . pleasures of all sorts . . . and anything, anything that interrupts and confounds the tapping of typewriters and filing of letters and forging of links and chains, binding the Empire together . . . Hail, happiness! kingfisher flashing from bank to bank, and all fulfilment of natural desire, whether it is what the male novelist says it is; or prayer; or denial; hail! in whatever form it comes, and may there be more forms, and stranger. (264-5)

As the 'splendid fulfilment of natural desire' and with something of the erratic, pulsing rhythms of the semiotic itself, the kingfisher 'darts of a sudden from bank to bank'. Though the narrator wishes the stream would flow 'as the rhyme hints ''like a dream''', the rhyme gets lost in the utilitarian 'binding together' of society, as the materiality of sound is subdued to the ideality of meaning. The stream the kingfisher flashes across becomes the stream of our own life. Though desire and its fulfilment could be more multiform and stranger than the male novelist allows, 'our usual lot' cannot sustain the dream; 'Alive, smug, fluent, habitual', we sustain the Empire, repressing the unconscious and its dreamwork. After this brief efflorescence of pleasure, the symbolic order again rivets down this moment of rupture. The stream of society once more flows on, just as the Thames resumed its usual flow after its carnivalistic interruption in the Great Frost. The shade of the trees 'drowns the blue of the wing of the vanishing bird when he darts of a sudden from bank to bank'. As the terrain of the unconscious, dreams expose the self as fissured. Immersion in dreams threatens the self established by identification with the mirror image: 'hail not those dreams which bloat the sharp image as spotted mirrors do the face in a country-inn parlour; dreams which splinter the whole and tear us asunder and wound us and split us apart in the night when we would sleep'. The eruption of desire threatens the 'forging of links and chains' of the symbolic, and must be checked. For Freud, drives are fundamentally dual, positive and negative, 'charges' and 'stases'; their process is, he posits, governed by the death-instinct.[23] *Orlando,* too, evokes a homeostatic state in the grip of the death instinct: 'folded, shrouded, like a mummy . . . prone let us lie on the sand at the bottom of sleep'. But again the pulsations of desire break the stasis. 'Blue, like a match struck', the kingfisher 'flies, burns, bursts the seal of sleep': 'now flows back refluent like a tide, the red, thick stream of life again; bubbling, dripping'. Such oscillations mark out precisely the place of Kristeva's *chora,* which is 'no more than the place . . . where [the subject's] unity succumbs before the process of charges and stases that produce him'. But the constraints of social structures check the drives, create momentary arrests and stases. The marks of these stases in the drives are thus integrated into the symbolic order, and the semiotic can be seen to shape the symbolic as an 'underlying causality'.[24] Or, in *Orlando*'s own version of this process, 'we rise, and our eyes (for how handy a rhyme is to pass us safe over the awkward transition from death to life) fall on . . .' (265-6). Here the music abruptly stops, and the semiotic interlude ends as our eyes fall on Orlando's first-born child, the only childbirth in all Woolf's novels.

With the 'shrinkage' which Orlando remarks as Edward succeeds Victoria, the fantastic aspect of the book also diminishes as a result of the author's loss of detachment towards the object of her writing. Authorial identification with Orlando strengthens as the narrative reaches the former's historical present and her own immediate concerns. As John Graham points out:

> Along with this reduction of Orlando and her *milieu* to the proportions of actual life runs a steady transfer of their fabulous aura to the events of the past which she now recalls. Yet these events are carefully robbed of their absurdity . . . . Fable must become history, for we are intended to take this resurrection of the dead not in the irreverent spirit with which we took the Great Frost, but in the spirit of a solemn vision.[25]

But the aesthetic strength of the book is not in making history vivid but rather in rupturing history itself by the laughter of an outsider, of a woman excluded from the historical. For 'when we write of a woman, everything is out of place—culminations and perorations; the accent never falls where it does with a man' (280-1). The success of the early part of *Orlando* derives from this stance, which

Woolf also adopts in *A Room of One's Own,* where she looks at patriarchal institutions 'with pleasurable obliqueness', with a consciousness that 'splits off'.[26] Woolf herself worried over *Orlando*'s disunity: 'I began it as a joke and went on with it seriously. Hence it lacks some unity' (*WD,* 128). In fact, the deflation of burlesque and the fantastic had begun with the onset of the eighteenth century, though its effects are only gradually felt. Since this 'serious' tone slowly sets in after *Orlando* has become a woman, it seems that Woolf's feminist concerns ultimately drive her into earnestness. She becomes a victim of the 'self-consciousness' she had so often deplored in others.

This diminishing of the fantastic also takes the form of the text's increasing inclination towards metaphor. As I remarked above, the narrative principle of *Orlando* is initially metonymy (or contiguity). The concept of androgyny is realised metonymically, and the narrative itself moves fast geographically and temporally. Woolf points to this feature of the novel in speaking of its 'plain sentences', 'the externality', of never having got down to the depth (*WD,* 118, 136). But the novel is none the less drawn towards the end into the 'depth' of metaphor and symbol. Since, as Jackson argued, 'the fantastic is *not* metaphorical' and 'does not create images which are "poetic" [but rather] produces a sliding of one form into another, in a metonymical displacement',[27] *Orlando* necessarily abandons fantasy and embraces metaphor in the same gesture, thus in the end conforming to the canons of what Woolf considered the 'serious' side of her literary project. What began as a fantastic joke ends up foreshadowing her next book: 'something abstract poetic next time . . . *Orlando* leading to *The Waves*' (*WD,* 128, 105).

'Images, metaphors of the most extreme and extravagant twined and twisted in his mind' (*O,* 36). Though the text is permeated with metaphor from the start, it remains highly self-conscious about them. The biographer often makes defensive gestures, baring the mechanism of metaphor as 'extreme and extravagant' rather than trying to exploit its powers of poetic symbolisation: 'Now the Abbey windows were lit up and burnt like a heavenly, many-coloured shield (in Orlando's fancy): now all the west seemed a golden window with troops of angels (in Orlando's fancy again)' (51). Orlando himself, as a would-be poet, ponders the problems of metaphor and the discrepancy between language and the thing itself. As a boy, he deplores the fact that 'green in nature is one thing, green in literature is another', that 'nature and letters seems to have a natural antipathy' (18). In his passion for Sasha, he discovers that 'Ransack the language as he might, words failed him. He wanted another landscape, and another tongue' (45). His difficulty is not a contingent matter of the limits of a particular language, but rather a problem of language as such. He is trapped by the circularity and figural nature of language: 'Another metaphor by Jupiter!'

> 'Why not say simply in so many words . . . . A figure like that is manifestly untruthful', he argued, '. . . And if literature is not the Bride and Bedfellow of Truth, what is she? Confound it all', he cried, 'why say Bedfellow when one's already said Bride? Why not simply say what one means and leave it'? (94)

He rejects the seductive, semiotic pleasures of alliteration—Bride and Bedfellow—for the rigours of ideal meaning, yet sheer literalism fares no better. Apparently, 'the grass is green and the sky is blue', but when Orlando looks he sees: 'the sky is like the veils which a thousand Madonnas have let fall from their hair; and the grass fleets and darkens like a flight of girls fleeing the embraces of hairy satyrs' (94). Ironically, sensuous particularity can only be approached by metaphor. Whether he speaks bluntly or sophisticatedly, Orlando remains embroiled in language, which—metaphorical or literal—has always already displaced the thing itself; 'Both are utterly false' (95). One never escapes metaphor; seeing is always seeing *as*. Orlando 'compared the flowers to enamel and the turf to the Turkey rugs worn thin . . . . Everything, in fact, was something else' (131).

Towards the end of the book this self-consciousness or even self-ridicule in relation to metaphor disappears completely. The early excessive use of similes, which openly bares the principle of metaphor (similarity), changes into an indulgence in metaphor proper. The final resonant symbol of 'the wild goose' is given its imagistic foundations in the penultimate chapter, with its 'wild birds' feathers', 'smooth, glinting plumage'. Orlando sees a single feather fall into 'a silver pool, mysterious as the lake into which Sir Bedivere flung the sword of Arthur' (223). Through this connection with the Arthurian sword, the various images of plumage are related to the possibility of some ultimate truth. In *To the Lighthouse* Lily expressed her wish that a hand would part the waters of the lake so that the meaning of life would be revealed (*TL*, 276). Just as her struggle as painter merges with this quest for meaning, so too does the wild goose represent all that Orlando tries to body forth in her poetry: 'Always it flies fast out to sea and always I fling after it words like nets . . . and sometimes there's an inch of silver—six words—in the bottom of the net. But never the great fish who lives in the coral groves' (282). The text here shows a curious intertwining of metaphor and metonymy. It offers an important symbol, but slides from one form to another, from goose to fish in a metonymical displacement with the sea as a point of contiguity. A similar interchange between sea and sky occurs in the final episode where Shelmerdine lands on shore. He may have 'grown a fine sea captain' (295), but arrives back by plane and leaps to the ground as if he were its captain. At this moment 'a single wild bird' springs up over his head: '"The wild goose . . ." Orlando cries' (295). If previously the goose flew out to sea, directions are now reversed: Shelmerdine, whose associations are all with the sea, has flown back from the sea as the wild bird. However, in both cases this metonymical development is not elaborated, certainly not as a possible springboard for the fantastic (and the potentially subversive implications of a 'wild goose chase' are also muted).

The fact that the narrative has reached the present is a major factor in diminishing the scope of the fantastic. In 1928 'Orlando started . . . . For what more terrifying revelation can there be than that it is the present moment?' (268). Does this not also allude, self-referentially, to the disturbance the biographer/author feels in confronting the present in writing? Roland Barthes writes that narrative is only possible in the past tense:[28] a biographical story of the present moment is impossible, a point where writing has to stop. Both novelist and protagonist receive with 'a great shock' the announcement of the present hour by the clock. 'We survive the shock' only 'because the past shelters us on one side and the future on another'. For Orlando, the present is always a giddying 'narrow plank' from which she might 'fall into the raging torrent beneath' (268-9). This is indeed the characteristic experience of time for Woolf's women. Orlando's clock recalls the menacing strokes of Big Ben in *Mrs. Dalloway*. At one level the hours operate in that novel as narrative connecting points, threading various characters' lives together, but they are also mercilessly 'shredding and slicing, dividing and subdividing' as they impose an objective order on the lived flux of experience (*MD*, 113). Mrs. Ramsay too senses time's irrevocability as she hears the sound of the falling waves with 'an impulse of terror'. For her too, the present is dangerous. Safety resides only in the past, 'since it happened twenty years ago, and life, which shot down even from the dining-room table in cascades, heaven knows where, was sealed up there, and lay, like a lake, placidly' (*TL*, 145).

> it cannot be denied that the most successful practitioners of the art of life . . . somehow contrive to synchronise the sixty or seventy different times which beat simultaneously in every normal human system so that when eleven strikes, all the rest chime in unison, and the present is neither a violent disruption nor completely forgotten in the past. (*O*, 274)

Since Orlando is obviously not one of these successful practitioners, the present is either violently disruptive or completely erased in the past. Neither Orlando, Clarissa nor Mrs. Ramsay can experience time as necessary development from past through present towards a willed future. For them, present and future are discontinuous, with no dialectical relation to each other. There is no grasp of history as meaningful process: the past is merely an isolated space in which life is 'sealed up . . . like a lake, placidly', or which engulfs the present. When Orlando sits in Queen Elizabeth's armchair, the past revives as a vista, 'as a tunnel bored deep into the past'. But when the clock strikes four, 'the gallery and all its occupants fell to powder' (287). Past and present prove mutually incompatible, each erasing the other in turn.

Orlando's inability to structure time into a meaningful teleology arises from the fact that as a woman she is excluded from the temporal order itself—from history, politics, society. After becoming a woman, she initially welcomes this position of outsider set over against the 'rule and discipline of the world'. Against the political order, she asserts the value of 'contemplation, solitude, love' (146). This is clearer still in the manuscript version of the novel:

> surely our choice is better than theirs: poverty, insignificance, nakedness: [those are] the [humble] garments which cover us with

invisibility & allow us to escape from all the [ties of pomp] & circumstance: to pass lonely & free as clouds where we are unnoted; to hover there . . . lost in contemplation; to [escape from] the [O] odious ceremonies, disciplines (here they come to slip from mankind) who are as busy with their ceremonies & disciplines; & thus enjoy the most exalted of all states of mind.

Here Woolf more explicitly offers Orlando's alienation from political and social affairs as freedom, as Madeline Moore's note points out.[29] But this escape from 'disciplines' also entails 'insignificance', 'invisibility'—namely the silence and marginality to which women are so often consigned. History is made elsewhere by others without Orlando (woman) having anything to do with it. Since her life has been shaped by patriarchal structures of which she has no grasp, time seems to her to come from an unknowable future and to race into an unknown past. The present is then the precarious 'narrow plank' between these two unknowns. For Orlando, history is alien to the living moment of the present: ' [the house] belonged to time now; to history; was past the touch and control of the living' (286). The present is a place of rapture and terror equally. In it *jouissance* may suddenly subvert 'the rule and discipline of the world', but it is also the place where the shocks of past and future are borne. Hence, 'braced up and strung by the present moment', Orlando is also afraid, 'as if whenever the gulf of time gaped and let a second through some unknown danger might come with it' (288).

The temporal discontinuity which Orlando lives is related to her being a woman and thus outside history, but it is also clearly connected with the difficulties of modern urban perception. In the capitals of advanced technological societies many aspects of life depend on processes beyond personal understanding and control. Modern city life is made possible by the separation of people from the sites of production of commodities and from the requisite scientific processes. Advanced technology, specialisation, and the immense scale of urban life are beyond the individual's grasp. Hence Orlando's amazement: 'I rise through the air; I listen to voices in America; I see men flying—but how it's done, I can't even begin to wonder' (270). This sense that one's life is governed by unknown social mechanisms destroys any possibility of wholeness of identity as well as the possibility of totalising history as teleology. The discontinuity of time and the fragmentation of the self are interrelated in the novel: 'for if there are . . . seventy-six different times all ticking in the mind at once, how many different people are there not—Heaven help us—all having lodgement at one time or another in the human spirit?' (277). Raymond Williams cites Orlando's drive from London to her country house as 'characteristic imagery of the urban preoccupation': 'in Virginia Woolf the discontinuity, the atomism, of the city were aesthetically experienced, as a problem of perception which raised problems of identity'.[30]

> Nothing could be seen whole or read from start to finish. What was seen begun . . . was never seen ended. After twenty minutes the body and mind were like scraps of torn paper tumbling from a sack and, indeed, the process of motoring fast out of London so much resembles the chopping up small of identity which precedes unconsciousness and perhaps death itself that it is an open question in what sense Orlando can be said to have existed at the present moment. (276)

This problem of fragmented identity is, as Williams points out, conventionally resolved on arrival in the country. Just before Orlando is 'entirely disassembled', 'green screens were held continuously on either side, so that her mind regained the illusion of holding things within itself'. One may draw a psychoanalytical parallel here. As the baby first gains control of its motility and then constructs the self as a unitary whole by identification with its mirror image, so Orlando regains the 'illusion' of a total self by the 'green screens' of the Kent countryside.

Orlando seeks 'what some people call the true self' or 'the Key self, which amalgamates and controls' all the selves she has it in her to be (279). Evoking such heterogeneous possibilities, the biographer demolishes the idea of a single, unitary identity. Woolf again takes up this theme in the essay 'Street Haunting'. Each person has 'instincts and desires which are utterly at variance with his main being, so that we are streaked, variegated, all of a mixture':

> Am I here, or am I there? Or is the true self neither this nor that, neither here nor there, but something so varied and wandering that it is only when we give the rein to its wishes and let it take its way unimpeded that we are indeed ourselves? Circumstances compel unity; for convenience sake a man must be a whole. (CE, 4:161)

The theme of the impossibility of totalising the incongruous components of the individual was treated in *Jacob's Room*. That novel was a shuffling of the discontinuous, fragmentary part-selves of Jacob in the hope of some symbolical fusion. But what the text finally offered us was only Jacob's room in London as a frame for sustaining the continuity of Jacob as a person, and even the room itself had to be left empty. In *Orlando* the great country house and estate successfully totalises Orlando's many part-selves. The house is origin and continuity, the origin as continuity. As she enters the lodge gates Orlando becomes 'what is called, rightly or wrongly, a single self, a real self' (*O, 282*). Yet she also sighs that 'the house was no longer hers entirely. . . . It belonged to time now; to history' (286). She, the living present, cannot be part of the temporal flow, precisely because she is a woman and therefore excluded. Palmerston's judgement declared that the estate descends on the heirs male of her body; Orlando will have to abandon the house, because history excludes her. In *Jacob's Room* the hero never returns to his room. History has destroyed him because in Woolf's novels there can be no involving, constructive relationship between history and the living individual.

Returning to her origin, Orlando achieves the command of a 'single self': 'masterfully, swiftly, she drove up the curving drive' (282). Since the house, like the 'other' in the mirror-stage, bolsters identity, even at the dangerous moment of the clock's striking the hour, 'she kept, as she had not done when the clock struck ten in London, complete composure (for she was now one and entire . . .)' (288). But we should note that this 'self' is characterised by certain images of fluidity which distinguish it from a fixed self of monolithic rigidity. As she at last achieves wholeness of self, Orlando feels as if 'all is contained as water is contained by the sides of a well . . . as if her mind had become a fluid that flowed round things and enclosed them completely' (282-3). This mode of perception—gentle envelopment rather than penetration at a single point, using all the senses rather than just sight—was, as I pointed out above, also the concern of Lily in *To the Lighthouse*. The scenery observed by the 'fluid' subject in *Orlando* is also presented in water images: 'the falling turf of the park whose fall was so gentle that had it been water it would have spread the beach with a smooth green tide', 'so she . . . watched the vast view, varied like an ocean floor' (282-3, 292).

Though she attempts to sustain her (relatively) unitary thetic self 'with great alertness of movement' and by walking 'more briskly than she liked', Orlando encounters an experience which thoroughly subverts this 'positioned' self: 'a raised saucer of pink flesh where the nail should have been' on the carpenter's thumb (289). Unpleasant this may be, but it hardly accounts in naturalistic terms for the violence of Orlando's reaction. I suggest that a psychoanalytic reading is necessary to account for the deeper forces this sight releases. 'Braced and strung up by the present moment', the self that can totalise the contradictory perspectives of Orlando's being depends on the secure separation of subject and object, inside and outside. It can master and know the world only so long as these rigid binary distinctions are held in place; thus the world Orlando sees now is 'miraculously distinct' (288). However, she then sees the 'pink flesh', that vulnerable inside which should have been covered by the fingernail (the tough carapace of the outside). Her revulsion derives from the sudden, unexpected emergence of the inside. This transgression of the borderline, this confusion of what should have been separated, instantly destabilises the security of the ego and its self-constitutive demarcations of inside and outside. Her ego is overthrown in a fit of disgust which is perhaps related to what Kristeva terms the 'abjection' roused by any ambiguity that ignores a border, rules, location, that confuses identity or system.[31] In this state of abjection, with its unstable relations of object and subject, Orlando's ego dissolves catastrophically, and then unconsciousness threatens in a moment of faintness. In this 'moment's darkness' that which had been repressed in the present emerges: 'she was relieved of the pressure of the present. There was something [which] is always absent from the present'. 'Terror' and 'beauty' at once, it is 'something one trembles to pin through the body', though it itself 'has not body' (289). In contrast to the 'miraculously distinct' and focused world of the thetic subject, 'the shadow of faintness' reveals ' a pool of the mind' (294).

'Furthest from sight', there is no clear distinction of subject and object, things are 'misty', nothing is detailed or distinct. This is a world of metonymy and metaphor: 'everything was partly something else', 'things . . . made the strangest alliances and combinations' (290). This is the terrain with which 'art and religion' are connected, a timeless world governed and syncopated by oceanic rhythms: 'Her mind began to toss like the sea'

(289-90). 'This pool or sea', with its shifting and dissolving forms, its labile rhythms, is surely an image of the Kristevan semiotic itself, representing a lapse back from the individuation of the Oedipus into the maternal realm of oceanic indifferentiation.

'She now looked down into this pool or sea in which everything is reflected . . . .' If art is 'the reflections which we see in the dark hollow at the back of the head when the visible world is obscured for the time' (290), that is, when the specular ego is in abeyance, then Orlando's poem 'The Oak Tree' is her furthest achievement in this direction. She climbs the path to the oak tree itself in order to perform 'symbolical celebrations' and pay homage to it. But this symbolical intention—to bury the book as tribute—is abandoned because 'the earth was so shallow over the roots' and anyway she finds it 'silly' (291). I have argued that towards its end the book begins a quest for metaphor and symbol, entailing a rapid abandonment of the fantastic and its principle of metonymy. But in this final episode the principle of metonymy 'revolts' and rejects the symbolic gesture. As if the author had become aware that the book has turned serious in spite of her initial intention to have a 'joke', she thwarts an act of burial that would have been a literal enactment of metaphorical depth, a 'reconciliation' of language and Nature. The poem's leaves are ruffled disconsolately by the wind, an appropriately casual and metonymical end to Woolf's venture into the fantastic.

CHAPTER 6

The Waves

On completing *The Waves*, Woolf wrote: 'What a long toil to reach this beginning—if *The Waves* is my first work in my own style!' (*WD*, 176). For though the novel is continuous with her rejection of Edwardian fiction in quest of some inner vision, it also marks an attempt to check the 'liquid' mode of writing of *To the Lighthouse*. Woolf notes that one reviewer had remarked a crisis in her style—'now so fluent and fluid . . . like water'— and wonders whether she can check 'that disease' (137). In the diary entries for *The Waves* she records her desire for a new solidity and depth. She aspires to penetrate deep, vertically, rather than pursue a 'liquid' expansion on the surface.[1] Hence the narrative consciousness that had sponsored the 'fluent and fluid' mode of *To the Lighthouse* must be interrogated in the later novel.

In *Jacob's Room* the narrator made her appearance in a meditation on the difficulties of being a woman ten years older than Jacob, and is thus foregrounded from the start. In *Mrs. Dalloway* and *To the Lighthouse* the narrator 'disappears', merging with the consciousness of the characters. Free indirect speech allows a narrative consciousness of such versatile subjectivity that there is no longer a single subject; discourse hovers suspended between authorial consciousness and characters' minds. In *The Waves* this chameleon style is replaced by the device of the dramatic monologue. However, as has often been pointed out, the interior monologues of this novel are very different from the 'stream of consciousness' which this device is normally used to effect; consciousness does not here spill unmediatedly on to the page. Borrowing T.S. Eliot's formula, Jean Guiguet terms these monologues a 'poetic correlative': 'a way of writing, a style . . . to obtain an equivalent to the sort of reality she is trying to express'. Hermione Lee also stresses stylisation rather than immediacy: 'a formal rhythmic monologue subjugates the representation of personality or action to a series of physical images which are made to stand for a state of mind'. The violence of Lee's language—subjugated, made to stand—testifies to liberal humanist assumptions about character which, I shall argue below, the novel itself rejects, but does at least register its formal innovations. One critic, remarkably, calls *The Waves* 'the most firmly rooted in stream of consciousness of all her books'.[2] But this is only true in the sense that a narratorial stream of consciousness existed in Woolf's early, inchoate plan of the book; it disappeared swiftly as she elaborated her idea.

The development of the structure of the book in her diary runs as follows. First a 'man and a woman' sit at a table talking, but then 'she might talk, or think. . . . Perhaps the man could be left absolutely dim' (*WD*, 108). Yet, still unable to start *The Moths* (her original title), Woolf has another idea: 'A mind thinking. . . . In its leaves she might see things happen. But who is she? I am very anxious that she should have no name. I want ''she'''. A month later: 'All sorts of characters are to be there. Then the person who is at the table can call out anyone of them at any moment; and build up by that person the mood, tell a story'. Later still she asks herself: 'Who thinks it? And am I outside the thinker!' (*WD*, 142-6). As these entries suggest, in the first drafts there indeed existed an unidentified figure, 'the lonely mind' (*H*, 6, 9). Its sexual identity is deliberately blurred: 'sex could not be distinguished in this very early light' (*H*, 42). Then, as if to increase the obscurity, Woolf 'hoods' the figure; it becomes only 'an eye in the hooded tent' (69). As if in answer to her own question—'Am I outside the thinker?'—the author is indeed situated outside this shadowy mind. Sentences tend to begin: 'if there was a person . . .', 'suppose there was someone . . .', 'if there was an eye . . .' (*H*, 89, 113, 124). But the eye is effaced as third-person description gives way to first-person monologue. Woolf noted: '*The Waves* is I think resolving itself (I am at page 100) into a series of dramatic soliloquies (*WD*, 159), and the shift seems to take place after page 192 of the holograph. In the terms of Woolf's earlier novels, we might say that the hitherto detached narrative consciousness interfuses with the speech of the characters, insinuates itself into their very phrases and rhythms. But this does not adequately describe the overall effect of *The Waves*. For it is in the end not the characters' but the *narrator's* consciousness that is elaborated, the former being only a 'poetic correlative' for some wider consciousness that envelops and exceeds them.

The continuities across Woolf's career have been clarified by the publication of the holograph draft of *The Waves*, which reveals thematic relationships with early stories like 'An Unwritten Novel' and 'The Mark on the Wall' that are less apparent in the final text. The original title—*The Moths*—is itself a recurrent Woolfian image, denoting the 'uncircumscribed spirit' that flits briefly into the light of narrative consciousness only to veer away again before it can be definitively grasped. Also prominent in the draft is that problematic of signs and meaning which I traced above in *Jacob's Room* and related short stories. It is necessary to decipher 'a mysterious hieroglyph, always dissolving' (*H*, 2), made by the purple crescent pattern on the wings of an 'enormous moth' on the wall. In quest of a meaning impeded by the opacity of the signifier, the text has to face the still more troubling prospect that the signified may not be just postponed but absent from the start:

'some bird pattered out a few irrelevant bars of ~~so pure a~~ ~~blank~~ sound so blank ~~so pure~~ that all meaning seemed emptied out of it'. This is the purity of kenosis not plenitude, and the rest of the page evokes a world of allegory in the sense I defined in Chapter 2. The world, drained of immanent significance, dissolves into unrelated fragments, 'as if the mind of the very old person man or woman, had gone back to the dawn of memory; & ~~had not been~~ without being been able to finish any sentence . . . without attempting to make a coherent story' (*H*, 2). But though the text here disowns the ambition of totalisation, that impulse in fact remains incorrigible. 'The power that centralises' collects shards and shreds from the debris, 'attempting to make a whole . . . thinking them into one story'. It sets itself the task of discovering 'in the folds of the past' or in 'such fragments as time having broken the . . . perfect vessel' (*H*, 6-9). The last phrase looks forward to the Grail motif implicit in Percival's name.

As a chain of images, associations, speculations, incited by the moth, the operations of the narrating mind in the early pages of the draft recall 'The Mark on the Wall'. Woolf's earlier narrator meditated on the fictional 'image of oneself' created in solitude:

> we are looking into the mirror . . . and the novelists of the future will realise more and more the importance of these reflections, for of course there is not one reflection but an almost infinite number; those are the depths they will explore, those the phantoms they will pursue (*HH*, 43)

If we interpret this in the light of Lacan's mirror stage, it seems that the narrator seeks to fix the identity in a single specular image only to find a radical process of splintering and fission begin. The subject's instability afflicts the object too. In this inchoate world, an apparently harmless metaphor shows a dangerous tendency to metamorphose its object. The copula of metaphor—X is Y—assumes ontological rather than merely rhetorical force. 'In this dim light one thing very easily suggests another. The creases of the table cloth might be waves endlessly sinking and falling'; 'how can I be sure that it is a cupboard there; it is a mountain slope' (*H*, 63, 114). In so far as Woolf aspires to a 'feminine' writing that avoids the complementary pitfalls of both feminist realism (old form, new content) and schizophrenic modernism (new form, 'no' content), she must do justice to both the systematic and the centrifugal impulses. Feminist realism offers a challenge to patriarchy at one level, but only confirms it at a deeper level (in forms and categories of representation). But an absolute rejection of the symbolic would precipitate psychosis and so radically divorce itself from the patriarchal system as to lose all possibility of exerting pressure for change on it: *Finnegans Wake* emblematises this danger. I shall argue that *The Waves* occupies the difficult 'between' of these two unpalatable options, maintaining a precarious dialectic between identity and its loss, the symbolic and its unrepresentable Other—an unsettling and unsettlable alternation prefigured in the sexual metamorphoses of *Orlando*.

The Waves opens with the dawn sky and seascape. Towards the end of the book Bernard, his self now limitlessly enlarged to 'a whole universe', returns to this scene (*W*, 207). Thus the interludes are also images or dreams which occur inside the narrative consciousness—'a mind thinking' (*WD*, 142). This mind looks reflexively at itself, at its own 'shadow' which might hold 'Something? Nothing?', and starts to explore its very beginnings (*W,* 207). The book inscribes the emergence of subjectivity and the process of its consolidation. Its scenic details serve as metaphor for the life process of the characters, and the first interlude evokes an undivided state before the subject appears: 'The sea was indistinguishable from the sky . . . Gradually as the sky whitened a dark line lay on the horizon dividing the sea from the sky' (5). In this prefiguration of the birth of self-consciousness there appears the recurrent image of a 'veil' or 'fabric' associated with the mind or being itself. This membrane or veil which contains or simply is consciousness develops Woolf's famous definition of life as 'a semi-transparent envelope surrounding us from the beginning of consciousness'. Her account in 'A Sketch of the Past' of memory at the very dawn of consciousness reveals the origin of the image: 'the feeling . . . of lying in a grape and seeing through a film of semi-transparent yellow' (*MB,* 65).

The last lines of the interlude evoke a still obscure state before the birth of meaning: 'all within was dim and unsubstantial. The birds sang their blank melody outside' (*W,* 6). The draft offers a more explicit image of the birth of the human subject:

> that
> ~~these~~ waves were . . . many mothers, & again
> of many mothers . . . endlessly sinking and falling,
> & lying prostrate, & each holding up, ~~like—~~
> > pass
> as the wave ~~hold~~ its crest . . . a child. (*H,* 9-10)

> For every wave, ~~before it sunk~~ sank ~~held up, &~~ cast a
> child from it; before it sunk into the obscure body
> of the sea. (*H,* 10)

> The little bodies wriggled &
> turned & twisted, curiously mobile & restless,
> [—] uneasy, ill-directed, shooting out arms & legs, — for
> there could be no doubt that these whiffs of spray, these
> pinkish balls, were, now that the light burnt a
> > greener
> little clearer, ~~children~~, new born babies, tossed ~~by the~~
> from the top of the waves, cast off by the rapidity
> of the sea . . . the worm like, eel like, half conscious yet

> animals
> blindly impulsive & violent actions of these little bald ~~brats.~~
> And soon the beach was covered with their markings.
> Soon they were staggering across the sand, & leaving foot prints
> . . . all across . . . its blankness. (*H*, 62)

This realm of inchoate motility, constituted by impulsive movements of muscles—Kristeva's *chora*—is not yet regulated into patterns of signification, though the world is pregnant with the possibility of meaning. 'There seemed to be beginnings or endings of meaning everywhere' (*H*, 61).

In a dimness in which 'one could scarcely distinguish anything', the children are mere 'pullulating', 'bubbling', 'pinkish rings of flesh': 'And how discriminate?' (60-3). In this amorphous pre-subjectivity the monologues are dominated by semiotic elements. The characters in the novel see vivid detached shapes and colours; a two-beat rhythm—'in and out', 'up and down', 'one, two; one, two; one, two'—pulses across their monologues. From this primitive state, separation and difference emerge. In the Latin class Neville discovers that 'each tense . . . means differently. There is an order in this world; there are distinctions, there are differences in this world, upon whose verge I step. For this is only a beginning' (*W*, 15). Absorbing lexical and syntactic organisation, namely entry into the symbolic order, is also the beginning of subjectivity: Bernard makes 'a wonderful discovery'—'I am myself, not Neville' (170). Each character 'elaborates' and 'differentiates' him or herself, using their friends to measure their own stature, for in youth self-identity is asserted ferociously (65, 83). The 'film of semi-transparent yellow' which for Woolf envelops human being has now solidified: 'A shell forms upon the soft soul, nacreous, shiny, upon which sensations tap their beak in vain' (181). 'The being grows rings; identity becomes robust' (186).

But self-identity is never fixed once and for all. It is a continuous intermixture, a dispersal and reassembly of diverse elements, Kristeva's subject in process. Woolfian 'personality' is never essentialist, though her work is often a quest for the essence of a character. The quest always involves a sense of the impossibility of fixing the essence: there is no inherent substantiality to the personality, which turns out to be the concurrence of all surrounding elements. *Jacob's Room* affirms that 'part of this is not

Jacob but Richard Bonamy—the room; the market carts; the hour; the very moment of history' (*JR,* 71), and Bernard ponders: 'what am I? There is no stability in this world. . . . We are forever mixing ourselves with unknown quantitites' (*W,* 84). 'Abnormally aware of circumstances', he is 'made and remade continually . . . there is something that comes from outside and not from within' (55, 96). Identity can never be a pure immanence. As the narrator of 'Street Haunting' remarks, 'circumstances compel unity; for convenience sake a man must be a whole' (*CE,* 4:161), and Bernard's self is an effect of the gaze of the other: 'To be contracted by another person into a single being—how strange' (*W,* 64). Alone once more, no longer impinged upon by the demands of the other, this sense of identity fades out. But even this is not a once and for all dissolution, for 'it steals in through some crack in the structure—one's identity. I am not part of the street—no, I observe the street. One splits off, therefore' (82). The separation of oneself, as subject, from the environment coincides with the acquisition of language. In psychoanalytical terms, subjectivity is achieved with the acceptance of the third term (the Name-of-the-Father), namely, the comprehension of mediation, the separation of word from the thing itself. This ability to erect himself as subject against object makes language possible for Bernard, 'a natural coiner of words': 'striking off these observations spontaneously, I elaborate myself: differentiate myself' (82-3). Continual alternation between an integrated assertion of identity and its dissolution makes Bernard a would-be novelist. 'Underneath, and, at the moment when I am most disparate, I am also integrated' (55). Only with such integration of selfhood in the thetic phase is language possible, yet, paradoxically, it also threatens his writing: 'The real novelist, the perfectly simple human being, could go on, indefinitely, imagining. He would not integrate, as I do (58). This is a local overemphasis, however, for as Kristeva argues, 'without the completion of the thetic phase no signifying practice is possible', and art must 'not relinquish the thetic even while pulverising it'. An 'unstable yet forceful positing of the thetic' is crucial for poetic practice. What is at stake is Kristeva's impossible dialectic: a permanent alternation between identity and its loss.[3] Here too Woolf's utopian idea of androgyny is affirmed. Partially caricaturing himself, Bernard describes himself as androgynous: '"joined to the sensibility of a woman" . . . "Bernard possessed the logical sobriety of a man"';

'the double capacity to feel, to reason' (55). For Woolf, writing should be such an androgynous alternation, an impossible dialectic which aims to be 'integrated' at the moment of maximum dispersal. Her ambition is to summon 'silence' into the order of speech, to reintroduce the repressed into an order made possible only by that exclusion of 'the other'.

Bernard is most acutely aware of the vagrant nature of selfhood, 'not one and simple, but complex and many' (55). But in fact most of the characters in *The Waves* confront the same query: 'what am I?'. Neville may boast that 'I am one person—myself', but he too soon encounters the ultimate uncertainties of identity: 'I do not know myself sometimes, or how to measure and name and count out the grains that make me what I am'. The frontiers of self and other blur as they had earlier done in the case of Bernard himself: 'As he approaches I become not myself but Neville mixed with somebody—with whom?—with Bernard? . . . Who am I?' (60). Though Susan represents a 'purely feminine' simplicity of 'love and hate', she too agonises, 'But who am I . . .?' (70). Louis assumes a rigidly definite identity: 'I, and again I, and again I. Clear, firm, unequivocal, there it stands, my name' (118). His is the egotistic, assertive self of Mr. Ramsay, Charles Tansley or Miss Kilman, the kind of domineering self categorised—and condemned—as typically male in *A Room of One's Own*. As an efficient agent of imperialist capitalism, Louis necessarily embodies this hated 'masculine' ego—'Acrid, suspicious, domineering, difficult' and 'formidable' (85). He reveres authority and orderly progress, erasing individual differences in the name of generality. Clearly he belongs to that realm of voracious ego and proto-Fascism that Woolf most hates. Yet this domineering self is in fact a frantic defensive manoeuvre prompted by Louis' inferiority complex as 'the weakest, youngest', an 'alien, external' colonial (he is Australian). More generally, the machismo of the aggressive self is a rejection of its own 'feminine' dependence on the maternal, of a difference or heterogeneity inherent in the self.[4] Though he respects Susan and desires the maternal safety she represents, Louis in fact chooses Rhoda, who has no trace of the maternal, as his lover. He has to imperiously sever himself from the mother. The memory of initial union with the mother is a threat to his ego and gender identity, though he can never finally escape it. In a powerful image he evokes his disgust and guilt at his former dependence: 'I am like some vast sucker, some glutinous, some adhesive, some insatiable mouth' (143). The mother must be rejected as abject, for only by this 'abjection' can the human being constitute itself as subject, separating out from its object.[5] In actual fact multiple and heterogeneous, Louis as subject must strive all the more to shore up a unitary selfhood: 'But now I am compact . . . all the furled and close-packed leaves of my many-folded life are now summed in my name' (119). Determined to be 'a full-grown man', he aims to impose his ego on the world, 'for if I deviate . . . I shall fall like snow and be wasted' (119). Sara Ruddick aptly applies to him the description of the policeman in *Jacob's Room*—'stiff from force of will'.[6] His will for integration extends to the whole world, indeed to the whole of human history. His megalomaniac ambition is to produce some vast totalisation, a poem which will plait into 'one cable the many threads . . . of our long history, of our tumultuous and varied day', resolving the 'discrepancies and incoherencies' (143-4). Only such a subjection of the entire universe to reason and order could secure the integrity of the threatened self. 'If I do not nail these impressions to the board and out of the many men in me make one . . . then I shall fall like snow and be wasted' (121).

When Louis speaks of the necessity to unify many selves, he reminds us of Rhoda who is precisely destined to fall and be wasted. As a child, she alone cannot write the answer in the mathematics lesson: 'But I cannot write . . . . The figures mean nothing now. Meaning has gone. The clock ticks. . . . Look, the loop of the figure is beginning to fill with time; it holds the world in it . . . . The world is entire, and I am outside of it, crying ''Oh save me, from being blown for ever outside the loop of time!'' '' (15). The symbolic order is a temporal order, as Kristeva insists in *About Chinese Women:* 'For the speaking animal, it is the clock of objective time: it provides the reference point, and, consequently, all possibilities of measurement, by defining a past, a present, and a future'.[7] While the other children, inserted into the symbolic, form a stable relationship with words and figures each in his or her own way, Rhoda does not. She cannot say this or that, yes or no, in the decisive way that Susan or Jinny can. 'But I lie; I prevaricate', and she is conscious, beyond her own difficulties with language, of everybody's 'lying tongues'; lies are not just contingent stratagems but structural to discourse. 'Broken into separate pieces', Rhoda can neither judge, name, nor be logical: 'I am not composed enough . . . to make even one sentence. What I say is perpetually contradicted' (76-7). 'Composed' has both its straightforward implication that she is nervous, and also a more radical sense, for Rhoda is not formed into the unified subject that could wield speech; she is merely 'separate pieces'. Her uneasy relationship with language and exclusion from time mutually imply each other. Kristeva argues that 'there is no time without speech. Therefore, no time without the father. That's what the father means: sign and time'.[8] 'Rhoda has no father' (14), and is accordingly excluded from and rejects genealogical continuity, temporal order, the clock of objective time. Later Bernard images full entry into the symbolic order as a clock which expands and contracts in an unswerving rhythm:

> Opening and shutting, shutting and opening, with increasing hum and sturdiness, the haste and fever of youth are drawn into service until the whole being seems to expand in and out like the mainspring of a clock. . . . And the little fierce beat—tick-tack, tick-tack—of the pulse of one's mind took on a more majestic rhythm. . . . We are the continuers, we are the inheritors, I said, thinking of my sons and daughters . . . .
>
> (183)

Louis too uses the image of 'the common mainspring. I watch it expand, contract; and then expand again' (68) to evoke the tempo of life in his eating house, but he, unlike Bernard, feels alienated from the temporal structure he observes. Both Rhoda and Louis contradict Bernard's momentary conviction 'that we marry, that we domesticate' within the 'machine' of the symbolic order (183).

The two figures who refuse/are unable to take their place in the passing on of a family lineage are both instances of unsuccessful repression of the mother. Louis and Rhoda share a self-image as 'the youngest', 'the most naked', and accordingly seek protection. Louis' vulnerable dependence on the mother provokes guilt and disgusted rejection, as I pointed out above, but at the same time he has 'an immeasurable desire that women should sigh in sympathy' (91). Rhoda yearns for 'mothers from whose wide knees skirts descend' protectively (76). At moments the text inscribes the images of union with and separation from the mother with moving explicitness. Neville when exhausted longs 'to rejoin the body of our mother from whom we have been severed' (165). Bernard remembers the first day at school as 'a second severance from the body of our mother', and, travelling on the train, he conceives of London as 'some ponderous, maternal, majestic animal' into whose flanks he will 'explode' (89, 80).

Driven out of the socio-temporal order, Rhoda lives a fragmented time. For her, 'one moment does not lead to another': 'they are all violent, all separate; and if I fall under the shock of the leap of the moment you will be on me, tearing me to pieces. I have no end in view'. Maturation and teleology are thus impossible: she cannot believe that she will 'grow old in pursuit and change' (93). Nor does the book as a whole subscribe to notions of maturity or purposive change. 'Nobody, I thought, ever changes the attitude in which we saw them first, or the clothes' (193): Bernard's opinion is a fundamental tenet of the novel itself. The style and vocabulary of the six characters do not change from the first monologues to the last; images which serve as indices to distinguish the six are repeated throughout the text. Fragmentariness is as characteristic of the time of the book as of Rhoda. Woolf composed by 'moments'. Her aim was

> to give the moment whole; whatever it includes. Say that the moment is a combination of thought; sensation; the voice of the sea. Waste, deadness, come from the inclusion of things that don't belong to the moment; this appalling narrative business of the realist: getting on from lunch to dinner: it is false, unreal, merely conventional. (*WD*, 139)

The doctrine of the 'moment' is also explicated in 'A Sketch of the Past'. 'Exceptional moments' involve a 'sudden violent shock' which ruptures the 'sealed vessels' of being, tearing one out of the ruck of the mundane—'non-being', 'non-descript cotton wool'—into either absolute despair or a fulfilling sense of wholeness (*MB*, 122, 70-1). Such aspects of life as eating, washing, cooking, everyday business are regarded as superfluity. On the level of fictional form, this mundane sequence is the narrativity of the realist novel which Woolf had been denouncing since 'Modern Fiction'; it is a materiality ('cotton wool') which blots out the light. *The Waves* enacts a denigration of 'general sequence' both formally and thematically. Bernard's attitude to 'the usual order' is profoundly ambivalent:

> observe how dots and dashes are beginning, as I walk, to run themselves into continuous lines, how things are losing the bald, the separate

identity that they had as I walked up those steps . . . . The world is beginning to move past me like the banks of a hedge when the train starts, like the waves of the sea when a steamer moves. I am moving too, am becoming involved in the general sequence when one thing follows another and it seems inevitable that the tree should come, then the telegraph-pole, then the break in the hedge. And as I move, included and taking part, the usual phrases begin to bubble up . . . . (*W,* 134)

This general sequence is more often resented as something that, impeding 'the moment', is viewed as dead matter, stifling truth and light ('cotton wool'). Even when Bernard welcomes it, he does so with an undertone of scorn or condescension, as when he talks of the complacent life of little shopkeepers. 'Life is pleasant. Life is good. The mere process of life is satisfactory . . . . Something always has to be done next. Tuesday follows Monday; Wednesday Tuesday . . . . So the being grows rings; identity becomes robust' (185-6). But for *The Waves* identity is as constrictive as it is desirable. Though Bernard says, 'Heaven be praised . . . we need not whip this prose into poetry' (186), this is not without a sort of resignation. Conventional plot is the macrostructural equivalent of the sentence in linguistic microstructure, and Woolf is similarly dissatisfied with the linearity of language itself, which is powerless to render the polymorphous nature of experience. As Woolf writes elsewhere, 'Every moment is the centre and meeting-place of an extraordinary number of perceptions which have not yet been expressed. Life is always and inevitably much richer than we who try to express it' (*CE,* 2:229). Language necessarily fails to give the moment whole, for the 'I' exists in discourse only by repressing the body, the unconscious, desire and pleasure.

Woolf's dissatisfaction with plot, sequence, narrativity is, in short, a protest against the symbolic, which by excluding multi-sensory living experience calls into being the unconscious. Her constant though strictly speaking impossible aim is to write about what escapes the symbolic order. In *The Voyage Out* Terence aspires to write a 'novel about Silence', about the domain outside speech (*VO,* 262). Woolf's rudimentary ideas for *The Waves,* her desire to abolish story, naming, specificity of time and place, all indicate this impulse towards a 'beyond' of the symbolic (*WD,* 142-3). Rhoda is incapable of establishing the thetic subject and is thus terrified of it; her abhorrence of the social is largely shared by the novel itself. 'You stand embedded in a substance made of repeated moments run together; are committed, have an attitude, with children, authority, fame, love, society; where I have nothing. I have no face' (*W*, 158). Woolf hoped that women's literature would cultivate 'poetry', as *The Waves* itself does: 'Why admit anything to literature that is not poetry?' (*WD*, 139). In 'The Narrow Bridge of Art' she adumbrates a kind of book which will encompass the elements that the novel, drama and poetry of the past could not accommodate; it is realised in *The Waves*, 'a playpoem' (*WD*, 137). Poetry, in this usage, involves reaching 'beyond the personal and political relationships' (*CE*, 2:147). The novel of the future will 'resemble poetry in this that it will give not only or mainly people's relations to each other and their activities together . . . but it will give the relation of the mind to general ideas and its soliloquy in solitude. . . . We long for some more impersonal relationship' (2:225).

The Waves accordingly refuses to be 'embedded' and 'committed' in the socio-temporal, symbolic order. There is little evidence of development or history in the book. Its time is either the detached moment or a 'substance made of repeated moments' contained within no humanist or religious framework. It might be termed an 'agnostic' time, where one constantly confronts 'abysses of infinite space' and in which human history is, humblingly, just 'one inch of light': 'And we ourselves, walking six abreast, what do we oppose, with this random flicker of light in us that we call brain and feeling, how can we do battle against this flood; what has permanence?' (*W*, 160-1).[9] Bernard's phrases closely parallel Rhoda's awareness that 'nothing persists': 'I am whirled down caverns, and flap like paper against endless corridors' (93). Neither experience nor history can constitute a meaningful continuity, on however modest a scale. During the visit to Hampton Court, Neville seems briefly to recover historical continuity: 'Unreasonably, ridiculously . . . as we walk, time comes back . . . . I am become a subject of King George' (161). He places himself in a particular flow of time which carries the specific values of a once extant society, in sharp contrast to Bernard who sees the King as a ludicrous mannikin 'with a golden teapot on his head' set against the 'whirling abysses of infinite space'. But as Neville's adverbs—unreasonably, ridiculously—already suggest, historical continuity cannot be sustained. Of the six characters Louis seems most to have a sense of history, and seeks in his poetry 'to realise the meeting-place of past and present' (48). But he in fact erases historical particularity to the blandness of the general concept. 'Too universal', he adds up people 'like insignificant items in some grand total which he is for ever pursuing' (66). In order to console himself in the mediocre present, he seeks to establish continuities from the past, in the end to assert the *sameness* of past and present from the viewpoint of 'theeternal procession' (119). For Louis, modern 'women going with attaché cases down the Strand' essentially *are* the women 'who went with pitchers to the Nile' (119). But this violent homogenisation is only the mirror-image of the historical fragmentation the other characters experience, and it too abolishes significant teleologies.

Time in this novel will not conform to canons of constructive development; it is discrete rather than continuous, or cyclical rather than linear. Bernard summarises its nature in the image of the falling drop, whose forming represents habitual behaviour within a quotidian routine. 'Shave, shave, shave . . . . The drop fell'.

> The drop falling has nothing to do with losing my youth. This drop falling is time tapering to a point. Time, which is a sunny pasture covered with a dancing light, time which is widespread as a field at midday, becomes pendant. Time tapers to a point. As a drop falls from a glass heavy with some sediment, time falls. These are the true cycles, these are the true events. (131)

Experience generates mere habit, veiling truth; its practical comforts efface the latter's harsh necessity. Moments of being are muffled in 'cotton wool' as 'I would go through that familiar ritual and wrap myself in those warm coverings' (132-3). When one phase of life reaches the maximum possible accumulation of habit it falls like an excessively heavy drop of water and completes itself. It does not lead with any cumulative progression or even connection into the next phase, just as it owed nothing to the previous one; it simply amounts to 'shedding one of my life-skins' (134). In the interval between one drop falling and the next forming, a covering 'veil' falls and offers an all too brief glimpse of truth. But 'the drop falls; another stage has been reached. Stage upon stage. And why should there be an end of stages? and where do they lead? To what conclusions?' (133).

This scepticism towards progressive time and Woolf's rejection of realist narrative are two aspects of the same anti-symbolic stance. For time and narrative order are sustained by the logical, unified subjectivity (Kristeva's thetic subject) that is constituted in the repression of 'the senses of sight, of sound, of touch—above all, the sense of the human being, his depth, and the variety of his perceptions, his complexity, his confusion, his self, in short' (*CE,* 2:158-9). Though he is a born story-teller, Bernard comes to believe in story less and less. In quest of 'the true story, the one story to which all these phrases refer', he must at last concede: 'But I have never yet found that story. And I begin to ask, Are there stories?' (133). He rejects classical canons of narrative. 'It is a mistake, this extreme precision, this orderly and military progress; a convenience, a lie', for 'there is always deep below it . . . a rushing stream of broken dreams, nursery rhymes, street cries, half-finished sentences and sights—elm trees, willow trees, gardeners sweeping, women writing—that rise and sink' (181). He here articulates the text's own desire to embody this stream beneath the civilised surfaces of the socio-symbolic order, though in it 'there is nothing one can fish up in a spoon; nothing one can call an event'.

In his final monologue Bernard declares his weariness with 'beautiful phrases' and 'neat designs of life' (169). He can tell a story only by a Coleridgean suspension of disbelief or a philosophy of 'as if': 'Let us pretend that we can make out a plain and logical story . . .' '(178). Linguistically gifted, he none the less despairs, in the face of the complex heterogeneity of beings, of rendering them adequately in language. Yet despite his distrust of 'logical story' and ordered 'biographic style' (184), he does not repudiate them altogether, since they after all serve to hold one within civilisation and sanity. One cannot so unreservedly despise the symbolic codes 'laid down like Roman roads across the tumult of our lives, since they compel us to walk in step like civilised people with the slow and measured tread of policemen though one may be humming any nonsense under one's breath at the same time— ''Hark, hark, the dogs do bark'', ''Come away, come away, death''' (184). The social system regulates wanton desire or vagrant dreams, achieving on its grander scale the efficiency of Bernard's humble clock. Its guardians, like the policeman in *Jacob's Room* or William Bradshaw, tell one to 'keep straight on' by ignoring 'the chasms in the continuity of our ways' (*JR,* 95), and its marvels of efficiency, like the ambulance which so impresses Peter Walsh, bolster the health of society by eliminating the 'insanity' of Septimus Smith.

But the Roman or biographic style cannot fish up the tumult of our lives, its rushing stream of broken dreams. As Woolf notes in 'Street Haunting', it dare not 'leave the straight lines of personality' with its gig-lamps symmetrically arranged in order to deviate into 'footpaths that lead beneath brambles and thick tree trunks into the heart of the forest' (*CE*, 4:165). Bernard reflects: 'Here again there should be music. Not that wild hunting-song, Percival's music; but a painful, guttural, visceral, also soaring, lark-like, pealing song to replace these flagging, foolish transcripts' (*W*, 177). Percival's music, hunting down its object with unwavering determination, partakes of, rather than challenges, the linearity of language itself. Later Bernard describes linear orderliness as 'military progress' (181). In this chain of associations—Roman roads, policemen, hunting, Percival, the military—the smooth teleology of narrative plot and male agressivity or even totalitarianism are clearly connected. It is this order which persecutes Rhoda. Without 'attitude . . . children, authority, fame, love, society', her life is merely 'the white spaces that lie between hour and hour' and is consigned to non-being by the symbolic order (158, 145). Bernard seeks a music close to the body, primitive (guttural and visceral) but also rhythmical and joyous (the pealing of a soaring lark). If ordered transcription, elaborate style and logical story are 'masculine', we may regard this utopian alternative as 'feminine'. 'What is the use of painfully elaborating these consecutive sentences when what one needs is nothing consecutive but a bark, a groan?' (178). He wishes to get back behind the construction of language, to 'a howl; a cry' which would be prior to syntax; 'a little language such as lovers use, words of one syllable such as children speak when they come into the room and find their mother sewing' (209). This language of and for the maternal presence would then be the Kristevan semiotic. The novel itself endorses Bernard, deploying discrete groups of words and isolated images rather than syntactical elaboration. Hence the fragmentation of the writing of *The Waves:* short sentences strung loosely together by semi-colons, the juxtaposition of nouns, its patterns of repetition.

The very frustration that such effects produce in the reader testify to the deeply ingrained forces of those conventions of plot and sequence which the novel regards as produced by the 'totalitarianism' of the logocentric mind. Woolf defines the modern age as 'an age incapable of sustained effort, littered with fragments'. And yet she defends modernism, for it stimulates the senses of sight, hearing, touch, of perceptual multiplicity or confusion, whereas past literature had been unable to express a mind 'full of monstrous, hybrid, unmanageable emotions' (*CE*, 2:219). Her dissatisfaction with the literary tradition and its contemporary Edwardian representatives is by now gender-specific, not generational. Though fragmentation of the psyche is the general experience of modernity, the woman writer sees it as a positive force of heterogeneity, unlike her male counterparts who tend to look nostalgically back to some pre-Renaissance 'unified sensibility'.

Dissatisfaction with unitary selfhood is frequently articulated by the characters of *The Waves*, who have a strong sense of the self as multiple and heterogeneous. Experiencing himself as 'unconfined and capable of being everywhere on the verge of things and here too' (207), Bernard seems to experience a megalomaniac inflation of the ego rather than its dissolution, as in Rhoda's case. However, inflation of the ego and its dissemination come in the end to the same thing, as is indicated by the fact that this experience of Bernard's only arises in the death of his self. Neville also experiences the expansionist ego—'To myself I am immeasurable'. But such elation is again close to dissolution, to a radical indifferentiation of self and world: 'a net whose fibres pass imperceptibly beneath the world. My net is almost indistinguishable from that which it surrounds. It lifts whales—huge leviathans and white jellies, what is amorphous and wandering' (152). Even Louis' near manic investment in the fixity of the self in fact testifies to the insidious force of pressures working always for its dissolution. 'I smoothed my hair when I came in, hoping to look like the rest of you. But I cannot, for I am not single and entire as you are' (91). But it is Rhoda, not knowing how to make 'the whole and indivisible mass' called life, who feels most persecuted by those who live in self-unity (93). She endures agony in going 'through the antics of the individual', yearning for those 'moments when the walls of the mind grow thin' and 'we might blow so vast a bubble that the sun might set and rise in it and we might . . . cast off and escape from here and now' (158-9). Her dream parallels Bernard's vision towards the end of the novel, and this illimitable consciousness beyond individuality in turn suggests the narrative consciousness of the text itself, in which scenery, characters, monologues have their being.

Abolition of the limiting walls of individuality can be experienced either as the infinitising or the dissolution of the self; denial of unity can be a polymorphously perverse enjoyment of multiple selves or the agony of the fragmented self. Neville's ego perishes in the rushing crowd; Bernard in solitude is 'dissolved utterly' and becomes 'featureless and scarcely to be distinguished from another' (159); Rhoda is undone by her fellow human beings who pierce her with a 'million arrows'. The sense of psychic breakdown even produces hallucinations of corporeal disintegration: 'More cruel than the old torturers, you will let me fall, and will tear me to pieces when I am fallen'; 'I am broken into separate pieces' (159, 76). For as Lacanian theory shows, it is the body which founds the unitary identity of the human subject; coherence is bestowed upon the infant by the specular image of corporeal unity with which it identifies. Rhoda, predictably, hates looking-glasses, for the image urges her to congeal into identity. Yet still she has to experience her totality outside her, over there in the mirror; identity as a whole is experienced in alienation. This impassable abyss or *béance* between mirror-image and self threatens her: 'Alone, I often fall down into nothingness . . . I have to bang my head against some hard door to bring myself back to the body' (31). The most intense crisis of this kind occurs at the puddle:

> I came to the puddle. I could not cross it. Identity failed me. We are nothing, I said, and fell. I was blown like a feather, I was wafted down tunnels. Then very gingerly, I pushed my foot across. I laid my hand against a brick wall. I returned very painfully, drawing myself back into my body over the grey, cadaverous space of the puddle. (46)

Between the image of herself on the surface of the water and her actual self lie 'crevices' and 'fissures', from which the 'emerging monster' leaps and menaces her, 'With intermittent shocks, sudden as the springs of a tiger, life emerges heaving its dark crest from the sea. It is to this we are attached; it is to this we are bound, as bodies to wild horses' (47). In this realm anterior to the symbolic an

169

unfocused aggressivity menaces the nascent ego: the ego is in continual struggle with the alter ego in binary relationship.

When the transcendental ego is threatened with dissolution, the mirror phase is reversed in phantasies of corporeal disintegration, a terror not peculiar to Rhoda. 'Little bits of ourselves are crumbling', remarks Bernard (166). Louis describes the others at the dinner party in lurid terms: 'The flames leap over their painted faces, over the leopard skins and the bleeding limbs which they have torn from the living body' (100). In *The Waves* even casual experiences like taking the Tube become major psychic traumas, involving violent images of being 'dissevered by all those faces' (127). Falling into crevices or nothingness, being torn to morsels by others—such images closely parallel Rhoda's psychotic fears, as does the vision of the dead man with his throat cut which had terrified Neville as a child and represents for him the 'unintelligible obstacle' or 'doom' which he cannot bypass (17-8). The very intensity with which the six characters seek to compose unity among themselves testifies to their obsession with the disintegration of the body, for 'we suffered terribly as we became separate bodies' (171). Recalling their dinner together in his last soliloquy, Bernard reflects dolefully: 'We saw for a moment laid out among us the body of the complete human being whom we have failed to be, but at the same time, cannot forget' (196). Though they attempt to assert individuality, 'like separated parts of one body and soul', Percival makes them aware that such efforts are false. They create one 'circle', 'this globe': 'do not let the swing door cut to pieces the thing that we have made' (104). This achievement is repeated at the second dinner party. Occurring at a communion meal in both instances, the unification into one body and the concomitant satisfaction of oral impulses perhaps suggests a fantasy return to primitive fusion at the breast.

Also marked by a certain disintegration is the 'body' of *The Waves* itself, whose formal characteristics I have already noted. Though the laws of syntax are never finally shattered, the novel does create in the reading an effect of fragmentariness, of a radical lack of sequential momentum. It abounds with short sentences, organised in an often simple syntax, in contrast to the 'chameleon style' of the earlier novels which sprawls through a meandering syntax. In his major study of poetic syntax, *Articulate Energy,* Donald Davie identifies three poetic traditions. The tautly

organised 'strong lines' of eighteenth-century verse contrast
clearly with the radically fragmented syntax of, say, Ezra Pound,
but between these two poles Davie identifies a third alternative:
'pseudo-syntax, a play of empty forms'.[10] For in Symbolist poetry,
syntax is on the surface intact, yet in fact carries no charge of
meaningful articulation; the verse is structured according to
principles of sound, rhythm, imagery. It is such a syntax that
Woolf's novels operate, and *The Waves* in particular. Syntax is
conspicuously subordinated to an organisation of rhythm, of
phonic or semantic repetition:

> There is a dancing and a drumming, like the dancing and the drumming
> of naked men with asseagais. (100)

> doors will open and shut, will keep on opening and shutting . . . . (111)

> I am no longer young. I am no longer part of the procession. Millions
> descend those stairs in a terrible descent . . . . Millions have died.
> Percival died. I still move. I still live. (137)

> This is the prelude, this is the beginning. I glance, I peep, I powder . . . .
> This is my calling. This is my world. All is decided and ready; the
> servants, standing here, and again here, take my name, my fresh, my
> unknown name, and toss it before me. I enter. (73)

Repetition of the personal pronoun between adjectives—'my fresh,
my unknown name'—is a recurrent stylistic oddity, and shows
repetition at work in the microstructures of the novel's language as
well as orchestrating whole pages at a time.

Since it produces strong rhythmic effects, repetition foregrounds
the materiality of language at the expense of linear narrative
development. By reintroducing words or phrases or redeploying a
simple, emphatic syntactic structure, repetition and tautology
activate the paradigmatic axis of language, which is usually
excluded by the developmental urgency of the syntagmatic chain,
and in so doing they begin to dissolve the syntagma. *The Waves*
shows a consistent reluctance to give up the paradigmatic
substitutions which in practice have to be repressed as the 'Other'
in order that meaning may be produced along the syntagmatic
chain. The novel explores the vertical axis, playing associational
variations on a single signifier which, as Saussure argues, 'will

unconsciously call to mind a host of other words' from the paradigm.[11] Lacan contends that 'strict coherence in the syntagmatic chain provides a position for the transcendental ego', and thus to unleash the paradigm, to juxtapose rather than subordinate signifiers, threatens that security.[12] *The Waves* manipulates discrete clusters of words or isolated images which are not neatly pigeon-holed in a syntactic hierarchy. Its philosophy of language is articulated by Bernard, who is tired of stories and phrases that 'come down beautifully with all their feet on the ground': 'what one needs is nothing consecutive but a bark, a groan' (169, 178). Thus the reappearances of the recurrent set images of each character are not governed locally by logical connections or narrative necessity. Woolf noted: 'this is the right way of using them [images and symbols]—not in set pieces, as I had tried at first, coherently, but simply as images, never making them work out; only suggest' (*WD*, 169). On this showing, Donald Davie's description of Symbolist poetry, as functioning 'by the arrangement of images, letting the meaning flow unstated, as it were, from the space between them', again has a bearing upon *The Waves*. He concludes 'that dislocation of syntax is essential to all poems written in this tradition'. The novel as such perhaps exercises stronger syntagmatic constraints than lyric poetry, but though Woolf does not dislocate syntax, even in Rhoda's extreme assertions of psychic breakdown, she goes a long way towards *emptying* syntax of its function of articulation across the novel as a whole. Yet the novel is divided about the consequences of this. Bernard rejects sequentiality, but also knows that 'without [it] we should be undone' (*W*, 166); syntax constitutes a 'Roman road' which maintains the self within sanity and civilisation. In this phase Bernard would agree with Davie (who has Pound's *Cantos* in mind) that 'to dislocate syntax in poetry is to threaten the rule of law in the civilised community'.[13] Yet both he and the novel retain a desire to pursue the paradigmatic, to 'play ducks and drakes with all these phrases' (184).

The arrangement of the monologues is a further device contributing to the novel's effect of broken stasis. Though described by its author as a 'play-poem', the novel has no dramatic impetus. The monologues are not addressed to each other, they achieve no dramatic interaction, they follow one another within a general chronology that does not establish close local links of logic or sequence. Whether the units are sentences or monologues, *The Waves* tends not to establish syntagmatic relations of implication, causality or subordination. The monologues are organised by parataxis rather than syntaxis. Laid in juxtaposition, they do not aim for tight closure in the larger syntagmatic chains of the novel, and the reader is again deprived of the fixed subject position of Kristevan 'thesis'; the resultant anxiety emerges in the reading as frustration and tedium. These effects are reinforced by the lack of drama *within* as well as between the speeches. Rhythm rather than dramatic interaction was Woolf's major concern in this 'series of dramatic soliloquies': 'the thing is to keep them running homogeneously in and out, in the rhythm of the waves' (*WD*, 159). The hard, external linguistic mode of the monologues denies the reader the pleasures of 'inwardness', of the intimate access to subjectivity that the stream of consciousness afforded. Dislocation of syntax may be recuperated as a more faithful transcription of a disordered but still basically homogeneous (even lyrical) subjectivity; this has been the fate of Pound's *Pisan Cantos*. Woolf avoids this danger, first by emptying rather than fracturing syntax, and second by a rhetoric of externality that rebuffs her reader's empathy.

The Woolfian novel must convey the uncircumscribed spirit 'whatever aberration or complexity it may display . . . however disconnected and incoherent in appearance' (*CE*, 2:106-7). But even so she was worried about the fragmentation of *The Waves*, for 'everything in a work of art should be mastered and ordered' as well (2:228). In February 1930 she wondered 'if I shall pull this book off! It is a litter of fragments so far' (*WD*, 154). In one sense, the novel has a very rigid form: it is structured by the temporally progressive interludes, which effect a rough parallelism between the sun's position and the phase of the characters' lives. But this sclerotic framework can perhaps be seen as an opportunistic concession to the 'disabilities' of contemporary readers. 'My difficulty is that I am writing to a rhythm and not to a plot', Woolf commented: 'the rhythmical . . . is completely opposed to the tradition of fiction and I am casting about all the time for some rope to throw to the reader' (*L*, 4:204). Another rope for the reader is Bernard's last soliloquy, in which Woolf intended to effect a synthesis and 'absorb all those scenes' (*WD*, 162). Yet this long soliloquy results only in a restatement of all the previous scenes without throwing any new light on them, and thus multiplies the reader's monotony. After pulverising the 'false, unreal, merely conventional' narrative sequence into 'moments' (*WD*, 139), Woolf now worries about a possible excess of fragmentation. From Julia Kristeva's viewpoint, such anxiety is a necessary component of art's creation: 'a text, in order to hold together as a text . . . requires a completion [*finition*], a structuration, a kind of totalisation of semiotic motility. This completion constitutes a synthesis that requires the thesis of language in order to come about, and the semiotic pulverises it only to make it a new device' (*RPL*, 51). The more Woolf destroys the thesis, the more rigid control she in another sense requires. If she dissolves the sequentiality of narrative, she must also introduce a more rigid, almost rebarbative, formal sequence. If she lets rhythm empty syntax, the syntax now none the less becomes far more stiff and straightforward, losing its earlier meandering qualities. The overall effect shifts from the 'fluent and fluid' to 'solidity' (*WD*, 176).

Woolf repeatedly records in her diary an extreme pressure of difficulty in writing *The Waves*, and this difficulty is encountered in turn by the reader. She comes to rely on rhythm to weld the book into a unity, though it was precisely rhythm that had fragmented it in the first place. 'what it wants is presumably unity. . . . Suppose I could run all the scenes together more?—by rhythms chiefly' (*WD*, 163). Throughout *The Waves* effects of rhythm pulse, pass, recur; rhythmic patterns or images of in/out, up/down, rise/fall appear innumerably: 'Lifts rise and fall; trains stop, trains start as regularly as the waves of the sea' (*W*, 139). I have already noted Bernard and Louis' use of the image of the regularly expanding and contracting mainspring. Bernard announces that 'the rhythm is the main thing in writing', and Neville concurs: 'Now begins to rise in me the familiar rhythm; words that have lain dormant now lift, now toss their crests, and fall and rise, and fall and rise again. I am a poet, yes' (57-9). In 'A Letter to a Young Poet' Woolf expands on the significance of rhythm in the writing of poetry, and the essay is also relevant to *The Waves*, her 'playpoem'. She meditates on 'the most profound and primitive of instincts, the instincts of rhythm': 'All you need now is to stand at the window, and let your rhythmical sense open and shut, open and shut, boldly and freely, until one thing melts in another' (*CE*, 2:191). Most primitive and profound of instincts, rhythm is central to Kristeva's semiotic, which becomes more or less integrated into the signifier. After the acquisition of language it remains a necessary accompaniment to adult speech or even the highest flights of rational thought. It breaks through the thetic in *The Waves,* subduing all the elements conventionally expected in a novel. Repetition and tautology, multiplied for the sake of rhythmical wave-effects, persistently hinder linear narrative development. Local effects of inertia ultimately evoke a universe of entropy, a term which is pejorative only from the teleological viewpoint that the text puts in question. '''What is lost? What is over?'' And ''Over and done with'', I muttered, ''over and done with'', solacing myself with words' (*W,* 131). 'A child playing—a summer evening—doors will open and shut, will keep opening and shutting . . .' (111).

The conventional concept of character is no less eroded, for the same rhythms and images traverse all six figures and blur the boundaries of self; a kind of choric dimension is given even to the most intimate self-revelation. 'The tautology is there for the sake of the rhythm and is not in character', and Hermione Lee concludes that *The Waves* is difficult 'to read as a novel, in that the emphasis on rhythm overwhelms distinctions of characters'.[14] If rhythm is the most primitive of instincts, repetition is hardly less so. 'The compulsion to repeat is an ungovernable process in the unconscious', and in the theory of *Wiederholungszwang* Freud finally sees repetition 'as the expression of the most general character of the instincts'.[15] *The Waves* gives the rein to unconscious discourse, allowing the semiotic to play dissolvingly across the discourse. But repetition then reconstitutes a new mode of unity of its own, which can be felt by contrasting the dour uniformity of *The Waves* to the flowing, polyphonic richness of Woolf's earlier novels.

Her second and more thematic device to give unity to the text is the figure of Percival. A charismatic personality, he is the hero who generates 'common feeling' or 'communion' by smoothing away the pugnacious assertion of egotistic differences. As in *To the Lighthouse* the epiphanic moment—'a globe whose walls are made of Percival, of youth and beauty'—occurs during a dinner-party, and is again contrasted to an 'outside' of Darwinian Nature, of dangerous flux: 'do not let the swing door cut to pieces the thing that we have made, that globes itself here, among these lights' (104). But whereas Mrs. Ramsay is a passive guardian of the human interior, Percival is a male hero whose mission is to spread the light into benighted regions of the world; he intends to solve 'the Oriental problem' by opposing 'a sense of the uselessness of human exertion' (97). The symbolic moment is thus experienced as the triumph of civilisation over natural flux. Leaving the restaurant, the diners 'stride not into chaos, but into a world that our own force can subjugate and make part of the illumined and everlasting road' (105). In the second reunion at Hampton Court, with the characters now middle-aged and Percival dead, the moment of illumination blazes only fitfully. The sense of ungovernable flux is more acute, the 'illimitable chaos' more menacing than previously (160).

After the death of Percival, the centre cannot hold, and in his role as absent centre this later hero clearly has strong affinities with Jacob Flanders. Adored by the other characters, Percival himself is silent; his mind, like Jacob's, is a lacuna in the text. Like his predecessor, he possesses an enviable lack of self-consciousness: 'Not a thread, not a sheet of paper lies between him and the sun' (35). His attraction is precisely this immediacy and solidity; like Jacob, he approaches an ideal unity of form and being. His death too is a Fall, casting doubt on the human project of shaping Nature into meaning. 'His horse tripped. He was thrown' (107), and he dies an obscure and pointless death. Both texts are deeply ambivalent about the relation—cause or effect?—of the hero's death to the fallen world, but because in *The Waves* the lives of the characters extend beyond Percival's death, it is their interpretation, which sees his death as cause, that predominates. The 'centre' of the world has become 'empty' (109, 111, 194). The name Percival evokes the Grail legend, and critics have pointed out various parallels between the two Percivals: both are failed heroes, not having lived up to their original promise. Moreover the Grail Percival (as opposed to Gawain) not only fails in the quest, but actually brings forth the Waste Land.[16]

Maria DiBattista has pointed out the abundance of 'veils' in *The Waves*, both as descriptive metaphors and as narrative technique. She argues that the veil masks the narrator whose power and voice control the ensuing narrative. Veils are 'narrative garments, strategies, and ploys that permit the ''she'' behind *The Waves* to speak'. She also reminds us that Percival's name 'denotes in its original French, to pierce the veil (perce-voile)', and regards it as an inspired choice of name for the hero of a narrative so concerned with the powers of dissimulation and obsessed with the recovery of a lost past (the memory of Thoby Stephen).[17] Inconspicuously but persistently, the text is indeed full of images of veil, net, film, fabric, which serve either for metaphors of consciousness and its delicate film of nerves and perceptions, or for the system of signs which constitutes and is constituted by consciousness or, finally, for the muffling layer of daily habit. This series of images thus rejoins the famous luminous halo and semi-transparent envelope. As *perce-voile*, Percival signifies a hole punched through the veil of consciousness. Lacking self-consciousness, he is a lacuna in the discourse or consciousness of the text. As I suggested in relation to *Jacob's Room*, such immediacy is the Edenic identity of signifier and signified; in *The Waves* Percival is the condition of possibility of their coincidence. His death aborts both the symbolic ideal and the utopian community, which are the two modes of organically fusing the disparate and contingent.

However, Percival is ambivalent in the same way as Jacob. For if the veil is truly an envelope surrounding us from the beginning of consciousness, then to pierce this 'veil of being' (209) is to risk death, and Percival's name foreshadows his own premature end. 'Pierce the veil' suggests the fundamental aggressiveness of this masculine hero and carries suggestions of the male's penetration of the hymen. Associations of heroic violence pervade the images in which the characters think of Percival. For Neville, he is the equal of 'Alcibiades, Ajax, Hector': 'they loved riding, they risked their lives wantonly' (129). In contrast to the others, Percival is a man of action, a born 'leader' (26), a guardian of standards and rules rather than an open, receptive sensibility; he reminds Louis of 'some medieval commander' (26). Neville's association of Percival with the classical world for his 'straight nose', his 'blue and oddly inexpressive eyes', his 'upright and indifferent' stance, points both to his physical splendour and his less attractive potential as 'an admirable churchwarden. He should have a birch and beat little boys for misdemeanours' (25). For Percival is in the end a typical representative of patriarchy and imperialism. He will resolve the Oriental problem 'by applying the standards of the West, by using the violent language that is natural to him' and becoming 'a God' in India (96). His nobility and magnificence shade off into more sinister patriarchal qualities: aggression, oppressiveness, domination. Dubbed 'conventional' by Bernard (88), Percival embodies qualities that the patriarchy values, and will assist their social diffusion. His death is then both poignant and ironic, as was Jacob's. As an eminent representative of a crass patriarchy, he deserves what he gets, yet he is also the system's victim, denied by it any glimpse of an alternative and thus still worth mourning. The text's ironic critique is articulated by Bernard, who reflects after Percival's death: 'I should be able to place him in trifling and ridiculous situations . . . I must be able to say, "Percival, a ridiculous name"' (110). It is crucial for the novel's final position that the centre that Percival once was is emptied. Bernard again: 'he sat there in the centre. Now I go to that spot no longer. The place is empty' (109).

Adored but absent, Percival's task is to serve, argues DiBattista, 'as a decoy figure whose function it is to divert attention from the novel's real center, the "She" not the "He" who successfully pierces the veil'. She contends that 'displacement and dissimulation are necessary to avoid all those censors of private feminine dreams', and relates this to Woolf's treatment in *Three Guineas* of St. Paul's pronouncement that women should veil themselves. But her argument is not wholly convincing, for at this stage of Woolf's career, with several successful books and her identity as a woman writer affirmed in *A Room of One's Own,* displacement and dissimulation hardly seem necessary any longer to enable her to write. If there is such a need, it is perhaps rather to avoid her own self-consciousness as a woman which, she often argues, is harmful to artistic creation. DiBattista further maintains that 'the disguised presence and subject of the novel is the "real novelist"—Virginia Woolf, the woman writing in the seclusion of Rodmell-Elvedon'.[18] She is right to relate Percival to the issue of women's writing, but he relates to it as absent centre, not as disguise.

To examine the Elvedon episode will clarify the issue. After his visit as a child, this half-imaginary land haunts Bernard: 'That is Elvedon. The lady sits between the two long windows, writing. The gardeners sweep the lawn with giant brooms' (12). This 'unknown land' lies 'down below, through the depth of the leaves', which merge with the novel's wave imagery: 'The waves close over us. The beech leaves meet above our heads' (11). The episode is deeply connected with the question of writing. It is while Bernard is 'making phrases' to console Susan that he makes his exploration into Elvedon, and when they return from this dreamland he composes a poem. The image of the lady writing and the gardeners sweeping recurs continually to him. DiBattista claims that this woman writing is the disguised subject of the novel, and Sara Ruddick also interprets her as an 'androgynous yet recognisably female narrator'.[19] Bernard's occasional generalisation of the lady to 'women writing' suggests that what is symbolised here is indeed female creativity. The men in the scene are ambivalent figures. As gardeners, they control Nature and provide a security in which the women can write, yet they are also reduced to the menial tasks that are conventionally allotted to women (sweeping). Bernard 'cannot interfere with a single stroke of those brooms. . . . Nor with the fixity of that woman writing' (170-1). As 'an unknown land' or 'ladies' garden', Elvedon seems to figure a utopia of feminine writing.

A passage from 'The Mark on the Wall' throws light on this Eden:

> Yes, one could imagine a very pleasant world. A quiet, spacious world, with the flowers so red and blue in the open fields. A world without professors or specialists or housekeepers with the profiles of policemen, a world which one could slice with one's thought as a fish slices the water with his fin. . . . How peaceful it is down here, rooted in the centre of the world and gazing up through the grey waters, with their sudden gleams of light, and their reflections—if it were not for Whitakers Almanack—if it were not for the Table of Precedency! (*HH*, 46)

This utopian realm is liberated from the male standards which still govern our lives but whose hegemony, Woolf writes earlier, has been crumbling since the First World War. This, like Elvedon, is a subaqueous world, and the fish is a recurrent image in Woolf for female thought quickly scared into hiding by the masculine point of view; in *A Room of One's Own* the narrator's 'little fish' is cowed by the Beadle who protects the turf of the college; in 'Professions for Women' the girl, 'impeded by the extreme conventionality of the other sex; cannot let her fish swim freely as she needs to if she wants to write' (*CE*, 2:287-8). Female imagination only flourishes in this underwater realm, in the stream which lies deep beneath realism's 'orderly and military progress' which Bernard had condemned as 'a mistake . . . a convenience, a lie' (*W*, 181).

Bernard counterposes an alternative mode of being to a linearity which is both narrative and the general social order supporting/supported by this literary form. He vindicates the suppressed 'rushing stream of broken dreams, nursery rhymes, street cries, half-finished sentences and sights—elm trees, willow trees, gardeners sweeping, women writing' (181). The Roman roads of conventional biographic style 'compel us to walk in step like . . . policemen' (184)—more particularly, like the policeman of *Jacob's Room*, controlling the traffic and repressing wayward impulses 'by force of will', and it is of this oppressive order that Percival is the major representative. Percival, narrativity and the patriarchy must be simultaneously dislodged to allow Elvedon and women's writing to emerge: hence the centre that Percival occupies must be emptied. There is, as Bernard remarks, 'nothing one can call an event' (181), and this describes Woolf's own aims in writing *The Waves:* 'not trying to tell a story . . . do away with exact place and time' (*WD*, 142-3). In a self-reflexive gesture the text figures in Elvedon its own project. The woman writing is indeed the narrator of the book, that 'mind thinking' or 'she' (*WD*, 142-3), who had initially existed but receded from the text in its final version, and is ultimately the author of the book, Woolf herself.

Immersed in the underworld beyond the socio-symbolic order, Bernard is granted a revelation—'one of those sudden transparencies through which one sees everything' (*W*, 171)—which he tries to elaborate into a phrase or poem: 'the pigeon beats the air with wooden wings' (13). In a system of images that first appeared as the wild goose and great fish in *Orlando,* Bernard's epiphany is symbolised as bird or fish. In his 'moments of escape' from the quotidian sequences of life in Rome, 'a fin turns': 'This bare visual impression is unattached to any line of reason, it springs up as one might see the fin of a porpoise on the horizon. Visual impressions often communicate thus briefly statements that we shall in time to come uncover and coax into words. I note under F., therefore, ''Fin in a waste of water''' (134-5). Here again the novel refers back to its own inception, for *The Waves* itself was an attempt to net 'that fin in the waste water which appeared to me over the marshes' as Woolf completed *To the Lighthouse (WD,* 169). Associated with the 'essence of reality', the image of the fin comes to her as, 'driven by loneliness and silence from the habitable world', she sinks to 'the bottom of the vessel' (*WD*, 148, 132)—just as Bernard reached Elvedon by sinking through the leaves/waves. But the eruption of a hidden meaning is alternately benevolent and sinister. 'Frightening and exciting', it entails isolation, 'agony', 'terror', and yet remains 'the most necessary thing to me: that which I seek' (*WD*, 101, 132). There is a sense of adventurous liberation from the self fixed in the socio-symbolic sequence, but also a fundamental fear of nothingness, and the visual image varies according to the local balance of ambivalent values. It may emerge as 'the fin of a porpoise', a conventionally friendly creature, or as the jutting 'spine' of some dangerous sea-monster. This latter sinister vision haunts Rhoda: 'with sudden intermittent shocks, sudden as the springs of a tiger, life emerges heaving its dark crest from the sea . . . it is to this we are bound, as bodies to wild horses . . . the emerging monster to whom we are attached' (*W*, 47).[20] In a further ramification of this system of images, the fin becomes an uncontrollable horse, thereby connecting with Percival's fatal accident, and with the riderless horse which appears towards the end of *Jacob's Room* (*JR*, 167).

The power of language governs whether 'reality' emerges as benevolent or menacing. If it can be successfully encircled by language, 'coaxed' into a coherent symbol, then meaning can be created/retrieved and the human mind triumph over insensate Nature. In 'A Sketch of the Past' Woolf's reflections on a childhood revelation illuminate the relations between the epiphanic moment and the power of words:

> I feel that I have had a blow; but it is not, as I thought as a child, simply a blow from an enemy hidden behind the cotton wool of daily life; it is or will become a revelation of some order; it is a token of some real thing behind appearances; and I make it real by putting it into words. It is only by putting it into words that I make it whole; this wholeness means that it has lost its power to hurt me; it gives me, perhaps because by doing so I take away the pain, a great delight to put the severed parts together . . . it is a constant idea of mine; that behind the cotton wool is hidden a pattern . . . .(*MB*, 72)

To synthesise in the instantaneity of the symbol and volatilise matter to transparency become a *raison d'être* of both literature and life. When Woolf fails in this, as in two other childhood 'exceptional moments', she is thrown into 'a state of despair', 'a peculiar horror and a physical collapse' (71-2). Language is both the means by which and the zone in which the shock of submarine impulses or the 'illimitable chaos' of *The Waves* may be humanely mastered. It aims to retrieve experience 'from the formlessness with words' in 'a fight against the green woods and green fields and sheep advancing with measured tread, munching' (*W,* 191-2)—a vision of Nature's depredations that harks back to the 'Time Passes' section of *To the Lighthouse.* It was 'the presence of these enemies' that incited Bernard, even as a child, to explore Elvedon (170).

'Beneath the surface of a stream' is the place of a potential revelation that might optimally be synthesised in language into a meaningful whole, but also of danger. Bernard expresses the positive wish for immersion in this realm beyond the symbolic order:

> to visit the profound depths; once in a while to exercise my prerogative not always to act, but to explore; to hear vague ancestral sounds of boughs creaking, of mammoths; to indulge impossible desires to embrace the whole world with the arms of understanding—impossible to those who act. (81-2)

But these pre-civilised depths beneath the Roman roads have also, as the imagery of mammoths and ancestral sounds here suggests, a darker aspect as the dangerous flux of Darwinian Nature: 'the green woods and green fields' modulate into an 'unfeeling universe' or 'the waste of immeasurable seas' (192, 199, 201). One enters this realm by casting off the thetic self of action and will, but this is simultaneously to abandon the human project of constructing chaos into a livable order. Freedom from 'the burden of individual life' (80) is also a state of impotence which leaves one buffeted by the forces of Nature. Rejecting 'deliberate' or 'reasonable' transcripts, Bernard calls for 'a painful, guttural, visceral, also soaring, lark-like, pealing song' (177), yet the text cannot so readily hold these two moments—guttural and lark-like—of its utopian ideal together. To enter the semiotic realm of dreams, 'unborn selves' or 'old, half-articulated ghosts', is also to unleash a threateningly pre-human self: 'the old brute . . . the savage, the hairy man who dabbles his fingers in ropes of entrails;

and gobbles and belches; whose speech is guttural, visceral' (205). Alert to the dangers of primitivism, the novel halts before giving free rein to this Darwinian savage, this 'illimitable chaos' *within* the self. The novel needs to dissolve the rigid, premature totalities of patriarchal 'consecutive sentences', yet without abolishing the project of totality altogether; it both desires *and* fears the 'bark, a groan' which seems the only possible alternative to the suave schematisations of the symbolic order. Bernard at last finds it impossible to live 'without a self, weightless and visionless . . . without illusion' (202-3). His final soliloquy is increasingly pessimistic as it contemplates the disastrous consequences of a collapse of the thetic self that had initially been desired.

The extreme enactment of the negative aspects of rejecting the symbolic and the thetic are seen in Rhoda, who suffers a dispersal of the self of pathological proportions. Excluded from the domain of propositions and positionality, she exists (if this is indeed the right word for her tenuous mode of being!) only in the margins of the symbolic order, in 'the white spaces that lie between hour and hour' (145). Associated with whiteness and emptiness, outside time and logic, Rhoda marks out the locus of a feminine space, that non-symbolisable Other that must be repressed but none the less exist for a normative discourse to be installed. Such a 'discourse' is not organised around the self-present centre that sustains phallocentric meaning, but is infinitely decentred. Yet Bernard finds language impossible without a self and Rhoda sinks psychotically beneath the waves. A feminine discourse of the white spaces remains strictly a contradiction, impossible except as silence.

Feminine writing would put into discursive circulation that which normative writing represses, the realm outside the Cartesian subject. In 'On Being Ill' Woolf draws attention to this realm. As the body asserts itself in the state of illness, language suddenly reveals its normally repressed materiality:

> In health meaning has encroached upon sound. Our intelligence dominates over our senses. But in illness, with the police off duty, we creep beneath some obscure poem by Mallarmé or Donne . . . and the words give out their scent and distil their flavour, and then, if at last we grasp the meaning, it is all the richer for having come to us sensually first. (*CE*, 4:200)

The self is pluralised; there return 'embryo lives which attend us in early youth until ''I'' suppressed them'. With reason and responsibility in abeyance, we become 'sudden, fitful, intense'; the sick are 'outlaws', escaped from 'paternal government' (199). Illness releases the characteristics of the submarine world that Bernard visits, the feminine that is repressed as disruptive by patriarchal Law. Liberated into a rich polyvalence, this realm is always in Woolf also menacing because it is near to, or simply is, a Nature that nullifies all human values into chaos. Elvedon is a hostile country' (*W*, 12) as well as utopia.

A difficult poise must be effected, since feminine writing must be sufficiently inside language not to succumb to Nature but also outside it in the sense of dissolving its reified unities. As *A Room of One's Own* maintains, it is fatal to be either a man or woman pure and simple (*RO*, 157). In the early stages of *The Waves* Woolf planned to use 'a man and a woman' talking as the narrative consciousness, and even if the man was later to be left 'absolutely dim', (*WD*, 108), his existence was still necessary, just as in Elvedon there must be gardeners as a counterpart to the woman writing. It is, appropriately, the androgynous Bernard, conjoining 'the logical sobriety of a man' and 'the sensibility of a woman' (*W*, 55), who discovers Elvedon. He also later absorbs the consciousnesses of the other five characters and even at last takes the place of the narrative consciousness itself, in which the whole discourse—interludes and monologues—had taken place. 'Day rises; the girl lifts the watery fire-hearted jewels to her brow . . .' (207). Bernard's discourse subsumes the interludes themselves, and he in a sense becomes identified with the woman writing in Elvedon. His androgyny is necessary for a feminine discourse to be heard at all. To make the feminine 'white spaces' conspicuous, to make silence heard, the letter and voice are necessary, even though they also threaten to quell what they enable. There must be, in Kristeva's words, ' a constant alternation between time and its ''truth'', identity and its loss, history and the timeless, signless, extra-phenomenal things that produce it. An impossible dialectic: a permanent alternation: never the one without the other'.[21] The condition of possibility of feminine writing is this alternation between the formation of the thetic subject and regression to the pre-Oedipal stage, to the *jouissance* of an as yet undissociated mother and child. As androgyne, Bernard lives precisely this endless oscillation. 'Having dropped off satisfied like a child from the breast, I am at liberty now to sink down, deep, into what passes, this omnipresent, general life'. As the regressive image of contented suckling suggests, he sinks to 'the profound depths' of the Imaginary in which there is no solidity, no distinction, no time but dreams: 'the passage of undifferentiated faces . . . drugs me into dreams; rubs the features from faces. People might walk through me'. 'Unmoored . . . from a private being', he retrieves the Imaginary identification with the whole: 'to embrace the whole world with the arms of understanding'. Then, in the next stage of the dialectic, Bernard gropes his way out of the Imaginary, separating and safeguarding from the world of objects 'one's identity. I am not part of the street—no, I observe the street. One splits off, therefore'. He resumes command over language, generating one story after another; thus he 'elaborates' and 'differentiates' himself (81-3).

This oscillation never comes to an end—'one moment free; the next, this' (207)—for it is the very process of androgyny. But the dialectic is charged with ambivalence, and a final value can never be assigned to either of its phases. Under one aspect, dissolution of the self is liberation from the limits of personal identity, freedom from 'false phrases'. In this stage Bernard expands in fantasy, 'unconfined and capable of being everywhere on the verge of things' (207), and attains a radical Keatsian negative capability. But he wonders whether such 'dissipation', 'endless throwing away', this becoming an 'immeasurable sea' (201), is 'a sort of death' or, positively, presages 'a new assembly of elements' (198). For dissolution may also threaten one with becoming 'part of that unfeeling universe', which is Rhoda's unenviable fate; it is potentially the defeat of humanity by 'the sea; the insensitive nature' (*WD*, 153). Bernard's ambivalence towards the dialectic of self and its dissipation emerges in his simultaneously thanking and cursing the gaze of the other which forces him to re-collect his self from dispersal: 'Curse you then . . . I must haul myself up . . . must push my arms into the sleeves . . . tired as I am, spent as I am' (*W*, 210). The image of pushing arms into sleeves is in part the reassumption of daily routine, but perhaps as a gesture of penetration (weary though it may be) also suggests a return to the phallic position and self-possession which underpin such routines. But 'must, must, must' are also 'merciful words'; though 'we pretend to revile', without them 'we should be undone' (166). He must perforce undergo a permanent alternation between the formation and dissemination of the self, 'the incessant rise and fall and fall and rise again' (211). This dangerous, impossible dialectic is the existential reality of androgyny. The rhythm of the sea as a metaphor of the semiotic *chora*—its patterns and pulses of one/two, in/out, rise/fall—cuts across the syntax of sentences and plot throughout the text, yet without dissolving them completely. Only in this form can the Kristevan alternation realise itself.

How indeed is it possible to actualise a feminine writing that is not organised around phallocentric identity and positionality, but would none the less not just be lost in silence? How, in the terms of Woolf's imagery, deviate from the 'straight lines' of the Roman roads into the 'brambles and thick tree trunks into the heart of the forest', and yet not simply abandon oneself to a valueless Nature or flux? The struggle to preserve both these moments or modes of being constitutes Bernard's 'perpetual warfare, it is the shattering and piecing together'. Reassembling the scattered jigsaw of identity, Bernard asserts himself against 'the stupidity of nature', once more challenges 'the immeasurable sea' (191, 201).[22] The ambivalences and oscillation I have traced recur in Woolf's own comments on the ending of the novel. On the one hand, she aims 'to show that the theme effort, effort, dominates; not the waves: and personality: and defiance'. But on the other hand, 'I am not sure of the effect artistically; because the proportions may need the intervention of the waves finally so as to make a conclusion' (*WD*, 162). And the waves, which are both a Darwinian 'insensitive nature' (153) and a warm, fecund bath of semiotic energies, a kind of primordial maternal body, of course do complete the novel. The waves are, thematically, the dissolution of human order, which has both its negative and positive (feminist) aspects, but *formally* the affirmation of an authorial will to totality, to thetic positionality. '*The waves broke on the shore*' (*W*, 211). The last sentence of the novel sustains the impossible dialectic of an androgynous feminine writing to the very end, formally reintegrating a subject that it thematically disseminates.

CONCLUSION

A New Subjectivity

I will conclude this study with a brief examination of the direction
that Woolf's work takes after *The Waves,* which I regard as the
high point of her achievement in terms of the dialectic of symbolic
and semiotic, and of the convergence of modernism and feminism.
Throughout the 1920s, as I argued in my first chapter, Woolf's
feminism was 'suppressed' by her modernist aesthetic. On the one
hand, both feminism and modernism have a common antagonist;
they challenge the dominant, phallocentric mode of discourse and
the masculine social order which it underpins. On the other hand,
modernism and feminism are in some ways at odds: the symbolist
version of modernism, which Woolf embraced, rejects feminist
anger, 'self-consciousness', explicit polemical statement, all of
which supposedly denature writing.[1] But the historical and
personal pressures of the 1930s (see *WD,* 268, 288, 292)
prompted Woolf to write her most outspokenly feminist books, *The
Years* and *Three Guineas.* Her long-held symbolist aesthetic with
its claim that art 'must not mean but be' is rejected, and *Three
Guineas* even comes close to being propaganda. The underlying
theme of both books is the same, not surprisingly given that Woolf
considered *The Years* and *Three Guineas* to be one book (295):
they maintain that 'the public and private worlds are inseparably
connected' (*TG,* 258), and that in both spheres it is the 'infantile
fixation' of the Father that destroys 'freedom and justice'. If *The
Years* limits itself almost rigorously to the private realm, only
evoking the public through its more intimate counterpart, this is
not done to reduce or bracket out the public realm, but rather to
show how one sphere is constricted by the other; the same principle
operates in both, and thus the private is political and vice versa.

187

Woolf contends that this is 'for us [women] a very important connection' (258). It is, indeed, the very pivot of her argument, which links the issue of feminism to that of anti-fascism. Though *Three Guineas* was read enthusiastically by many contemporary women, it was the least well received of her works among her own circle: 'my own friends have sent me to Coventry over it' (*WD*, 308). But their contempt at its 'silly' argument, its 'tenuous' logic in connecting women's rights and anti-fascism and its 'inadequate' suggestions (*QB*, 2:205) is clearly embarrassment at a radicalism whose implications they dared not face. For the book deconstructs the conventional oppositions private/public, English liberalism/German and Italian fascism, on which the very identity of Woolf's social circle was constructed. The severe, almost hysterical criticisms from the enemy Leavisite camp, in Queenie Leavis' 'Caterpillars of the Commonwealth Unite' in *Scrutiny*, betray a similar inability to think beyond the categories of this ideological framework.[2] Woolf sees in the Fascist dictator—regardless of nationality—'the quintessence of virility, the perfect type of which all the others are imperfect adumbrations'; it is 'Man himself' (*TG*, 257) who menaces the contemporary world with 'tyranny; brutality; torture; the fall of civilisation; the end of freedom' (*Y*, 418). It is only the work of recent feminist critics which, by breaking with the underlying assumptions of Woolf's contemporary readers, has allowed these two late books to stand forth in their full stature. In contrast to the earlier image of a secluded, politically naïve lady here venturing into territory of which she knew nothing, Carolyn G. Heilbrun affirms her 'transformation': 'in Woolf's fifties, with great work behind her, she would no longer fear either expression of her anger or its effects on the men who overheard her'. American feminists have been particularly important in re-establishing Woolf as a political thinker. Naomi Black, for instance, has offered a Woolf squarely placed within the network of 'social feminism' by excavating her long involvement—dating back to her younger days—in the women's movement—and it is to this context that these late works belong.[3]

The 'Present Day' section of *The Years* is poised ambivalently between the optimism of the older and the pessimism of the younger generation. While Eleanor and Kitty revel in the 'happier', 'freer' present day, Peggy and North think wistfully of the Victorian days as 'so peaceful and so safe' (351). Whereas the older generation rejoices over the lifting of patriarchal oppression from the private sphere, the younger generation finds the same tyranny looming in the public realm, though now in the form of fascist war. Yet despite the atmosphere of frustration throughout the novel, which comes to its focus in the younger generation's bleak *Weltanschauung, The Years* ends with Eleanor's optimistic vision: a young man and woman getting out of a cab and entering a house together. This image, as in *A Room of One's Own,* carries the value of androgyny, for there too 'unity had been restored by seeing two people come together and get into a taxi-cab' (*RO,* 145). History, however, bears out the pessimists, and in *Between the Acts* the ideal of androgyny seems further than ever away from reality. The theme of rape recurs throughout the book, as in the newspaper report of a rape with which Isa is obsessed and in allusions to the myth of Procne Philomela and Swinburne's treatment of it.[4] The novel ends with Giles and Isa's 'fight, as the dog fox fights with the vixen, in the heart of darkness' (*BA,* 256). Far removed though this may be from the optimism of the couple descending from the cab, the book none the less ends on a note of hope. In what follows I shall examine the grounds of this hope for a new life after the possible apocalypse of world war, this hope for a continuity across the great chasm of imminent mass-destruction, which sustains the buoyant, almost euphoric atmosphere of the novel despite the sombreness of its theme.

As I have argued throughout this book, Woolfian androgyny involves a *dialectic* of symbolic and semiotic, of man and woman—or, in Kristeva's phrase, 'never the one without the other'. Hence Woolf never radically destroys the symbolic and its thetic subject. For her, it constitutes one of the poles necessary for the dialectic movement of her writing, a framework to work against. But as she worked on *Between the Acts* during the war, she wrote poignantly in her diary: 'the writing "I" has vanished' (*WD,* 336). The symbolic is thus destroyed by the war which is, in a grim irony, only the extreme expression of its own masculine principle. During this period Woolf often notes in her diary the disappearance of 'the protecting and reflecting walls' of the 'standards—which have for so many years . . . thickened [her] identity'. She now has 'no surroundings', 'no standard to write for: no public to echo back; even the "tradition" has become transparent' (337, 9). In the novel itself the pageant representing the present shows 'civilisation (the wall) in ruins' and man and woman struggling to rebuild it (*BA*, 212). There is only vacancy where were once the 'walls' that constrained, resisted but also therefore energised her own project of androgyny as impossible dialectic, 'a constant alternation between time and its "truth", identity and its loss'.

Now that one of the poles of androgyny has crumbled, hope is invested solely in its counterpart, the fertile ocean of the semiotic, which now emerges as a sort of last ditch utopian hope. The semiotic is figured in the novel as primeval swamp rather than ocean. As Lucy reads her 'Outline of History', she is fascinated by the primordial age before difference appears, when the continents are still one. The 'unifier' in contrast to her brother Bart, the 'separatist', Lucy nullifies both spatial and temporal differences and lives in the vision of pre- and post-history: 'she was given to increasing the bounds of the moment by flights into past or future' and thus she sees 'a beast in a swamp' as well as God (14, 31). As William Dodge remarks to her, 'you don't believe in history' (203). But this nullification of history, distance, difference is the formal as well as thematic principle of the book. The book mixes modes of writing—play, poetry, prose—and breaks down such categorisations as reality and artifice, nature and the human or, at the social level, 'gentles and simples'. Prehistoric images and rhythms recur throughout the book, creating the effect that Gillian Beer has well described—'the simultaneity of the prehistoric in our present moment'.[5] During the pageant Miss La Trobe hears the bellowing of the cows: 'it was the primeval voice sounding loud in the ear of the present moment . . . . The cows annihilated the gap; bridged the distance; filled the emptiness and continued the emotion' (165-6). This archaic voice turns out to be the call of the mother, for one of the cows has lost her calf; this is as we should expect, since the semiotic reaches into the most primitive, pre-Oedipal relation to the maternal. The book ends with yet another evocation of the prehistoric, and thus implies a hope for some fundamental continuity which might overcome the gap produced by the mass-destruction of war.

As Gillian Beer argues, 'pre-history implies a pre-narrative domain which will not buckle to plot'; Woolf's resistance to the evolutionary account (his/story) of the world is thus profoundly connected with her renunciation of fictional plot.[6] As the title of the novel—the intervals in the progression of a story—already suggests, the semiotic or in this novel more specifically the 'prehistoric' disrupts conventional narrative in ways familiar from earlier novels. Miss La Trobe's remark is true of *Between the Acts* as well as of her own pageant: 'Don't bother about the plot: the plot's nothing' (109). For the plot of world history seems to have proven itself a failure. Now that civilisation, tradition, standards are in ruin, the firm ligatures of the symbolic order are loosened, and its thetic subject is dispersed by the primordial semiotic forces, as when in the outdoor pageant 'the wind blew away the connecting words of their chant' (98). There thus comes about a certain libertarian euphoria in the novel, 'the airy world' in Woolf's own phrase (*WD*, 292). The values both of meaningful linear plot and of organic unity are swept away with the thetic subject. The text is a litter of word-plays, recollected fragments of poems, snatches of nursery rhymes, yet as with the rhythms, rhymes and refrains that run through Isa's mind, these cannot shape themselves into any kind of elegant whole. Prose, poetry and drama, the categories of nature/human, artifice/reality, physical/psychological are abruptly juxtaposed to create a collage-like effect.[7] Throughout the book, the symbolic function of language is subordinated to the semiotic, to the more primitive play and pleasure of the signifier. As the text notes of its own pageant, 'It didn't matter what the words were; or who sang what. Round and round they whirled, intoxicated by the music' (113). Surcharged with an excess of either signifier or signified, words stray from their mundane, communicational functions. Even for Giles, the least literary figure in the book, 'words this afternoon ceased to lie flat in the sentence. They rose, became menacing and shook their fists at you' (74). More generally, as Hermione Lee notes, characters articulate their inner thoughts 'in scraps of rhyme': 'their conversations, though on such apparently trivial subjects . . . are lyrical and resonant, partly because of a strong sense of rhythm which turns conversations into recurring tunes'.[8]

Unable to make anything out of the pageant, Isa decides not to bother about its plot: 'The plot was only there to beget emotion. There were only two emotions: love and hate' (109). Isa's crisis is that of her century; 'what remedy', the novel asks, 'was there for her at her age—the age of the century, thirty-nine . . .?' (26).

'Abortive was the word that expressed her' (21): fragments of remembered phrases and rhythms or rhymes for her own verse run through her mind, but she lacks the thetic force that could compel them into significant unity. Regressing from the unifying fixed position, she is dominated by the more archaic drives of the semiotic—'Love and hate—how they tore her asunder!'—and she longs for 'a new plot' to be invented (252). The semiotic drives thus appear both in such characteristic dualisms and as a primeval force in the very texture of the language and in the theme of the book, for 'the semiotic activity', Kristeva argues, 'is, from a synchronic point of view, a mark of the workings of drives (appropriation/rejection, orality/anality, love/hate, life/death) and, from a diachronic view, stems from the archaism of the semiotic body'.[9] In the by now familiar oceanic rhythms and imagery, '"Yes", Isa answered, "No", she added. It was Yes, No. Yes, yes, yes, the tide rushed out embracing. No, no, no, it contracted' (251). This yes/no is her answer to the Reverend Streatfield's remark: 'we act different parts but are the same' (251). Both the reader of the novel and the audience of the pageant oscillate similarly between yes/no, sameness/difference, continuity/ disruption or what the novel terms 'Unity—Dispersity' (235). The text too is organised around such dual drives, just as the sun on the day of the pageant alternately shines 'embracing every flower' and 'withdrew' (30). Expressing alternating impulses of appropriation and rejection, such dualisms are the bearers of fundamental oral and anal drives which are structured around the mother's body, the ordering principle of the semiotic *chora*. The apocalyptic question of communal survival hinges on this dualism. In the primeval matrix of the *chora*, there does not yet fully exist an identity or subject: the subject is both generated and negated, but only from this dual play of drives—assimilative and destructive—will a subject in the full sense finally emerge. Formally and thematically, then, the novel is situated in such a semiotic *chora*, and it ends by implying the hope of a birth of 'another life' out of prehistoric darkness, 'before roads were made, or houses' (256).

Between the Acts is not an obviously feminist text, unlike its predecessors *The Years* and *Three Guineas*, but given that it not only fears but also relies on the apocalypse to provide a clean sweep of a man-made civilisation, it clearly carries a strong feminist charge. E.M. Forster once remarked bewilderedly of Woolf's feminism that 'society is man-made' and therefore 'she, a woman, had no responsibility for the mess'.[10] This feminine stance is best represented within the novel by Lucy Swithin. 'Foolish, free' (59), mocking Giles in his role as stockbroker, she escapes from temporal suffering by virtue of her atemporal vision. Giles, on the other hand, is a typical English liberal of the type whose inherent complicity with the fascist enemy Woolf had sought to articulate in *Three Guineas*. His masculinity—'the muscular, the hirsute, the virile' (127)—is stressed throughout the novel and excites the homosexual William Dodge. His exemption of his father, a retired Indian civil servant, from the criticism of the feckless 'old fogies' who won't act despite the imminent war, reveals a virulent imperialist masculinity frustrated by the political situation; it is further exacerbated by the mockery and contemptuous criticism of his aunt and wife. The familiar Woolfian image of the policeman yet again represents the authoritarian rigidity of the male ego which underpins both capitalist imperialism and fascism. Giles identifies himself with the pageant's Victorian policeman who, accidentally pointing at Lucy, accuses a vagrant pedestrian of a disturbance of public order. The polarity of women's ahistorical vision beyond the constraints of anthropocentricity and men's time-bound views is further illuminated by the contrast of the two pictures in Pointz Hall. For while the portrait of the family ancestor generates a vociferous discussion of family history and episodes, the picture of the nameless lady leads the beholder into 'emptiness, silence', 'what was before time was' (47).

As she worked on the drafts of the novel Woolf noted in her diary: '"I" rejected: "We" substituted: to whom at the end shall there be an invocation?' (*WD*, 289). In the spirit of the Reverend Streatfield's remark at the end of the pageant that difference is ultimately subsumed in identity, the theme of primeval unity which runs throughout the book becomes the symbol and guarantee of a post-individualist future on the other side of the apocalypse brought about by the rapacious male 'I'. Stylistically too, the carnivalesque mixture of genres suggests the possibility of some new post-individualist mode of social community, as does the uncanny ability of characters in this novel to converse without speaking. Lucy's 'volatile' existence seems to be in accordance with that Irigarayan principle of 'the fluid' that I discussed above in connection with *To the Lighthouse*. Standing 'between two fluidities [air and water]' (239), she protects from her brother Bart her private vision of 'the sea on which we float', which suggests the possibility of transcending the rigid individualist ego and its carapace of 'reason': 'surely every boat sometimes leaks?' (240). In *The Waves* Bernard had already wished for 'the world without a self', and from the 1930s onwards Woolf's work articulates an intensifying rejection of the liberal, individualist consciousness that she regards as the male tradition. She was appalled, James Naremore writes, at what 'liberal democracy (identified with the masculine ego) had done to the human spirit'.[11] *The Years* condemns the possessive ego and expresses a dream of some potentially collective future—'another world, a new world' in which people 'live differently' (*Y*, 456)—though what is ultimately enacted in the novel is the difficulty and failure of the dream. The book's ending posits a future which belongs to a totally different kind of subject—one well beyond the limited categories of bourgeois consciousness. At the end of Delia's party the caretaker's children sing, but to most of their patronising middle-class audience, 'the rhythm seemed to rock and the unintelligible words ran themselves together almost with a shriek'. Eleanor, however, opens herself with a cautious optimism to this strange adumbration of future possibility: 'It was impossible to find one word for the whole. ''Beautiful?'' she said, with a note of interrogation' (*Y*, 465). In the essay 'The Leaning Tower' (1940—a paper originally read to a W.E.A. group), Woolf's recognition of the death of middle-class culture is, similarly, neither despairing nor nostalgic but rather anticipates hopefully 'a world without classes or towers' after the war (*CE*, 2:178).

Woolf's increasing commitment to a post-individualist subjectivity emerges explicitly in the book she planned after *Between the Acts*, which was first called *Reading at Random*, later *Turning Pages*. This was to have been a work of literary history. It would exemplify 'a new critical method' which is 'less composed; more fluid and following the flight . . .' (*WD*, 337); it would, in short, extend to criticism the formal innovations already explored in her fiction. From the drafts and sketches of the first two chapters 'Anon' and 'the Reader', we can follow through her interest in 'the world beneath consciousness; the anonymous world to which we can still return', 'which still exists in us, deep sunk, savage, primitive, remembered', 'the song beneath'—namely, the semiotic.[12] Now preoccupied with the possibilities of survival beyond apocalypse, Woolf here equates the instinct for song with the 'instinct for self-preservation' (403), and regards it as a possible saving force in the imminent last days of her civilisation. In the beginning was not the Word but rather the song of 'innumerable birds' on the boughs which covered prehistoric Britain; then the voice of Anon breaks the silence. This 'wondering voice', 'sometimes man; sometimes woman' (382), predates individuation and the social division of labour between writer and audience, and articulates a communal instinct towards song. The map which Woolf drew of the evanescent emergence and growth of human consciousness, especially its aesthetic creativity, in *The Waves* is here transposed from the individual to the collective level. In the notes for *Reading at Random,* we read: 'The song . . . the call to our primitive instincts./Rhythm–Sound. Sight' (374). Since in the distant aeons of prehistory the subject once emerged, Woolf finally reposes on the fact that the semiotic matrix, which still persists in us 'deep sunk', may again be capable of this feat of gestation—and that a 'new plot' or human narrative may differ from the previous one, the fallen realm of his/story. In *Between the Acts* Miss La Trobe is a modern Anon: she attempts to tap the archaic reservoir of collective emotions and memories in order to produce a new human narrative. Working on a new play, she first allows herself to lapse into the waters of the semiotic: 'From the earth green waters seemed to rise over her. She took her voyage away from the shore' (*BA*, 246). The semiotic 'mud became fertile' with 'words of one syllable', 'words without meaning' (247-8)—precisely the kind of language yearned for in *The Waves* by Bernard who denounces neatly organised rhetorical language as false. In a close parallel to the beginning of 'Anon' (which Woolf was then writing), the first creative impulse seems to be carried by flights of birds, for 'suddenly she was pelted with starlings'. Miss La Trobe then 'heard the first words of her new play' (248), her inspiration coinciding with the end of the novel.

Between the Acts, Woolf's final novel, and the draft of 'Anon' represent a courageous gaze into and beyond apocalypse: they trace threads of possibility across military devastation, and chart intimations of the hope for a new human—a *truly* human—subjectivity. In his biography Quentin Bell records Woolf's unexpected 'imperturbability' and 'serenity' during the last days of her life, despite the strain of the war; but he then predictably interprets this 'euphoric interval' as part of her mental illness (*QB*, 2:221). Yet it seems to me that it is rather a resigned aloofness from Forster's 'man-made mess', as in the diary's 'growing detachment from the hierarchy, the patriarchy' (*WD*, 361), and the hope for some true change on the other side of a radical break. Julia Kristeva argues that the reactivation of the pre-Oedipal phase, the flight from the symbolic paternal order, may result in male laughter but that 'A woman has nothing to laugh about when the paternal order falls'.[13] Does she not? Or might not she, too, find cause for laughter there—in liberation from the patriarchal order? At any rate, Woolf remained cheerful. Her laughter made a strong impression on Elizabeth Bowen, who visited her in February 1941. 'Where did the laughter end and the darkness begin?' asks Quentin Bell (*QB*, 2:224) or, as we might rephrase this, where does the prehistoric psychic stratum, the tie to the mother, change from the pleasantly fecund semiotic sea to a dangerous swamp or the 'black lava' which Kristeva claims lies in wait for a woman? Kristeva herself invokes Woolf's laughter in *About Chinese Women:* 'I think of Virginia Woolf, who sank wordlessly into the river, her pockets weighted with stones. Haunted by voices, by waves, by lights, in love with colours—blue, green—seized by a sort of bizarre gaiety that brought on the fits of strangled, hooting, uncontrollable laughter remembered by Miss Brown'.[14] Does the 'call of the mother', then, only generate 'voices, ''madness'', hallucinations', as Kristeva claims? If this is indeed so in the case of our present mode of subjectivity, then it is all the more urgent to pursue the project of forging a new kind of subjectivity for which the call of the mother and the fall of the paternal order would *not* mean its foundering.

Notes

Preface

1. See '''No more horses'': Virginia Woolf on art and propaganda', *Women's Studies*, 4, No. 2/3, 1977, 265-90; and B. Carroll, '''To crush him in our country'': the political thought of Virginia Woolf', *Feminist Studies* 4, No. 1, 1978, 99-129. Jane Marcus has also edited two collections of criticism on Woolf: *New Feminist Essays on Virginia Woolf* (London, 1981) and *Virginia Woolf: A Feminist Slant* (Lincoln, Nebraska and London, 1983).

Chapter 1

1. 'Modern Novels' was published in *The Times Literary Supplement* on 10 April 1919 and reprinted slightly revised in *The Common Reader* (1925) as 'Modern Fiction', the version which is now generally known. The revision involves only slight changes of phrasing, the only major difference being that the famous remark that 'life is not a series of gig-lamps symmetrically arranged' does not appear in the first version. I will therefore use 'Modern Fiction' as my text, but will treat it as written in 1919 in my discussion.
2. See *Virginia Woolf's Reading Notebooks* ed. Brenda R. Silver (Princeton, 1983), pp. 18-19.
3. R. Brimley Johnson, *Some Contemporary Novelists (Women)* (London, 1920), pp. xiv-xv.
4. Elaine Showalter, *A Literature of their Own: British Women Novelists from Brontë to Lessing* (London, 1978), p. 242.
5. Dorothy Richardson, *Pilgrimage* 1, (London, 1979), p. 9.
6. David Lodge, *The Modes of Modern Writing: Metonymy and the Typology of Modern Literature* (London, 1977), p. 177.
7. Richardson, *Pilgrimage* 2, (London, 1979), p. 210.
8. *The Diary of Virginia Woolf*, Vol. II, ed. Anne Olivier Bell (London, 1978), Appendix II: 'The Intellectual Status of Women', pp. 339-42.
9. *Woolf: Women and Writing*, ed. Michèle Barrett (London, 1979), p. 67.

10. Stephen Heath, *The Sexual Fix* (London, 1982), pp. 141-2.
11. Julia Kristeva, 'Oscillation between Power and Denial' in *New French Feminisms*, ed. Elaine Marks and Isabelle de Coutivron (Amherst, 1980), p. 165.
12. Mary Jacobus 'The Difference of View' in *Women Writing and Writing about Women*, ed. Mary Jacobus (London, 1979), p. 20.
13. Hélène Cixous, 'Castration or decapitation', *Signs: Journal of Women in Culture and Society*, Vol. VII, No. 1, 1981, p. 54; and 'The Laugh of the Medusa' in *New French Feminism, op. cit.*, p. 254.
14. Stephen Heath, 'Difference', *Screen*, Vol. XIX, No. 3 (Autumn 1978), pp. 77-8; *The Sexual Fix, op. cit.*, p. 118.
15. Woolf, *The Pargiters: The Novel-Essay Portion of 'The Years'*. ed. Mitchell A. Leaska (London, 1978), p. xxxiii.
16. Showalter, *op. cit.*, pp. 289, 296, 318, 291.
17. Georg Lukács, *The Meaning of Contemporary Realism*, trans. John and Necke Mander (London, 1963), pp. 26, 46.
18. Showalter, *op. cit.*, p. 296.
19. Anika Lemaire, *Jacques Lacan*, trans. David Macey (London, 1977), p. 177.
20. Gillian Beer, 'Beyond Determinism: George Eliot and Virginia Woolf' in Jacobus, *op. cit.*, p. 90.
21. This psychoanalytic account of the emergence of the subject is based on a fundamentally masculine model, and has come under strong criticism from feminist theoreticians. Psychoanalytic theories of the female subject and of female sexuality have been offered by women analysts like Irigaray, Chodorow and Chassegut-Smirgel. These emphasise the crucial significance of the daughter's attachment to the mother, which Freud initially recognised but failed to explore adquately.
22. Cixous, 'Castration or Decapitation', p. 54.
23. Heath, *The Sexual Fix*, p. 135.
24. May Sinclair, 'The Novels of Dorothy Richardson', *The Little Review*, Vol. IV, No. 12 (April 1918), p. 6. For 'liquid flow' see the account of an as yet untranslated work by Irigaray in Jane Gallop, *Feminism and Psychoanalysis: The Daughter's Seduction* (London, 1982), pp. 39, 42. For 'white ink' or 'milk' see Cixous 'Laugh of the Medusa', p. 251.
25. Beer, *loc. cit.*, pp. 95-6. See also her discussion in *Virginia Woolf: A Centenary Perspective*, ed. Eric Warner (London, 1984), p. 107.
26. Julia Kristeva, *Revolution in Poetic Language*, trans. Margaret Waller (New York, 1984), p. 41. Hereafter referred to as *RPL*.
27. Kristeva, cited in Sherry Turkle, *Psychoanalytic Politics: Freud's French Revolution* (London, 1979), p. 82.
28. Allon White, 'Expositions and Critique of Julia Kristeva', Stencilled Occasional Paper, CCCS, The University of Birmingham, pp. 16-17.
29. Toril Moi, *Sexual/Textual Politics*, 'New Accents' (London, 1985), pp. 171-2.
30. Luce Irigaray, 'This Sex Which Is Not One', in *New French Feminisms, op. cit.*, p. 100. Cixous, 'The Laugh of the Medusa', p. 248, n. 3.
31. Kristeva, 'Woman Can Never Be Defined', in *New French Feminisms, op. cit.*, pp. 137-8.

32. Kristeva, *About Chinese Women,* trans. Anita Burrows (London, 1977), pp. 27-30.
33. Kristeva, 'Oscillation between Power and Denial', p. 166; see also *About Chinese Women, op. cit.,* p. 39.
34. Kristeva, *About Chinese Women, op. cit.,* pp. 30, 38.

Chapter 2

1. Roland Barthes, 'Lecture', trans. Richard Howard, *Oxford Literary Review,* Vol. IV, No. 1 (Autumn 1979), p. 36. On Lacan's difficult concept of the 'Real', see Lemaire, *op. cit.,* p. 41.
2. Lodge, *op. cit.,* p. 183.
3. Hermione Lee, *The Novels of Virginia Woolf* (London, 1977), pp. 81-3.
4. Paul de Man, *Blindness and Insight: Essays in the Rhetoric of Contemporary Criticism,* second edn. (Minneapolis, 1983), pp. 192. 189, 192. Frank Lentricchia, *After the New Criticism* (London, 1980), p. 6.
5. Jacques Derrida, *Of Grammatology,* trans. Gayatari Sivak (Baltimore and London, 1974), p. 12.
6. See the entry in Martin Pegler, *The Dictionary of Interior Design* (New York, 1966). The technical term for the motif is 'aegicram' or 'aegicranes'.
7. Derrida, *op. cit.,* pp. 11, 136.
8. From Hegel's *Lectures of Aesthetics,* cited in Mowbray Allan, *T.S. Eliot's Impersonal Theory of Poetry* (Lewisburg, 1974), pp. 25-6.
9. T.S. Eliot, *Selected Essays,* third edn. (London, 1951), p. 145.
10. Lentricchia, *After the New Criticism, op. cit.,* p. 6.
11. T.S. Eliot, 'London Letter', *The Dial,* 71 (August 1921), pp. 216-7.
12. Cited in Terry Eagleton, *Walter Benjamin, Or Towards A Revolutionary Criticism* (London, 1981), p. 4.
13. F.R. Leavis, *Revaluation* (Harmondsworth, 1972), pp. 193-4.
14. Jacques Derrida, 'Difference', *Speech and Phenomena and Other Essays on Husserl's Theory of Signs,* trans. David B. Allison (Evanston, 1973), p. 143.
15. For the 'aura', see Walter Benjamin, *Illuminations,* ed. Hannah Arendt (Glasgow, 1973), p. 190, 223ff.
16. In *CE,* 2:167 she notes that nineteenth-century 'conditions' 'lasted, roughly speaking, till the year 1914'. See also her claim that 'the war withered a generation before its time' in 'New Novels' (1920), cited in Jane Marcus, 'Art and Anger', *Feminist Studies,* Vol. IV, No. 1 (February 1978), p. 96.
17. Fredric Jameson, *Marxism and Form: Twentieth-Century Dialectical Theories of Literature* (Princeton, 1971), p. 72.
18. Derrida, *Of Grammatology, op. cit.,* pp. 39-40.
19. In *The Voyage Out* Rachel's death soon after exploring a South American wilderness also suggests the precariousness of the human in the face of a meaningless Nature. Gillian Beer demonstrates the close affinity between the description of the jungle in the novel and a passage from Darwin's *The Voyage of the Beagle* and offers a full discussion of the implications of

Darwin's work for Woolf in 'Virginia Woolf and Pre-history', in *Virginia Woolf: A Centenary Perspective, op. cit.,* pp. 99-123.
20. See my discussion of Lily Briscoe's relation to such aesthetic minimalism, p. 109 below.
21. Paul Fussell, *The Great War and Modern Memory* (New York, 1975), p. 230.
22. 'Phallogocentric' combines the concepts of 'phallocentrism' and 'logocentricism'. The latter refers to the dominance of the *logos* (word) in reason and the conceptualisation of the world. The former refers to the privileged place accorded to the phallus in language, psychoanalysis and Western thought generally. Condensed together, they name the fundamental principle of Western rationality.
23. Lee, *Novels of Virginia Woolf, op. cit.,* pp. 74-6.
24. Roland Barthes, *The Pleasure of the Text,* trans. Richard Miller (New York, 1975), p. 32.

Chapter 3

1. *QB,* 2:106 and *L.* 3:136.
2. See Otto Jesperson, *The Philosophy of Grammar* (London, 1924), pp. 291-2.
3. David Daiches argues that 'for' is 'a word which does not indicate a strict logical sequence, at least not in its popular usage, but does suggest a relationship which is at least half-logical', *Virginia Woolf,* revised edn. (New York, 1963), p. 72.
4. Erich Auerbach, *Mimesis: the Representation of Reality in Western Literature,* trans. Willard R. Trask (Princeton, 1968), p. 532.
5. J. Hillis Miller, 'Virginia Woolf's All Souls' Day: The Omniscient Narrator in *Mrs. Dalloway*' in *The Shaken Realist: Essays in Modern Literature in Honour of F.J. Hoffman,* ed. Melvin Friedman and John B. Vickery (Louisiana, 1982), pp. 100-27.
6. 'After ''To the Lighthouse'' in *A Selection from Scrutiny,* ed. F.R. Leavis, Vol. II (Cambridge, 1968), pp. 97-100.
7. Kristeva, 'Oscillation', *loc. cit.,* p. 166.
8. Phyllis Rose, *Woman of Letters: A Life of Virginia Woolf* (London, 1978), p. 125.
9. To Ethel Smyth, Woolf wrote: 'how can you imagine how much sexual feeling has to do with an emotion for one's mother!' Cited by Jane Marcus in her 'Thinking Back Through Our Mothers' in *New Feminist Essays, op. cit.,* p. 14.
10. Juliet Mitchell, *Psychoanalysis and Feminism* (London, 1974), p. 116.
11. The Shelley quotation is in 'Mrs. Dalloway in Bond Street' in *Mrs. Dalloway's Party: A Short Story Sequence by Virginia Woolf,* ed. Stella McNichol (London, 1973), p. 22. In this short piece, from which the novel developed, the theme of losing integrity and purity as one grows is more explicit.

12. Kristeva, *Polylogue* (Paris: Editions du Seuil, 1977), p. 79, cited in Josette Féral, 'Antigone or the Irony of the Tribe', *Diacritics* (September 1978), p. 12.

14. I use this phrase in its generalised, non-psychoanalytical sense. 'It should be pointed out that this expression is often employed in a loose way as a description of a woman with allegedly masculine character traits—e.g. authoritarianism—even when it is not known what the underlying phantasies are'. J. Laplanche and J.-B. Pontalis, *The Language of Psycho-Analysis,* trans. Donald Nicholson-Smith (London, 1973), p. 312.

15. Raymond Williams, 'The Bloomsbury Fraction', *Problems of Materialism and Culture: Selected Essays* (London, 1980), p. 156.

16. The French term *jouissance* carries a wide range of meaning: enjoyment in the sense of legal or social possession, pleasure, and the pleasure of sexual climax. Lacan uses the word emphasising the *totality* of enjoyment covered by it—simultaneously sexual, spiritual, physical, conceptual.

    Kristeva similarly uses the word to denote a total joy which 'also, through the working of the signifier . . . implies the presence of meaning (*jouissance = J'ouis sens* = I heard meaning), requiring it by going beyond'. See Kristeva, *Desire in Language: A Semiotic Approach to Literature and Art,* ed. Leon S. Roudiez (Oxford, 1980), p. 16. In Kristeva's work, purely sensual or sexual pleasure is covered by the term *plaisir.*

17. See the preface to the first edition of *Mrs. Dalloway.* In a letter Woolf wrote 'Septimus and Mrs. Dalloway should be entirely dependent upon each other' (*L,* 3:189).

18. In the novel, 'life' and 'death' do not have one fixed value; they constantly interchange positive and negative signs. Septimus' suicide is positive, while the 'life' the doctors uphold is corruption and lies. Elsewhere 'life' is joy and pleasure and death their negation.

19. Gilles Deleuze and Felix Guattari, *Anti-Oedipus: Capitalism and Schizophrenia* (New York, 1977), p. 2.

Chapter 4

1. Lodge, *op. cit.,* p. 177.

2. Gillian Beer, 'Hume, Stephen and Elegy in *To the Lighthouse*', *Essays in Criticism,* Vol. XXXIV, (1984), p. 48.

3. Roland Barthes, *S/Z,* trans. Richard Miller (London, 1974), p. 160.

4. Jonathan Culler, 'Jacques Derrida' in *Structuralism and Since: From Lévi-Strauss to Derrida,* ed. John Sturrock (Oxford, 1979), p. 178.

5. John Mepham, 'Figures of desire: narration and fiction in *To the Lighthouse*', in *The Modern English Novel: the reader, the writer and the work,* ed. Gabriel Josipovici (London, 1976), p. 174.

6. Sigmund Freud, *New Introductory Lectures on Psycho-Analysis,* trans. James Strachey (London, 1953), p. 115. See also Gallop, *Feminism and Psychoanalysis, op. cit.,* p. 65.

7. Jacques Derrida, *Positions,* trans. Alan Bass (London, 1981), p. 41.

8. See Lemaire, *Lacan, op. cit.*, p. 87.

9. Luce Irigaray, 'This Sex Which Is Not One', in *New French feminisms, op. cit.*, pp. 100-1.

10. Derrida, *Of Grammatology, op. cit.*, p. 12.

11. Woolf, *Three Guineas*, pp. 107, 121.

12. Derrida, *Of Grammatology, op. cit.*, p. 147.

13. Irigaray, *loc. cit.*, p. 104.

14. See Hanna Segal, *Klein* (Glasgow, 1979), p. 66.

15. Claude Lévi-Strauss, *Structural Anthropology*, trans. Claire Jacobson and Brooke Grundfest Schoepf (London, 1969), p. 215.

16. See Eliot, 'Marie Lloyd', in *Selected Essays*, pp. 456-9. For Woolf's comments on her see *QB*, 2:77.

17. Gayatri Spivak, 'Unmaking and Making in *To the Lighthouse*', in *Women and Language in Literature and Society*, ed. Sally McConnell-Ginet and others (New York, 1980), pp. 310-11.

18. Susan Squier points out the ambiguous value of domestic labour in Woolf's work: women's household drudgery is 'a product of oppressive patriarchal culture', but at the same time it guarantees 'privacy' from male interruption and gives women a certain space of freedom to engage themselves with the 'satirical critique of society' which had banished them to it. 'A Track of Our Own: Typescript Drafts of *The Years*' in *A Feminist Slant, op cit.*, p. 207.

19. See the account in Gallop, *op. cit.*, Chs. 3 and 6.

20. Irigaray, *loc. cit.*, pp. 104-5. Italics in the original are omitted.

21. Auerbach, *Mimesis, op. cit.*, p. 532.

22. Gallop, *op. cit.*, p. 121.

23. *Ibid.*

24. T.E. Hume, *Speculations*, ed. Herbert Read (London, 1960), p. 134.

25. It is more common to associate the phallic with the Father. However, the notion of the 'woman with a penis' can be seen even in Freud's early article 'On the Sexual Theories of Children' (1908). Melanie Klein developed this concept, proposing a totally different genesis for it. See the relevant entries in Laplanche and Pontalis, *The Language of Pyscho-Analysis*. Gallop, *op. cit.*, p. 115.

26. Kristeva, *Polylogue*, cited in Gallop, *op. cit.*, p. 117.

27. Jacques Lacan, *Écrits*, trans. Alan Sheridan (London, 1977), p. 288.

28. On the issue of an unworked grief in Woolf herself which Lily solves vicariously, see Mark Spilka, 'Lily Briscoe's Borrowed Grief', *Virginia Woolf's Quarrel with Grieving* (Lincoln, Nebraska and London, 1980), pp. 75-109.

29. Gallop, *op. cit.*, p. 114 n. 1, p. 115. On this 'structural weakness' see also Nancy Chodorow, *The Reproduction of Mothering* (Berkeley and Los Angeles, 1979) and Dorothy Dinnerstein, *The Mermaid and the Minotaur* (New York and London, 1976).

30. Also see above pp. 45-6, 116.

31. Lemaire, *Lacan, op. cit.*, p. 86.

Chapter 5

1. Maria DiBattista, *Virginia Woolf's Major Novels: The Fables of Anon* (New Haven and London, 1980), p.115.
2. Rosemary Jackson, *Fantasy: the Literature of Subversion,* 'New Accents' (London, 1981), p. 3.
3. Showalter, *op. cit.,* p. 282.
4. Jackson, *op. cit.,* p. 41.
5. Showalter, *op. cit.,* pp. 264, 289.
6. Jacobus, 'The Difference of View', *loc. cit.,* p. 20.
7. Kristeva, *About Chinese Women, op. cit.,* p. 38.
8. Nancy Topping Bazin, *Virginia Woolf and the Androgynous Vision* (New Brunswick, New Jersey, 1973), p. 132.
9. Jackson, *op. cit.,* p. 42.
10. Cited in Cora Kaplan, 'Language and Gender', in *Papers on Patriarchy* (Brighton, 1976), p. 36. Kaplan remarks: 'Metonymy is a dominant trope in women's poetry, since it is a way of referring to experience suppressed in public discourse'.
11. Jackson, *op. cit.,* p. 16. See also Kristeva on Bakhtin, 'Word, Dialogue and Novel', in *Desire in Language, op. cit.,* pp. 64-91.
12. Heath, 'Difference', *loc. cit.,* pp. 65-6.
13. Eagleton, *Walter Benjamin, op. cit.,* p. 138. DiBattista, *op. cit.,* p. 120.
14. Kristeva, *About Chinese Women, op. cit.,* p. 38.
15. See Jackson, *op. cit.,* pp. 20, 28, 82.
16. Freud's question is cited in E. Jones, *Sigmund Freud: Life and Work,* Vol. II (London, 1953). p. 468. Lacan repeats it in 'God and the *Jouissance* of The Woman. A Love Letter', in *Feminine Sexuality: Jacques Lacan and the ecole freudienne* (London, 1982), p. 146.
17. 'In both *Encore* and *Télévision* Lacan repeatedly asserts that "woman does not exist"'. Gallop, *op. cit.,* p. 34.
18. Jameson, *Marxism and Form, op. cit.,* p. 374; *The Political Unconscious: Narrative as a Socially Symbolic Act* (London, 1981), p. 136.
19. *QB,* 2:118. See Rose, *Woman of Letters, op. cit.,* especially Ch. 8.
20. Kristeva, *About Chinese Women, op.cit.,* p. 36.
21. Kristeva, *RPL,* p. 79.
22. Kristeva, *About Chinese Women, op. cit.,* p. 34.
23. See Freud, *Beyond the Pleasure Principle,* and 'Death Instincts' and 'Pair of Opposites' in *The Language of Psycho-Analysis, op. cit.*
24. Kristeva, *RPL,* p. 28; *About Chinese Women, op. cit.,* p. 34.
25. John Graham, 'The "Caricature Value" of Parody and Fantasy in *Orlando* ', in *Virginia Woolf: A Collection of Critical Essays,* ed. Claire Sprague (Englewood Cliffs, N.J., 1971), p. 114.
26. Jacobus, 'The Difference of View', *loc. cit.,* p. 19.
27. Jackson, *op. cit.,* p. 82.
28. Roland Barthes, *Writing Degree Zero,* trans. Annette Lavers and Colin Smith (New York, 1968), pp. 30-1.
29. Manuscript of *Orlando,* reprinted in *Twentieth Century Literature: Virginia*

Woolf Issue, Vol. XXV, No. 3/4 (Fall/Winter 1979), p. 316. Madeline Moore's note is on p. 342, n. 17.

30. Raymond Williams, *The Country and the City* (Frogmore, St. Albans, 1975), p. 290.
31. Kristeva, *Powers of Horror: An Essay on Abjection,* trans. Leon S. Roudiez (New York, 1982), especially Chs. 1 to 3.

Chapter 6

1. She writes: 'the difficulty of digging oneself in there, with conviction . . . I press to my centre . . . I could perhaps do B's soliloquy in such a way as to break up, dig deep . . . that very condensed book *The Waves* . . . I think *The Waves* is anyhow tense and packed' (*WD,* 149, 151, 165, 171, 174).
2. Jean Guiguet, *Virginia Woolf and her Works,* trans. Jean Stewart (New York, 1976), p. 286; Lee, *The Novels of Virginia Woolf, op. cit.,* p. 163; Melvin Friedman, cited in Lee, p. 160.
3. See Kristeva, *RPL,* 63, 69, 62; *About Chinese Women, op. cit.,* p. 38.
4. Coppelia Kahn reveals a parallel defensive rejection and then struggle and interaction with the feminine element in *King Lear.* See 'Excavating "Those Dim Minoan Regions'': Maternal Subtexts in Patriarchal Literature', *Diacritics* (Summer 1982), pp. 32-41.
5. See Kristeva, *Powers of Horror, op. cit.*
6. Sara Ruddick, 'Private Brother, Public World', in Jane Marcus, *New Feminist Essays, op. cit.,* p. 206.
7. Kristeva, *About Chinese Women, op. cit.,* p. 34.
8. *Ibid.,* p. 35.
9. Gillian Beer's account of Woolf's struggle with non-anthropocentric concepts of the universe in *To the Lighthouse* also bears upon *The Waves.* She notes of the earlier novel: 'Language can never be anything but anthropocentric', and hence the book's doubts about and struggles with language. 'Hume, Stephen and Elegy in *To the Lighthouse', loc. cit.,* p. 48.
10. Donald Davie, *Articulate Energy: An Inquiry into the Syntax of English Poetry* (London, 1976), p. 10.
11. Ferdinand de Saussure, *Course in General Linguistics,* trans. Wade Baskin (Glasgow, 1974), p. 123.
12. Cited in Anthony Easthorpe, *Poetry as Discourse,* 'New Accents' (London, 1983), p. 142.
13. Donald Davie, *Purity of Diction in English Verse* (London, 1967), p. 92.
14. Lee, *op. cit.,* p. 164.
15. See Laplanche and Pontalis, *op. cit.,* pp. 78-80.
16. Jessie Weston argues that the *Gawain* versions of the Grail legends, in which the hero attempts to restore the Waste Land, are older than the *Perceval* 'in which the ''Wasting'' is brought about by the action of the hero'. *From Ritual to Romance* (New York, 1957), p. 63.
17. DiBattista, *op. cit.,* pp. 150-2.
18. *Ibid.,* pp. 159-60.

19. Sara Ruddick, *op. cit.*, p. 200.
20. Quentin Bell records one of Woolf's 'short but violent mental tremor[s]', of which she wrote: 'now the old devil has once more got his spine through the waves' (*QB*, 2:100).
21. Kristeva, *About Chinese women, op. cit.*, p. 38.
22. In the diary Woolf notes: 'when I wake early I say to myself Fight, fight' (*WD*, 148). 'Modern Fiction' itself ends on a little-remarked note of pugnacity. The first part of the essay argues that the false totalities of realist narrative must be dissolved into a passive, Impressionistic receptivity. But this process of deliquescence may go too far. The essay finally turns round on itself and valorises a native English instinct to 'enjoy and fight', to impose a 'vision', over the spiritually subtilised but helpless 'inconclusiveness' of the Russians (*CE*, 2:109).

Conclusion

1. Susan J. Leonardi argues for the convergence of modernist and feminist concerns in Woolf's search for a 'new language'. The latter's rejection of the 'hierarchical sentence', together with the anthropocentric view of the universe underpinning and underpinned by it, is the common concern; but for Woolf and other women modernists, language, which is after all male, fails to express women's reality. 'Bare Places and Ancient Blemishes: Virginia Woolf's Search for New Language in *Night and Day*', *Novel*, Vol. 19, Winter 1986.
2. Queenie Leavis points out that Woolf's proposals involve 'a thorough-going revolution', 'a regular social reorganisation'—as if Woolf herself were not fully aware of this. Leavis then offers sympathy to 'the unfortunate men who are to marry these daughters of educated men' in the new society. She concludes: 'The position with regard to further female emancipation seems to be that the onus is on women to prove that they are going to be able to justify it, and that it will not vitally dislocate . . . the framework of our culture', *Scrutiny*, Vol. 7, No. 2, September 1938, pp. 203-14.
3. Heilbrun, 'Virginia Woolf in her Fifties' in *Virginia Woolf: A Feminist Slant, op. cit.*, pp. 238, 237. Black, 'Virginia Woolf and the Women's Movement', *ibid.*, pp. 180-97.
4. See the discussion of the two stories of a swallow and a nightingale in Madeline Moore, *The Short Season Between Two Silences: The Mystical and the Political in the Novels of Virginia Woolf* (Boston, London and Sydney, 1984).
5. Beer, 'Virginia Woolf and Pre-History', in *Virginia Woolf: A Centenary Perspective, op. cit.*, p. 111.
6. *Ibid.*, p. 103.
7. Woolf notes in her diary: 'it's to be a dialogue: and poetry: and prose; all quite distinct. No more closely written books' (*WD*, 285-6). '. . . all waifs and strays—a rambling capricious . . .'(*WD*, 289-90).
8. Lee, *op. cit.*, p. 208.

9. Kristeva, 'From One Identity to Another' in *Desire in Language, op. cit.,* p. 136.
10. E.M. Forster, *Virginia Woolf* (The Rede lecture, 1941), (Cambridge, 1942), pp. 8, 23.
11. James Naremore, 'Nature and History in *The Years'* in *Virginia Woolf: Revaluation and Continuity,* ed. Ralph Freedman (Berkeley, Los Angeles and London, 1980), p. 262.
12. '''Anon'' and ''The Reader'': Virginia Woolf's Last Essays', ed. by Brenda R. Silver in *Twentieth Century Literature: Virginia Woolf Issue, op. cit.,* pp. 385, 381, 404. Subsequent page references are included in my text.
13. Kristeva, *About Chinese Women, op. cit.,* pp. 29-30.
14. Kristeva, *ibid.,* p. 39. 'Brown' here seems to be an error for Bowen.

Index

abjection, 150, 160
aesthetics, T.S. Eliot's, 34-5; female, 2;
  modernist, and feminism, 5, 8, 14,
  187; realist, 13; symbolist, 39;
  V.W.'s, ix-x, 29
allegory, 29-30, 35, 38-9, 42, 45, 84-5,
  102, 115, 154. *See also* symbol;
  metonymy; writing
Allen, Mowbray, 34
ambivalence, 28, 30, 37, 40-1, 43, 47,
  53, 66, 72, 85, 88, 91, 99, 112, 115,
  128, 177, 185-6. *See also*
  indeterminacy
androgyny, 22-3, 120-1, 137; and
  heterogeneity, 9-10, 12, 130-2;
  Showalter's critique of Woolfian, 12,
  120-1; and writing, 158-9, 184-6,
  189-90
'Angel in the House', 111-13
Arnold, Matthew, 39
Arthurian legend, 109, 144
Auerbach, Erich, *Mimesis*, 57, 106
aura (W. Benjamin), 38
avant-garde, 4, 20, 21

Bakhtin, Mikhail, 123
Barthes, Roland, 13, 24, 50, 87, 145
Bazin, Nancy Topping, *Virginia Woolf
  and the Androgynous Vision*, 15, 121
Beer, Gilian, 14, 16, 85, 190, 199n19
Bell, Quentin, ix, 117, 195-6
Benjamin, Walter, 36, 38
Bennett, Arnold, 3, 7, 16, 26, 28; anti-
  feminism of, 5-6
Beresford, J.D., ix
binary oppositions, 9, 12, 85, 117, 121,
  141, 188, 192. *See also under*

deconstruction
bisexuality, 9, 10-11. *See also*
  adrogyny
Black, Naomi, 188
Bloomsbury, 74
body, 34, 62-3, 70-1, 74, 170; as
  materiality of the signifier, 30, 36-7,
  49, 76, 88; mother's, 14-15, 22, 67,
  70, 79, 98, 101, 107-8, 161, 186,
  192; and representation, 16, 71, 104,
  107-8, 113-15, 134, 163; and
  woman, 21, 45, 70, 93
Bowen, Elizabeth, 196
Brecht, Bertolt, 14
British Empire, 65, 139, 141
Brontë, Emily, 136
Brontë, Charlotte, 2; *Jane Eyre*, 68, 119

carnival, 123-6, 141
castration, 47, 52, 69, 87-9, 125
castration complex, 14
capitalism, 13, 20, 65, 74, 77, 135, 159,
  193
chora, 18, 21, 63, 73, 79, 142, 157,
  186, 192; sea imagery for, 63, 73,
  81-2, 150-1, 190, 192, 196; swamp
  imagery for, 73, 190, 195-6. *See also*
  semiotic
Cixous, Hélène, 10, 15, 21
class, middle, 7, 49, 75, 194; lower, 21,
  101
Coleridge, Samuel Taylor, 29
consciousness, 61, 177; birth of, 156,
  195; female, 2; splitting in the female,
  10, 22, 95, 121, 127, 143. *See also
  under* subject

207

Index

209

nature of their present situation

Professor Ilan Pappe, University of Exeter, Israeli historian
and author of *The Ethnic Cleansing of Palestine* (2007)

'This book provides one of the best introductions to the Israel/Palestine
conflict. It reveals what mainstream media in the West seeks to conceal
from the public: that Israel has an apartheid regime which has been
obsessed with demographic racism and ethnic cleansing for six decades.
The book provides an indispensable context for understanding the origins

and consequences of the conflict. It also makes by far the most compelling case for "peace with justice-not apartheid".'

'Is Israel an apartheid state? The answer to this question has enormous implications for how states and international civil society should act towards a country that bills itself as the moral guardian of the memory and lessons of the Nazi Holocaust – that is why it is so heavily contested. But there is no doubt that Israel is constituted as a "Jewish state". The problem is that half the population it controls – the indigenous Palestinians – is not Jewish. In this carefully researched book, Ben White demonstrates that indeed Israel could have become and could not continue to be a "Jewish state" unless it used discriminatory tactics that resemble and often surpass those of apartheid South Africa. At a time when Israel appears to regard any action against Palestine's indigenous people – no matter how violent and illegal – as justified, this book is essential reading for those who want to deepen their understanding beyond soundbites and spin.'

'Ben White's new book *Israeli Apartheid: A Beginner's Guide* is a useful introduction to a vital debate. To understand the challenges of the current situation in the Middle East we must revisit the long and often painful journey that led from the creation of Israel to the 40-year-long occupation of the Palestinians. This challenging new work unpicks some of the myths of that story and forces us all to look again at the reality of current Israeli policy towards the Palestinians.'

'There are always those who say the conflict in Palestine is too complicated for anyone to dare engage with it, much less understand it. Yet here is the book which answers them, and it does so with a rare intelligence and fine line of argument. Drawn from a rich range of sources, Ben White's *Israeli Apartheid: A Beginner's Guide* takes on the most complex arenas of injustice and contested history, and renders them accessible, lucid, and morally compelling. Never compromising on the facts, its narrative both enlightens and inspires. If you want to learn about Palestine, start here.'

'An essential guide for understanding the reality of Israeli apartheid – both the history, and the day to day reality.'

> **Eyal Weizman**, Israeli architect and author of
> *Hollow Land: Israel's Architecture of Occupation* (2007)

'I am impressed by Ben White's clear-minded journalism and analysis. I have quoted from an article of his in a speech to the House of Commons. I feel sure his book will be of value in understanding the attitudes behind the Middle East division.'

> **Harry Cohen**, Labour Member of Parliament
> for Leyton and Wanstead

'White's book helps us see much more clearly both what is happening in Israel/Palestine but also what we must do about it. If you really care about peace in the Middle East, read this book. Then commit yourself to supporting non-violent proactive ways to bring justice with peace for both Israelis and Palestinians.'

> **Rev. Stephen Sizer**, author of *Zion's Christian Soldiers* (2007)

'Ben White provides a lucid and essential account of the roots, nature and development of Israeli apartheid and the continued resistance – home grown or international. His work cleverly unites the relevant past to the unbearable present, and provides a solid presentation of the ongoing struggle to rid the Zionist state of its racially selective "democracy". His writing is dispassionate, clear and thoroughly substantiated, as is the case with all of his work.'

> **Ramzy Baroud**, editor of the *Palestine Chronicle* website,
> journalist and author of *The Second Palestinian Intifada* (2006)

'Ben White presents a book to be used and not only read. It is to be used by all those who are interested in taking a political and historic journey into the Palestinian-Israeli conflict and who are involved in moving beyond the historic narratives into creating a future where peace prevails in the Middle East.'

> **Sami Awad**, Executive Director of Holy Land Trust,
> Bethlehem, Palestine

'This is not a story for the faint of heart but it is a necessary story, rarely told with such candour. This is also one of those rare books that will permanently change a reader's view of the world and inevitably force us to ask about our own country's complicity in this occupation.'

> **Gary M. Burge**, PhD, Wheaton College and Graduate School,
> author of *Whose Land? Whose Promise?* (2003)

'Ben White is an unusually measured and thoughtful commentator on the Israel/Palestine question. There aren't many writers on the region whose work demands attention for the quality of its insight and reliability of its research, but Ben is one of them.'

Arthur Neslen, author of *Occupied Minds* (2006)

'In this book Ben White provides important insights on the history and emergence of the State of Israel while simultaneously documenting the suffering, dispossession and dispersion of the Palestinian people from lands they controlled for hundreds of years. For the earnest scholar and serious student of the Israel/Palestine question, his research will prove most valuable.'

Rev. Alex Awad, professor at Bethlehem Bible College and pastor of East Jerusalem Baptist Church

'Western governments, including my own – Australia – have largely fallen for Israel's "victim" propaganda, and blame the Palestinians for what has happened. This book is a well documented rejoinder and should be read by all with a genuine concern for peace with justice for all the peoples of historic Palestine.'

Dr Kevin Bray, Member of the National Council of Churches of Christ in Australia, Chair of the Canberra Ecumenical Working Group on Palestine-Israel and Chair of Australians for Justice and Peace in Palestine

'This is a very honest, clear and powerful book bringing us face to face with the reality of what Israel has done and is doing to the Palestinians. It would be convenient to ignore it. It would be convenient to assume Ben has got it wrong – that it's not quite that bad. Sadly it is and we ignore it at everyone's peril.'

Garth Hewitt, Canon of St George's Cathedral, Jerusalem

'Ben White has a passionate commitment to justice and to facing difficult facts. This book is likely to produce strong reactions, but it will also hopefully provoke real thought.'

Simon Barrow, Co-director, Ekklesia (UK-based think tank)

Israeli Apartheid

A Beginner's Guide

Second Edition

Ben White

PlutoPress
www.plutobooks.com

First published 2009 by Pluto Press
345 Archway Road, London N6 5AA and
175 Fifth Avenue, New York, NY 10010

Second edition published 2014

www.plutobooks.com

Distributed in the United States of America exclusively by
Palgrave Macmillan, a division of St. Martin's Press LLC,
175 Fifth Avenue, New York, NY 10010

British Library Cataloguing in Publication Data

A catalogue record for this book is available from the British Library

ISBN   978 0 7453 3463 9   Paperback
ISBN   978 1 7837 1026 3   PDF eBook
ISBN   978 1 7837 1028 7   Kindle eBook
ISBN   978 1 7837 1027 0   EPUB eBook

Library of Congress Cataloging in Publication Data applied for

This book is printed on paper suitable for recycling and made from
fully managed and sustained forest sources. Logging, pulping and
manufacturing processes are expected to conform to the environmental
standards of the country of origin.

10 9 8 7 6 5 4 3 2 1

Typeset from disk by Stanford DTP Services, Northampton, England
Text design by Melanie Patrick
Simultaneously printed digitally by CPI Antony Rowe, Chippenham, UK
and Edwards Bros in the United States of America

إلى الصامدين

To the steadfast ones

Contents

Maps, Figures and Photographs

Acknowledgements

A lot of people have worked hard to make this book what it is, and for that I am very grateful. I cannot thank everyone here as much as I would like, and there are many dear friends and family who helped simply with their friendship and support. An especial thanks though to the following who gave invaluable assistance, advice and encouragement:

Roger van Zwanenberg and all the team at Pluto Press – particularly Robert Webb.

Andy Sims, Alex Awad, Lizzie Clifford, Jonathan Cook, Ilan Pappe, Khaled Hroub, Glen Rangwala, Jonathan Kuttab, Arthur Nelsen, Suhad Bishara at Adalah; John Dugard, Paul Higgins, Penny Julian, Karma Nabulsi, Isabelle Humphries, Ramzy Baroud and the Palestine Chronicle; Philip Rizk, Colin Chapman, Washington Report on Middle East Affairs (WRMEA); Daoud Badr at the Association for the Defense of the Rights of Internally Displaced Persons in Israel (ADRID); Stephen Sizer, Shaza Younis, Daoud Nassar, Institute for Middle East Understanding (IMEU); Professor Gary Burge, Juliette Bannoura at the Applied Research Institute of Jerusalem (ARIJ); Muzna Shihabi and Ashraf Khatib at the Negotiations Affairs Department; the Palestinian Academic Society for the Study of International Affairs (PASSIA); Waseem Mardini and the Foundation for Middle East Peace (FMEP); Amnesty International; the United Nations Office for the Coordination of Humanitarian Affairs in the OPT (OCHA); and Sami Mshasha at the United Nations Relief and Works Agency for Palestine Refugees in the Near East (UNRWA), Jerusalem.

Foreword

John Dugard

Perhaps the most striking aspect of the Israel/Palestine conflict is that it is so little discussed in the West, particularly in the United States. Unlike the human rights situation in Zimbabwe, Sudan, Burma, Tibet and Cuba it is a taboo topic in most quarters. Whereas human rights in apartheid South Africa was vigorously debated in the media, universities, churches, shareholders meetings and social and professional gatherings the subject of human rights in the Occupied Palestinian Territory (OPT) is studiously avoided. This contrasts with the position in Israel itself, where all issues are examined and debated in the media and public life. As Special Rapporteur to the Human Rights Council (previously Commission for Human Rights) on the Human Rights Situation in the OPT, I spoke in Israel to the Knesset on house demolitions, at the Hebrew University of Jerusalem on human rights violations in the OPT and at other meetings on controversial aspects of the conflict. But in the West one is not so welcome to express opinions on this subject. It seems that one can address real issues in Israel itself without the risk of being labelled as anti-Semitic but in the West it is not so. In many quarters any frank criticism of Israel's treatment of the Palestinians is viewed as anti-Semitic.

The failure to discuss and debate the conflict presents a serious problem as until it is fully aired the conflict will not be resolved. Herein lies the value of the present work. Unlike the many available comprehensive and scholarly studies of the conflict which inevitably have a limited readership, this book highlights the key issues of the conflict in a short and highly readable study, in which brevity is not achieved at the expense of a serious analysis of Israeli law and practice or a proper treatment of the historical record. All the principal topics at the heart of the conflict are addressed: the treatment of Palestinians both within Israel itself and the OPT, why Palestinians reject the notion of a 'Jewish state', is Israel a democracy, is Gaza still occupied by Israel, the plight of Palestinian refugees, the expansion of settlements, the Wall presently being constructed in the OPT, checkpoints etc., etc. In short the book is an ideal reader for informed debate about the conflict.

Many will take issue with the comparison with apartheid. Ben White does not, however, say that apartheid and Israel's treatment of Palestinians are exactly the same. What he says is that they have certain similarities, that they resemble each other. That is why he calls it Israeli apartheid. It is Israel's own version of a system that has been universally condemned. Of course there are differences, as White freely admits. Apartheid in South Africa was a regime of institutionalised race discrimination in which a white minority sought to maintain domination over a black majority, whereas Israeli apartheid is concerned with the discriminatory treatment of a minority of Palestinians in Israel itself and the discriminatory treatment of Palestinians in the OPT under a regime of military occupation that, unlike apartheid, is tolerated by international law. But, as White points out, there are similarities. He rightly says that 'The common element of both legal systems is the intention to consolidate and enforce dispossession, securing the best land control over natural resources for one group at the expense of another.' Control is achieved in Israel/Palestine by many of the same devices employed in apartheid South Africa: colonisation or the settlement of land owned by the indigenous population; territorial fragmentation of the OPT by a process of Bantustan-isation; restrictions on movement by a strict system of permits and checkpoints that brings to mind the much-hated pass system of apartheid, but probably exceeds the pass system in severity; house demolitions, military brutality and the arrest and imprisonment of political opponents. Control is also achieved by means not employed by the apartheid regime: a wall/fence/barrier (whatever you like to call it) that divides and separates people; a system of separate and unequal roads for Israelis (who get the best roads) and Palestinians (who get the poor roads); and a deliberately manufactured humanitarian crisis that has reduced the Palestinian people to a state of poverty and despair. This last difference is perhaps the most striking. Whereas the Israeli military occupation of the OPT has resulted in the destruction of houses, agriculture and businesses, the impairment of schools, universities, hospitals and clinics, damage to electricity plants, water supplies and other amenities, and the subjection of the Palestinian people to poverty, the apartheid state, in order to promote a pretence of equal treatment, built houses, schools, universities, businesses, hospitals, clinics and provided water to the black population. It sought to advance the material welfare of the black people while denying political rights. Israel, on the other hand, denies political rights to Palestinians and at the same time undermines their material welfare – in violation of its obligations as an occupying power under international humanitarian law.

Israel has been condemned for its policies in the OPT by numerous United Nations resolutions and by the International Court of Justice, in an advisory opinion of 2004 in which it held that the wall Israel is constructing in Palestinian Territory is illegal and should be dismantled. But no serious attempt is made by the West to compel Israel to comply with its international obligations. As White correctly states 'Israel has been exempted from sanction for breaking international legal norms.' In this respect the response of the international community differs substantially from its response to apartheid. The General Assembly of the United Nations called for widespread economic sanctions on South Africa, the Security Council imposed a mandatory arms embargo, every effort was made to compel South Africa to comply with an advisory opinion of the International Court of Justice condemning apartheid in Namibia, and states, corporations and civil society imposed various forms of sanctions. This too is an issue that must be addressed if the credibility of the Rule of Law is to be maintained.

Ben White's book is no stranger to controversy. It considers issues that many in the West would like to see swept under the carpet. But the Palestinian issue is one that threatens international peace and cannot be avoided. The present book, by presenting the issues that need to be considered in a readable, but highly informative, manner will, it is hoped, stimulate an awareness of the plight of the Palestinian people. Until this is fully understood and appreciated a just settlement of the conflict will remain as elusive as ever.

John Dugard

Professor of Law, Centre for Human Rights, University of Pretoria; Visiting Professor of Law, Duke University, North Carolina; Former Special Rapporteur to the Human Rights Council on the Human Rights Situation in the Occupied Palestinian Territory.

Preface to the Second Edition

Just weeks after I had finished writing the manuscript for *Israeli Apartheid: A Beginner's Guide* in 2008, Israel launched an unparalleled attack on the Gaza Strip, pummelling the fenced-in enclave for three weeks. The impact of this massacre, both at the time and as the war crimes were documented and published, was to spur many in trade unions, faith communities, on campuses and elsewhere to mobilise against Israeli apartheid for perhaps the first time.

Since then, the situation on the ground has continued to get worse, while internationally, solidarity with the Palestinians has grown and pressure on Israel in various government and non-governmental contexts has increased.

This new, updated edition of the book is intended to reflect these developments. In the last half decade, Israel has continued to build in and expand its network of illegal settlements in the West Bank, the Apartheid Wall remains, and Palestinians are being pushed off their land in places like the southern Hebron Hills and the Jordan Valley. The Gaza Strip remains largely cut off from the West Bank, subject to blockade by both Israel and to a lesser extent Egypt.

Inside the pre-1967 borders, Palestinian citizens of Israel have been the target of explicitly nationalistic and discriminatory legislation, shining on a light on Israeli ethnocracy and everyday racism (the topic of a second book I have since written, *Palestinians in Israel: Segregation, Discrimination and Democracy*). Worse still, tens of thousands face forced expulsion in the Negev, victims of Israel's long standing policies of 'Judaisation'.

Meanwhile, the call from Palestinian civil society in 2005 for a global campaign of Boycott Divestment Sanctions (BDS) has been heard and taken up by students, charities and unionists with a speed that has greatly alarmed Israel and its lobbyists. The last few years have also seen a development of, and increased familiarity with, an analytical framework of apartheid and colonialism, reflected here in an expanded introductory chapter.

A new edition also provides the opportunity to update statistics and sources, as well as cover important changes, particularly with regards to the Gaza Strip. But all the elements of the first edition that were most appreciated remain, such as the Frequently Asked Questions section.

More and more people are seeing Israel's policies for what they are: forms of segregation and structural discrimination that need to be resisted not excused. The best feedback I had after the 2009 publication of the first edition was from people who said that the book had helped them understand the issues with a new clarity, and that they wanted to do something in response.

Today, that is exactly what I hope this new edition will also achieve – introduce the past and present of Israel's apartheid regime and ethnic cleansing of Palestinians, point towards a better future based on decolonisation, return and equality, and act as a springboard for readers to take action in their own communities.

Map 1   General map of Palestine/Israel

Source: Keith Cook, in Jonathan Cook, *Blood and Religion*,
London: Pluto Press, p. xv.

Introducing Israeli Apartheid

> Supporters of Israel present Zionism as an ideology of liberation of the Jewish people, but for Palestinians, Zionism, as it has been practiced and as they have experienced it, has been precisely apartheid.[1]

Approaching the Israeli-Palestinian conflict for the first time can be a confusing experience. There seem to be such widely varying points of view, contradictory versions of history, and utterly opposing explanations for the root of the problem. Why is this? One of the main reasons for this difficulty is the fact there are disagreements over Israel's origins.

In this book, the truth of Israel's past and present is laid bare; the ethnic cleansing, land grabs, discriminatory legislation and military occupation. This reality is very different from the typical tale of a small, brave nation, forced from the very beginning to fight for survival against implacable, bloodthirsty enemies; a country that has made mistakes but has always done its best to achieve noble aims with pure means.

What can explain such a profound difference? Pro-Israeli propaganda in the West has had a huge impact, but there is a more fundamental reason. 'Security' has been the justification for all manner of Israeli policies, from the population expulsions in 1948, to the Separation Wall over 60 years later. Defence, so it goes, is why Israel is forced to take certain measures, however unpleasant they may be.

Indeed, Israel argues, it alone is a country that fights for its very survival. Even putting aside Israel's vast military strength, why would Israel's existence as a Jewish state be so objectionable to Palestinians? Unlike today's slick apologists, the early Zionists were refreshingly honest about the reality of their mission, as we will see more of in Part I.

Ze'ev Jabotinsky was one of the foremost Zionist leaders and theoreticians, a man who has more streets in Israel named in his honour than any other historical figure.[2] In perhaps his most famous essay written in 1923, Jabotinsky was clear about one thing: 'Zionist colonization, even the most restricted, must either be terminated or carried out in defiance of the will of the native population'.[3] Why? Simply put, history shows that 'every indigenous people will resist alien settlers'.[4]

This book has been written in order to describe clearly and simply what Zionism has meant for the Palestinians, how Israeli apartheid has been implemented and maintained, and suggestions for how it can be resisted. In this task, I am indebted to the many academics, writers and journalists who have researched, documented and witnessed the unfolding of Israeli apartheid in Palestine.

Part I begins with a concise history of the development of Zionist settlement and theory, particularly with how it related to the Palestinians. There is then a summary of the key historical events of the Nakba, the Palestinian Catastrophe of 1948, when the aim of a Jewish state in Palestine was realised.

Part II will clearly define the main areas of Israeli apartheid and the contradictions of a so-called 'Jewish democratic' state. Dispersed through Parts I and II will be small 'stand alone' boxes with personal stories of how individual Palestinians are affected by a given aspect of Israeli apartheid.

Part III is the section in which ways to resist Israeli apartheid are discussed, with details of existing initiatives that should hopefully encourage you, the reader, to think of your own ideas. Finally, the book concludes with a 'Frequently Asked Questions' section in which doubts or criticisms of the book's main thrust will be asked and answered. But first, we are going to take a look at the definition of apartheid in international law, and the similarities and differences between South African apartheid and Israel.

DEFINING APARTHEID

> For the purpose of the present Convention, the term 'the crime of apartheid', which shall include similar policies and practices of racial segregation and discrimination as practised in southern Africa, shall apply to the following inhuman acts *committed for the purpose of establishing and maintaining domination by one racial group of persons over any other racial group of persons and systematically oppressing them* ... [emphasis added][5]
>
> Article II, International Convention on the Suppression and Punishment of the Crime of Apartheid, UN General Assembly Resolution 3068, 30 November 1973

While South Africa is most associated with apartheid (and is the context from which the term originates), the crime of apartheid actually has a far broader definition. This is important in the case of Israel, since even putting aside the similarities and differences to the South Africa case specifically, we have some kind of measure by which to assess Israel's policies past and present towards the Palestinians.

In 1973, the UN's General Assembly adopted the International Convention on the Suppression and Punishment of the Crime of Apartheid, which meant agreeing on a detailed description of what exactly 'the crime of apartheid' looked like. From this list of 'inhuman acts', there are some particularly worth highlighting:

- Denial to a member or members of a racial group or groups of the right to life and liberty of person … by the infliction upon the members of a racial group or groups of serious bodily or mental harm, by the infringement of their freedom or dignity, or by subjecting them to torture or to cruel, inhuman or degrading treatment or punishment.
- Any legislative measures and other measures calculated to prevent a racial group or groups from participation in the political, social, economic and cultural life of the country … [including] the right to leave and to return to their country, the right to a nationality, the right to freedom of movement and residence …
- Any measures including legislative measures designed to divide the population along racial lines by the creation of separate reserves and ghettos for the members of a racial group or groups … the expropriation of landed property belonging to a racial group …

As will be described in Parts I and II of this book, Israel has been, and continues to be, guilty of these crimes, which are all the more serious for having been 'committed for the purpose of establishing and maintaining domination by one racial group of persons over any other racial group of persons'.

There are other reference points for a legal framework for apartheid. The International Convention on the Elimination of All Forms of Racial Discrimination of 1969 – to which Israel is a signatory – condemns 'segregation and apartheid' and state parties 'undertake to prevent, prohibit and eradicate all practices of this nature in territories under their jurisdiction'.[6]

Then there is the 1977 Protocol Additional to the Geneva Conventions which in Article 85 includes within a list of 'grave breaches' the 'practices of "apartheid" and other inhuman and degrading practices involving outrages upon personal dignity, based on racial discrimination'.[7]

More recently, the Rome Statute of the International Criminal Court (ICC) was adopted in 1998 at an international conference.[8] Israel was actually one of seven countries (out of 148) to vote against the statute. The ICC Statute includes the 'crime of apartheid' in a list of 'crimes against humanity', going on to describe apartheid as:

> inhumane acts … committed in the context of an institutionalized regime of systematic oppression and domination by one racial group over any other racial group or groups and committed with the intention of maintaining that regime …

Therefore, even before a consideration of the similarities and differences between Israel and apartheid South Africa, there is a clear set of criteria for what constitutes the crime of apartheid under international law with which we can assess Israel's policies since 1948.

Recently, the apartheid analysis has gained traction in a number of quarters. Palestinian activists have been promoting a combined apartheid-colonialism-occupation analysis, exemplified by a 2008 paper produced by the Boycott National Committee (BNC).[9] The following year, the Human Sciences Research Council of South Africa (HSRC) published an extensive study conducted by a group of international scholars and legal practitioners titled 'Occupation, Colonialism, Apartheid?: A re-assessment of Israel's practices in the occupied Palestinian territories under international law'.[10]

In 2011, the Russell Tribunal on Palestine held its South Africa session – the third of four total hearings conducted by the popular court between 2010 and 2012. The focus was on whether Israel's policies amounted to a system of apartheid, an assessment that was made on the basis of three main elements drawn from international law: two distinct racial groups, inhuman acts, and systematic, institutionalised domination.[11] One of the expert witnesses, Dr David Keane, has written usefully about the nature of the 'racial groups' definition from the point of view of international law:

> the meaning of a racial group for the purposes of the [International Convention on the Elimination of All Forms of Racial Discrimination] is a broad and practical one. If a group identifies itself as such, and is identified as such by others, for example through discriminatory practices, then it comes under the protection of the Convention … Ultimately who is or is not a racial group under international law is not a scientific question, but a practical one.[12]

Another significant NGO to develop a case for apartheid has been Ramallah-based legal centre Al-Haq, who in their 2013 report on discriminatory water policies concluded that 'the threshold for apartheid is met because the inhuman acts, committed against Palestinians through the denial of access to water in the OPT, are carried out systematically in the context of an institutionalised regime with the intent of establishing and maintaining Jewish-Israeli domination over Palestinians as a group'.[13]

Finally, the UN's Committee on the Elimination of Racial Discrimination (CERD) in its March 2012 conclusions, issued as part of a periodical review, slammed Israel for a variety of policies on both sides of the Green Line – demarcating between Israel and the post-1967 Occupied Territories – and noted the existence of 'segregation between Jewish and non-Jewish communities', a lack of 'equal access to land and property', and 'home demolitions and forced displacement'.[14] CERD's report said:

> The Committee draws the State party's attention to its General Recommendation 19 (1995) concerning the prevention, prohibition and eradication of all policies and practices of racial segregation and apartheid, and urges the State party to take immediate measures to prohibit and eradicate any such policies or practices which severely and disproportionately affect the Palestinian population in the Occupied Palestinian Territory and which violate the provisions of article 3 of the Convention.

This was the first such condemnation made by CERD since the apartheid era in South Africa.

Interestingly, Israeli leaders have also talked in terms of apartheid, but as a way of warning about what might happen in the future.[15] Yet the situation they describe is actually already happening, and has been happening, since the post-1967 occupation began. See, for example, remarks made by then-Defence Minister Ehud Barak in 2010:

7

As long as in this territory west of the Jordan river there is only one political entity called Israel it is going to be either non-Jewish, or non-democratic. If this bloc of millions of Palestinians cannot vote, that will be an apartheid state.[16]

THE SOUTH AFRICA COMPARISON

If Palestinians were black, Israel would now be a pariah state subject to economic sanctions led by the United States.[17]

Observer, October 2000

White settlers in South Africa, like Zionist pioneers, colonised a land already inhabited. As in South Africa, the settlers in Palestine expelled the indigenous population, some two-thirds of the Palestinians in the land that became Israel in 1948, took possession of their properties and legally segregated those who remained.[18]

Leila Farsakh, *Le Monde Diplomatique*, 2003

It seems to me that the Israelis would like the Palestinians to disappear. There was never anything like that in our case. The whites did not want the blacks to disappear.[19]

Mondli Makhanya, editor-in-chief of the
South African *Sunday Times*, July 2008

Israel was compared to South African apartheid long before Jimmy Carter wrote his bestseller *Peace not Apartheid*. While the legal infrastructure that enforced apartheid South Africa differs substantially from the relevant Israeli legislation, there are also strong similarities.[20] The common element of both legal systems is the intention to consolidate and enforce dispossession, securing the best land control over natural resources for one group at the expense of another.

Architect and academic Lindsay Bremner has observed that while in the popular imagination apartheid in South Africa meant walls, fences and barbed wire separating blacks and whites, in fact:

> it was the countless instruments of control and humiliation (racially discriminatory laws, administration boards, commissions of inquiry, town planning schemes, health regulations, pass books, spot fines, location permits, police raids, removal vans, bulldozers) ... that delineated South African society during the apartheid years and produced its characteristic landscapes.[21]

As will be seen in Part II, this kind of description is all too familiar for Palestinians inside Israel, and the Occupied Palestinian Territories (OPT), for whom – like black South Africans – 'daily acts and rituals' become 'acts of segregation and humiliation'.[22]

In a bitter irony, important parts of the so-called 'peace process' of the 1990s, which saw limited Palestinian 'self rule' in a small percentage of the OPT, have actually strengthened the comparison with apartheid South Africa. In 1959, South Africa passed a law designed to promote 'self-government' amongst blacks in sealed-off 'reservations'.[23] Reading this description by the late Israeli journalist Tanya Reinhart, the similarities with the situation in the OPT since the 1990s are striking:

> The power in each of these entities was bestowed to local flunkies, and a few Bantustans even had elections,

Parliaments, and quasi-governmental institutions ... The Bantustans were allowed some symbols of sovereignty: a flag, postage stamps, passports and strong police force.

In 1984, Desmond Tutu noted that the Bantustans, in territory 'arbitrarily carved up for them by the all mighty White Government' deprived of 'territorial integrity or any hope of economic viability' were basically intended to 'give a semblance of morality to something that had been condemned as evil'.[24] 'Fragmented and discontinuous territories, located in unproductive and marginal parts of the country' with 'no control' over natural resources or access to 'territorial waters' – as we shall see, this is a frighteningly spot-on description of the OPT today.[25]

It is not just the policies and tools of repression and control where there are parallels. Modern-day Israel also echoes Pretoria's diplomats of decades gone by when it comes to propaganda and defending the indefensible. Like South African diplomats of the 1980s, Israel's representatives today claim that a boycott hurts Palestinian workers.[26] In addition, Israeli leaders today sound the alarm about Palestinian birth-rates and the prospect of a democratic one-state solution in the same sort of 'national suicide' discourse as once used by apartheid's defenders in South Africa.[27]

However, to describe Israel as an apartheid state 'does not mean equating Israel with South Africa'.[28] Indeed, any comparison should highlight both 'corresponding developments' as well as 'obviously different circumstances'.[29] One particularly striking difference is the fact that the apartheid regime in South Africa meant the rule of a white minority over a sizeable black majority; in 1913, when 'the first segregation laws were passed', the indigenous blacks made up 'more than 75% of the total labour force'.[30]

The other main difference is that Israel has not practised so-called 'petty' apartheid – in other words, there are no public toilets marked 'Jews' and 'Non-Jews'. Palestinian citizens of Israel have full voting rights and there are a small number of elected Palestinians in the Israeli legislature (the Knesset). This is because had the 'discrimination against Palestinians been written into Israeli law as specifically as discrimination against Blacks' was written into South African law, then 'outside support would surely be jeopardized'.[31]

There is one key difference between Israel and apartheid South Africa that Zionists definitely do not trumpet. While in apartheid South Africa, the settlers 'exploited' the 'labour power' of the dispossessed natives, in the case of Israel, 'the native population was to be eliminated; exterminated or expelled rather than exploited'.[32] It could be said that Zionism has been *worse* for the indigenous population than apartheid was in South Africa – Israel needs the land, but without the people.

In a conversation between Israeli historian Benny Morris and Palestinian American academic Joseph Massad, the latter compared Israel to South Africa by way of its 'supremacist rights'.[33] Morris said this was 'ridiculous', responding that throughout Zionism's history, Zionists 'would have much preferred Palestine to be empty of Arabs with therefore no need for Jews to be supreme over anybody. They simply wanted a Jewish state.'

Morris's objection to the term 'supremacist' is revealing, as it flags up the problem that has haunted Zionism until today. South African apartheid had a critical internal contradiction: while aiming 'at setting racial groups apart', it also 'acknowledged their dependency'.[34] Zionism, on the other hand, has tried 'disappearing' the Palestinians from Palestine in theory and in practice, yet they are still there.

THE FRIENDSHIP BETWEEN ISRAEL AND APARTHEID SOUTH AFRICA

Over the years there was a good deal of warmth between the respective leaders of the South African apartheid regime and Israel. South Africa's Daniel Malan was the first prime minister to visit Jerusalem in 1953, but long before Israeli statehood was proclaimed, a personal friendship had thrived between Chaim Weizmann, who became Israel's first president, and Jan Smuts, South African prime minister and senior military leader for the British.[35] Weizmann often turned to Smuts in times of crisis – and 'both men took for granted the moral legitimacy of each other's respective position'.[36]

Israel's warm ties with the apartheid regime began in earnest in the mid 1970s, with military technology and intelligence-sharing central to the alliance.[37] Over a period of about 15 years, examples of the close relationship included a 1975 pact signed by Shimon Peres and then-South African defence minister P.W. Botha, while in the mid 1980s, the Israeli defence industry was helping the isolated apartheid regime circumvent international sanctions.

Israel's 'collaboration with the racist regime of South Africa' eventually led to a 1984 UN General Assembly Resolution specifically condemning 'the increasing collaboration by Israel with the racist regime of South Africa'.[38] While many countries supported apartheid, what is interesting in the case of Israel is the extent of the shared empathy. In the early 1960s, for example, Hendrik Verwoerd, the South African prime minister, shared his own view that 'the Jews took Israel from the Arabs after the Arabs had lived there for a thousand years. Israel, like South Africa, is an apartheid state.'[39]

In 1976, then-South African Prime Minister John Vorster – a man who had been a Nazi sympathiser in World War II – was afforded a state banquet during a visit to Israel. At the official welcome, Israel's Yitzhak Rabin made a toast to 'the ideals shared by Israel and South Africa: the hopes for justice and peaceful coexistence'.[40] The following year, the *Official Yearbook of the Republic of South Africa* noted that 'Israel and South Africa have one thing above all else in common: they are both situated in a predominantly hostile world inhabited by dark peoples.'[41]

IN CONCLUSION

Increasingly, Israelis, Palestinians, South Africans and international observers are pointing out the parallels between apartheid South Africa and Israel. Several prominent South Africans have expressed their solidarity with the Palestinians, denouncing what they see as a similar (or worse) structure of oppression to the apartheid regime many of them fought against.

In 2002, veteran anti-apartheid figure and human rights campaigner, Archbishop Desmond Tutu made headlines with his article 'Apartheid in the Holy Land'.[42] Describing himself as 'deeply distressed' after a trip to Palestine/Israel that had reminded him 'so much of what happened to us black people in South Africa', the Archbishop affirmed that 'Israel will never get true security and safety through oppressing another people.'

In 2007, the UN Human Rights Rapporteur John Dugard, South African legal professor and apartheid expert, said that

'Israel's laws and practices in the OPT certainly resemble aspects of apartheid', echoing other South African trade union leaders, politicians, church groups and academics.[43] Western media correspondents have also made the comparison.[44]

Even Israeli politicians and commentators are now talking about apartheid, or more specifically, the risk of Israel facing a similar civil rights struggle that eventually prevailed in South Africa.[45] Indeed, albeit from quite a different perspective on the matter, Israel's foreign ministry predicted in 2004 that if the 'conflict with the Palestinians is not resolved', Israel 'could turn into a pariah state, on a par with South Africa during the apartheid years'.[46]

It is important to realise, however, that to compare the situation in Palestine/Israel to apartheid South Africa is not to try and force a 'one size fits all' political analysis where there are clear differences, as well as similarities. Rather, any such comparison is useful in so far as it helps sheds light – in Israel's case – on a political system that is based on structural racism, separation and dominance.

Moreover, as the rest of this book explains, even leaving aside the specific comparison with South Africa, Israel's past and present policies towards the indigenous Palestinians fully meet the aforementioned definition of apartheid laid out in international law – and urgently need to be treated as such by the international community.

Part I: Israeli Independence, Palestinian Catastrophe

We have forgotten that we have not come to an empty land to inherit it, but we have come to conquer a country from people inhabiting it.[1]

Moshe Sharett, Israel's second prime minister

'Ben-Gurion was right …Without the uprooting of the Palestinians, a Jewish state would not have arisen here.'[2]

Benny Morris, Israeli historian

In August 1897, in the Swiss city of Basle, a meeting took place that would have profound and disastrous consequences for the Palestinians – though they were not present at the event, or even mentioned by the participants. The First Zionist Congress, the brainchild of Zionism's chief architect Theodor Herzl, resulted in the creation of the Zionist Organization (later the World Zionist Organization) and the publication of the Basle Programme – a kind of early Zionist manifesto.

Just the year before, Herzl had published 'The Jewish State', in which he laid out his belief that the only solution to the anti-semitism of European societies was for the Jews to have their own country. Writing in his diary a few days afterwards, Herzl predicted what the real upshot would be of the Congress:

At Basle I founded the Jewish State. If I said this aloud today, I would be answered by universal laughter. In five years perhaps, and certainly in fifty years, everyone will perceive this.[3]

Herzl's Zionism was a response to European anti-semitism and, while a radical development, built on the foundations of more spiritually and culturally focused Jewish settlers who had already gone to Palestine on a very small scale. At the time, many Jews, for different reasons, disagreed with Herzl's answer to the 'Jewish question'. Nevertheless, the Zionists got to work; sending new settlers, securing financial support and bending the ear of the imperial powers without whose cooperation, the early leaders knew, the Zionist project would be impossible to realise.

At the beginning of the twentieth century, the population of Palestine was around 4 per cent Jewish and 96 per cent Palestinian Arab (of which around 11 per cent were Christian and the rest Muslim).[4] Before the new waves of Zionist settlers, the Palestinian Jewish community was 'small but of long standing', and concentrated 'in the four cities of religious significance: Jerusalem, Safed, Tiberias and Hebron'.[5] As new Zionist immigrants arrived, with the help of outside donations, French experts were called upon to share their experience of French colonisation in North Africa.[6]

An early priority for the Zionists was to secure more land on which to establish a secure, expanded, Jewish community. In 1901, the Jewish National Fund (JNF) was founded, an organisation 'devoted exclusively to the acquisition of land in Palestine for Jewish settlement'.[7] The JNF was destined to play a significant role in the history of Zionism, particularly as the land it acquired, by definition, 'became inalienably Jewish, never to be sold to or worked by non-Jews'.[8]

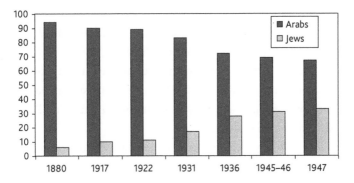

Figure 1 Palestinian population, 1880–1947

Source: *Facts and Figures About the Palestinians*, Washington, DC:
The Center for Policy Analysis on Palestine, 1992, p. 7.

The land purchased by the JNF was often sold by rich, absentee land-owners from surrounding Arab countries. However, much of the land was worked by Palestinian tenant farmers, who were then forcibly removed after the JNF had bought the property. Thousands of peasant farmers and their families were made homeless and landless in such a manner.[9]

The Zionists knew early on that the support of an imperial power would be vital. Zionism emerged in the 'age of empire' and thus 'Herzl sought to secure a charter for Jewish colonization guaranteed by one or other imperial European power'.[10] Herzl's initial contact with the British led to discussions over different possible locations for colonisation, from an area in the Sinai Peninsula to a part of modern day Kenya.[11] Once agreed on Palestine, the Zionists recognised, in the words of future president Weizmann, it would be under Britain's 'wing' that the 'Zionist scheme' would be carried out.[12]

The majority of British policy-makers and ministers viewed political Zionism with favour for a variety of reasons. For an empire competing for influence in a key geopolitical region of the world, helping birth a natural ally would reap dividends. From the mid nineteenth century onwards, there was also a tradition of a more emotional and even religious support for the creation of a Jewish state in Palestine amongst Christians in positions of influence, including Lord Shaftesbury and Prime Minister Lloyd George.[13]

Britain's key role is most famously symbolised by the Balfour Declaration, sent in a letter in 1917 by then Foreign Secretary Arthur Balfour to Lord Rothschild. The Declaration announced that the British government viewed 'with favour the establishment in Palestine of a national home for the Jewish people' and moreover, promised to 'use their best endeavours to facilitate the achievement of this object'. At the time, Jews were less than 10 per cent of Palestine's population.[14]

In the end, the role of the imperial powers proved crucial. For all the differences between some in the British foreign policy establishment and members of the Zionist movement – as well as the open conflict between radical Zionist terror groups and British soldiers – it was under British rule that the Zionists were able to prepare for the conquest of Palestine. Ben-Gurion once joked, after visiting the Houses of Parliament in London, 'that he might as well have been at the Zionist Congress, the speakers had been so sympathetic to Zionism'.[15]

Differences between the Zionist leaders of various political stripes were essentially tactical. As Ben-Gurion explained, nobody argued about the 'indivisibility' of 'Eretz Israel' (the name usually used to refer to the total area of the Biblical 'Promised Land').[16] Rather, 'the debate was over which of two routes would lead quicker to the common goal'. In 1937, Weizmann told the British high commissioner that 'we shall expand in the whole country in the course of time ... this is only an arrangement for the next 25 to 30 years'.[17]

A LAND WITHOUT A PEOPLE ...

There is a fundamental difference in quality between Jew and native.[18]

Chaim Weizmann, Israel's first president

The Zionist leadership's view of the 'natives' was unavoidable – 'wanting to create a purely Jewish, or predominantly Jewish, state in an Arab Palestine' could only lead to the development 'of a racist state of mind'.[19] Moreover, Zionism was conceived as a Jewish response to a problem facing Jews; the Palestinian Arabs were a complete irrelevance.

In the early days, the native Palestinians were entirely ignored – airbrushed from their own land – or treated with racist condescension, portrayed as simple, backward folk who would benefit from Jewish colonisation. One more annoying obstacle to the realisation of Zionism, as Palestinian opposition increased, the 'natives' became increasingly portrayed as violent and dangerous. For the Zionists, Palestine was 'empty'; not literally, but in terms of people of equal worth to the incoming settlers.

The early Zionist leaders expressed an ideology very similar to that of other settler movements in other parts of the world, particularly with regards to the dismissal of the natives' past and present relationship to the land. Palestine was considered a 'desert' that the Zionists would 'irrigate' and 'till' until 'it again becomes the blooming garden it once was'.[20] The 'founding father' of political Zionism, Theodor Herzl, wrote in 1896 that in Palestine, a Jewish state would 'form a part of a wall of defense for Europe in Asia, an outpost of civilization against barbarism'.[21]

Many British officials shared the Zionist view of the indigenous Palestinians. In a conversation, the head of the Jewish Agency's colonisation department asked Weizmann about the Palestinian Arabs. Weizmann replied that 'the British told us that there are some hundred thousand negroes and for those there is no value'.[22]

Winston Churchill, meanwhile, explained his support for Jewish settlement in Palestine in explicitly racist terms. Comparing Zionist colonisation to what had happened to indigenous peoples in North America and Australia, Churchill could not 'admit that a wrong has been done to those people by the fact that a stronger race, a higher grade race, or, at any rate, a more worldly-wise race, to put it that way, has come in and taken their place'.[23]

The Zionist movement was passionately opposed to democratic principles being applied to Palestine, for obvious reasons. As first Israeli Prime Minister Ben-Gurion admitted in 1944, 'there is no example in history of a people saying we agree to renounce our country'.[24] At the beginning of British Mandate rule in Palestine, the Zionist Organization in London explained that the 'problem' with democracy is that it

> too commonly means majority rule without regard to diversities of types or stages of civilization or differences of quality ... if the crude arithmetical conception of democracy were to be applied now or at some early stage in the future to Palestinian conditions, the majority that would rule would be the Arab majority ...[25]

As late as 1947, the director of the US State Department Office of Near Eastern and African Affairs warned that the plans to create a Jewish state 'ignore such principles as self-determination and majority rule', an opinion shared by 'nearly every member of the Foreign Service or of the department who has worked to any appreciable extent on Near Eastern problems'.[26]

THE 'TRANSFER' CONSENSUS

'Disappearing' the Arabs lay at the heart of the Zionist dream, and was also a necessary condition of its realization.[27]

Tom Segev, Israeli journalist and historian

If there are other inhabitants there, they must be transferred to some other place. We must take over the land.[28]

Menahem Ussishkin, chairman of JNF, member of the Jewish Agency, 1930

There was a logical outcome to the Zionist view of the indigenous Palestinians. As Israeli historian Benny Morris described it, 'from the start, the Zionists wished to make the area of Palestine a Jewish state'.[29] But 'unfortunately' the country already 'contained a native Arab population'. The 'obvious and most logical' solution was 'moving or transferring all or most of the Arabs out of its prospective territory'.[30]

How this ethnic cleansing was achieved is described later on, but for now, it is important to realise just how central the idea of 'transfer' (the preferred euphemism) was to Zionist thinking and strategising. The need to ethnically cleanse Palestine of its native Arabs was understood at all levels of the Zionist leadership, starting with Ben-Gurion himself. More than a decade before the State of Israel was born, the Zionist leader told the 20th Zionist Congress that 'the growing Jewish power in the country will increase our possibilities to carry out a large transfer'.[31]

Forcing out the Palestinians was only a problem for Ben-Gurion in terms of practicalities, as he did 'not see anything immoral' in 'compulsory transfer'.[32] By 1948, Ben-Gurion was 'projecting a message of transfer', and had created a consensus in favour of it.[33] A few months after becoming Prime Minister of the new state, Ben-Gurion said that 'the Arabs of the Land of Israel' had 'but one function left – to run away'.[34]

Ben-Gurion was not the only leader explicit about the need to ethnically cleanse Palestine. Joseph Weitz, JNF Director of Land and Forestry for 40 years, was passionate about the need for transfer. In a meeting of the so-called 'Committee for Population Transfer' in 1937, Weitz pointed out that:

> the transfer of Arab population from the area of the Jewish state does not serve only one aim – to diminish the Arab population. It also serves a second, no less important aim which is to evacuate land presently held and cultivated by the Arabs and thus to release it for the Jewish inhabitants.[35]

Weitz was a key influence on pre-state Zionist 'thinking and policy', 'well-placed to shape and influence decision-making regarding the Arab population on the national level and to oversee the implementation of policy on the local level'.[36] Others with powerful positions in the Zionist movement expressed their support for transfer, such as the director of the Jewish Agency (JA)'s immigration department, who told a JA Executive meeting in 1944 that the 'large minority' (the Palestinian Arabs) set to be inside Israel 'must be ejected'.[37]

That almost 'none of the Zionists disputed the desirability of forced transfer – or its morality' should not be a surprise: 'transfer was inevitable and inbuilt into Zionism – because it sought to transform a land which was 'Arab' into a 'Jewish' state'.[38] It explains the 'virtual pro-transfer consensus' in the JA Executive, and indeed, the support for transfer amongst the Zionist leadership's leading lights in the 1920s, 1930s and 1940s.[39]

In fact, the historical evidence that we *do* have regarding the Zionist desire for 'transfer' probably only represents a fragment of the total amount. Early on, Zionist leaders learned that 'under no circumstances should they talk as though the Zionist program required the expulsion of the Arabs' since 'this would cause the Jews to lose the world's sympathy'.[40] Thus while in public, 'discretion and circumspection' were necessary, 'in private, the Zionist leaders were more forthcoming'.[41]

Sometimes, there was more overt self-censorship. For example, the Jewish press coverage of the 20th Zionist Congress 'failed to mention that Ben-Gurion, or anyone else, had come

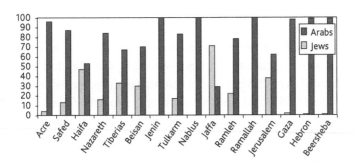

Figure 2   Palestinian population by subdistrict in 1946

Source: Walid Khalidi, *Before Their Diaspora*, Washington, DC: Institute for Palestine Studies, 1984, p. 239.

out strongly in favour of transfer', and when the Zionist Organization published the official text of the addresses given at the Congress, 'controversial' sections were omitted.[42] Those taking minutes in meetings of Zionist organisations could be asked to 'take a break' 'and thus to exclude from the record discussion on such matters' such as 'transfer'.[43]

THE CALM BEFORE THE STORM

By the time that Britain had decided to get out of Palestine and hand the problem over to the United Nations, the Zionists were ready for the revolutionary moment they knew was necessary to create a Jewish state in Palestine. Effective Zionist lobbying, particularly in the USA, combined with an ineffective strategy from the Arabs, meant that when it came to the vote, 33 nations voted in favour of partition, 10 abstained and 13 rejected the plan.[44]

Partition was not the reasonable compromise it can sound like. The Palestinian Arabs were more than two thirds of the population of Palestine, and were a majority in all but one of the 16 subdistricts (Figure 2).[45] Jews owned around 20 per cent of the cultivable land, and just over 6 per cent of the total land of Palestine.[46]

Despite the fact that Jews were a clear minority in terms of both population and land ownership, the Partition Plan handed over 55.5 per cent of Palestine to the proposed Jewish state (Israel would later increase that by strength of arms to 78 per cent). The Palestinian Arabs would make up almost half the population of the new Jewish state, territory even set to include the Negev which was 1 per cent Jewish.[47] The Jewish state would include prime agricultural land and '40 percent of Palestinian industry and the major sources of the country's electrical supply'.[48]

Given that the indigenous Palestinians, without their consultation, were set to lose more than half their country to a settler population who explicitly wished to alienate the land from the Arabs forever, it has taken quite a feat of propaganda to represent the Palestinian rejection of 'Partition' as inflexible and irrational.

At the time, there were a few dissenting voices, Jews who opposed the violent conquest of Palestine and instead favoured sharing the land with the Palestinian Arabs.[49] But by the time of the unilateral declaration of Israeli statehood in May 1948, the vast majority of the Zionist leadership was prepared for the forced 'transfer' they knew was necessary for the old propaganda slogan of a 'land without a people' to become a darkly self-fulfilling prophecy.

Far from being weak and outnumbered, a British military intelligence assessment in 1947 had 'estimated that an embryonic Jewish state would defeat the Palestinian Arabs' even if they were secretly helped by neighbouring Arab states.[50] Throughout the war, in fact, Jewish forces 'significantly outnumbered all the Arab forces' sometimes by nearly two to one.[51]

THE NAKBA (CATASTROPHE)

The dismantling of Palestinian society, the destruction of Palestinian towns and villages, and the expulsion of 700,000 Palestinians ... was a deliberate and planned operation intended to 'cleanse' (the term used in the declassified documents) those parts of Palestine assigned to the Jews as a necessary pre-condition for the emergence of a Jewish state.[52]

Henry Siegman, *New York Review of Books*

Another prominent left-winger stated: 'I don't have any problem with the fact that we threw them out, and we don't want them back, because we want a Jewish state.'[53]

Cited by Meron Benvenisti, in *Sacred Landscape*

The term 'ethnic cleansing' is a relatively recent addition to the English language, originating from conflict in the Balkans in the latter part of the twentieth century. Using the expression can immediately conjure up televised images of faraway wars and horrific brutality; but an exact definition is surprisingly hard to come by.

In 1993, *Foreign Affairs* journal carried an article on the subject, where the author admitted the difficulty in pinning down a definition.[54] Nevertheless, he concluded that 'at the most general level', ethnic cleansing is 'the expulsion of an "undesirable" population from a given territory due to religious or ethnic discrimination, political, strategic or ideological considerations, or a combination of these'.

The following year, the *European Journal of International Law* published a piece by Drazen Petrovic about identifying a 'methodology' of ethnic cleansing.[55] Petrovic noted that it is probable the term had its origin 'in military vocabulary', where 'cleaning' a territory is used 'in the final phase of combat in order to take total control of the conquered territory'. 'Ethnic' is added because 'the "enemies" are considered to be the other ethnic communities'.

On the local level, ethnic cleansing policies include 'the creation of fear, humiliation and terror for the "other" community' and 'provoking the community to flee', with the overall aim being 'the extermination of certain groups of people from a particular territory, including the elimination of all physical traces of their presence'.

Even more revealingly for our focus on Palestine in 1948, Petrovic also differentiates between the short- and long-term goals of ethnic cleansing policies. In the short term, the goal 'could be effective control over territory for military or strategic reasons', but long term, the objective is 'the creation of living conditions that would make the return of the displaced community impossible'.

The Palestinian Catastrophe ticks all of the boxes. The Zionist leadership understood it (we have already read about their pre-war strategising on the matter), as did the soldiers on the ground. In the Jewish military plans, Palestinian villages became 'enemy bases', their inhabitants 'dehumanised in order to turn them into "legitimate targets" of destruction and expulsion'.[56]

Some Zionist propagandists, unable to sustain any longer the long-standing lie that the Palestinians were told to leave by the Arab armies or simply left of their own volition, now try and suggest that the absence of documents signed by the Zionist leadership ordering blanket expulsions is somehow proof the ethnic cleansing never occurred.

In reality, once you dig beneath the surface, there is no shortage of evidence of orders from superiors to units on the ground. Moreover, it is now well known that Ben-Gurion 'usually resorted to a nod and a wink' rather than 'explicit orders', keenly and 'constantly aware of how history would judge his deeds'.[57] Israel's prime minister did, however, keep track in his diary of the so-called 'occupied and evicted villages'.[58]

The word 'cleansing' in Hebrew, *tihur*, was on 'every order that the High Command passed down to the units on the ground', while individual villages were either ordered to be 'cleansed' or 'destroyed'.[59] Haganah (the official pre-state Jewish armed forces) orders in April 1948 were 'explicitly calling for the "liquidation" [*hisul*] of villages'.[60] A standard operational order of May 1948 instructed the army company concerned:

> to expel the enemy from the villages... to clean the front line ... To conquer the villages, to cleanse them of inhabitants (women and children should [also] be expelled), to take several prisoners ... [and] to burn the greatest possible number of houses.[61]

An important role in the ethnic cleansing of Palestine was played by the so-called 'Plan Dalet', adopted by the Haganah military leaders in March 1948. The aim of the plan was 'to clear the interior of the country of hostile and potentially

Photograph 1   Palestinians leaving their homeland after the Arab-Israeli war of 1948 (UNRWA photo, 1948).

hostile Arab elements', and thus 'permitted and justified the forcible expulsion of Arab civilians'.[62] In May, Ben-Gurion wrote a letter to the Haganah brigade commanders to remind them that 'the cleansing of Palestine remained the prime objective of Plan Dalet'.[63] By the end of March, the head of the Haganah had already appointed a 'Committee for Arab Property' charged with managing the increasing number of empty Palestinian villages and homes.[64]

Khaled Diab

'I remember everything. On the night of October 27, 1948, it became clear that the village would soon fall to the Israeli army. The people fled in fear of a massacre similar to the several others that happened in villages like Deir Yassin, where more than 100 men, women and children were murdered in cold blood by Israeli forces. All those who could walk across the Galilee Mountains to Lebanon did. But due to the birth of my sister one month before, my parents couldn't walk the distance to Lebanon, so they stayed. After more than 20 hours of walking in fear we arrived in Lebanon. We slept under trees with a blanket that was given to us. We thought we would be in Syria for a few weeks, only until we were allowed to return home.'

Source: Institute for Middle East Understanding, 'Untold stories: Khaled Diab', 9 April 2008, http://imeu.net/news/article008407.shtml.

MASSACRES AND EXPULSIONS

In another meeting Ben-Gurion stated, 'We decided to clean out Ramle.'[65]

Tom Segev

Creating terror and panic amongst civilians through atrocities – as well as direct, forced expulsions – are an integral part of an ethnic cleansing campaign. Estimates for the number of massacres carried out in 1948 vary – 24 is one suggestion, 33 another.[66] Some atrocities, when dozens of Palestinians were executed at a time, are easier to agree on as constituting a 'massacre'. But there were also many cases of random killings: 'two old men are spotted walking in a field – they are shot. A woman is found in an abandoned village – she is shot.'[67]

Massacres were significant because of the way in which they created a general sense of panic amongst neighbouring villages and towns, and a subsequent increase in Palestinians who fled their homes in fear (unbeknown to them at the time, never to return). Deir Yassin remains one of the most notorious massacres, where between 100 and 120 villagers were murdered, including families shot down 'as they left their homes and fled down alleyways'.[68]

Deir Yassin was far from being an isolated case of the deliberate murder of civilians. In the village of Khisas, for example, in December 1947, Jewish forces 'randomly started blowing up houses at the dead of night while occupants were still fast asleep', an attack that killed 15 villagers.[69] After the incident received unwelcome international attention, Ben-Gurion publicly apologised – only a few months later to include the assault 'in a list of successful operations'.

Across the country, Palestinians were terrorised into leaving. In Mejd al-Kroom, twelve men were randomly selected and shot dead in front of the others, while in Safsaf, 70 Palestinians were murdered in front of the villagers who had not already run for their lives.[70] In Dawayima in October 1948, 'villagers were gunned down inside houses, in the alleyways and on the surrounding slopes as they fled' (80–100 died).[71]

The massacres were often a prelude to the emptying of individual villages. While many Palestinians left their homes through fear of the advancing Zionist forces, some were forcibly driven from their communities by soldiers. A notorious case in point was the ethnic cleansing of Ramla and Lydda in the summer of 1948, two neighbouring Palestinian cities actually outside the intended borders of the Jewish state.[72]

In Lydda, the military assault ended with a handful of Israeli soldiers and hundreds of Palestinians dead. Shortly after conquering both towns, Israeli soldiers began expelling the population. Yitzhak Rabin, a commander at the time, had asked Ben-Gurion what should be done about the inhabitants, to which the prime minister responded dismissively, 'Expel them.'[73]

In Ramla, the Israeli soldiers banged on the doors of houses with 'the butts of their guns' shouting through bullhorns 'go to Ramallah!'[74] Altogether, an estimated 50,000 Palestinians were forced to march to the West Bank, with some of the refugees dying on the road 'from exhaustion, dehydration and disease'.[75] In Lydda, which became the Israeli town of Lod, around 98 per cent of the Palestinian population were expelled.[76]

Other communities experienced a similar fate, with incidents of emptied villages mined to prevent Palestinians returning, shots being fired over fleeing civilians to 'encourage' their flight, and columns of refugees targeted with mortar fire and makeshift bombs dropped by aircraft – all 'to speed them on their way'.[77]

Despite the mass of available evidence from eyewitnesses, survivors, perpetrators and historians, Zionist apologists have tried to confuse the issue about why the Palestinian refugees left their homes. One oft-repeated lie is that the refugees were simply responding to orders by advancing Arab forces, a propaganda claim tied up with the idea that the nascent Israeli state was fighting a desperate war of self-defence.

In fact, the ethnic cleansing of Palestine began *before* Israel unilaterally declared independence, and before the Arab states had (half-heartedly) joined the battle. An estimated half of the eventual total of dispossessed Palestinians had been 'cleansed' before the 'Arab-Israeli' war even began.[78]

In a period of less than seven weeks leading up to Israel's creation and the Arab-Israeli war, 200 Palestinian villages 'were occupied and their inhabitants expelled'.[79] From 15 May to the time of the first truce in June, a further 90 villages were 'wiped out'. Even before that, starting in December 1947, the evacuation of Palestinians from their towns and villages was principally due to Jewish 'attacks or fear of impending attack'.[80] It was a pattern that would continue through April–June of 1948, when every 'exodus occurred during or in the immediate wake of military assault'.[81]

Historian and Middle East specialist, Charles D. Smith affirms that during the war with the Arab states, 'the Israelis embarked on a deliberate policy of ousting Arabs from the territories they took over'.[82] Israeli historian Ilan Pappe observes that 'not allowing people to return to their homes after a short stay abroad is as much expulsion as any other act directed against the local people with the aim of deportation'.[83] Historian Benny Morris, likewise, makes it clear where responsibility lies:

> Above all, let me reiterate, the refugee problem was caused by attacks by Jewish forces on Arab villages and towns and by the inhabitants' fear of such attacks, compounded by

expulsions, atrocities, and rumours of atrocities – and by the crucial Israeli Cabinet decision in June 1948 to bar a refugee return.[84]

SHOOTING THE HARVESTERS

Even as Israel was concluding armistice agreements with the Arab states, there were acts of ethnic cleansing. In January 1949, almost 1,000 Palestinians were expelled, while others were 'transferred' to other villages inside the new Jewish state.[85] A couple of months later, a further few hundred Palestinians were expelled from two villages, usually forcibly taken to the West Bank in trucks.[86] In June, up to 1,500 Palestinian refugees

---

Nimr Khatib

'So the people of Mujaydil were forced to flee… While we were escaping there was shooting at us. Of those who escaped through the main road to Nazareth … four or five young men were killed and wounded… Some other people stayed in their hideaway… a great number of them were killed in the olive groves… The old people and children who couldn't run away and escape … hid in the Latin monastery till the next day, [when] the army vehicles arrived and took them and let them down on the edge of Nazareth. We heard that the old men and women who could not leave the houses and didn't get to Nazareth – after a period of time their families crept into al-Mujaydil and found them dead, killed in the houses. And from that time they sealed off al-Mujaydil and not one of the people was allowed to enter…'

Source: Nakba Oral Histories, as told to Isabelle Humphries, *Washington Report on Middle East Affairs*, May–June 2008, pp. 28–9, http://www.wrmea.com/archives/May-June_2008/0805028.html.

---

were violently 'pushed across the border' in one night, while in November, an estimated 1,500–2,500 Bedouin were again 'pushed' over the border.[87]

A striking example of these 'belated' expulsions was the experience of the Palestinian city of Majdal. The majority of the town's population had fled in fear of the advancing Jewish forces, but some had remained. In November 1948, around 500 were expelled from Majdal to the Gaza Strip.[88] During 1949, hundreds of Palestinians managed to return to the town, but meanwhile, the Israeli government was busy settling new Jewish families there.[89]

These remaining Palestinians were put under military government, 'concentrated and sealed off with barbed wire and IDF guards in a small, built-up area commonly known as the "ghetto"'. The formal transfer of the town's 'undesirable' population was completed between June and October of 1950, so that eventually, there was an 'Arab-free Majdal'.[90] This became the Israeli port city of Ashkelon.

The problem faced by Israeli authorities in Majdal, of a returning Palestinian population, was a challenge faced in other parts of the country. These returning refugees were dubbed 'infiltrators'. Having gone to such trouble to 'cleanse' Palestine of its unwanted natives, the Israeli leadership was not prepared to tolerate even a piecemeal return; Prime Minister Ben-Gurion once said 'he viewed the infiltration problem "through the barrel of a gun"'.[91]

Typically, there was the 'security' excuse, justified by the incidents of persons crossing the border into Israel in order to carry out armed attacks. However, between 1949 and 1956, at least 90 per cent of all 'infiltrators' were motivated by social or economic concerns: they wanted to return home, search for relatives, harvest their crops and recover lost possessions.[92]

Israeli armed forces were brutal in their response to the returning refugees. Women and children, who had only crossed the frontier by a matter of a few hundred yards to gather crops, were murdered. Those 'wounded by patrols or ambushes were often killed off on the spot'.[93] The estimates for the total number of 'infiltrators' killed up to 1956 range between 2,700 and 5,000; the 'great majority of them unarmed'.[94]

WHEN THE DUST CLEARED

It would be an offence against the principles of elemental justice if these innocent victims of the conflict were denied the right to return to their homes while Jewish immigrants flow into Palestine and indeed, at least offer the threat of permanent replacement of the Arab refugees.[95]

Count Folke Bernadotte, United Nations Palestine mediator, assassinated in Jerusalem the day after his report was published in September 1948

The policy was to prevent a refugee return at all costs ... In this sense, it may fairly be said that all 700,000 or so who ended up as refugees were compulsorily displaced or 'expelled'.[96]

Benny Morris, Israeli historian

Physically preventing the return of refugees, however, was just one small part of a far bigger plan to make the ethnic cleansing a permanent fact and secure Palestinian land for the Jewish state. In June 1948, JNF director Josef Weitz had a meeting with Prime Minister Ben-Gurion in order to share the recommendations of the Transfer Committee. According to Weitz, Ben-Gurion 'agreed to the whole line'.[97]

There were five specific proposals: destroy villages as much as possible, prevent Palestinians cultivating their land, settle Jews in some of the villages and towns, enact tailor-made legislation and employ propaganda against a return. The legislation carried out will be examined in more detail in Part II, as Israel first categorised the refugees' land as 'absentee property' before transferring it all to the state Development Authority.[98]

Initially, however, the most fervent concentration of activity was focused on destroying the emptied villages, parcelling out their land to neighbouring Jewish settlements and, in some cases, directly repopulating Palestinian towns with Jews. The number of Palestinian villages and towns ethnically cleansed range from over 350 to more than 500 (often depending on what is classified as a recognised community) (Map 2).[99]

While the exact numbers differ, the overall scale of the Zionist conquest is clear. Around 87 per cent of the Palestinians who had lived in what was now Israel had been removed, while the majority of the Negev's Bedouin population, numbering around 65,000 in the 1922 census, 'were expelled in successive waves after 1948'.[100] An estimated four in every five Palestinian towns and villages inside Israel were either totally destroyed, or immediately settled by Jews.[101]

Benny Morris records how the number of Jewish settlements in Palestine increased by almost 50 per cent between 1947 and 1949, with most built on Palestinian land.[102] Other estimates are that 95 per cent of new Jewish settlements established between 1948 and 1953 were on absentee Palestinian property.[103] Former Israeli deputy mayor of Jerusalem, Meron

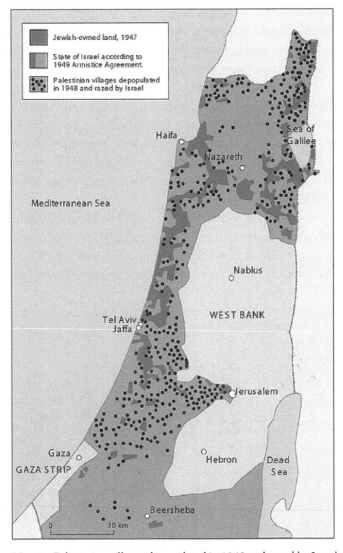

Legend:
- Jewish-owned land, 1947
- State of Israel according to 1949 Armistice Agreement
- Palestinian villages depopulated in 1948 and razed by Israel

Haifa

Sea of Galilee

Nazareth

Mediterranean Sea

Nablus

Tel Aviv
Jaffa

WEST BANK

Jerusalem

Gaza

GAZA STRIP

Hebron

Dead Sea

Beersheba

0   30 km

Map 2   Palestinian villages depopulated in 1948 and razed by Israel

Source: Adapted from Palestinian Academic Society
for the Study of International Affairs (PASSIA).

37

Benvenisti, has written of how, by mid 1949, 'two-thirds of all land sown with grain in Israel was abandoned Arab land'.[104]

In some cases, Palestinian towns emptied by atrocities and expulsions were more or less immediately resettled by the Israeli government with Jews. Ramle and Lydda, whose Palestinian population had been forced to trek eastwards, had a combined population of over 16,000 Jewish settlers by March 1950.[105] In 1949, Jewish immigrants were even settled in Deir Yassin. The dedication ceremony for the new settlement was attended by 'several Cabinet ministers, the two chief rabbis and Jerusalem's mayor'.[106]

An important part of Israel's effort to 'disappear' Palestine was changing the names on the map. Ben-Gurion appointed a Negev Names Committee, saying that Israel was 'obliged' for 'reasons of state' to remove Arabic names.[107] Between May

Photograph 2   Palestinian refugees in Jordan, in the aftermath of the 1967 war (UNRWA photo by G. Nehmeh, 1968).

1948 and March 1951, the Jewish National Fund's 'Naming Committee' 'assigned 200 new names'.[108]

POSTSCRIPT: THE SECOND 'NAKBA' OF 1967

No factual and necessarily brief account can, however, portray the overwhelming sense of bewilderment and shock felt by the inhabitants of the areas affected by the hostilities as the cataclysm swept over them.[109]

> UNRWA General-Commissioner,
> UN General Assembly, June 1967

While the 1948 Nakba condemned hundreds of thousands of Palestinians to enforced exile and dispossession, it is often forgotten that during the 1967 Six Day War, Israel was able to expel many more Palestinians. Around 300,000 Palestinians fled or were expelled from the Gaza Strip and West Bank, the vast majority from the latter territory.[110] Like the Nakba, many of these refugees (some of whom had already been expelled in 1948) had been 'forcibly evicted from their homes', their villages bulldozed to ensure that they would not be able to return'.[111]

In 1967, the conditions did not exist for executing a repeat of the mass exodus on the scale of, or greater than 1948; in particular, there was far more international scrutiny. Israeli forces therefore resorted to a more psychological campaign of fear. The UN's on the ground investigator noted 'persistent reports of acts of intimidation', including the use of loudspeakers on cars recommending the population go to Jordan.[112]

Others have described how 'Israeli buses and trucks were made available to tens of thousands of frightened Palestinians who were warned to vacate their homes and flee or remain to find they had no home'.[113] At least half of those who left the West Bank were already UN registered refugees, while in Jericho, 90 per cent of the population fled their homes.[114] Ultimately, of the thousands who fled the West Bank, less than 8 per cent were allowed by Israel to return.

Apart from the general attempt at 'encouraging' population flight, there were also several incidents of more direct ethnic cleansing. In Jerusalem's Old City, just days after its conquest, Israel targeted the eight-centuries-old Moroccan Quarter, ordering out hundreds of Palestinian families and demolishing all the homes.[115] The area then became the spacious plaza that exists until today in front of the Wailing Wall.

Meanwhile, in the Latroun area of the West Bank, close to the border with Israel proper, three villages were depopulated and destroyed. The Palestinian residents:

> were first told to leave their homes and gather in an open area outside the villages. At around nine in the morning, they were instructed over loudspeakers to march toward Ramallah. There were some eight thousand of them.[116]

An Israeli observer described how 'men and women, children and old people, had been forced to walk, in the stifling heat of over 30 degrees Centigrade, towards Ramallah, a distance of 30 km'.[117] The army then wasted no time, 'immediately' beginning to destroy the homes. In their place, Israel later built the recreational 'Canada Park', administered by the Jewish National Fund.[118]

The village of Beit Awa also met a similar fate. At 5.30am on 11 June, the 2,500 inhabitants were ordered out of their homes by Israeli forces, who told them 'to take two loaves of bread and to go to the hills surrounding the village'.[119] Two hours later, the troops started to demolish the houses 'with dynamite and bulldozers'. Three hundred and sixty homes were destroyed before a fraction of the original population was permitted to return.[120]

Qalqilya, a substantial West Bank city (now penned in behind Israel's Separation Wall), was fortunate to survive the 1967 occupation at all. As it was, 850 of the city's 2,000 dwellings were destroyed by the Israeli army, 98 per cent of them after the actual fighting had finished.[121] One returning resident described how 'the streets were devastated and there were no features to identify the city as ours'.[122]

Perhaps the biggest localised population movement was in the Jordan Valley, on the eve of war home to three large refugee

Photograph 3   Some of the tens of thousands of Palestinian refugees who fled the West Bank for Jordan in 1967 (UNRWA photo by G. Nehmeh).

camps clustered near Jericho. One Israeli who visited the camps soon after the war described them as 'ghost towns'.[123] Only a few of the camps' inhabitants were allowed back by Israel; the Jordan Valley's population fell by 88 per cent. Israel's first settlements in the OPT were in the Jordan Valley.[124]

ISRAELI INDEPENDENCE, PALESTINIAN CATASTROPHE: THE MAKING OF APARTHEID

Over the course of a generation, Palestine disappeared from the map. By 1970, just over 70 years since the Basle congress launched Herzl's dream of a Jewish state, Palestinian society had been shattered:

- Around half of all Palestinians were living outside of Palestine as dispossessed, denationalised refugees, prevented from returning home.
- One in seven Palestinians were living as second-class citizens in a state that defined itself as the homeland of the Jews.
- One in three Palestinians were living under military rule, increasingly subject to a regime of apartheid separation designed to facilitate the colonisation of the OPT by Israeli settlers. (Over half of the OPT population were themselves refugees from 1948.)

For political Zionism to come to fruition – for a Jewish state to be created in Palestine – it was necessary to carry out as large a scale as possible ethnic cleansing of the country's unwanted Arab natives. But even in 1948, and especially in 1967, Israel was unable to fully 'cleanse' the land of the Palestinians. As a result, Israel's fallback position was to implement an apartheid regime of exclusion and discrimination. Where the dispossession had been most effective – inside Israel's pre-1967 borders – apartheid could be less explicit. But in the OPT, home to a vast majority of Palestinians, Israeli apartheid had to be overt and iron-fisted. In Part II, we will examine conditions for Palestinians living in both Israel and the OPT.

Photograph 4 Dheisheh refugee camp, West Bank
(Andy Sims, http//www.andysimsphotography.com).

Part II
Israeli Apartheid

In 'Introducing Israeli Apartheid' we looked at a definition of apartheid under international law, and noted some of the useful comparisons with apartheid South Africa. In Part I, we saw how the Zionist settlement in Palestine developed, how the key figures directing the project for Jewish statehood were clear in their intention to expel the indigenous Palestinian Arabs, and how this dream became reality with the Palestinian Catastrophe in 1948.

Part II is concerned with describing just how Israeli apartheid has been maintained for the last 60 years; legally, practically, and what it has meant for the day to day lives of Palestinians inside Israel and the OPT. The first section deals with the way in which Israel has been able to regulate and legalise its system of apartheid, with a focus on the Palestinians inside the Jewish state. The second section examines the nature of Israel's occupation of the West Bank, Gaza Strip and East Jerusalem since 1967, a story of land theft, colonisation and ethnic separation.

ISRAEL: A STATE FOR SOME OF ITS CITIZENS

As a Zionist State, the State of Israel, contrary to other states, must regard itself as the State of a people the majority of which is not concentrated within its borders.[1]

Eliezer Schweid, 1970

One of the defences offered by apologists for Israel in the West is that Israel is unfairly 'singled out' amongst the countries of the world for condemnation. In fact, Israel is indeed a 'unique' case, but not in the way the propagandists like to acknowledge. Israel is not a state of all its citizens, like for example Britain, the USA or France, but rather a state for *some* of its citizens: Jews. Moreover, it is not just the state of its Jewish citizens: it identifies itself as the state of *all* the Jews worldwide, no matter where they live.[2]

Israel is in many respects admirably democratic, in terms of the electoral process and accountability, a robust legal system, as well as freedom of the press. Yet there is a fundamental contradiction at its core. As former Prime Minister Shamir put it, 'the Jewish state cannot exist without a special ideological content. We cannot exist for long like any other state whose main interest is to insure the welfare of its citizens.'[3]

This contradiction of a 'Jewish and democratic' state is highlighted by the distinction within Israeli law between citizenship and nationality.[4] All Israeli citizens (*ezrahut* in Hebrew) have equal rights in theory. But only its Jewish citizens are nationals (*le'um*) – because the whole purpose of political Zionism is a state for the Jewish nation. So, in fact, there is no such thing as 'Israeli' nationality in Israeli law, a distinction concealed by the fact that in Western democracies, 'citizenship' and 'nationality' are most commonly used inte changeably.

This facet of Israeli law has been highlighted in the courts, when individuals have sought to challenge the status quo. In 1970, Israel's Supreme Court supported a district court judge's denial of the existence of an 'Israeli' nationality.[5] The district judge explained his decision by declaring that there 'is no Israeli nation that exists separately from a Jewish nation'.

More recently, a group of Israelis tried to again bring the issue to the court's attention. One of the petitioners, Professor Uzzi Ornan, explained the inherent 'anti-democratic' nature of the citizenship/nationality distinction in Israel:

Most countries have citizens who categorize themselves not only according to their country of origin, but by ethnic, religious or cultural affiliation as well; however, all are considered to be of the same nationality...Imagine the uproar amongst the Jewish communities in the US or France, if the authorities tried to list 'Jewish' or 'Christian' in any official document.[6]

A 'Jewish democracy', as Israel describes itself, is thus a contradiction in terms, and it is clear which part of the equation has precedence when it really matters. In 1985, with Shimon Peres as prime minister, an amendment was passed to a Basic Law (one of nine that are the closest thing Israel has to a written constitution) prohibiting participation in elections to the Knesset for candidates who 'expressly or by implication' oppose 'the existence of the State of Israel as the state of the Jewish people'.[7] In addition, the Knesset Speaker can prevent a bill from even being discussed if it is judged to be anti-'democratic' or goes against Israel as a Jewish state.[8]

Palestinian citizens are also targeted by the state should they seek to resist Israel's ethnocracy. The Shin Bet security service sees part of its role being to 'thwart the activity of any group or individual seeking to harm the Jewish and democratic character of the State of Israel, even if such activity is sanctioned by the law'.[9] This includes going after individuals 'conducting subversive activity against the Jewish identity of the state'.[10] An example of this attack on dissent is the 2010 trial and imprisonment of Ameer Makhoul, a veteran community leader and activist who was warned the year before his arrest by a Shin Bet agent that he would 'have to say goodbye to his family'.[11]

In recent years Palestinians inside Israel have published serious, in-depth studies into the inherent discrimination of a Jewish state (also see Part III). The reaction was instructive: the *Jerusalem Post*'s editorial saw the call for a 'democratic, bilingual and multicultural' state as 'enticing and deceptive'.[12] A distinguished diplomat and academic condemned one constitutional draft as a plan 'for Israel's annihilation as a Jewish state' coated 'in the outward trappings of human rights and justice'.

What could be so threatening about a constitution based on human rights and justice? Adalah, 'the legal centre Arab Minority Rights in Israel', who authored one of the recent studies, noted that 'the reaction of the Israeli establishment … has been one of hysteria', characteristic of colonial regimes, which viewed any challenge to their constitutional structure, based on repression, as a strategic threat:

> Such was the reaction of the Apartheid regime in the 1950s when the African National Congress proposed the Freedom Charter, in which it demanded the transformation of South Africa into a state of all its citizens …[13]

INCLUSION AND EXCLUSION

> One certain truth is that there is no Zionist settlement and there is no Jewish State without displacing Arabs and without confiscating lands and fencing them off.[14]
>
> Yeshayahu Ben-Porat,
> *Yediot Aharonot* newspaper, 14 July 1972

Veteran Israeli·activist Dr Uri Davis wrote in his seminal book *Apartheid Israel* how, in 1950, 'the Israeli Knesset passed two defining laws': the Absentee Property Law, 'defining the boundaries of exclusion', and the Law of Return, 'defining the boundaries of inclusion'.[15]

The Law of Return has been described, in the absence of an Israeli constitution, as one of the state's 'most fundamental documents', defining 'the nation's raison d'etre' – namely, to be the national home for all Jewish people the world over.[16] In the words of Ben-Gurion, the Law has 'nothing to do with immigration laws' found in other countries.[17] The significance of the Law of Return is that since its passing:

Jews have been entitled to simply show up and declare themselves to be Israeli citizens ... Essentially, all Jews everywhere are Israeli citizens by right.[18]

At the same time as it offered automatic entry to Jews the world over, the State of Israel took a significant step toward consolidating in law the dispossession that had been previously effected at the barrel of a gun. Around six months after Israeli independence had been declared, a Custodian of Absentee Property was appointed and given 'absolute powers' over the lands and properties belonging to the Palestinian refugees.[19]

The Absentee Property Law of 1950 declared land to be 'abandoned' if the owner or owners were absent for even just one day from November 1947. Naturally, this included all the Palestinians pushed over the borders of the new Jewish state. The singular purpose behind this definition of 'absentee property' was 'to justify the taking of Arab lands and buildings for the sake of consolidating Israel's hold on the bulk of the land area'.[20]

The Israeli government sent inspectors out to Palestinian communities throughout the 1950s and 1960s 'to claim the land of those who could be defined as absentees on behalf of the Custodian'.[21] In 1953, the Knesset passed the Land Acquisition (Validations of Acts and Compensation) Law which confirmed the government's title to the land previously classified as 'absentee'.[22]

While it was the Absentee Property Law and subsequent legislation which proved to be the primary means by which Israel confiscated Palestinian land, there are many other examples of laws being used to transfer property into Jewish possession. Crucial to the way in which Israel consolidated its apartheid regime in the early years of statehood was the military rule placed over the remaining Palestinians until 1966.

The 'Defense (Emergency) Regulations' law meant that around 85 per cent of the Palestinians inside Israel lived under full martial law.[23] The military government was responsible for curfews, dividing the Galilee into 58 administrative sections, and implementing a 'permit' system for travel between them. The Regulations were also used to confiscate Palestinian land.

All in all, since 1948, Israel has passed 30 statutes that 'expropriated and transferred land from Palestinian citizens to state (Jewish) ownership'.[24] While most large-scale dispossession was carried out in the early years of the Israeli state, even in the 1990s, legislation like the 'Public Purposes Ordinance' was being used to confiscate hundreds of thousands of dunams – a unit of land measurement equivalent to 1,000 square metres – of private Palestinian land.[25]

By the mid 1970s, the average Palestinian community had lost around 65–75 per cent of its land.[26] Palestinian loss was Jewish gain: 350 of the 370 new Jewish settlements established between 1948 and 1953 were on Palestinian land.[27] Almost 200,000 Jews moved into empty Arab towns and villages, while in so-called 'mixed cities', Palestinians were concentrated in specified 'Arab quarters'.[28]

The legal infrastructure of Israeli apartheid is more sophisticated and complicated than that of apartheid South Africa, and necessarily so. For 'had discrimination against Palestinians been written into Israeli law as specifically as discrimination against Blacks is written into South African law, outside support would surely be jeopardized'.[29] The key

---

Hussein Mubaraki

'I am from al-Nahr, in the district of Akka, a village of 420 people. The village was 6,000 dunams (1,500 acres), including a river. It was a village rich in water, with fertile lands. Every day we had a wagon full of oranges, lemons and other produce which would go out to the cities, to Akka and Haifa…

[In 1948] we fled to Abu Snaan village … no, first we went to Tarshiha – then they hit Tarshiha with planes – and we came here … Just two or three families from our village found shelter here, not more … the rest are in Lebanon …

Military rule was like this: they made the military rule so that when we came from al-Nahr to here we couldn't go [back] there – it was a military zone … So that people couldn't go. If people went they would put them in prison. If you entered the military zone … that's what happened. In order to take the land …'

Source: Nakba Oral Histories, as told to Isabelle Humphries, *Washington Report on Middle East Affairs*, May–June 2008, pp. 28–9, http://www.wrmea.com/archives/May-June_2008/0805028.html.

---

then is to understand the role played by the so-called 'National Institutions' and in particular the legal mechanisms related to land ownership in Israel.

VEILING APARTHEID

Dr Uri Davis relates Israel's dilemma: on the one hand, 'the new state was politically and legally committed to the values of the Universal Declaration of Human Rights, the Charter of the United Nations Organization, and the standards of international law'.[30] Yet on the other hand, the 'driving force underpinning the efforts of political Zionism' was definitely not 'liberal democratic'.

While the 'key distinction' in Israeli apartheid is between 'Jew' and 'non-Jew', this is rarely explicitly stated in the text of Knesset legislation.[31] Instead, there is a 'two-tier structure' which 'has preserved the veil of ambiguity over Israeli apartheid legislation for over half a century'. The first tier is the Zionist institutions – the Jewish National Fund (JNF), the World Zionist Organization (WZO) and the Jewish Agency (JA) – that exist for the benefit of Jews.

The second tier is the way in which these institutions are 'incorporated into the body of the laws of the State of Israel', and in particular, 'the body of strategic legislation governing land tenure'.[32] This way, an organisation like the JNF, whose own constitution outlines the group's purpose as 'settling Jews' on the land, is assigned responsibilities and authority normally reserved for the government.

The benefits of this two-tier system are clear, as Ben-Gurion himself acknowledged. Israel's first prime minister described how the Zionist Organization 'is able to achieve what is beyond the power and competence of the State' which is precisely 'the advantage of the Zionist Organization over the State'.[33]

The JNF, as has already been described in Part I, was the organisation that took charge of land purchasing in the early days of Zionist colonisation. But with the creation of the State of Israel, the JNF did not go out of business. By October 1950, the government sale of land to the JNF had tripled its holdings, including around 40 per cent of Palestinian 'abandoned' land.[34]

The JNF was assigned three crucial roles in the Israeli apartheid infrastructure: firstly, it became a significant landholder in its own right; secondly, it was 'assigned specific tasks in the state that were by their nature governmental functions'; and thirdly, the JNF was given 'shared responsibility with the state for managing Israel Lands, now over 93 per cent of all land in Israel'.[35]

The body that oversees the management of some 93 per cent of Israeli land is the Israeli Land Authority, which replaced the previous Israel Lands Administration in land reforms passed in 2011. The JNF preserved the influential role it had previously enjoyed, with its representatives granted 6 of the 13 seats on the new Land Authority Council.[36] Thus the JNF, which directly owns 13 per cent of land in Israel, also shapes the policy of the ILA – and this, an organisation that in its own words:

> is not a public body that works for the benefit of all citizens of the state. The loyalty of the JNF is given to the Jewish people and only to them is the JNF obligated. The JNF, as the owner of the JNF land, does not have a duty to practice equality towards all citizens of the state.[37]

Furthermore, as part of the reforms, the JNF received thousands of acres of land in the Negev and Galilee in exchange for its land in urban areas, with the Land Authority administering the lands 'in a manner that will preserve the principles of the JNF'. The JNF proudly touted the reforms as allowing the organisation to 'to continue to develop the land of Israel on behalf of its owners – Jewish people everywhere'.[38]

A defining moment in legislating for a permanent apartheid was the Basic Law: Israel Lands passed by the Knesset in 1960.[39] Along with the 'Israel Lands Law' passed at the same time, this legislation established a truly comprehensive land regime in Israel for really the first time since 1948.

At the time, the chair of the Constitution, Law and Justice Committee told the Israeli lawmakers that 'the reasons for recommending this law, as far as I understand it, are to provide a legal cover for a principle that at its core is religious, and that is "the land shall never be sold, for the land is mine"' (quoting Leviticus 25:23).[40] A JNF report in 1973 described the 1960 Basic Law as giving 'legal effect to the ancient tradition of ownership of the land in perpetuity by the Jewish people'.[41]

Through the 1950s and into the early 1960s, the Israeli legislature passed laws that regularised the intimate relationship between the state and Zionist institutions like the WZO and the JA.[42] The JA, for example, an explicitly Zionist organisation that exists for the benefit of Jewish people, was given responsibilities normally reserved for the state, with regards to immigration and rural settlement within Israel's 1967 borders.[43]

Another way that Palestinian citizens of Israel are excluded by the apartheid regime is through the 'selection committees' that set the criteria for who can live in almost 70 per cent of Israel's towns.[44] These towns are under the authority of regional councils who have control over around 80 per cent of all the land. Applicants are assessed for 'social suitability' – by a committee made up of government and community representatives, and a senior official of the JA or WZO. The role of these committees was formalised in 2011 with the passing of legislation applying to around 42 per cent of all Israeli towns.[45] The law was denounced by Human Rights Watch as 'yet more officially sanctioned discrimination', and by legal rights group Adalah as instituting 'an apartheid-like regime in housing'.[46]

Photograph 5   Palestinians in Israel on an ADRID march in
May 2008 (Ben White).

TO BE A PALESTINIAN IN THE JEWISH STATE

The Palestinians who managed to stay inside the borders of the new Israeli state were faced with a shattered society – the majority of their compatriots were now refugees, their property confiscated. Rebuilding after such a trauma was made all the more difficult by the military government the Israeli government maintained over its Palestinian citizens for almost 20 years.

This martial law resembled the kind of all-pervasive intrusion experienced by Palestinians living under military rule in the OPT since 1967. Travel permits, curfews and political arrests were defining characteristics of a regime that for a generation stunted the Arab community's natural growth, prevented the development of an independent political consciousness and fragmented society.

All of which was no accident. Yehoshua Palmon, who in the first years of the Israeli state served under the Minister of Minorities and then as advisor to the prime minister on 'Arab affairs', assisted with the day-to-day running of the military government over the Palestinians. Years later, Palmon described his approach:

I opposed the integration of Arabs into Israeli society. I preferred separate development ... The separation made it possible to maintain a democratic regime within the Jewish population alone.[47]

Another Arab affairs advisor from the 1960s, Uri Lubrani, was frank about the state's relationship to the natives: 'we give them tractors, electricity, and progress, but we take land and restrict their movement ... if they [Arabs] would remain hewers of wood perhaps it would be easier to control them'.[48]

While the military rule over Israel's Palestinian citizens finished in 1966, other fundamental components of the apartheid structure have remained constant to this day.

One such characteristic of Israeli state policy is the so-called 'Judaisation' of areas where it is deemed there are too many Palestinians and too few Jews, done by confiscating land from Arabs and creating new Jewish settlements. Two particular regions have been the focus of such efforts; the Negev and the Galilee.

One notable example was the creation of Jewish 'Upper Nazareth' overlooking Palestinian Nazareth in the Arab-dominated Galilee. In 1953, one government official crystallised the official thinking of the time:

> The only chance of making Nazareth a partially Jewish city is by consolidating the [state] institutions there. It is a colonizing act with difficulties, but without it we will not be able to Judaize Nazareth.[49]

The Israeli government used a law called the 'Land (Acquisition for Public Purposes) Ordinance' in order to confiscate 1,200 dunams in and around Nazareth in 1954, claiming that the seized land would indeed be used in the public interest.[50] In the end, only 9 per cent of the land was used for government offices, with the rest forming the foundations of 'Upper Nazareth'.[51]

Other examples of this 'Judaisation' strategy include placing 'lookout' settlements 'around the Galilee to watch over Arab villages' and planting trees 'to guard against Arab encroachment on land'.[52] As a Jewish Agency planner explained, 'the goals of the hilltop Jewish communities' were: 'to prevent Arabs from "taking over" government lands, keep Arab villages from attaining territorial continuity and attract a "strong" population to the Galilee'.[53] In 2002, the JA announced major plans to encourage a total of 350,000 Jews to move to the Galilee and Negev, in order to guarantee 'a "Zionist majority" in those areas'.[54] Two years later, the Housing Ministry revealed plans to establish Jewish settlements in the Negev to 'block' the 'expansion' of Bedouin communities.[55]

Racist Israeli state policies are so commonplace that even outside observers can take for granted what in other contexts would be considered absurd or even outrageous. Thus the BBC can note how a Jewish town in the Galilee was set up by the JA 'as a bulwark against the surrounding Israeli Arab villages', or the *Washington Post* can record that Karmiel emerged as a 'Zionist response to the large Arab population in the Galilee', without outcry.[56]

This is just one way in which the Palestinian citizens of Israel are systematically discriminated against. Between 1957 and 1972, the proportion of the government's total development budget allocated to the Arab sector ranged from 0.2 to 1.5 per cent.[57] By 2008, the budget allocation for Arabs had increased to just 4 per cent, despite the fact that Palestinian citizens are one in five of the population, and half of Arab families are below the poverty line.[58]

Not only do the Palestinians within Israel live as second-class citizens in terms of land ownership and development budgets, but they are also frequently reminded that Israeli society considers their very presence to be a danger. This is commonly referred to as the 'demographic threat', a rather bland expression given that it is used to label Palestinians as dangerous on account of not being Jewish.

Discussing the 'threat' posed by the continued existence of Palestinians within Israel's borders and in the Israeli-controlled OPT is commonplace amongst Israeli politicians, military leaders, academia and the general public. In 2002, the Israeli government reconvened the previously defunct Demography Council, in order to specifically find solutions to the 'problem'.[59]

As the Israeli journalist Gideon Levy has pointed out, it is entirely illegitimate to talk of a 'demographic threat': 'Imagine what would happen if a discussion were held in the United States or Europe on "the worrisome natural growth of the Jews"', he points out.[60] Yet this is exactly the kind of language routinely employed to discuss the Palestinians in Israel. In 2005, a drop in the Arab birth rate was viewed as a success to be celebrated, with a senior Finance Ministry official quoted as saying that 'we are reversing the graph, to defend the Jewish majority in the country'.[61]

The *Ha'aretz* report said the drop was 'a clear result of the cutbacks in child support allocations over the past two years', before quickly adding that 'the cutbacks were driven by economic, not demographic reasons'. Just a couple of months later, however, the same newspaper reported that government officials had told the leader of a political party that the reduced child allowance was motivated by 'the desire to reduce the Arab birth-rate'.[62]

In Israel, there is no shame for the most senior of political leaders to describe one group of citizens as a threat on the basis of their ethnicity – as ex-prime minister Netanyahu did in 2003 – or to openly discuss how to make sure Israel 'remains Jewish', as then-prime minister Sharon did in 2005.[63] Press coverage of the latter's remarks noted that Israel's National Security Council had 'recently formulated a plan for "improving the demographic situation in Israel"'. It is in fact no obstacle to a successful political or military career to hold openly racist views regarding the Palestinians.[64]

The racism facing Palestinians in the Jewish state is found in both the legal structure and the rhetoric of political, religious and military leaders. One study in the late 1990s found 20 discriminatory laws, while legal rights NGO Adalah has an online database of what it describes as 'more than 50 Israeli laws that discriminate against Palestinian citizens of Israel in all areas of life'.[65] Even the US State Department sees Israel as practising 'institutional and societal discrimination'.[66]

Over the last decade, there has been a new push to advance and pass nationalistic and discriminatory laws in the Knesset.[67] Some initiatives have not advanced beyond the debate stage, while others have become law – all contributing to an atmosphere of heightened hostility towards Palestinian citizens (and indeed, also to non-Jewish African refugees and migrants).[68]

These recent developments include one of the more strikingly openly racist pieces of legislation. In 2003, the Knesset passed the 'Nationality and Entry into Israel Law' which bans Palestinians from the OPT who marry Israeli citizens from gaining residency or citizenship status.[69]

This 'temporary' law has since been repeatedly renewed by the Knesset, and in 2004 it already affected between 16,000 and 24,000 families, separating husbands and wives from their spouses and children.[70] The legal rights centre Adalah, in a 2008 press release marking yet another extension of the law, noted that 'no other state in the world denies the right to conduct a family life on the basis of national or ethnic belonging'.[71]

In 2012, Israel's Supreme Court upheld the ban on family unification, with Justine Asher Grunis writing in the majority verdict that 'human rights are not a prescription for national suicide'.[72]

There is one final feature of life for a significant number of Palestinians living in the Jewish state that encapsulates their inferior status in political Zionism: legal invisibility. There are two ways in which Palestinians inside Israel and their dwellings are rendered 'invisible': the unrecognised villages and the 'present absentees'.

Unrecognised villages are communities of Palestinians that the Israeli state has refused to officially acknowledge exist.[73] The Planning and Building Law of 1965 categorised the land on which a number of Palestinian villages lay as 'non-residential', thus making their presence illegal: 'the authorities simply pretended they were not there'. With no official status afforded to their communities, the residents receive no government services and their homes are targets for demolition.

There are dozens of such unrecognised villages inside Israel, with the majority concentrated in the south amongst the Bedouin of the Negev.[74] The total number of Arabs affected is around 70–90,000, disconnected from water, electricity, sewerage and the telephone network, and 'prohibited from developing infrastructure'.[75]

At the time of writing, the Israeli government seems set on a new plan that threatens dozens of unrecognised communities with demolition, leading to the forced expulsion of tens of thousands.[76] Designed to concentrate Palestinian Bedouin citizens in state-approved shanty towns, the so-called Prawer Plan is ethnic cleansing in the name of 'development'.[77]

There are also thousands of Palestinian individuals who the Israeli state classifies as internal refugees. In 1948, this group left their homes and towns but remained in what became Israel.

Yet under Israeli legislation, having been 'absent' from their home for even a short period of time, they lost their land and property. So although citizens, these Palestinians 'were forcibly prevented from reasserting possession over property declared to have been "abandoned"', and are called 'present absentees'.[78]

Around one in four Palestinian citizens of Israel are 'present absentees'.[79] The battle of the residents of two villages, Kafr Bir'im and Iqrit, to return home is instructive about the relationship between Israeli apartheid and the native Arabs.[80] Originally evicted by the Israeli army in November 1948, the Christian Palestinian villagers were assured that their removal was for 'temporary' security purposes.

By 1951, the villagers had still not been allowed home, and so they filed a claim in the Israeli High Court of Justice. Three months later, the army declared Kafr Bir'im a 'closed' military area requiring special permits for entry, and then in December, with the case still before the court, the army detonated every house in Iqrit. In 1953, the remaining houses of Kafr Bir'im were destroyed by the army. The lands of both villages were confiscated, declared 'state lands', and made available for Jewish development.

Since then, the persistence of the villagers has occasionally raised the profile of their case. In the mid 1990s, a government committee suggested a deal that the villagers rejected on the grounds that it severely restricted both the numbers allowed back and the amount of land to be recovered. When the case has come before the Israeli cabinet, such as in 1972 and 2001, the response has been the same: the villagers are refused permission to return on the grounds of 'security', and out of fear that it would set a 'precedent' for the other Palestinian present absentees.

PALESTINIANS INSIDE ISRAEL: CONCLUSION

Perhaps the core of Israeli apartheid as it affects the country's Palestinian citizens is the 'exclusionary land regime', a reflection of the historic objective of political Zionism: the land of Palestine without the Palestinians.[81] The three main tools of this regime are: physical dispossession; the system for 'the ownership and administration' of 'public' land; and the bureaucratic arrangements 'regulating land development and land-use planning'. The open racism faced by Palestinian citizens of Israel is simply a result of the central contradiction inherent in the idea of a 'Jewish democratic' state.

THE OCCUPATION

As mentioned briefly at the end of Part I, the necessity of the ethnic cleansing of the indigenous Palestinians presented Israel with a challenge after it occupied the rest of Palestine in 1967 (the West Bank, East Jerusalem and Gaza Strip). Excepting mass expulsions (unfeasible in terms of Israel's international relations and regional context), Israel would have to live with a massive Palestinian majority in the OPT. In order to maintain dominance over land access and natural resources therefore, and in order to keep the Palestinians fragmented and weakened, Israel had to develop an apartheid regime in the Occupied Territories far more explicit than what had already been in place since 1948.

Israel was faced with a problem, however, in that the international community viewed the Palestinian territories conquered in 1967 as occupied and only under temporary Israeli control, pending a peace agreement. International and humanitarian law also laid out strict provisions for what an occupying power could or could not do in the territory under control.

Faced with these obstacles, maintaining an apartheid regime to control the Palestinians had to be a gradual, unspoken and duplicitous process. Sometimes Israel has simply ignored what weak international protest emerged; other times Israel has resorted to legal fictions, or encouraged a religiously radical settler movement whose 'outposts' turn into official colonies. Most commonly, Israel resorted to hiding behind the excuse of 'security' considerations, slowing down or speeding up the pace of the colonisation according to 'peace process' sensitivities or periods of Palestinian violence.

Over the last half century, Israel has effectively integrated the conquered area with the pre 1967 territory, through a 'matrix of control' that incorporates Jewish colonies, settler-only roads, checkpoints, military bases, no-go zones and water resources.[82] The following is an overview of the mechanisms and character-istics of Israeli apartheid in the OPT.

LAND THEFT

> We enthusiastically chose to become a colonial society ... engaging in theft and finding justification for all these activities.
>
> Michael Ben-Yair, March 2002[83]

The main characteristic of Israel's rule in the OPT since 1967 has been land theft. Israel has tried to veil its rapacious land seizures with a veneer of legality and 'due process'. Thus in the aftermath of the 1967 war, the Israeli military introduced a number of 'Military Orders' designed to ease the takeover of Palestinian property.[84]

Israel has replicated inside the OPT many of the same land confiscation policies and laws that it used after 1948.[85] There was an added impetus after 1979, when 'government agencies started a large-scale project of mapping and land registration in order to discover public lands to which Israel could lay claim'.[86] If a Palestinian could not prove both private ownership and present use (i.e. if it was public land), it was seized.

An Amnesty International report in 1999 detailed how successive Israeli governments have manipulated the question of 'public land' for massive scale colonisation, including the cynical way in which Israeli authorities depend on Ottoman land legislation dating back to 1858.[87] Even more cynically, Palestinians have been subjected to discrimination based on prohibiting 'alien persons' from 'building on or renting state lands'. Ironically, while immigrants under the Law of Return (i.e. Jews) are given full rights, the definition of 'alien' includes almost the entire Palestinian population in areas occupied after 1967.

The pace of Israeli colonisation has varied, though both Likud *and* Labor governments have aggressively pursued substantial confiscation policies. Moreover, even during the years of the Oslo 'peace process', the Israeli government confiscated around 35,000 acres in the West Bank, 'much of it agricultural and worth more than $1 billion', in order to expand the settlements and build their bypass roads.[88] Between 1995 and 1999, Israel confiscated land equivalent to the size of London every year.[89]

By the mid 1980s, Palestinian cultivated land in the West Bank had dropped by 40 per cent.[90] By the spring of 2000, six months before the Second Intifada began, the Special Rapporteur for the UN's Commission on Human Rights estimated that since 1967, Israel had confiscated 60 per cent of the West Bank, a third of the Gaza Strip and a third of Palestinian land in Jerusalem.[91] In 2013, it was revealed that just 0.7 per cent of designated 'state land' in the West Bank had been allocated to Palestinians (a policy thus specifically denying Palestinians access to 23 per cent of the West Bank).[92]

Nabil Saba

'In 1972 the Israeli soldiers came to my family's home at the top of Beit Jala, and offered to buy the land from my father. We refused. So almost every day and night they would come to the house, to threaten us, to intimidate us. They would take me and my brothers to jail. They falsely accused us of supporting the guerrillas with 300 dinars, which was a lot of money in those days. They beat my brother in jail.

The Israelis would come to our home and put me and my brothers up against a wall. Then they would ask my mother which one of us she wants to see killed first. My mother would cry. After a year, we left the house, taking most of our belongings with us. We thought we would be away just temporarily; we left out of fear.

The soldiers came and demanded the keys. They wanted to occupy one room in the house, they said, to stop the guerrillas. After that, they stopped us going back to the house. I've never been back since.

If I were to go back, I would have a heart attack to see Israeli housing there. There were grapes, fig trees; they were all bulldozed, like you see them doing to the olive trees. My father, before he died, said he wished he could sleep just one more night in his house. I will never forget those words.'

Source: Interview with author.

SETTLEMENTS

There seems no doubt that the settlement project has been conceived, stimulated and implemented by the Government of Israel; colonization has not been a spontaneous popular movement taking place in the face of governmental resistance or indifference. Furthermore, this policy has been energetically followed for over 40 years by all administrations from 1967 until the present time.[93]

Amnesty International, 1999

[Ariel] Sharon, flying over the Occupied Territories once remarked: 'Arabs should see Jewish lights every night from 500 metres.'[94]

Eyal Weizman, *Hollow Land*

The land that Israel continues to confiscate from the Palestinians in the OPT is largely given over to illegal colonies of settlers and their infrastructure (Map 3). Since 1967, Israel has established more than 130 officially recognised settlements in the West Bank (including East Jerusalem), as well as the Gaza Strip's 16 settlements dismantled in 2005 (not to mention dozens of 'unofficial' outposts).[95] As for the number of residents, there are now well over half a million settlers in the West Bank and East Jerusalem combined, with the West Bank settler population hitting 350,000 in mid 2012.[96]

It is important to note that all the settlements are illegal under international law, a damning verdict returned time and again by bodies such as the United Nations and the International Court of Justice at The Hague. Although the Israeli government – and pro-Israel propagandists in the West – often try and cloud the issue, or claim that there is genuine legal disagreement, in 1967 the Israeli government itself was told that the settlements would be illegal.

In a 'Top Secret' memorandum, the Israeli Foreign Ministry's legal counsel concluded that 'civilian settlement in the

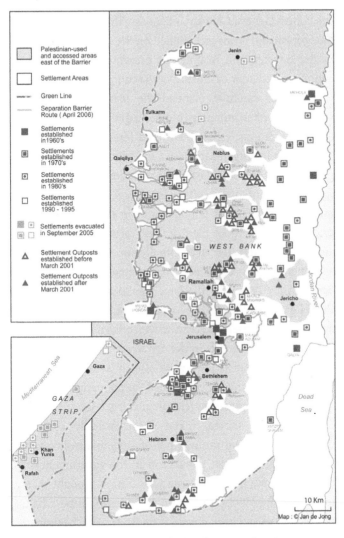

Map 3 Settlements established and evacuated 1967–2008

Source: Foundation for Middle East Peace.

administered territories contravenes the explicit provisions of the Fourth Geneva Convention', noting that the prohibition is 'categorical and is not conditioned on the motives or purposes of the transfer, and is aimed at preventing colonization of conquered territory by citizens of the conquering state'.[97]

Israel has carefully planned the location of important settlements, often grouping colonies together to form 'blocs' in strategic locations, especially around Jerusalem. In 1983, the World Zionist Organization and the Ministry of Agriculture prepared a settlement 'Master Plan' that 'envisaged the eventual incorporation of the West Bank into Israel, aiming "to disperse maximally large Jewish population in areas of high settlement priority..."'.[98] The goal, then, of these 'facts on the ground' is to create areas that Israel can eventually annex.

Sometimes it is assumed that settlement construction has been mainly driven by the Israeli political 'right', especially the religious zealots. In fact, over the decades there has been a remarkable consensus across the spectrum. For example, by the time that Labor left power ten years after the 1967 war, 'about 50,000 Israeli Jews were already settled in the new Jewish neighbourhoods established on the peripheries of the occupied areas annexed to Jerusalem'.[99]

What Labor started, Likud enthusiastically continued, more than doubling the number of settlements and almost quadrupling the settler population in the government's first term of office.[100] However, one would have thought that, at least after the 1993 Oslo Accords, there would be a halt, if not reduction, in Israeli colonisation. In fact, in the years that followed, the number of settlers *doubled* – including a 50 per cent rise to 147,000 settlers between 1993 and 1996 when Labor was in power.[101]

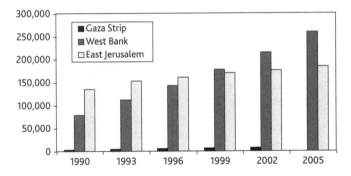

Figure 3   Settler population growth in the OPT, 1990–2005

Source: FMEP, http://fmep.org/settlement_info/settlement-info-and-tables/
stats-data/comprehensive-settlement-population-1972-2006.

Photograph 6   Har Homa settlement, outside Bethlehem in the
West Bank, May 2008 (Ben White).

69

Daoud Nassar

'We have been fighting to keep our land from the Israeli military since 1991. If anyone "claimed" to own the land he had to go and present his case to a military court. Some had no papers or documents to prove ownership and so lost their land.

When the [Second] intifada started the settlers wanted to confiscate the land. Sometimes they came with machine guns. One time I showed a settler my papers showing ownership of the land, and he said that he had papers from God. They tried to open a road through the land, they uprooted our trees, pulled down fences, broke water tanks, but we just kept mending everything. Now we try and keep a permanent presence here.

Our project here is called "Tent of Nations", a place to bring different religions, cultures and nationalities together. There are a lot of projects in Area A and B but this is not where it is important to do something. If we don't do something like this in Area C then the land might just be taken one day.'

Source: Interview with author.

'BYPASS ROADS'

> The roads regime, which is based on separation through discrimination, bears clear similarities to the racist apartheid regime that existed in South Africa until 1994.[102]

> B'Tselem report, 2004

An integral part of Israeli colonisation in the OPT is the network of bypass roads that link up colonies and further fragment Palestinian land. By 2000, these roads had a total length of 340 kilometres and took up 51.2 square kilometres in the West Bank.[103] Jeff Halper, of the Israeli Committee Against Home Demolitions, has described how these bypass roads are 'lined on both sides with "sanitary" margins that eliminate all Palestinian homes, fields and orchards in their path', incorporating 'the West Bank into Israel's national highway system'.[104]

The bypass roads, intended to serve Israeli citizens rather than Palestinians, are governed according to a discriminatory regime ranging from banning Palestinians to partial restrictions like physical obstacles and/or special permits.[105] In 2005 and 2006, new Israeli plans surfaced for the 'upgrade' of the bypass system, 'creating a Palestinian state of enclaves, surrounded by walls and linked by tunnels and special roads'. This 'would create an "apartheid" road network for Palestinians in the West Bank' whereby 'existing roads would be reserved for Jews, linking their settlements to each other and to Israel'.[106]

At around the same time, practical steps began to be taken by the Israeli occupation authorities to enforce the separation, with the Israeli military blocking 'Palestinians from driving on the main artery through the West Bank'. Apparently, the government approved plan would culminate in the barring of 'all Palestinians from roads used by Israelis in the West Bank', the purpose being 'total separation between the two populations'.[107]

By 2008, Israel was finding it hard to keep up even the pretence of democracy. For the first time in its history, the High Court of Justice issued an interim decision on a specific road (Route 443) that meant the closing of a road in the OPT to Palestinians, purely 'for the convenience of Israeli travellers'.[108] In an article about the 'two-tier road system', the *New York Times* quoted Limor Yehuda, attorney for the Association for Civil Rights in Israel, mentioning *that* word – 'apartheid'.[109]

Photograph 7   Bypass road south of Jerusalem, with olive trees ready for removal, July 2006 (Ben White).

Photograph 8   Palestinian man with his ID and Israeli military travel permission slip (Andy Sims, http://www.andysimsphotography.com).

Photograph 9   Rubble placed by the IDF to block Palestinian access,
west of Bethlehem, May 2008 (Ben White).

CHECKPOINTS AND CLOSURE

The checkpoint system belongs entirely to the Israeli
unwillingness to give up all of the territory of the West
Bank, including all of the settlements. The checkpoint
system is aimed at ensuring Israeli control over the lives of
the Palestinians.[110]

Yitzhak Laor

[The checkpoints'] function is to send a message of force and
authority, to inspire fear, and to symbolize the downtrodden
nature and inferiority of those under the occupation.[111]

Meron Benvenisti

Across the OPT there are hundreds of Israeli obstacles to
Palestinian freedom of movement, from manned checkpoints

to blocked roads and iron gates. The majority of these obstacles, including major, permanently manned checkpoints, are not on the Green Line, but rather restrict or completely prevent the free flow of pedestrians and traffic from one Palestinian town and city to another. The United Nations painstakingly documents the quantity and type of obstacles, which also include trenches, earth mounds, the Separation Wall (more later) and random or 'flying' checkpoints.

In December 2012, the UN's Office for the Coordination of Humanitarian Affairs (OCHA) in Jerusalem estimated there to be more than 500 obstacles in the West Bank.[112] OCHA also pointed out how 'these measures are frequently implemented in an unpredictable way', meaning that 'the total number of closure obstacles present at a given time, although indicative, does not fully capture the relative severity of the closure regime'.[113]

Israel claims that the checkpoints are there to fight terrorism. It is difficult, however, to understand what 'security' rationale there can be for preventing Palestinians from reaching their own weddings or blocking a village's only access road. An editorial in *Ha'aretz*, however, suggested that 'encirclement, or more bluntly, siege, of Palestinian villages' lacking 'even a pretense of having a security purpose' is in fact 'a real tool of severe and collective punishment'.[114]

The checkpoints and other obstacles are one way that Israel enforces the policy of 'closure' on the occupied Palestinians, a series of 'restrictions placed on the free movement of Palestinian people, vehicles and goods'.[115] Enforced 'by a complex bureaucratic-military travel permit system and a two-colour car licence plates system', 'closure' can be: internal (of towns and villages in the OPT); external (of the border between Israel and the OPT); or external including international crossings.

Figure 4   Births at military checkpoints

Shaza Younis

'I am a student at university in Nablus. But my family and I live in Jenin, and so I must make the difficult journey to Nablus through Israeli checkpoints. I never know how long it will take me to make this journey each time. Once, I left Jenin in the middle of the afternoon, and reached the checkpoint. Hundreds of cars were waiting, and the weather was so cold, so we continued walking to reach the other side. When I reached the soldiers, one of them suddenly pushed me down to the ground, claiming that I crossed the line. Then another Palestinian man walked forward and pushed this soldier, and so many soldiers attacked him, hitting him, and then taking him away – where I don't know.'

Source: Interview with author.

Contrary to the claim by some that this kind of collective punishment only became necessary with the suicide bombings of the Second Intifada, closure has been imposed by Israel on the OPT 'since the early 1990s', and 'is much too far-reaching to be seen as an ad hoc measure linked to Palestinian security performance'.[116] Between 1994 and 1999, Israel imposed a total of 499 days of closure; while by 1998, less than 4 per cent of Palestinians from the West Bank and Gaza Strip had permission to enter Jerusalem.[117]

THE SEPARATION WALL

The course of the wall clearly indicates that its purpose is to incorporate as many settlers as possible into Israel.[118]

> John Dugard, law professor and UN Special Rapporteur
> to the Human Rights Council on the Human Rights
> Situation in the Occupied Palestinian Territory

In 2003, Israel began work on the Separation Wall in the West Bank and East Jerusalem, a major development in the geography and control mechanisms of the occupation. The International Court of Justice's (ICJ) advisory ruling (see below) explained that the term 'Wall' was satisfactory, though in different places it features a 25 feet high wall, razor wire, trenches, sniper towers, electrified fences, military roads, electronic surveillance and buffer zones of up to 100 metres in width.[119]

The current route of the Wall is over 710 km in length, which as of July 2013 was 62 per cent complete, with 10 per cent under construction.[120] Around 85 per cent of the total length of the projected Wall lies inside the West Bank, with 9.4 per cent of West Bank and East Jerusalem land being caught between the Barrier and the Green Line.[121] The tens of thousands of Palestinians trapped in this 'no man's land' are isolated from the rest of the West Bank and require 'permission' to stay in their homes.[122]

The Separation Wall is also illegal. In a landmark case, the ICJ at The Hague ruled in July 2004 by 14 to 1 that 'the construction of the wall being built by Israel, the occupying power, in the occupied Palestinian territory, including in and around East Jerusalem, and its associated regime, are contrary to international law'.[123] The ICJ also ruled (14 to 1) that Israel is obliged to stop the Wall's construction, dismantle what has already been done, and 'make reparation for all damage caused by the construction of the wall'.

The ICJ decision came after the Separation Wall had already been condemned by numerous human rights organisations, including the International Committee of the Red Cross, who in an unusually strong statement in February 2004 denounced the Wall as '"contrary" to international law'.[124]

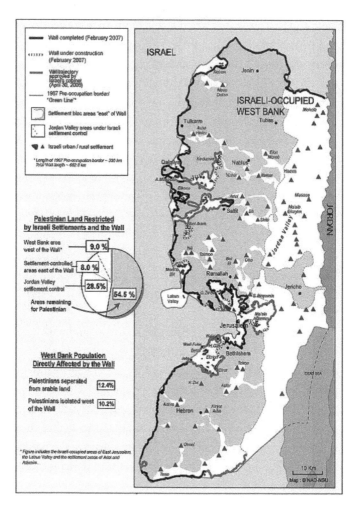

Map 4 Israel's Wall and settlements (colonies), February 2007

Source: PLO's Negotiation Affairs Department.

Amnesty International had already given their view the year before: construction of the Wall 'must be halted immediately' they said.[125]

The main justification given by the Israeli government and its apologists for the Wall is security, and specifically, Palestinian suicide bombers. Even as a 'security measure', the Wall is of debatable significance. For example, in late 2007, over 1,200 Palestinians were bypassing the Wall to work without permits in Israel on average *every week*.[126] While the Wall has contributed to a sharp drop in Palestinian attacks inside Israel, the Israeli security service itself attributed this improvement in 2006 to the ceasefire unilaterally implemented by Palestinian armed groups.[127]

The collective punishment of a population in the name of 'security' is, of course, expressly forbidden by the Geneva Conventions. Yet the best answer to those who pretend, like Sharon, that 'the terror built the fence', is to produce a map of the route.[128] The Wall's path does not lie on Israel's border with the OPT, but instead loops around to include the most important colonies on the 'Israeli' side. According to data from Israel's Interior Ministry, more than 75 per cent of all settlers will be included to the west of the Wall, by its present route (Map 4).[129]

The logic of the Wall is to grab as much land as possible, with as few Palestinians as possible. That is according to the Wall's main designer, Danny Tirza, who told the *Washington Post* in 2007 that 'the main thing the government told me in giving me the job was to include as many Israelis inside the fence and leave as many Palestinians outside'.[130] Tirza is himself a settler, 'who believes Israel has a historic right to the land between the Mediterranean Sea and the Jordan River'.

The Wall has had a devastating effect on Palestinians' ability to maintain their way of life. Neighbouring villages are now hours away, or completely unreachable. The first phase land grab alone, in the northern district of the West Bank, was 95 per cent prime agricultural land, including citrus and olive trees, cropland and pasture.[131] The land closed off by the Wall contains, 'coincidentally', 65 per cent of the West Bank Palestinians' water sources.[132]

Jayyous is one village that has been particularly affected by the Wall. David Bloom described in a piece for *The Nation* in 2004 how 'seventy percent of the villagers' farmland – and all their irrigated land – has ended up on the western side of Israel's "security fence"'.[133] The physical separation has paved the way for progressive, bureaucratic dispossession:

Once, 300 Jayyous farmers went to their lands every day. Then the wall was built. At first the gates were open. Then the Israelis placed locks and chains on them. Then they started locking the gates, only opening them for about fifteen or twenty minutes at a time. On October 2 the Israeli West Bank military commander, Gen. Moshe Kaplinsky, declared the area between the wall and the Green Line to be a closed military zone … [and] the rules of the seam zone require that no Palestinian can enter without a permit issued by Israel. However, Israeli citizens and those eligible to be citizens under the Law of Return are allowed to enter.

The situation in Jayyous is part of the 'new geographical and bureaucratic reality' created by the Wall 'for hundreds of thousands of Palestinians in the northern West Bank'.[134] But it's not just the north of the OPT; in East Jerusalem, an enormous concrete wall slices through Palestinian neighbourhoods,

Photograph 10   The Separation Wall in Bethlehem, September 2005
(Andy Sims, http://www.andysimsphotography.com).

while in Bethlehem, the north of the city has been turned into a ghost town.

Palestinian resistance to the Wall has been brutally suppressed. In numerous villages across the West Bank, demonstrations and other expressions of popular opposition have been met with tear gas, rubber-coated metal bullets, beatings, and live ammunition. More than 20 Palestinians have been killed in protests against the Wall, and hundreds injured.[135] Israeli soldiers have also targeted villages seen as 'trouble spots' for harassment, night raids and arrests.

EAST JERUSALEM

[Israel's] main concern seems to be to ensure that this conquest of Jerusalem be the last one.

The Economist[136]

> We break up Arab continuity and their claim to East Jerusalem by putting in isolated islands of Jewish presence in areas of Arab population … Our eventual goal is Jewish continuity in all of Jerusalem.[137]
>
> Uri Bank, Moledet party

After capturing East Jerusalem in 1967, Israel moved quickly to make the conquest an unquestionable – and irreversible – fact on the ground. The very same month, the Israeli parliament passed legislation extending Jerusalem's municipal boundaries to include the newly occupied territory.[138] This act of effective annexation has never been recognised as legal by the international community.

The annexation amounted to over 1,700 acres of East Jerusalem and the West Bank, and around a third of the land was also expropriated – most of it privately owned Palestinian property.[139] This land was then used for illegal settlement construction; by 2001, around 47,000 housing units had been built for Jews on this expropriated land – 'but not one unit for Palestinians'.[140]

A key Israeli goal in Jerusalem is to increase the proportion of the Jewish population, though until now, one in three of the city's residents are Palestinian (this increases to over 50 per cent on land annexed in 1967).[141] In order to win the 'demographic' battle, Israel physically isolates East Jerusalem from the West Bank, discriminates in land and housing plans, revokes Palestinian residency rights and neglects East Jerusalem infrastructure.[142]

Amir Cheshin served as Senior Advisor on Arab Community Affairs and Assistant to Teddy Kollek, Mayor of Jerusalem from

1965 to 1993. In his book, he gives an insider's perspective on Israel's racist discrimination, writing how:

the 1970 Kollek plan contains the principles upon which Israeli housing policy in east Jerusalem is based to this day – expropriation of Arab-owned land, development of large Jewish neighbourhoods in east Jerusalem, and limitations on development in Arab neighbourhoods.[143]

Thus when Ariel Sharon dedicated a new house of Jewish families in the Old City's Muslim Quarter in 1992, declaring, 'We have set a goal for ourselves of not leaving one neighbourhood in East Jerusalem without Jews', he was not speaking as an 'extremist' individual, but as a man in tune with official policy.[144]

The Palestinians of East Jerusalem have different identity cards to West Bank Palestinians. They are not Israeli citizens, but are under Israeli law, considered 'residents'.[145] Furthermore, their 'right' to residency can be revoked by Israel, if certain criteria are not met; in 2006 alone, over 1,300 East Jerusalem Palestinians had their residency rights revoked.[146] In this way, 'Israel treats them like other non-naturalised immigrants, though it was Israel, in effect, that immigrated to them'.[147]

Since so much land is deliberately 'off-limits' for Palestinian development, there is a huge housing shortage (in stark contrast to the willingness with which the Israeli government expands or initiates illegal Jewish colonies). Palestinians are also routinely denied permission to build, and are 'therefore faced with a choice': either build and risk demolition, or buy outside the municipality and 'in so doing lose their status as citizens of Jerusalem'.[148] Between 2004 and April 2013, 448

Palestinian homes built without permits were demolished, leaving 1,752 people homeless.[149]

WATER

Since the military occupation began in 1967, the Palestinians have been systematically discriminated against when it comes to accessing and using the water resources of their own land. On an annual per capita basis, 'Israelis consume more than four times as much water as Palestinians', while the aquifer that is the only water source for West Bank residents is left with only 17 per cent for Palestinian usage, after Israel takes the rest for its own cities and settlements.[150]

The Israeli military authorities have 'largely forbidden Palestinians from drilling new wells or rehabilitating old ones', as well as enforcing restrictions on the depth Palestinian pumps are allowed to reach down to – restrictions, of course, that do not exist for the settlements.[151] The settlements in fact continue to play a double role in denying Palestinians access to their water resources.

Firstly, the settlers use hugely disproportionate amounts of water, compared to the Palestinian towns and villages around them. In the heat of the summer in 1997, for example, the settlers of the Kiryat Arba colony were allocated more than eight times as much water per person as the Hebron Palestinians forced to live alongside this group of extremists protected by an occupation army.[152]

Secondly, the very location of the colonies is related to Israel's intentions of permanently holding on to those parts of the West Bank that would grant control over water resources like aquifers. In an interview in 2001, Ariel Sharon admitted that 'it's not by accident that the settlements are located where they are', adding that 'come what may' Israel must hold on to territory including the 'hill aquifer'.[153] Marwan Bishara, a Palestinian writer and researcher, noted that 'the map of the settlements looked like a hydraulic map of the territories'.[154]

In 2009, Amnesty International published a report on what it called Israel's 'discriminatory' control of water access and usage, 'restrictions ... denying hundreds of thousands of Palestinians the right to live a normal life'.[155] The report also noted that 'the Israeli army's destruction of Palestinian water facilities ... is often accompanied by other measures that aim to restrict or eliminate the presence of Palestinians from specific areas of the West Bank'.[156] In other words, part of a policy of ethnic cleansing.

DETENTION AND TORTURE

In light of the large number of those arrested and detained for a short time with very little interrogation, and the consistent use of degrading treatment, Amnesty International is concerned that the aim of the large-scale arrests may have been to collectively punish and to degrade and humiliate Palestinians not involved in armed opposition.[157]

Amnesty International, May 2002

Israel administratively detains Palestinians for their political opinions and non-violent political activity.[158]

B'Tselem

Since 1967, around 800,000 Palestinians have at one time or another been arrested by Israel.[159] During 'Operation Defensive Shield' in 2002, the Israeli army detained around 15,000 Palestinians across the West Bank, 6,000 of whom were still in prison by the end of 2003.[160] The number of prisoners, who are mostly held in jails inside Israel rather than the Occupied Territories, of course varies. As of 1 July 2013, support group Addameer cited 5,071 Palestinian prisoners from the OPT in Israeli jails, including almost 200 children.[161]

On average, 500–700 Palestinian children, 'some as young as 12 years', are 'detained and prosecuted in the Israeli military court system' every year.[162] The abuse of Palestinian children by the Israeli military is well documented. In 2012, a UK government-backed delegation of senior lawyers produced a report on child detainees citing several violations of international law, while the following year, the UN Committee on the Rights of the Child said that 'Palestinian children arrested by (Israeli) military and police are systematically subject to degrading treatment, and often to acts of torture'.[163]

Taken from their home or workplace by an occupation army, some Palestinians are not even able to defend the charges brought against them. That is because Israel holds hundreds of Palestinians under 'administrative detention', a polite name for keeping someone prisoner 'without trying them and without informing them of the suspicions against them'.[164]

Military commanders in the West Bank can detain someone 'for up to six months if they have "reasonable grounds to presume that the security of the area or public security require the detention"', the interpretation of which is left to the army.[165] This sentence can be renewed every six months, indefinitely, while the hearing is carried out without the detainee or their attorney being privy to the evidence. The number of Palestinians being held by Israel in administrative detention at any given time fluctuates; at the end of 2002, it was more than 1,000, while in July 2013, the figure was 136.[166]

Palestinian prisoners are routinely abused, both during their initial capture as well as in detention. In fact, it was only in 1999 that the Israeli High Court of Justice ruled against the use of torture during interrogations.[167] But a crucial loophole was left, meaning that security agents would not be held criminally responsible for applying prohibited 'physical pressure' if 'it is subsequently found that the methods were used in a "ticking-bomb" case'.[168]

Human Rights Watch noted that in 2002, the Israeli General Security Service (GSS) 'had up to that point employed "exceptional interrogation means" against ninety Palestinians':

> The readiness of the Attorney General to grant 'necessity defense' requests, along with the fact that since 1999 no Israeli Security Agency or GSS officer has faced criminal or disciplinary charges for acts of torture or ill-treatment, appears to have led to an erosion of the restraints initially imposed by the 1999 ruling.[169]

So while the 1999 court decision made a significant difference, it comes as no surprise that a May 2007 detainees' survey by two Israeli human rights groups found that interrogations by Israeli Security Agency personnel 'routinely included mental and physical ill-treatment'.[170]

HOME DEMOLITIONS

> The demolition of Palestinian houses is inextricably linked with Israeli policy to control and colonize areas of the West Bank.[171]

Amnesty International, 1999

The demolition of Palestinian homes has always been part of the occupation. In 1971, 2,000 houses in Gaza were cleared under the command of Ariel Sharon 'to facilitate military control'.[172] During the First Intifada of the late 1980s to early 1990s, over 2,000 houses were destroyed, while in the Oslo 'peace process' years, almost 1,700 'illegal' Palestinian homes were demolished by court order.

Yet it was during the Second Intifada that home demolition truly became a weapon in Israel's war against the Palestinians, when an estimated 5,000 Palestinian homes were destroyed in military operations, with tens of thousands of others left uninhabitable.[173] Sometimes there are bursts of intense destruction, such as in May 2004, when '298 buildings were demolished and 3,800 people were made homeless' in the Gaza Strip.[174] Almost 9 per cent of Rafah's population lost their homes in the first four years of the Second Intifada.[175]

By May 2007, 'about 1900 Palestinian homes have been demolished by the Civil Administration for lack of proper permits' and more than 600 homes were demolished as punishment (the latter practice ceasing in 2005).[176] A UN report in May 2008 revealed that in the previous seven years, Israel denied 94 per cent of Palestinian building permit requests in the more than 60 per cent of the West Bank under direct Israeli military and administrative authority.[177] Between 2006 and April 2013, 3,427 Palestinians were left homeless by Israeli demolitions in the West Bank.[178] In 2012 alone, some 540 Palestinian-owned structures were demolished for lacking an Israeli-issued permit, displacing 815 Palestinians, over half of them children.[179]

Amnesty International documented how 'house demolitions are usually carried out without warning, often at night, and the

> **Fatima al-Ghanami**
>
> 'They came at 10 o'clock in the morning. They didn't notify us the day before in order to let us prepare. They came at the house from behind, not from the front. They took everything out – all the furniture and utensils, all our belongings. The house had four rooms and a bathroom and it cost 70,000 NIS to build. We couldn't do anything, we were totally helpless. Some of my sons were here, but they didn't protest or resist because we all knew that no matter what we did they'd demolish the house anyway. We also had to pay for a bulldozer to come and remove the mess they left of the ruined home. That cost us 700 NIS right there. Afterwards my sons built me this temporary shack, but now it also has a demolition order … When I got the first demolition order for the old house I was sure they would never come. Now I know better. I know they'll come and do it … They might come tomorrow, they might come anytime. If they demolish this place I have nowhere to go and no money left. I have no idea what I'll do.'
>
> Source: Human Rights Watch interview, from 'Off the map: land and housing rights violations in Israel's unrecognized Bedouin villages', March 2008.

occupants are forcibly evicted with no time to salvage their belongings. Often the only warning is the rumbling of the Israeli army's US-made Caterpillar bulldozers beginning to tear down the walls of their homes.'[180]

MILITARY BRUTALITY

Like all occupations, Israel's was founded on brute force, repression and fear, collaboration and treachery, beatings and torture chambers, and daily intimidation, humiliation, and manipulation.[181]

Benny Morris, 2001

Since the beginning of the occupation in 1967, Israel has regularly needed to suppress Palestinian resistance with military force. During the First Intifada (uprising), 1987–93, Israeli security forces killed over 1,000 Palestinians, one in five of them children.[182] A third of this eventual death toll had already been reached after nine months.[183] Around the world, people watched the images of occupying soldiers breaking the bones of Palestinians, responding to civil disobedience and stone throwing with beatings and bullets.

The Second Intifada, however, which began in September 2000, saw Israel deploying its military on a far greater scale. In the first few days of the Palestinian uprising known as the Second Intifada, and 'before the wave of terror attacks against Israelis even began', the Israeli army fired 1.3 million bullets, a statistic that casts doubt on the claim that IDF violence is a 'regrettable but necessary' response to Palestinian terror (Figure 5). [184] As Derek Gregory points out, with the outbreak of rioting and protests by the occupied Palestinians,

> The IDF responded with astonishing violence; no Israeli civilians were killed by Palestinians until November, but by October Israel had already deployed high-velocity bullets, helicopter gunships, tanks, and missiles against the Palestinian population.[185]

From 29 September 2000 to the end of May 2008, over 5,100 Palestinians were killed by Israeli forces (Figure 6).[186] Over 1,000 Israelis died in Palestinian attacks. To get some kind of perspective on the scale of Palestinian fatalities, the US equivalent would be the violent deaths of 385,000 people – or more than 120 '9/11's.

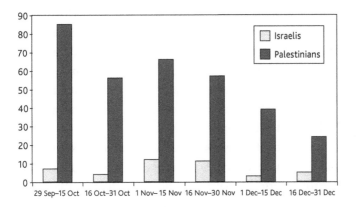

Figure 5   Second Intifada deaths,
29 September 2000–31 December 2000

Source: Middle East Policy Council, http://www.mepc.org.

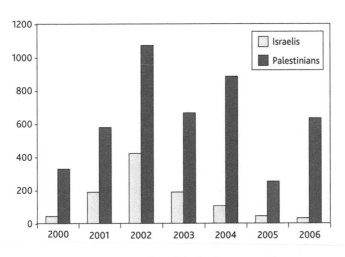

Figure 6   Second Intifada deaths, 2000–06

Source: Middle East Policy Council.

Some periods saw particularly high casualties, such as during Operation Defensive Shield in 2002 – the largest military operation in the West Bank since the 1967 war. Launched at the end of March after a string of bloody Palestinian suicide bombings, the Israeli army invaded the major Palestinian cities like Bethlehem, Ramallah, Nablus and Jenin, deploying tanks, bulldozers and helicopter gunships.

In a period of three weeks, around 500 Palestinians were killed and 1,500 were injured.[187] The operation was characterised by extensive curfews, the systematic destruction of Palestinian Authority infrastructure, and various documented human rights abuses and war crimes.[188]

The Gaza Strip has witnessed some of the most devastating IDF attacks and the worst human rights abuses. In May 2004, the Israeli military killed 45 Palestinians (including 38 civilians), and in six days made 575 people homeless.[189] Less than six months later, 'Operation Days of Penitence' saw more than 30 Palestinian children killed by Israeli forces in the first two weeks.[190] In the summer of 2006, after an Israeli soldier was captured by Palestinian fighters, Israel launched attacks that killed over 200 Palestinians in two months (including 44 children).[191]

In December 2008, and in the context of a blockade that is discussed in more detail below, Israel's launched an assault on the Gaza Strip that in terms of scale and devastation made previous massacres pale in comparison. The pretext was rocket fire, but what Israeli officials did not let on was that during the preceding Hamas-enforced ceasefire, rocket fire was reduced by 97 per cent compared to earlier in the year – a truce that ended with Israel's attack on 4 November 2008 killing six Hamas members.[192]

Over 22 days, the Israel military pummelled the Gaza Strip to such an extent that the International Committee of the Red Cross compared the devastation to 'the epicentre of a massive earthquake', with 'whole neighbourhoods' turned 'into rubble'.[193] For the first six days, the Israeli Air Force carried out over 500 sorties – an average of one every 18 minutes.[194]

During what was called 'Operation Cast Lead', the IDF killed some 1,400 Palestinians, including over 300 children (38 per cent of whom were under 11 years old).[195] Around 5,000 were injured. The Palestinian Centre for Human Rights and Al-Haq both estimated figures of over 80 per cent for the proportion of non-combatant deaths.[196]

More than 6,000 homes were totally destroyed or sustained major damage, with another 52,000 needing minor repair.[197] The UN Human Rights Council-commissioned Fact Finding Mission on the Gaza Conflict – referred to as the Goldstone report – concluded that Israel's attacks were 'directed by Israel at the people of Gaza as a whole, in furtherance of an overall policy aimed at punishing the Gaza population', in a 'carefully planned' assault intended 'to punish, humiliate and terrorise a civilian population'.[198]

Similar conclusions were reached by other observers. Amnesty International said that 'Israeli forces committed war crimes and other serious breaches of international law', including the shooting of 'children and women ... fleeing their homes in search of shelter'.[199] Human Rights Watch documented how Israel repeatedly fired 'white phosphorus shells over densely populated areas'.[200]

The Gaza Strip was subject to yet another onslaught in November 2012, in what the Israeli military referred to as 'Operation Pillar of Defense'. The eight-day-long attack killed at least 160 Palestinians, over a hundred of whom were civilians (including at least 30 children).[201] More than 1,000 were injured, of whom an estimated one third were children.[202]

There was also again widespread damage to property and civilian infrastructure. The UN estimated 450 houses destroyed or severely damaged, with 'bridges, schools, clinics, media offices and sports facilities' also all damaged.[203]

During the years of the Second Intifada, there were numerous documented cases of the deliberate murder of Palestinian civilians – including many children – by Israeli soldiers. According to Amnesty International, in 2003 alone the Israeli army killed more than 100 children (out of some 600 total Palestinian deaths that year).[204] By June 2013, almost 1,400 Palestinian children had been killed since 2000 'as a result of Israeli military and settler presence in the OPT'.[205] Some observers have concluded that the Israeli army was knowingly killing civilians, such as Physicians for Human Rights-USA, which after investigating the number of Palestinian deaths and injuries in the first months of the Intifada concluded that 'the pattern of injuries seen in many victims did not reflect IDF use of firearms in life-threatening situations but rather indicated targeting solely for the purpose of wounding or killing'.[206]

In Rafah, May 2004, siblings Asma and Ahmad al-Mughayr, aged 16 and 13 respectively, were both killed with a bullet to the head 'within minutes of each other on the roof-terrace of their home' as they took clothes off the drying line and fed the pigeons.[207] In a typical kind of response, the Israeli army immediately claimed that Asma and Ahmad had been killed by an explosion caused by Palestinian fighters. It is only when specific cases are investigated – normally by human rights groups or journalists – that the true facts come to light, and the IDF is forced to change its story.

On the rare occasion that the death of a Palestinian civilian is officially investigated, Israeli soldiers typically either escape discipline entirely, or receive a token, disproportionate punishment. According to Israeli NGO Yesh Din, a mere 3.5 per cent of the total 3,150 complaints filed against Israeli troops between 2000 and 2010 led to indictments.[208] One Israeli soldier later revealed that in his unit the attitude was, 'so kids got killed. For a soldier it means nothing. An officer can get a 100 or 200 shekel [£12.50–£25] fine for such a thing.'[209]

A particularly striking incident was the murder of 13-year-old Iman al-Hams, a schoolgirl from Rafah. In October 2004, she entered an area declared out of bounds by the Israeli army and shortly afterwards was riddled with bullets from automatic gunfire. Soldiers present at the time described how their commanding officer 'confirmed' the kill by shooting her in the head and emptying his magazine into her body.[210]

While this incident seems exceptional for its cold-blooded brutality, a B'Tselem staff member pointed out that 'disregard for human life and being trigger-happy is not exceptional at all' and that 'the exceptional part here is that it was documented'. In the end, the army acquitted the commander of Iman's death, accepting his defence that 'he fired into the ground near the girl after coming under fire in a dangerous area' – though without explaining 'why the officer shot into the ground rather than at the source of the fire'.[211]

In an extra twist, the commander in question was later *compensated* to the tune of over £10,000, as well as having all legal expenses reimbursed.[212] *Ha'aretz* noted that 'the judges who acquitted Captain R accepted his version of event [sic], in which he stated that the shots that he fired were not aimed directly at the girl's body ... and that he believed that the young girl posed a serious threat'. He has since been promoted to major.

During the Second Intifada, the Israeli military has also targeted the very fabric of Palestinian political, social and economic life. During Operation Defensive Shield, for example, the 'civilian infrastructure' of the Palestinian Authority (PA) was targeted, with the ransacking of PA ministries, the confiscation of hard disks, 'the burning of files and, more bizarrely, the wrecking of bathroom fixtures and upholstery'.[213] On several occasions, 'faeces were left in ministers' offices'.

Early in the Second Intifada, Palestinian boy Mohammad Al-Dura was filmed being shot to death, apparently by Israeli soldiers. Since then, the video has been the focus of a dispute

Photograph 11   The morning after an Israeli raid, Balata refugee camp, near Nablus, September 2006 (Ben White).

over an alleged manipulation of the footage. But writing in *Ha'aretz*, Gideon Levy pointed out the pettiness of the obsession with the Al-Dura film, when the general pattern of the murder of children is taken into account:

> Al-Dura became a symbol because his killing was documented on videotape. All the other hundreds of children were killed without cameras present, so no one is interested in their fate. If there had been a camera in Bushara Barjis' room in the Jenin refugee camp while she was studying for a pre-matriculation test, we would have a film showing an IDF sniper firing a bullet at her head. If there had been a photographer near Jamal Jabaji from the Askar camp, we would see soldiers emerging from an armored jeep and aiming their weapons at the head of a child who threw stones at them … it is certain that the IDF has killed and is killing children.[214]

SIEGE ON GAZA

> Israeli officials have confirmed … on multiple occasions that they intend to keep the Gazan economy on the brink of collapse without quite pushing it over the edge.[215]
>
> Secret US diplomatic cable, 2008

Israel imposed restrictions on the freedom of movement of Palestinians in the Gaza Strip as early as the 1990s, but a much more severe blockade was imposed following Hamas's electoral success in 2006 and then their defeat of Fatah in 2007 following violent clashes.

The goal of the blockade was clear, with an official in Israel's National Security Council confirming in 2007 that it was not about security, but rather to 'damage Hamas economic position in Gaza and buy time for an increase in Fatah support'.[216] The following year, then-prime minister Ehud Olmert said there was 'no justification' for allowing 'residents of Gaza to live normal lives while shells and rockets are fired from their streets and courtyards [at Israel]'.[217]

The key elements of Israel's lockdown of the territory – restrictions on imports, exports, and movement of people – remained in place until the summer of 2010, when following the murderous attack on the Gaza Freedom Flotilla, Israel sought to assuage international outrage by easing some of the measures.[218]

Yet core, punitive policies remained in place, especially with regards to what the Israeli military calls a "separation policy" designed to prevent goods and people moving between the Gaza Strip and West Bank. This has affected family life, studies, and businesses.[219]

As of July 2013, more than 70 per cent of the population in the Gaza Strip receives humanitarian aid, with an unemployment level of 31 per cent.[220] Exports from the Gaza Strip to the West Bank remain almost entirely prohibited – the territory's total exports dropped by 97 per cent between 2007 and 2012 (Figure 7).[221]

Monthly exports January–June 2013 amounted to 1.4 per cent of what exited monthly before 2007.[222] Israel permitted passage through Erez crossing for business people and medical patients, with a fraction of the pre-blockade numbers able to go in and out.

Palestinians' freedom of movement at the Gaza Strip's other crossing, Rafah, is now dependent on decisions taken by the Egyptian government, and relative ease or difficulty of passage

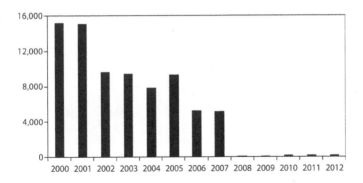

Figure 7   Exports from the Gaza Strip to the West Bank, 2000–12

has depended on the diplomatic and political dynamics between the authorities in Cairo and the Hamas government in Gaza.

Even at its best, the Rafah crossing has operated only patchily, and it is also no substitute for the facilities and capacity available at Israeli-controlled crossings such as Erez and Kerem Shalom.[223] Following President Mubarak's departure and the early political victories of the Muslim Brotherhood, Rafah became easier to use – with the military takeover of summer 2013, at the time of writing, there is a renewed closure of the Rafah border.[224]

Tunnels quickly emerged as a mainstay of the economy in Gaza, due to the conditions of the blockade. But this came at a cost: between 2007 and 2012, more than 170 Palestinian civilians were killed and over 300 injured working the tunnels between Gaza and Egypt.[225]

Israel's control over the Gaza Strip following the 2005 withdrawal of settlers and redeployment of troops has included attacks on fishermen working off Gaza's coast, as well as shooting attacks targeting civilians near the border fence.[226]

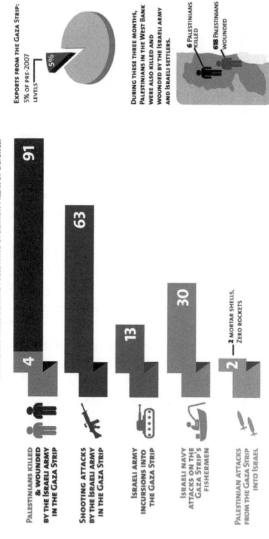

THIS INFOGRAPHIC SHOWS THE NUMBER OF ATTACKS ON THE GAZA STRIP BY THE ISRAELI MILITARY AND PALESTINIAN ATTACKS EMANATING FROM GAZA DURING THE THREE MONTHS FOLLOWING OPERATION PILLAR OF DEFENCE.

PALESTINIANS KILLED & WOUNDED BY THE ISRAELI ARMY IN THE GAZA STRIP — 4, 91

SHOOTING ATTACKS BY THE ISRAELI ARMY IN THE GAZA STRIP — 63

ISRAELI ARMY INCURSIONS INTO THE GAZA STRIP — 13

ISRAELI NAVY ATTACKS ON THE GAZA STRIP'S FISHERMEN — 30

PALESTINIAN ATTACKS FROM THE GAZA STRIP INTO ISRAEL — 2 — **2** MORTAR SHELLS, ZERO ROCKETS

EXPORTS FROM THE GAZA STRIP:
5% OF PRE-2007 LEVELS

5%

DURING THESE THREE MONTHS, PALESTINIANS IN THE WEST BANK WERE ALSO KILLED AND WOUNDED BY THE ISRAELI ARMY AND ISRAELI SETTLERS.

6 PALESTINIANS KILLED
618 PALESTINIANS WOUNDED

DATA FROM 22 NOVEMBER 2012 TO 21 FEBRUARY 2013. SOURCES: UNITED NATIONS OCHA, PALESTINIAN CENTRE FOR HUMAN RIGHTS, GISHA, PALESTINIAN AND ISRAELI MEDIA SOURCES.

Figure 8   Gaza ceasefire attacks, November 2012–February 2013

In 2010–11, for example, there were 30 documented cases over a 19-month period of the IDF shooting children near the fence, most of whom were 'shot whilst collecting gravel'.[227] To take another illustrative example, during three months of ceasefire beginning at the end of 'Operation Pillar of Defense' in November 2012, the IDF attacked Palestinian fishermen 30 times and conducted incursions into the Gaza Strip on 13 occasions.[228]

THE FRAGMENTATION OF PALESTINE

As far as I am aware, the imprisonment of a whole people is an unprecedented model of occupation – and it is being executed with frightening speed and efficiency.[229]

Tanya Reinhart, late Israeli academic and journalist

We would like this to be an entity which is less than a state, and which will independently run the lives of the Palestinians under its authority. The borders of the State of Israel, during the permanent solution, will be beyond the lines which existed before the Six Day War.[230]

Israeli prime minister Yitzhak Rabin in 1995
on Israel's view of the 'two-state solution'

Israeli colonisation and a decades-long military occupation have put immense pressure on Palestinian society in the OPT. The economy has been reduced to a stunted, aid-dependent shadow, a process that began long before the devastation of the Second Intifada. Post-Oslo, average unemployment rose by over 900 per cent between 1992 and 1996, while real per capita Gross National Product (GNP) fell by 37 per cent.[231]

That was nothing compared to the first two years of the Second Intifada, as the Palestinian economy experienced one of the deepest recessions in modern history, 'worse than the United States in the Great Depression or Argentina in 2001'.[232] By 2005, over 60 per cent of Palestinian households in the OPT were either in poverty or deep poverty, while the unemployment rate remained at just under 30 per cent in 2008.[233]

Collective punishment is routine, producing conditions designed to push Palestinians into leaving the land coveted by Israel. Israel's apartheid rule has territorially fragmented the OPT into an 'an archipelago of landlocked "sovereign zones"', subordinate Bantustans that Israeli architect Eyal Weizman describes as 'a permanently temporary Palestinian state'.[234]

Already by 2000, the West Bank had been fragmented into 227 separate enclaves, with only 17 per cent of the entire territory under full Palestinian control.[235] Around 88 per cent of these cantons were less than two square kilometres in size. The strategically placed colonies, the segregated roads, the Separation Barrier; Israel's iron grip on the OPT has only grown stronger with time.

> If one looks at a blueprint of a planned prison, it appears as if the prisoners own the place. They have 95% of the territory: the living areas, the work areas, the exercise yard, the cafeteria, the visiting area. All the prison authorities have is 5%: the prison walls, the cell bars, the keys to the doors, some glass partitions. The prison authorities do not have to control 20–30% of the territory in order to control the inmates.[236] (Jeff Halper, Israeli Committee Against House Demolitions)

Photograph 12 Qalandiya checkpoint near Ramallah, September 2005 (Andy Sims, htp://www.andysimsphotography.com).

PART II: CONCLUSION

Since 1948, Israel has maintained an apartheid regime over the territory it controls, whether inside the internationally recognised borders of the state or in the OPT since 1967 (Map 5). The nature of the apartheid regime in the OPT we have just considered (land theft, colonies, separate roads, the Wall, military brutality, etc.) is manifestly not simply a case of isolated human rights abuses, or even harsh restrictions in the name of security. The checkpoints, settlements and raids are all part of a systematic policy to consolidate and enforce Israeli apartheid in the territories.

The nature of Israel's system of control varies, according to the different dynamics on the ground and context-specific objectives. Inside the OPT, where the Palestinians vastly outnumber the settler population, a far more repressive regime

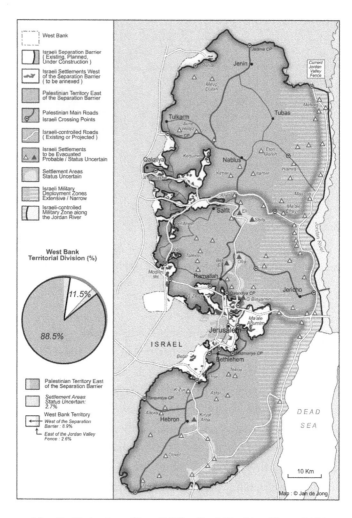

Map 5   Projection of Israel's West Bank Partition Plan – 2008

Source: Foundation for Middle East Peace.

is required to protect the colonisation process, compared to inside the Israeli state, where the Palestinian community is smaller and comparatively weaker.

Of course, around half of the entire Palestinian population as a whole are not ruled by Israel at all: they are the refugees and their descendants who were denationalised, expelled and forcibly kept out of their homeland by the first, dramatic acts of Israeli apartheid. Those who have remained are denied their basic freedoms as individuals and a people group, all in the name of the 'Jewish democratic' state.

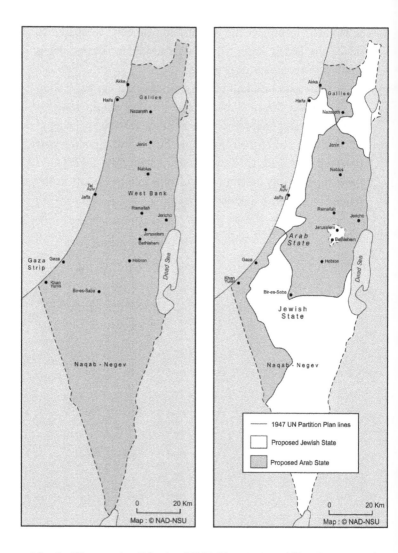

Map 6   Disappearing Palestine (PLO's Negotiations Affairs Department)

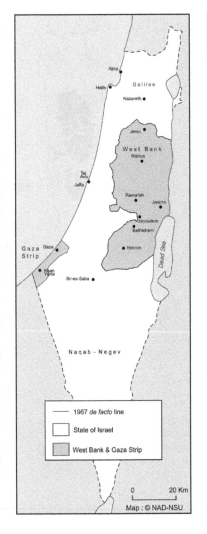

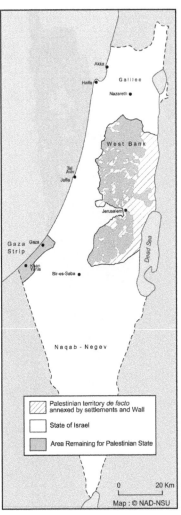

107

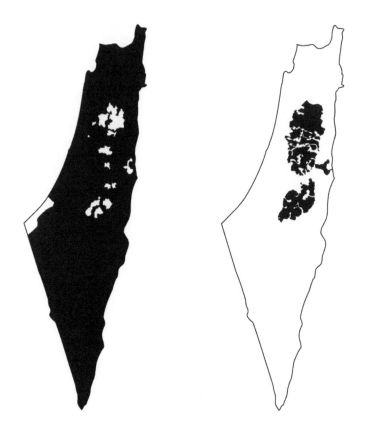

Map 7   Access 2013 (left to right) Israeli ID, West Bank ID,
Gaza Strip ID, stateless Palestinian refugee (arenaofspeculation.org)

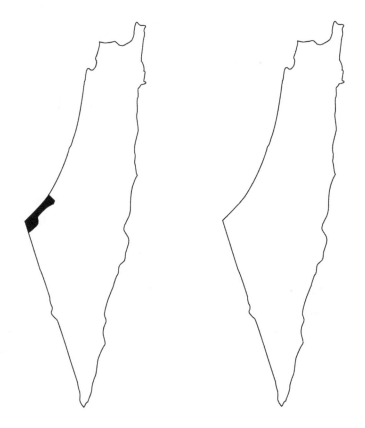

Part III
Towards Inclusion and Peace
– Resisting Israeli Apartheid

Resisting Israeli apartheid has always first and foremost been the work of the Palestinians who directly suffer the most. Families struggling over roadblocks with farm tools, villagers planting olive trees in groves surrounded by settlements, men waking at 4 am to queue at the checkpoints, activists living in fear of arrest or worse – ordinary people doing their best to live ordinary lives, confronting racism and colonial exclusion with defiance and dignity. But of course, defeating Israeli apartheid requires organised, committed and varied resistance strategies – locally and internationally.

Having introduced the concept of Israeli apartheid, how it came about and how it is being maintained, Part III of this book is intended to go a small way towards answering the question: 'What can we do about it?' Before discussing practical suggestions for international solidarity, however, we are going to have a brief look at a few organisations who are busy resisting Israeli apartheid where it matters the most: on the ground.

ON-THE-GROUND RESISTANCE

Adalah – the Legal Centre for Arab Minority Rights in Israel
Operating since 1996, Adalah ('justice' in Arabic) is at the forefront of legal efforts to challenge the system of Israeli apartheid. Independent, non-profit and non-sectarian, Adalah

represents the struggle of the Palestinian population inside Israel for individual and collective equal rights in all areas of life.

Its team of lawyers go to Israeli courts to file petitions on a wide range of issues: land access, planning rights, police accountability, budget discrimination and more. In 2012 Adalah worked on dozens of new petitions and follow up cases.[1] In summary, Adalah:

- Brings cases before Israeli courts and various state authorities.
- Advocates for legislation that will ensure equal individual and collective rights for the Arab minority.
- Appeals to international institutions and forums in order to promote the rights of the Arab minority in particular, and human rights in general.
- Organises study days, seminars and workshops, and publishes reports on legal issues concerning the rights of the Arab minority in particular, and human rights in general.[2]

'Adalah has been at the centre of some high-profile struggles, such as the ongoing campaign to hold accountable the Israeli police officers responsible for the deaths of 13 Palestinian citizens of Israel, killed in October 2000.[3] Adalah is also heavily involved with challenging the discriminatory land policies of the Jewish National Fund through the courts, and their website features many resources for those wishing to learn more, including a database of 'Discriminatory Laws in Israel'.[4]

While investing a lot of effort in particular court cases, the group has also continued to advocate what it sees are the fundamental changes that need to take place in Israel to guarantee equality for both Jew and Palestinian. To that end, Adalah published its 'Democratic Constitution' document in 2007, a document that in calling for a state privileging no religion or race over another, was condemned by Zionist apologists as calling for the 'destruction of Israel'.[5]

The Association for the Defense of the Rights of the Internally Displaced in Israel (ADRID)
In the context of the increasingly significant peace talks between Israel and the PLO in the early 1990s, Palestinians inside Israel began to worry that negotiations towards a comprehensive settlement were neglecting the concerns of the Palestinian people living as second-class citizens in the Jewish state.

In 1992, community activists held a meeting in Nazareth and agreed on the formation of an initial committee that would work for the rights of the present absentees.[6] This led to the first nationwide conference in 1995, when representatives of almost 40 destroyed villages met together, turning the committee into ADRID.[7]

ADRID emerged as an umbrella organisation with three main aims: firstly, to promote the right of return of the 'present absentees' to their villages; secondly, to unite the various disparate efforts of Palestinians in Israel already working towards this goal; and thirdly, to raise the profile of the plight of internally displaced Palestinians domestically and internationally.[8]

Since then, the group has gone from strength to strength. In 1998, on the 50th anniversary of the Nakba, thousands of internal refugees went on a march to an abandoned village, while in 2000, 850 participants attended a rally in Nazareth.[9]

Two years later ADRID was one of four international winners of 'The Body Shop Human Rights Award'.[10]

Uniting the various Arab institutions, political parties and religious bodies, ADRID's most celebrated annual event is the 'Return March' that takes place on Israeli Independence Day.[11] In 2008, on the state's 60th anniversary, thousands of Palestinian and Jewish citizens marched to the site of Safuriyya near Nazareth, a peaceful protest that ended with arrests and tear gas.[12] Throughout the year though, ADRID organises a variety of activities, and deserves much of the credit for the renewed steadfastness and determination of the Palestinian 'present absentees' to fight for their rights.

BADIL

While the official peace process has largely sidelined Palestinian refugees and Palestinian citizens of Israel, BADIL, a human rights organization in Palestine with a special focus on refugees and internally displaced persons, has worked hard at the grassroots and advocacy levels with the tough issues at the historic core of the conflict.[13]

Going strong since 1998, the centre emerged through 'recommendations issued by a series of popular refugee conferences in the West Bank and Gaza Strip'. It has maintained that grassroots and popular dimension through its activists-composed General Assembly, which elects BADIL's leadership.

According to BADIL, their 'vision, missions, programs and relationships' are defined by their 'Palestinian identity and the principles of international law', through which they seek 'to advance the individual and collective rights of the Palestinian people'. The organisation enjoys 'consultative status with UN ECOSOC, a framework partnership agreement with UNHCR' and is a member of various Palestinian networks on the ground, regionally, and globally.

Amongst their various activities, BADIL operates the Ongoing Nakba Education Centre, which 'aims to produce and make multi-media advocacy tools available to visitors, journalists, researchers, activists and the general public'.[14] The Centre is both a multimedia website, as well as a gallery, conference and library facility in Bethlehem.

In addition, BADIL also publishes analysis and updates in its publication *al-Majdal*, and conducts valuable research, such as its 2013 survey of Palestinian youth in historic Palestine, Jordan, Syria and Lebanon.[15] Keeping those links alive, as well as supporting solidarity strategies and campaigns like BDS (Boycott Divestment Sanctions), is what has made BADIL a go-to organisation for activists and academics alike.

Israeli Committee Against House Demolitions (ICAHD)

For over a decade, ICAHD has been focusing on one very specific aspect of Israeli apartheid: home demolitions and the discriminatory planning system which they physically enforce.[16] Founded by Israeli anthropologist professor Jeff Halper, the group's work ranges from rebuilding demolished Palestinian homes to campaigning domestically and internationally for Palestinian rights to be respected.

During the year, ICAHD organises 'working parties' of Jewish Israelis, Palestinians and international volunteers to help rebuild a demolished home. When possible, ICAHD members mobilise at the last minute to try and physically prevent the bulldozers from carrying out the demolition order. This 'hands on' experience with one aspect of Israeli apartheid has drawn ICAHD towards analysis and campaign work with a broader focus than just housing discrimination and demolitions.

ICAHD offer 'alternative' tours of East Jerusalem and the Occupied Palestinian Territories, in order to show people the 'facts on the ground'. For those who are not able to participate, ICAHD also provides information about the ever changing realities and policies to international diplomats and the media.

The organisation campaigns against the occupation, the violations of the Geneva Convention, and ultimately, the overall apartheid 'matrix of control' at the heart of Israeli colonisation efforts in the West Bank.[17] Halper's political analysis has been debate-shaping, highlighting Israel's exclusivist approach to the land, and providing a way to understand the evolving dynamic in the OPT.

In recent years, ICAHD has enjoyed successes and experienced challenges. It has chapters in the UK, USA and Norway, and in 2006, Halper was nominated for the Nobel Peace Prize for his work with the group.[18] But in 2008, ICAHD lost European Union funding, in what appeared to be a success for groups angry at ICAHD's role opposing Israeli apartheid.[19]

Popular Committees
In the last few years, the biggest threat facing thousands of Palestinians across the occupied West Bank has been the Separation Wall (see Part II). Communities have responded to this assault on their livelihoods by creating 'Popular Committees Against the Wall', grassroots, locally orientated initiatives intended to coordinate resistance to Israel's occupation policies.

Made up of those who are seen as trusted within the village the Committees also focus on Israeli land confiscation for settlements, a practice often closely tied up with the development of the Wall. There are Popular Committees all over the West Bank, including the Hebron and Bethlehem regions in the south, East Jerusalem, Ramallah and further up to the north.

In the village of Budrus, the first Committee was formed in the autumn months of 2003, quickly formulating rules for the organised protests against the Wall.[20] Other villages followed suit over the next couple of years, with perhaps the most famous example being Bil'in, in the Ramallah district.[21] Bil'in, whose story has often been covered by the international media, earned attention by forming a Popular Committee in early 2005, and organising regular non-violent demonstrations against the Wall.[22]

The Popular Committee in Bil'in has since organised international conferences held in the village that every year have attracted hundreds of delegates and notable figures (such as Palestinian political leaders and international politicians).[23]

The relative success of the Committee, whose members have penned internationally published articles and pursued the legal path in the Israeli courts, has also made them a target for harassment by the Israeli soldiers.[24] While the Popular Committee in Bil'in has made the most headlines, Palestinians in dozens of affected villages have mobilised to protect their fields and olive groves, knowing that in many cases, they are fighting for their continued existence in the land.

Popular Committees have also been behind new forms of protest, such as the 'Bab al-Shams' tent village established by hundreds of activists in January 2013 between Jerusalem and Ma'ale Adumim settlement.[25] Popular committees have also coordinated with activists inside Israel in order to carry out protests against issues like the Prawer Plan the expulsion of Bedouin Palestinian citizens in the Negev.[26]

Zochrot

While the remains of Palestinian villages, communities and mosques lie all over Israel, many Israelis today have no idea about the ethnic cleansing that took place in 1948, nor the 'hidden history' that lies beneath the surface of modern-day Israeli cities, picnic parks and forests.

Zochrot, Hebrew for 'remembrance', is an organisation made up of Israelis concerned with raising awareness of the Nakba amongst their own people. As a member put it, 'most Israelis don't want to know this word [Nakba]' or even 'hear it'.[27] The group is not just simply about education and history; it is also very much about challenging Israeli apartheid as it stands today.[28]

One of Zochrot's activities is the placing of signs that commemorate Palestinian villages destroyed by Israel during the Nakba in the places where these communities once stood. This can bring them into conflict with Jewish Israelis who object to such 'political' actions, or even the Jewish National Fund itself. One year, Zochrot put stickers up around Tel Aviv, placing the words 'I almost forgot – today is Nakba Day' in speech bubbles coming out of people's mouths.[29]

Zochrot takes groups of Israelis to visit the remains of destroyed Palestinian villages, trips that can also include Palestinian refugees sharing about what village life used to be like.[30] On their website, Zochrot explain the hope behind their work, that by

bringing the Nakba into Hebrew, the language spoken by the Jewish majority in Israel, we can make a qualitative change in the political discourse of this region. Acknowledging the past is the first step in taking responsibility for its consequences. This must include equal rights for all the peoples of this land, including the right of Palestinians to return to their homes.

PALESTINIANS FORGE NEW VENTURES

The political stagnation between Fatah and Hamas and the comatose peace process stand in stark contrast to a host of initiatives by Palestinians on the ground and in the Diaspora relating to a whole variety of issues. Together, they show ways in which new generations of Palestinians are taking action, rejecting approaches they see as inadequate, reconnecting across colonial borders, and providing resources and tools appropriate for community and solidarity mobilisation.[31]

In Palestine, a number of young activists have organised around questions such as national reconciliation, opposing Israeli plans for ethnic cleansing in the Negev, and voicing opposition to policies of the Palestinian Authority and Hamas.[32] Gaza Youth Break Out and the 15 March 2011 protests stand out, but more widely there are increased links between youth in the West Bank, Gaza, Israel and regional refugee camps which, in part, are due to the opportunities offered by social media.[33]

Another recent venture has been the campaign for elections for the PLO's Palestine National Council (PNC), and as part of that, a push for voter registration in different countries through Palestinian associations, networks and activists.[34] According to those behind the call, it is based on 'years of campaigning and organizing amongst Palestinians across the world, seeking a representative national institution that reflects the demands and positions of its people'.[35]

Other recent initiatives include Al-Shabaka, a 'Palestinian Policy Network' producing analysis and briefs with a focus on international law, human rights, and Visualising Palestine, which designs 'creative visuals to describe a factual rights-based narrative of Palestine/Israel'.[36] These organisations are making links amongst Palestinians, and between Palestinians and policy-makers and solidarity activists the world over.

INTERNATIONAL SOLIDARITY

While Palestinians and Israelis continue to resist apartheid on the ground, there is an indispensable role to be played by people around the world in realising a just peace in Palestine/Israel.[37] This small section will take a brief look at some of the possible strategies already being used by different groups around the world; there are many more ideas, and in every context, one tactic will be better than another.[38]

As with every movement, there can be disagreements about what strategies are the most effective or appropriate. The important point is that building a global campaign against Israeli apartheid that will really make a difference takes a whole variety of activities and strategies, by people from all walks of life: trade unions, religious groups, students, national politicians, students, town councillors, artists and many more besides.

At the back of this book there is a 'Resources' section where you will find a list of organisations and websites who work as part of the Palestine solidarity movement.

Boycott, divestment, sanctions

In 2005, a year after the International Court of Justice declared the Separation Wall to be illegal, a coalition of hundreds of

Palestinian political groupings, trade unions, community associations and NGOs, in Palestine and the Diaspora, launched a call for international activists to pursue strategies of Boycott Divestment Sanctions (BDS) as part of the Palestinian people's struggle for their rights.[39]

In several countries, there are ongoing efforts by various groups to institute Israeli apartheid-targeting boycotts. Some of these are 'consumer' boycotts, in other words, campaigns urging people not to buy products made in Israel, or sometimes just the illegal settlements. Some campaigners approach supermarket chains and ask them to ensure that any produce they stock from Israel has not come from colonies in the OPT.

Other boycotts can be of a more institutional nature, whereby a trade union or organisation urges its members to stop cooperating professionally with their relevant Israeli counterparts. There is also a campaign focusing on a cultural and sporting boycott of Israel, seeking to encourage the same kind of isolation experienced by the apartheid regime in South Africa.

Divestment means withdrawing an investment in Israeli companies or international companies that are profiting from doing business with apartheid. Although this could be done on an individual basis, it more commonly refers to the actions of a group – like a church denomination – that decides to sell its stock portfolio, or cancel some other kind of investment, in the offending company.

Sanctions are perhaps the most intense form of international pressure as they are enforced at the highest governmental levels. Broadly speaking, there are three kinds of sanctions: military, economic and diplomatic. Military sanctions include the cessation of arms sales to Israel, while economic pressure would mean cancelling preferential trade agreements that Israel currently enjoys with many individual nations, as well as collective blocs (like the European Union). Diplomatic sanctions means restricting or cutting official inter-government ties. For all of these, it is vital to lobby one's elected representative, raising the issue of Palestinian rights and demanding action be taken against the international law-breaking apartheid regime.

Since 2005, the BDS call has been taken up by activists and human rights campaigners the world over, making extraordinary progress considering the time scale and lack of resources. Consumer, academic and cultural boycott campaigns have all seen successes, as have ethical divestment initiatives.[40] For many activists, its strength has been the focus on its rights-based approach, the emphasis on enforcing accountability, and its origins with Palestinian civil society.[41]

In response, the Israeli government and lobby groups have begun to dedicate significant amounts of money and energy to fighting BDS, through expensive 'rebranding' advertising, smear attacks, legal threats, and propaganda trips for opinion-makers in different communities.[42]

Protest and education

For all the progress made in recent years with regards to awareness of, and participation in, the fight for justice in Palestine/Israel, there is still a lot more to be done. Protest marches, sit-ins, public lectures, film screenings, publicity stunts, subversive advertising, city twinning – there is a huge variety of creative options.

Supporting grassroots Palestinian and Israeli groups committed to resisting apartheid

Another excellent response to Israeli apartheid is to support the Israeli and Palestinian grassroots organisations that are committed to the struggle for justice. This could be in the form of direct financial giving, or perhaps by helping to raise awareness in your region or country of the work done by the group in question. Another way is to arrange a speaking event, or even a tour, so that representatives of these groups can come and share their experiences on the 'front lines' with international audiences.

Go there

Some people, from many different countries around the world, decide to actually visit Palestine/Israel, to see and understand the situation better, and to get involved with projects on the ground. This could be a short-term 'fact-finding' type trip or a longer term stay when there is time to invest personally in a particular initiative – such as a refugee camp community centre, environmental work, a group like ICAHD or a university. Of course, many go each year as pilgrims, and it is vital that 'Holy Land' tours include meetings with local Christian communities and exposure to the reality of life for Palestinians. While going there is not for everyone, seeing Israeli apartheid at first hand is a uniquely powerful experience, and those struggling against injustice on the ground welcome the solidarity.

TOWARDS A DIFFERENT KIND OF FUTURE

In what is deliberately intended to be an introduction to a big subject, this book does not have room for detailed descriptions of what a 'solution' either should or could look like in Palestine/

Israel. To some extent, the answer to the question about what the future must look like is contained by implication in this book's description of Israel's apartheid: a just, lasting peace for both peoples can surely only come about by removing the various elements of the apartheid regime.

It is important to remember that this is not about trying to go back in time, or trying to 'undo' things that cannot be undone. It is certainly not about wanting to make Jewish Israelis feel unwelcome in what is also their home. Put simply, the struggle against Israeli apartheid is about Palestinians having the same rights in the land as Jews do: all the rights they have been deprived of since Israel was built on the rubble of the Nakba.

When a permanent political settlement for the Israelis and Palestinians is discussed, the conversation often quickly turns to the 'two-state solution' and issues such as borders and Jerusalem – sensitive matters to be delicately negotiated. Most of this 'peace' talk is anything but, based on unawareness, or the deliberate concealing, of the reality of Israeli apartheid. It is incredible that diplomats and pundits can urge Palestinians to be more willing to 'compromise' as Israel continues its policies of colonisation and dispossession.

Peace for Israelis and Palestinians will not primarily emerge from the precise details of a geopolitical formula – the foundations of any such lasting, political settlement are human rights, dignity and justice. One of the biggest obstacles then is the persisting Zionist mindset – that informs practical policies – which sees Jews as having exclusive rights to the land. The Palestinian presence is tolerated, so long as the natives play by the rules.

As we have seen in this book, the result of this attitude towards the Palestinians is that even the most 'liberal' of

Israel's leaders have maintained or strengthened the apartheid system, ensuring that the Palestinian people remain scattered, denationalised and dispossessed. At the same time, Palestinian resistance to Israeli apartheid has too often suffered from crucial strategic errors as well as failing to acknowledge or reach out to the deep-seated fears of Jewish Israelis shaped by the Nazi Holocaust and anti-semitism.

In Part II, brief mention was made of some important documents put together by Palestinian community leaders inside Israel in the last few years. One of them was the 'Haifa Declaration', a paper prepared by the Mada Al-Carmel centre, with an emphasis that reflected the main thrust of the other draft constitutions and publications. The Declaration stated:

> our vision ... is to create a democratic state founded on equality between the two national groups ... [a solution that] would require a change in the constitutional structure and a change in the definition of the State of Israel from a Jewish state to a democratic state established on national and civil equality between the two national groups, and enshrining the principles of banning discrimination and of equality between all of its citizens and residents.[43]

The essence of this vision – democratisation, the dismantling of ethnocracy, a reimagining of self-determination – has begun to emerge in the Western mainstream as a critique of Israel's identity of a Jewish state, and a questioning of the 'two-state solution' orthodoxy.

While many analysts have questioned whether the two-state solution is realisable on the grounds of 'practicalities' (i.e. Israeli colonisation has advanced too far to be rolled back), others have suggested that some form of one-state framework would be the best means of realising the Palestinian people's full rights.

A good example of the growing prominence of this rethinking – which of course has a historical tradition and is thus more of a revival than an innovation – is the coincidental appearance of three related articles in March 2013 in the US media. These commentaries, by philosophy professor Joseph Levine for the *New York Times*, political scientist Ian Lustick in the *LA Times*, and human rights attorney Noura Erakat in *The Nation*, in different ways and from different perspectives critiqued Zionism and the idea of a 'Jewish state' in a way that until recently just did not appear in mainstream publications.[44]

Sadly, there are still those who advocate a compromise with Israeli apartheid, rather than its dissolution, arguing for 'realistic' expectations. The strange aspect of this approach, even leaving aside the morality of what it means for Palestinians, is that it assumes a peaceful future for Palestinians and Israelis can be built on injustice and domination. In fact, it will only be through dismantling Israeli apartheid, and guaranteeing the collective and individual rights of all the peoples of Palestine/Israel, that the people of the region can realise the kind of peaceful tomorrow previous generations have been denied.

Frequently Asked Questions

Isn't singling out Israel for criticism anti-semitic?
Racism that targets Jews, like all forms of racism, must be condemned and resisted. In fact, it is precisely this opposition to racism that motivates the critique of how Israel treats the Palestinians. Sadly, there are some genuine anti-semites who wish to try and use the peace and justice movement in Palestine/Israel to gain a platform for their ignorant bigotism. But this does not mean that to struggle against Israeli apartheid is anti-semitic.

To complain that Israel is being 'singled out' is at best illogical, and at worst, a deliberate attempt to shield Israel from criticism (itself a form of 'singling out'). Furthermore, Israel has been exempted from sanction for breaking international legal norms, benefitting from generous aid and preferential trade agreements from the USA and EU while doing so.

For the Palestinians, Zionism has meant expulsion, exile and subjugation – so of course they will 'single out' Israel, as will those who are in sympathy and solidarity with them. You wouldn't hear a Tibetan activist being accused of 'singling out' China – so why should Palestinians or their supporters be treated any differently, just because it's Israel?

Criticising certain Israeli government policies is one thing. But surely demonising Israel, and denying its very right to exist as a Jewish state is anti-semitic?
'Criticise but don't demonise', the defenders of Israeli apartheid will urge, meaning that only they can define the boundaries of

acceptable debate. Some pro-Israel advocates try to set limits when it comes to discussing Israel and accusing someone of 'demonising' Israel can be a very effective smear tactic. It discredits their opponent's viewpoint and motivations, and intimidates the undecided.

One of these 'taboo' subjects is the nature of Israel as a Jewish state. In fact, although 'anti-semitism' is often the charge levelled at critics, among Jewish Israelis there is also much disagreement about whether a state should be defined in ethno-religious terms. But ultimately, the question of Israel's 'right' to exist as a Jewish state is not simply a matter of debate and controversy. For the Palestinians, it is something far more fundamental:

> When you demand that Palestinians acknowledge the 'right' of Israel to exist as a Jewish state, you are asking them ... to acknowledge that it was and is morally right to do all the things that were and are necessary for the establishment of a Jewish state in Palestine, even though these necessary things include their own displacement, dispossession and disenfranchisement.[1]

To question the right of a state to exist at the expense of an entire group of people is not 'demonisation', and nor is it 'anti-semitic'. For Israel to be a Jewish state, the Palestinians must accept continued dispossession and second-class status in their own country, which is not a recipe for a lasting peace for either Palestinians or Jewish Israelis.

The English have England, and the French have France. Why deny the right of the Jews to a state of their own?
On the face of it this sounds quite reasonable, but only because of confusion over the nature of the relationship between the

Israeli state and Jews. For example, France is the state of the French, every French person is a citizen of France and all citizens of France are French.[2] Yet with Israel, the self-proclaimed state of all Jews worldwide, the same statement is impossible:

> Israel is the state of all the Jews; all Jewish persons are by definition citizens of Israel; and all citizens of Israel are ... Jews. The third part of the proposition is clearly empirically wrong; thus the assertion that Israel is as Jewish as France is French cannot be sustained.[3]

The analogy with Islamic states like Pakistan or Saudi Arabia is also a flawed one, even though both have Muslim majority populations and incorporate aspects of interpretations of Islamic law into the state institutions and legal framework. Yet while some states privilege one religion over another, no other country 'claims to be the sole global representative of the faith' or 'grants citizenship to people solely because of their religion (without regard to place of birth or residence)'.[4] Most importantly, the question 'Why deny the Jews to a state of their own?' is misleading, as it is not merely a hypothetical discussion. Israel has been established as a state for Jews the world over *at the expense* of the Palestinians.

Undeniably, you can find racism in Israeli society. But why don't you condemn the hate-preachers and racists in Palestinian society as well?
Of course, there are some Palestinians who hold to racist views, and this is entirely condemnable. Sometimes this can be specifically anti-Jewish racism, which is also unacceptable,

even taking into account the fact that Palestinians continue to be occupied, dispossessed and killed by a state that deliberately identifies itself as Jewish, and claims to act in the name of Jews everywhere.

So while any kind of racism is to be opposed and challenged, there is an important distinction to be made. Some people are content to highlight the loud-mouthed bigots that can be found in both Israeli and Palestinian societies, blaming them for preventing the 'moderate' majority from reaching a peaceful agreement.

In reality, while there are individual racist Palestinians and Israelis (like any society), an enforced Jewish superiority is intrinsic to the very fabric of a Zionist state in the Middle East. As detailed in Parts I and II of this book, ethnic and religious exclusivity are written into Israeli laws, and expressed every time the bulldozer blade cuts into a Palestinian home. It goes much deeper than the reprehensible beliefs of a few 'extremists'.

Isn't Israel the only democracy in the Middle East?

Israel certainly has many elements of a thriving democracy: the Declaration of Independence includes a pledge of equality for all regardless of race or religion; Palestinians inside Israel have the vote; there is a diverse, varied media. These features and others seem to make a favourable comparison with Israel's neighbours very easy. But scratch beneath the surface, and another picture emerges.

To praise Israel as a democracy is to forget the occupation. For over 40 years, Palestinians living under Israel's military occupation have been denied their right to self-determination, as they watch Jewish Israelis colonise their land. Israelis refer to the Occupied Territories as Judea and Samaira, or 'the Territories', and include the area in official maps of 'Israel'. In which case, under Israel's control are 4 million Palestinians without voting rights or any semblance of dignity. When Palestinians in the Occupied Territories did vote in parliamentary elections – for a polity with no effective jurisdiction over its territory – Israel's response was to boycott the government.

Moreover, as we have seen in Part II, even for Palestinian citizens of Israel, there is profound, institutionalised discrimination on the basis that they are not Jewish – the same reason why Palestinian refugees cannot return home. It's beginning to look like a strange sort of 'democracy'. In fact, it was Avraham Burg, former Knesset speaker and Jewish Agency for Israel chairman, who made clear the stark choice facing Israelis: it is either 'Jewish racism or democracy' – you can't have both.[5]

State discrimination against ethnicities and religions, in whatever form, is to be condemned, and most of Israel's Middle East neighbours are dictatorial and repressive. However, Israel cannot be spared from critique simply because there are other examples of non-democratic governments. Time and time again, Israel's defenders seek to divert attention by pointing to other human rights issues.

In 2005, Israel actually withdrew from the Gaza Strip. But instead of concentrating on building up an economy and demonstrating a desire for peace, haven't Palestinians responded to this painful concession with rocket fire and terrorism?

With the bitter political infighting, the images of Israeli settlers being physically dragged away by their 'own' soldiers, and the fulsome international praise, many were convinced that Israel's 'disengagement' in the summer of 2005 was a genuine compromise made for the sake of the peace process. International politicians and media commentators marvelled at how Ariel Sharon had become the 'man of peace' Bush believed him to be.

But in reality, the whole thing was a televised PR stunt. Israel was under international pressure to make a 'painful compromise' in the name of peace, and withdrawing from Gaza also offered the chance to relieve the 'demographic' pressure of controlling 1.4 million Palestinians. Moreover, Israeli leaders had made it perfectly clear that the redeployment meant simultaneously strengthening illegal settlements in the West Bank. In other words, it was more land, fewer Arabs.

Then-prime minister Ariel Sharon's own advisor later told an Israeli newspaper that the aim had indeed been to freeze the peace process. He boasted, 'Sharon can tell the leaders of the settlers that he is evacuating 10,000 settlers and in the future he will be compelled to evacuate another 10,000, but he is strengthening the other 200,000, strengthening their hold in the soil.'[6] In the aftermath of the pull-out, the Education Minister stressed frankly the importance of the 'window of opportunity' Israel had won itself to consolidate the major West Bank colonies.[7]

Sharon himself was also explicit about the strategy, telling the Knesset that 'whoever wishes to preserve the large Israeli settlement blocs under our control forever … must support the Disengagement Plan'.[8] A couple of months before the disengagement, the prime minister told an audience that the withdrawal from Gaza was done 'in order to strengthen those [areas] with a high strategic value for us'.[9] Days later, Sharon confirmed how 'at the same time' as withdrawing from Gaza, Israel was focusing its efforts on areas like 'greater Jerusalem' and 'the settlement blocs'.[10]

But even putting aside the real motivation, the Israeli government also tried to claim that now there were no settlers or soldiers with a permanent base in the Strip, there was no occupation, and thus no Israeli responsibility. The Israeli human rights group B'Tselem demolished this pretence:

> The laws of occupation apply if a state has 'effective control' over the territory in question … The broad scope of Israeli control in the Gaza Strip, which exists despite the lack of a physical presence of IDF soldiers in the territory, creates *a reasonable basis for the assumption that this control amounts to 'effective control,'* such that the laws of occupation continue to apply. *Even if* Israel's control in the Gaza Strip does not amount to 'effective control' and the territory is not considered occupied, Israel still bears certain responsibilities under international humanitarian law. [emphasis added][11]

In fact, Israel retained control over the Strip's borders, air space and territorial waters, the population registry, export and import abilities, and crossings.[12] Moreover, the Israeli military continued to routinely conduct ground raids inside the Strip, using the air force for assassinations, spying missions and collective punishment.

In 2006, the year after 'disengagement', the IDF fired some 14,000 artillery shells into the Gaza Strip.[13] During that July, following the capture of IDF soldier Gilad Shalit the previous month, Israel killed 163 Palestinians in the Strip, almost half of whom 'were not taking part in the hostilities' when they were killed (including 36 minors).[14] Then in 2008 and 2012 came the death and destruction of 'Operation Cast Lead' and 'Operation Pillar of Defense', onslaughts that killed hundreds of Palestinian men, women and children.

Moreover, since Hamas's success in the Palestinian Legislative Council elections of January 2006, Gaza had been totally isolated, subjected to an economically and socially devastating blockade which Israel continues to this day.

The legacy of over 40 years under occupation, plus a continued siege and punitive military operations; it is disingenuous to point to the giant prison that is the impoverished Gaza Strip, and blame 'the rockets'. Indiscriminate attacks on Israeli civilians by Palestinian armed groups are deplorable, but to consider Palestinian violence in isolation means ignoring both Israel's open intentions for the Gaza 'withdrawal' as well as the collective punishment Israel has inflicted on Gaza's 1.7 million Palestinians ever since.

When the Palestinians voted in 2006, they chose Hamas, a Muslim fundamentalist terror group sworn to Israel's destruction. How can the Israelis be expected to feel like making concessions?

Hamas was formed in 1987, 20 years into Israel's military occupation, and at the start of the First Intifada. Some Palestinians, paralleling regional trends, were disillusioned with leftist or secular parties, and looked for an alternative politics. Hamas's popular support has been typically connected to the buoyancy of the peace process. During the Oslo years, when hopes of progress were high, Hamas's popularity fell. During the brutal Israeli repression of the Second Intifada, however, support for a more militaristic, radical strategy increased.

Sometimes, Hamas is lumped together with al-Qaeda as part of a global Islamic jihad, despite the huge differences in origin, context, social base and aims. This clumsy analogy is often drawn for propaganda purposes, and sometimes made out of ignorance. In fact, Hamas has demonstrated a flexible approach to pragmatic politics similar to other parties and organisations. In the last few years, depending on circumstances, it has held to unilateral ceasefires and key leaders have even expressed a willingness to implicitly recognise Israel's existence as part of a genuine two-state solution.

That is not to say that there aren't individuals within the group who are more focused on a religious agenda than a political one, though unfortunately, the Israeli government has chosen to assassinate important Hamas moderates, only strengthening the hand of the hardliners. Some Hamas leaders and affiliated preachers have also been guilty of anti-semitic rhetoric, while others have noted the anti-semitism of the 1988 Charter. According to leading Hamas expert Khaled Hroub, however, this document has since 'become largely obsolete', while even at the time it was the work of one individual. This is not the only shift:

> The vague idea of establishing an Islamic state in Palestine as mentioned in the early statements of the movement was quickly sidelined and surpassed ... Hamas has developed, and is still developing, into a movement that is more and more preoccupied with current and immediate, and medium-term, goals.[15]

The reasons for the surge in support for Hamas at the ballot box in 2006 were nothing to do with an upswing in the number of Palestinians seeking an 'Islamic state'. Hamas had proven itself to be efficient in providing a number of vital services, such as health care and charitable support, in stark contrast to the corrupt Palestinian Authority. A vote for Hamas was also a rejection of the plans entertained by the international community, Israel and the Fatah-dominated PA, as well as a symbol of defiance after years of brutal Israeli repression.

People talk about the Palestinian refugees, but weren't a similar number of Jewish refugees kicked out of Arab countries and welcomed by Israel? Couldn't this be seen as a 'fair swap'?

The creation of the State of Israel led to two substantial population movements in the Middle East. Between 700,000 to 800,000 Palestinians fled or were expelled from their homes, and forbidden from returning by the new Jewish state, while from 1948 through to the 1970s, around 850,000 Jews left Arab countries, with the majority moving to Israel. But the rough equality in scale is just about the only similarity.

Israeli professor Yehouda Shenhav once wrote that 'any reasonable person' must acknowledge the analogy to be 'unfounded':

Palestinian refugees did not want to leave Palestine. Many Palestinian communities were destroyed in 1948, and some 700,000 Palestinians were expelled, or fled, from the borders of historic Palestine. Those who left did not do so of their own volition. In contrast, Jews from Arab lands came to this country under the initiative of the State of Israel and

Jewish organizations. Some came of their own free will; others arrived against their will. Some lived comfortably and securely in Arab lands; others suffered from fear and oppression.[16]

Some prominent Israeli politicians who themselves come from Arab countries reject the 'refugee' label. Former Knesset speaker Yisrael Yeshayahu once said 'We are not refugees. [Some of us] came to this country before the state was born. We had messianic aspirations.' Member of Knesset Ran Cohen, who emigrated from Iraq, made it clear: 'I came at the behest of Zionism, due to the pull that this land exerts, and due to the idea of redemption. Nobody is going to define me as a refugee.'[17]

As well as the fact that Jews in Arab countries were actively encouraged by the Zionist movement to move to Israel, there is another big problem with the 'swap' theory – timescale. Dr Philip Mendes points out how 'the Jewish exodus from Iraq and other Arab countries took place over many decades, before and after the Palestinian exodus' and 'there is no evidence that the Israeli leadership anticipated a so-called population exchange when they made their arguably harsh decision to prevent the return of Palestinian refugees'. Mendes also concludes his analysis by affirming that 'the two exoduses ... should be considered separately'.[18]

But the 'swap' idea is anyway illogical. One refugee's right – in the case of the Palestinians, a right affirmed by UN resolutions – cannot be 'cancelled out' by another's misfortune. Furthermore, 'the Palestinians were not at all responsible for the expulsion of the Jews from Arab countries' – while 'the

Palestinian refugee problem was caused by the Zionist refusal to allow the Palestinians to return to their homes'.[19]

Given the historical and logical flaws, the only way this analogy can be so tempting for some is its propaganda value. The World Organization of Jews from Arab Countries (WOJAC), for example, claim on their website that their mission is simply 'to document the assets Jewish refugees lost as they fled Arab countries'. Professor Shenhav, however, describes how WOJAC 'was invented as a deterrent to block claims harboured by the Palestinian national movement, particularly claims related to compensation and the right of return'.[20]

Dismayingly, but perhaps unsurprisingly, the US House of Representatives was persuaded to pass a bill in April 2008 that not only equated Jewish and Palestinian refugees, but also urged 'the administration to raise the issue every time the issue of Palestinian refugees is brought up'.[21] *The Economist* magazine described the non-binding resolution as having 'doubtful value', as well as showing 'once more the power of the pro-Israel lobby in Washington'.[22]

Haven't the Arab countries used the Palestinian refugees as a political football, leaving them to rot in refugee camps?
There is no question that the Palestinian refugees have received often shockingly bad, discriminatory treatment in neighbouring Arab countries such as Jordan, Syria, Lebanon and even the Gulf States. But the question implies that these Arab countries, which themselves still suffer from an underdeveloped infrastructure and other significant socio-economic problems, should have simply granted citizenship to hundreds of thousands (now millions) of refugees. In Western Europe, many citizens baulk at the idea of granting asylum to a pro-

portionately much smaller percentage – and this in countries well-equipped to embrace new immigrants.

Many of the Palestinians displaced from their villages by Israel in 1948 were peasant farmers. Cut off from their land and everything they knew, they were not at all equipped to make a living in an alien country with a scarcity of jobs. Finally, it should be remembered that the reason why so many Palestinian families became, and remain, stateless refugees is because Israel has refused to allow their return, destroyed hundreds of their communities and confiscated their properties.

Hundreds of thousands of Jews came to live in Israel as survivors of the Holocaust and because there was nowhere else for them to go. How can you simply label them as racist colonisers?

To describe Israel in terms of apartheid is not to dehumanise Israelis. In fact, the struggle for a just peace in Palestine/Israel emerges from insisting on the humanity of both Palestinians and Israelis. It's true that thousands of Jews fled to first Mandate Palestine, and then to Israel, escaping persecution in Europe and Russia. The majority of Jewish Israelis today, moreover, have been born in the land that they have every right to call home.

Anti-Jewish persecution certainly helps to explain how Zionism emerged, but cannot justify, or detract from, the realities of Israeli apartheid. It's not about name-calling, or denying how after the Holocaust, many European Jews felt like there was nowhere else for them to go. It is about recognising that the Palestinians also have a profound and deeply rooted attachment to their country and the question, then, is whether or not they will share that land as equals. At the same time as it is vital to respect and understand the impact and legacy of the Holocaust, it is also sadly necessary to refuse those who would manipulate and exploit Nazi crimes in order to justify the oppression of the Palestinians.

Why have the Palestinians continued to reject a compromise with Israel, from the very beginning of the state in 1948, to Arafat's 'No' at Camp David?

The myth of 'brave but peace-seeking' Israel always let down by violent, compromise-rejecting Arabs is powerful and enduring. Israel's defenders argue that if only the Palestinians had accepted partition in 1948, rather than seeking 'Israel's destruction', everything would have been different. Likewise, for the propaganda war of the Second Intifada, the Palestinians – and Arafat in particular – were said to have turned down a 'best ever' offer from Israel at Camp David, instead opting for violence.

Let's take a look at 1948 first. As we saw in Parts I and II, the real story of Israel's creation – the Nakba – is very different from the sanitised, Zionist narrative. When the UN proposed partition, Jews owned less than 7 per cent of the land, made up a third of the population – yet over half of the land of Palestine was assigned to the Jewish state. Moreover, even in its proposed borders, the Jewish state's population would be almost half Arab.

Ironically, while Palestinians are often accused of 'rejectionism', the Zionist leadership only accepted the idea of partition for tactical reasons. First prime minister Ben-Gurion described a 'partial Jewish state' as just the beginning: 'a powerful impetus in our historic efforts to redeem the land in its entirety.'[23] In a meeting of the Jewish leadership in 1938,

Ben-Gurion shared his assumption that 'after we build up a strong force following the establishment of the state – we will abolish the partition of the country and we will expand to the whole Land of Israel'.[24]

It should come as no surprise that 'the fear of territorial displacement and dispossession was to be the chief motor of Arab antagonism to Zionism'.[25] Palestinian Arabs had seen the Jewish proportion of Palestine's population triple from around 10 per cent at the end of World War I, while the Zionist leadership in Palestine made no bones about their political aims. A question worth asking, then, is whether you or I would simply accept the loss of our country, or if we too would be 'rejectionists'?

A similar question can be posed about events at the Camp David negotiations of 2000. Contrary to popular assumptions, 'Israel never offered the Palestinians 95 percent of the West Bank as reports indicated at the time'.[26] The 'generous offer' was just another incarnation of previous Israeli plans to annex huge swathes of the OPT, retaining major settlement blocs 'that effectively cut the West Bank into three sections with full Israeli control from Jerusalem to the Jordan River'.[27]

A similar story is told about Ehud Olmert's offer to Mahmoud Abbas in 2008, which has also become part of the narrative of Palestinian 'rejectionism' in the face of Israeli 'generosity'. The reality, of course, is somewhat different:

In 2008 Olmert made two offers to the Palestinians. In April he proposed that Israel annex 9.2% of the West Bank in exchange for Israeli territory equivalent of 5% of the West Bank. Then on 31 August he offered the Palestinian president Mahmoud Abbas a landswap in which Israel would annex 8.7% of the West Bank in exchange for Israeli territory equivalent of 5.5%. This second 'offer' was not a formal one: Olmert would not allow it to be presented to the broader negotiation teams. The maps he presented were reportedly 'similar to the Wall'.[28]

To question why the Palestinians have 'rejected' compromise is to look at the region's past and present from a particularly skewed perspective. Palestine has been wiped off the map, its land colonised and its people ethnically cleansed. Expecting those on the receiving end to be satisfied with the crumbs from the table is both unjust – and wishful thinking.

Glossary

Words in *italics* in the Glossary text have their own entry.

Annapolis Conference
A one day conference for Israeli-Palestinian negotiations, hosted at a US Naval Academy in Annapolis, Maryland, on 27 November 2007. It was organised by the Bush administration, and attended by Israeli prime minister Ehud Olmert, Palestinian president Mahmoud Abbas, President George W. Bush and numerous other international diplomats.

Areas A, B, C
The *Oslo Accords* divided up the *OPT* into three kinds of administration. Area A is under full *Palestinian Authority* control (less than 3 per cent), Area B is under Palestinian civil control and Israeli security control (25 per cent), while Area C is under full Israeli control (72 per cent).

Camp David
A rural retreat for the US President and location for the Israeli-Palestinian peace talks brokered by Bill Clinton in 2000. The Camp David talks ended without a final agreement, with the Americans, the Israelis (led by Prime Minister Ehud Barak) and the Palestinians (led by Yasser Arafat) blaming each other for the failure to close a deal.

Dunam

A unit of land measurement in Palestine: 1 dunam = 1,000 square metres or a quarter of an acre.

East Jerusalem – Occupied East Jerusalem

In 1967, Israel occupied the rest of Jerusalem, which since 1948 had been under Jordanian rule. Israel unilaterally expanded the municipal boundaries of the city, and illegally annexed East Jerusalem, a move that has not been recognised internationally. East Jerusalem, like the *West Bank*, is occupied territory.

Eretz Israel

The Hebrew term used to refer to the total area of the Biblical 'Promised Land' believed to have been given by God to the Jewish people, including all of Palestine/Israel and parts of neighbouring Arab countries.

Fatah

Founded in 1959 by Yasser Arafat and others, Fatah had become the main political party in the *PLO* by the late 1960s. Historically, Fatah has been happy to use both armed struggle and negotiations as strategies in the Palestinian national struggle. The current Palestinian president Mahmoud Abbas is a long-standing Fatah member.

Galilee

A region in the north of Israel with the highest national proportion of Palestinian citizens.

Gaza Strip

A small slice of territory bordering Israel, Egypt and the Mediterranean Sea, and considered part of the *OPT*. The Strip is home to around 1.4 million Palestinians, many of whom are registered refugees. In 2005, the Israeli government withdrew all settlers, and redeployed the army. In June 2007, after increasing tensions, *Hamas* overpowered its rival *Fatah* and secured political and security control over the Strip.

Green Line

Refers to the 1949 Armistice lines between Israel and the neighbouring countries. It effectively marks the division between territory accepted as Israel proper, and territory militarily occupied by Israel since 1967.

Hamas

Founded in the late 1980s during the First Intifada, a religious-nationalist liberation movement encompassing political activities, religious education, social and charitable services, and an armed wing targeting Israel. Considered a terrorist organisation by Israel and many in the international community due to its attacks on Israeli civilians, including the use of suicide bombings. An increase in popularity saw Hamas win the *Palestinian Legislative Council* elections in January 2006. A bitter rivalry with *Fatah* has often spilled over into violence.

Israel Defence Forces (IDF)

Israel's military, including ground, air and naval forces.

Jewish Agency (JA)

One of Israel's 'National Institutions', the JA became a kind of government-in-waiting for the Jewish community during the

British Mandate in Palestine, before receiving responsibilities for immigration and settlement by the Israeli state.

Jewish National Fund (JNF)
Founded at the beginning of the twentieth century to buy land in Palestine for Jewish colonisation. After 1948, the JNF was incorporated into the Israeli state's system of land ownership, increasing its holdings with the 'abandoned' property of Palestinian refugees.

Knesset
The Israeli legislature, located in West Jerusalem. An elected politician is referred to as a Member of Knesset (MK).

Labor
Founded in the 1960s, a left-of-centre Israeli political party whose leaders have included Yitzhak Rabin, Shimon Peres and Ehud Barak.

Likud
One of the biggest Israeli political parties, and ideologically right-wing. Famous leaders have included Prime Ministers Menachem Begin, Yitzhak Shamir, Binyamin Netanyahu and Ariel Sharon.

Nakba
Arabic for 'Catastrophe' and the term used by Palestinians to describe their ethnic cleansing and dispossession at the hands of the new Israeli state in 1948.

Negev
A desert region in the south of Israel, home to Bedouin Arabs.

Occupied Palestinian Territories (OPT)/Occupied Territories (OT)
Refers to the territories conquered by Israel in 1967, namely
the *West Bank*, *Gaza Strip* and *East Jerusalem* (although Israel
has unilaterally annexed the latter). The United Nations and
the International Court of Justice use the term 'Occupied
Palestinian Territories' (OPT), though they are often also
described as simply the Occupied Territories.

Oslo Accords
Signed in 1993 by Israeli prime minister Yitzhak Rabin
and *PLO* leader Yasser Arafat, the deal led to the creation of
the *PNA* and was intended to start a process of incremental
transfer of sovereignty to Palestinians in the *OPT*, and eventual
statehood.

Oslo (Peace) Process
The Oslo (Peace) Process began with secret talks between Israel
and the *PLO*, which led to the signing of the *Oslo Accords* in
1993. Since then, the Oslo Process has been used to describe
the subsequent agreements and the general framework
governing relations between Israel and the *PNA*.

Outposts
Unauthorised settler communities in the West Bank, 'illegal'
in the sense that they are not officially sanctioned by the
Israeli government. Often emerging from existing, authorised
settlements, outposts have historically developed into
fully-fledged colonies.

Palestinian National Authority (PNA)/Palestinian Authority (PA)
Created out of the *Oslo Accords*, the PNA (sometimes just
referred to as the PA) administers the parts of the *OPT* granted

varying degrees of autonomy (see *Areas A, B, C*). The president is Mahmoud Abbas and the prime minister at the time of writing is Salam Fayyad. This latter role is contested by *Hamas*, who contend that Ismail Haniyeh is the democratically elected prime minister (the *Hamas* government was dismissed by Abbas in June 2007 as part of the *Hamas-Fatah* conflict).

Palestinian Legislative Council (PLC)
The elected legislature of the *PNA*, albeit with the same limits with regards to sovereignty. In January 2006, *Hamas* won a majority in the PLC elections.

Palestine Liberation Organisation (PLO)
Founded in 1964 to fight for the Palestinian national struggle, the PLO aimed for the creation of a single, democratic and secular state in Palestine/Israel. In 1988, the PLO recognised the State of Israel, and in 1993, the group signed the *Oslo Accords* with Israel. Until his death in 2004, Yasser Arafat was PLO Chairman, and was succeeded by Mahmoud Abbas.

The peace process
The general term used to describe official, high level negotiations between Israeli and Palestinian political leaders since the early 1990s (initially in the context of the *Oslo Process*). It is now a more general term to describe ongoing, international diplomatic efforts to resolve the conflict, premised on the idea of dividing Palestine/Israel into one Jewish state and one Palestinian state.

Present absentees/internally displaced Palestinians
Present absentees/internally displaced Palestinians are internal refugees within the State of Israel who were declared

'absent' from their villages during the 1948 war and were prevented from returning to their property. Around one in four Palestinian citizens of Israel are internally displaced.

Separation Wall

The Separation Wall is the barrier being built by Israel in the *OPT* since 2003, ostensibly as a security measure. In 2004, the International Court of Justice ruled that the Wall is illegal and should be removed. The Court also said that the term 'wall' was perfectly appropriate, since no one word perfectly fits the combination of concrete wall, electric fences, gates, trenches and military-only roads.

Settlements – colonies

Jewish communities established by the Israeli government in the *OPT* since 1967, in contravention of international law. Some settlers are religiously motivated, but others are drawn by government financial incentives. The need to protect settlements is a core principle behind Israeli apartheid policies towards Palestinians in the *West Bank*.

West Bank

Territory that borders with Israel and Jordan, and under Israeli military occupation since 1967. Home to around 2.5 million Palestinians (including *East Jerusalem*), and to around 475,000 Israeli settlers living in illegal *colonies*. Major cities include Ramallah, Bethlehem, Nablus, Hebron, Jenin and Jericho.

World Zionist Organization (WZO)

Beginning in 1897 at the First Zionist Congress, the WZO served as the main organisation coordinating Zionist efforts at creating a state in Palestine. It is also one of Israel's 'National Institutions', and has an official relationship with the State of Israel.

Zionism

A political movement that emerged in nineteenth-century Europe seeking to create a Jewish state, founded by Theodor Herzl. A response to anti-semitism, the Zionist movement soon rejected other geographical locations, and sought to realise the objective of Jewish statehood in Palestine.

Israeli Apartheid: A Timeline

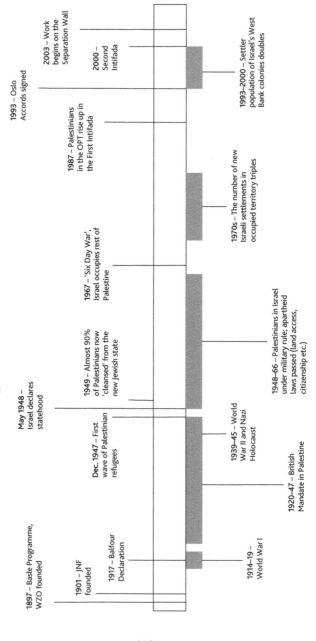

1897 – Basle Programme, WZO founded

1901 – JNF founded

1917 – Balfour Declaration

1914–19 – World War I

1920–47 – British Mandate in Palestine

1939–45 – World War II and Nazi Holocaust

Dec. 1947 – First wave of Palestinian refugees

May 1948 – Israel declares statehood

1949 – Almost 90% of Palestinians now 'cleansed' from the new Jewish state

1948–66 – Palestinians in Israel under military rule; apartheid laws passed (land access, citizenship etc.)

1967 – 'Six Day War', Israel occupies rest of Palestine

1970s – The number of new Israeli settlements in occupied territory triples

1987 – Palestinians in the OPT rise up in the First Intifada

1993 – Oslo Accords signed

1993–2000 – Settler population of Israel's West Bank colonies doubles

2000 – Second Intifada

2003 – Work begins on the Separation Wall

Resources

The author and publisher are not responsible for the content of websites.

NEWS

Al-Jazeera English (English version of the leading Arabic language news service): www.aljazeera.com/

Alternative Information Centre: www.alternativenews.org

BBC News (latest worldwide news): http://news.bbc.co.uk

Guardian: www.theguardian.com/world

Ha'aretz (Israeli newspaper, regularly updated news): www.haaretz.com

Inter Press Service: www.ipsnews.net

International Middle East Media Centre (IMEMC): www.imemc.org

Jerusalem Post (Israeli newspaper, regularly updated news): www.jpost.com

Jewish Telegraphic Agency: www.jta.org

Ma'an (Palestinian news agency): www.maannews.net/en

The National (UAE-based English language newspaper): www.thenational.ae

Palestine News & Info Agency (WAFA): http://english.wafa.ps

Palestine News Network (PNN): http://english.pnn.ps

Reuters: www.reuters.com/places/israel

Times of Israel (Israeli newspaper, regularly updated news): www.timesofisrael.com

Ynetnews.com (English site version of Israeli newspaper *Yediot Abaranot*): www.ynetnews.com

+972 (Israeli independent blog-based magazine): www.972 mag.com

ANALYSIS

The Electronic Intifada: http://electronicintifada.net

Institute for Middle East Understanding (IMEU): www. imeu.net

Institute for Palestine Studies: www.palestine-studies.org

Jadaliyya: www.jadaliyya.com

Middle East Monitor: www.middleeastmonitor.com

The Middle East Research and Information Project/Middle East Report: www.merip.org

MIFTAH (The Palestinian Initiative for the Promotion of Global Dialogue and Democracy): www.miftah.org

Le Monde Diplomatique: http://mondediplo.com

Mondoweiss: www.mondoweiss.net

Palestine Center: www.palestinecenter.org

Palestine Chronicle: www.palestinechronicle.com

Al-Shabaka, The Palestinian Policy Network
http://al-shabaka.org/

Washington Report on Middle East Affairs: www.wrmea.com

INFORMATION (E.G. MAPS, STATISTICS)

Applied Research Institute of Jerusalem: www.arij.org

Foundation for Middle East Peace: www.fmep.org

Palestinian Academic Society for the Study of International Affairs (PASSIA): www.passia.org

PLO Negotiations Affairs Department: www.nad-plo.org

UN's Office for the Coordination of Humanitarian Affairs –
Occupied Palestinian Territory: www.ochaopt.org

United Nations Relief and Works Agency for Palestine
Refugees in the Near East (UNRWA): www.un.org/unrwa/
english.html

Visualizing Palestine: www.visualizingpalestine.org

HUMAN RIGHTS AND NGOS

Adalah – The Legal Centre for Arab Minority Rights in Israel:
www.adalah.org/eng

ADDAMEER – Prisoner Support and Human Rights
Association: www.addameer.org

Al-Haq: www.alhaq.org

Alternative Tourism Group: www.atg.ps

Amnesty International: www.amnesty.org

Amos Trust: www.amostrust.org

Anarchists Against the Wall: www.awalls.org

The Arab Association for Human Rights: www.arabhra.org

The Association for Civil Rights in Israel: www.acri.org.il/eng

Association for the Defence of the Rights of the Internally
Displaced in Israel (ADRID)

The Association of Forty: www.assoc40.org

BADIL – Resource Centre for Palestinian Residency and
Refugees' Rights: www.badil.org

Bimkom – Planners for Planning Rights: www.bimkom.org

Breaking the Silence: www.breakingthesilence.org.il

B'Tselem – The Israeli Information Centre for Human Rights
in the Occupied Territories: www.btselem.org/English

Christian Aid: www.christian-aid.org.uk

Christian Peacemaker Teams: www.cpt.org/work/palestine

Ecumenical Accompaniment Programme in Palestine and Israel (EAPPI): www.eappi.org

Gisha – Legal Centre for Freedom of Movement: www.gisha.org

Gush-Shalom: www.gush-shalom.org

HaMoked – Centre for the Defence of the Individual: www.hamoked.org

Holy Land Trust: www.holylandtrust.org

Human Rights Watch: www.hrw.org

International Solidarity Movement (ISM): www.palsolidarity.org

Israeli Committee Against House Demolitions (ICAHD): www.ichad.org/eng

Ittijah (Union of Arab Community-Based Associations): www.ittijah.org

MachsomWatch: www.machsomwatch.org/en

Mada al-Carmel (Arab Center for Applied Social Research): www.mada-research.org

Medical Aid for Palestinians: www.map-uk.org

Middle East Fellowship: www.middleeastfellowship.org

Mossawa Centre – The Advocacy Centre for Arab Citizens in Israel: www.mossawacenter.org

Open Bethlehem: www.openbethlehem.org

Palestine Red Crescent Society: www.palestinercs.org

Palestinian Centre for Human Rights: www.pchrgaza.org

Palestinian Hydrology Group: www.phg.org

Physicians for Human Rights – Israel: www.phr.org.il/phr

Rabbis for Human Rights: http://rhr.israel.net

Refutrees: www.refutrees.org

Sabeel – Ecumenical Liberation Theology Centre, Jerusalem: www.sabeel.org

Ta'ayush – Arab-Jewish Partnership: www.taayush.org

War on Want: www.waronwant.org

Women in Black: www.womeninblack.org

Yesh-Gvul (There Is a Limit!): www.yeshgvul.org

Zochrot (Remembrance): www.zochrot.org

INTERNATIONAL SOLIDARITY AND CAMPAIGNING

Boycott Divestment Sanctions: http://bdsmovement.net

Palestinian Campaign for the Academic and Cultural Boycott
of Israel (PACBI): www.pacbi.org

Stop the Wall: www.stopthewall.org

UK

Al-Awda, The Palestine Right of Return – UK: www.al-awda.
org.uk

Architects and Planners for Justice in Palestine: http://apjp.org

Boycott Israel Network: www.boycottisraelnetwork.net

British Committee for the Universities for Palestine: www.
bricup.org.uk

The Council for Arab-British Understanding (CAABU): www.
caabu.org

Friends of Al-Aqsa: www.aqsa.org.uk

Friends of Bir Zeit University: www.fobzu.org

International Jewish Anti-Zionist Network: www.ijsn.net

Jews for Justice for Palestinians: www.jfjfp.org

Palestine Solidarity Campaign: www.palestinecampaign.org

Scottish Palestine Solidarity Campaign: www.scottishpsc.org.
uk

Twinning with Palestine: www.twinningwithpalestine.net

Canada

Canada – Palestine Support Network: www.canpalnet.ca

Coalition Against Israeli Apartheid: www.caiaweb.org

Palestine House Educational and Cultural Centre: www.palestinehouse.com

Solidarity for Palestinian Human Rights (individual campus chapters) The Palestine Right to Return Group: www.al-awda.ca

Not In Our Name (NION): Jewish Voices Opposing Zionism: www.nion.ca

USA

Adalah-NY, The Coalition for Justice in the Middle East: www.adalahny.org

Al-Awda, The Palestine Right to Return Coalition: www.al-awda.org

Jewish Voice for Peace : www.jewishvoiceforpeace.org

The Palestine Freedom Project: www.palestinefreedom.org

The Palestine Solidarity Movement: www.palestinesolidarity-movement.org

Students for Justice in Palestine: www.sjpnational.org

US Campaign to End the Israeli Occupation: www.endtheoccupation.org

South Africa

End the Occupation – South Africa: www.endtheoccupation.org.za

Palestine Solidarity Committee/South Africa: http://psc.org.za

Ireland

Ireland Palestine Solidarity Campaign: www.ipsc.ie

Australia

60 Years of Al-Nakba: www.1948.com.au

Coalition for Justice and Peace in Palestine: www.coalitionfor-palestine.org

The Australian Friends of Palestine: www.friendsofpalestine.org.au

Australians for Justice and Peace in Palestine: http://ajpp.wordpress.com

Australians for Palestine: www.australiansforpalestine.com

Notes

INTRODUCING ISRAELI APARTHEID

1. Mona N. Younis, *Liberation and Democratization*, Minneapolis, MN: University of Minnesota Press, 2000, p. 12.
2. 'Jabotinsky most popular street name in Israel', Ynetnews.com, 28 November 2007.
3. Nur Masalha, *Expulsion of the Palestinians*, Washington, DC: Institute for Palestine Studies, 2001, p. 28.
4. Avi Shlaim, *The Iron Wall*, New York: W.W. Norton, 2000, p. 13.
5. UN website, http://untreaty.un.org/cod/avl/ha/cspca/cspca. html (last accessed 8 August 2013).
6. Office of the United Nations High Commissioner for Human Rights website, www.ohchr.org/EN/ProfessionalInterest/ Pages/CERD.aspx (last accessed 8 August 2013).
7. International Committee of the Red Cross website, www.icrc. org/applic/ihl/ihl.nsf/Article.xsp?action=openDocument&do cumentId=73D05A98B6CEB566C12563CD0051E1A0 (last accessed 8 August 2013).
8. 'Rome Statute of the International Criminal Court', http:// untreaty.un.org/cod/icc/statute/romefra.htm (last accessed 4 September 2013).
9. 'United against apartheid, colonialism and occupation – dignity and justice for the Palestinian people', /www.bdsmovement. net/apartheid-colonisation-occupation (last accessed 8 August 2013).
10. 'South African study: Israel practicing apartheid and colonialism', EI, 9 June 2009, http://electronicintifada.net/ content/south-african-study-israel-practicing-apartheid-and- colonialism/3432 (last accessed 8 August 2013). Also see Virginia Tilley (ed.), *Beyond Occupation: Apartheid, Colonialism*

and International Law in the Occupied Palestinian Territories, London: Pluto Press, 2012.

11. Russell Tribunal website, www.russelltribunalonpalestine.com/en/sessions/south-africa/south-africa-session-%E2%80%94-full-findings/cape-town-session-summary-of-findings (last accessed 8 August 2013).

12. David Keane, 'Elements of the definition of apartheid: racial groups under international law', *Al Majdal*, Autumn 2011, www.badil.org/en/article74/item/1693-article-5 (last accessed 8 August 2013).

13. 'Water for one people only: discriminatory access and "water-apartheid" in the Occupied Palestinian Territory', www.alhaq.org/advocacy/topics/housing-land-and-natural-resources/695 (last accessed 8 August 2013).

14. UN's Committee on the Elimination of Racial Discrimination website, www2.ohchr.org/english/bodies/cerd/docs/CERD.C.ISR.CO.14-16.pdf (last accessed 8 August 2013).

15. For example, 'Olmert to Haaretz: two-state solution, or Israel is done for', 29 November 2007, www.haaretz.com/news/olmert-to-haaretz-two-state-solution-or-israel-is-done-for-1.234201 (last accessed 8 August 2013; 'Livni: without peace progress European boycott will move from settlements to rest of country', 2 July 2013, www.jpost.com/Diplomacy-and-Politics/Livni-European-boycott-of-settlement-goods-can-spread-to-all-of-Israel-318307 (last accessed 8 August 2013).

16. 'Barak: make peace with Palestinians or face apartheid', *Guardian*, 3 February 2010, www.guardian.co.uk/world/2010/feb/03/barak-apartheid-palestine-peace (last accessed 9 August 2013).

17. 'Israel must end the hatred now', *Observer*, 15 October 2000.

18. Leila Farsakh, 'Israel: an apartheid state?' *Le Monde Diplomatique*, November 2003.

19. *Ha'aretz*, 12 July 2008.

20. In an echo of Israeli land-ownership laws, the Native Land Act of 1913 and the Native Trust and Land Act of 1936 designated 93 and 87 per cent of South African land respectively off-limits

to native African acquisition. See John Quigley, *Palestine and Israel: A Challenge to Justice*, Durham, NC: Duke University Press, 1990, pp. 124–5.

21. Lindsay Bremner, 'Border/skin', in Michael Sorkin (ed.), *Against the Wall*, New York: The New Press, 2005, pp. 122–37 (123).

22. *Ibid.*, p. 129.

23. Tanya Reinhart, 'The era of yellow territories', *Ha'aretz*, 27 May 1994.

24. Desmond Tutu, *Hope and Suffering*, London: Fount Paperbacks, 1984, pp. 94–5.

25. Bremner, 'Border/Skin', p. 127.

26. 'Apartheid apologists respond to BDS with fake concern for Palestinians', *The Electronic Intifada*, 30 April 2012, http:// electronicintifada.net/blogs/ben-white/apartheid-apologists-respond-bds-fake-concern-palestinians (last accessed 9 August 2013).

27. 'Israel's demography obsession has historical echo', *The Electronic Intifada*, 13 January 2012, http://electronicintifada. net/blogs/ben-white/israels-demography-obsession-has-historical-echo (last accessed 9 August 2013).

28. Uri Davis, *Apartheid Israel,* London: Zed Books, 2003, p. 84.

29. Lorenzo Veracini, *Israel and Settler Society*, London: Pluto Press, 2006, p. 18.

30. Farsakh, 'Israel: an apartheid state?'

31. Roselle Tekiner, 'The "Who is a Jew?" controversy in Israel: a product of political Zionism', in Roselle Tekiner, Samir Abed-Rabbo and Norton Mezvinsky (eds), *Anti-Zionism: Analytical Reflections*, Brattleboro, VT: Amana Books, 1989, pp. 62–89 (71).

32. Moshe Machover, 'Is it Apartheid?', Jewish Voice for Peace website, 15 December 2004, www.jewishvoiceforpeace.org/ publish/article_417.shtml (last accessed 4 September 2013).

33. 'History on the line: Joseph Massad and Benny Morris discuss the Middle East', in Joseph A. Massad, *The Persistence of the Palestinian Question*, Oxon: Routledge, 2006, pp. 154–65 (163).

34. Bremner, 'Border/skin', p. 131.

35. Joel Peters, *Israel and Africa: The Problematic Friendship*, London: British Academic Press, 1992, p. 53.

36. N.A. Rose, *The Gentile Zionists: A Study in Anglo-Zionist Diplomacy, 1929–1939*, London: Routledge, 1973, p. 5; Richard P. Stevens, 'Smuts and Weizmann', *Journal of Palestine Studies*, Vol. 3, No. 1 (Autumn 1973).

37. See Sasha Polakow-Suransky, *The Unspoken Alliance: Israel's Secret Relationship with Apartheid South Africa*, New York: Pantheon, 2010.

38. A/RES/39/72.C, 'Policies of apartheid of the Government of South Africa', adopted at the 99th plenary meeting, 13 December 1984.

39. *Guardian*, 6 February 2006.

40. 'Brothers in arms – Israel's secret pact with Pretoria', *Guardian*, 7 February 2006.

41. Cited in Benjamin M. Joseph, 'Separatism at the wrong time in history', in Tekiner et al., *Anti-Zionism*, pp. 136–52 (136).

42. 'Apartheid in the Holy Land', *Guardian*, 29 April 2002.

43. 'Occupied Gaza like apartheid South Africa, says UN report', *Guardian*, 23 February 2007; see, for example, 'COSATU open letter in support of CUPE resolution on Israel', *MRZine*, 7 June 2006, and '"This is like apartheid": ANC veterans visit West Bank', *Independent*, 11 July 2008.

44. *Ha'aretz*, 21 February 2003; 'Why the BBC ducks the Palestinian story', *The Electronic Intifada*, 6 February 2004; 'Worlds apart', *Guardian*, 6 February 2006.

45. 'Israel risks apartheid-like struggle if two-state solution fails, says Olmert', *Guardian*, 30 November 2007; Meron Benvenisti, 'Bantustan plan for an apartheid Israel', *Guardian*, 26 April 2004; 'Ha'aretz editor slams Israel at UN conference', *JTA*, 30 August 2007; 'The war's seventh day', *Ha'aretz*, 3 March 2002.

46. 'Israel could become pariah state, warns report', Associated Press, 14 October 2004.

PART I: ISRAELI INDEPENDENCE, PALESTINIAN CATASTROPHE

1. 'What leading Israelis have said about the Nakba', Institute for Middle East Understanding, 9 May 2007, http://imeu.net/news/article001252.shtml (last accessed 4 September 2013).
2. *Ha'aretz*, 9 January 2004.
3. Anton La Guardia, *Holy Land, Unholy War*, London: John Murray, 2002, p. 7.
4. Justin McCarthy, *The Population of Palestine*, New York: Columbia University Press, 1990, p. 10.
5. Hussein Abu Hussein and Fiona McKay, *Access Denied*, London: Zed Books, 2003, p. 67.
6. Gershon Shafir, 'Zionism and colonialism', in Ilan Pappe (ed.), *The Israel/Palestine Question: A Reader*, Abingdon: Routledge, 2007, pp. 78–93 (83).
7. Abu Hussein and McKay, *Access Denied*, p. 67.
8. Charles D. Smith, *Palestine and the Arab-Israeli Conflict*, Fifth edn, Boston, MA: Bedford/St Martin's, 2004, p. 37.
9. Abu Hussein and McKay, *Access Denied*, p. 68; *ibid.*, p. 123.
10. La Guardia, *Holy Land, Unholy War*, p. 77.
11. Smith, *Palestine and the Arab-Israeli Conflict*, p. 36.
12. Isaiah Friedman, *The Question of Palestine: British-Jewish-Arab Relations, 1914–1918*, New Brunswick, NJ: Transaction Publishers, 1992, p. 197.
13. See Stephen Sizer, *Christian Zionism*, Leicester: Inter-Varsity Press, 2004.
14. Avi Shlaim, *The Iron Wall*, New York: W.W. Norton, 2000, p. 7.
15. Tom Segev, *One Palestine, Complete*, London: Abacus, 2002, pp. 395–6.
16. Baylis Thomas, *How Israel Was Won: A Concise History of the Arab-Israeli Conflict*, Lanham, MD: Lexington Books, 1999, p. 25.
17. Nur Masalha, *Expulsion of the Palestinians*, Washington, DC: Institute for Palestine Studies, 2001, p. 62.
18. Segev, *One Palestine, Complete*, p. 110.

19. Maxime Rodinson, *Israel: A Colonial-Settler State?* New York: Pathfinder Press, 2001, p. 74.

20. Arthur Hertzberg, *The Zionist Idea*, Philadelphia, PA: The Jewish Publication Society, 1997, p. 245.

21. *Ibid.*, p. 222.

22. Masalha, *Expulsion of the Palestinians*, p. 6.

23. Michael Makovsky, *Churchill's Promised Land: Zionism and Statecraft*, New Haven, CT: Yale University Press, 2007, p. 156.

24. Edward W. Said, *The End of the Peace Process*, London: Granta Books, 2000, pp. 313–14.

25. Segev, *One Palestine, Complete*, p. 119.

26. Donald Neff, 'Truman overrode strong State Department warning against partitioning of Palestine in 1947', *Washington Report on Middle East Affairs*, September/October 1994, www.wrmea.com/backissues/0994/9409074.htm (last accessed 4 September 2013).

27. Segev, *One Palestine, Complete*, p. 405.

28. Masalha, *Expulsion of the Palestinians*, p. 37.

29. Benny Morris, 'Revisiting the Palestinian exodus of 1948', in Avi Shlaim (ed.), *The War for Palestine*, Cambridge: Cambridge University Press, pp. 37–59 (39).

30. *Ibid.*, p. 40.

31. *Ibid.*, p. 43.

32. Masalha, *Expulsion of the Palestinians*, p. 117.

33. Interview with Benny Morris, *Ha'aretz*, 9 January 2004.

34. La Guardia, *Holy Land, Unholy War*, p. 188.

35. Masalha, *Expulsion of the Palestinians*, pp. 94–5.

36. Benny Morris, *The Birth of the Palestinian Refugee Problem Revisited*, Cambridge: Cambridge University Press, 2004, p. 131; Benny Morris, 'Yosef Weitz and the Transfer Committees, 1948–49', *Middle Eastern Studies*, Vol. 22, No. 4, October 1986, p. 523. Cited in Masalha, *Expulsion of the Palestinians*, p. 182.

37. Morris, 'Revisiting the Palestinian exodus of 1948', p. 47.

38. Segev, *One Palestine, Complete*, p. 405; Morris, *The Birth of the Palestinian Refugee Problem*, p. 60.

39. Morris, *The Birth of the Palestinian Refugee Problem*, p. 50.

40. Segev, *One Palestine, Complete*, p. 404; Benny Morris, 'For the record', *Guardian*, 14 January 2004.

41. Morris, *The Birth of the Palestinian Refugee Problem*, p. 41.

42. Morris, 'Revisiting the Palestinian exodus of 1948', p. 43.

43. *Ibid.*, p. 44.

44. Smith, *Palestine and the Arab-Israeli Conflict*, pp. 189–90; also see Kathleen Christison, *Perceptions of Palestine*, Berkeley, CA: University of California Press, 2001, pp. 61–94.

45. Rashid Khalidi, 'The Palestinians and 1948: the underlying causes of failure', in Shlaim, *The War for Palestine*, pp. 12–36 (12).

46. Smith, *Palestine and the Arab-Israeli Conflict*, p. 185.

47. Walid Khalidi, 'Revisiting the UNGA partition resolution', in Pappe, *The Israel/Palestine Question*, 2nd edn, pp. 97–114 (102–3).

48. Derek Gregory, *The Colonial Present*, Malden, MA: Blackwell Publishing, 2004, p. 86; Khalidi, 'Revisiting the UNGA partition resolution', p. 106.

49. For example, the Hebrew University's first Chancellor Judah Magnes and philosopher Martin Buber both advocated a binational solution.

50. Morris, *The Birth of the Palestinian Refugee Problem*, p. 33.

51. Avi Shlaim, 'The debate about 1948', in Pappe, *The Israel/Palestine Question*, pp. 139–60 (149).

52. 'Israel: the threat from within', *New York Review of Books*, Vol. 51, No. 3 (26 February 2004).

53. Meron Benvenisti, *Sacred Landscape*, Berkeley, CA: University of California Press, 2002, p. 328.

54. Andrew Bell-Fialkoff, 'A brief history of ethnic cleansing', *Foreign Affairs*, Summer 1993.

55. Drazen Petrovic, 'Ethnic cleansing – an attempt at methodology', *European Journal of International Law*, Vol. 5, No.3, 1994, pp. 342–59.

56. Ilan Pappe, *The Ethnic Cleansing of Palestine*, Oxford: Oneworld Publications, 2007, p. 89.

57. Morris, 'Revisiting the Palestinian exodus of 1948', p. 49; Benvenisti, *Sacred Landscape*, p. 121.

58. Pappe, *The Ethnic Cleansing of Palestine*, p. 147.

59. *Ibid.*, p. 72, p. 138.

60. Morris, *The Birth of the Palestinian Refugee Problem*, p. 235.

61. Cited in *ibid.*, p. 257.

62. Shlaim, *The Iron Wall*, p. 31.

63. Morris, *The Birth of the Palestinian Refugee Problem*, p. 172.

64. *Ibid.*, p. 361.

65. Segev, *One Palestine, Complete*, p. 511.

66. Interview with Benny Morris, *Ha'aretz*, 9 January 2004; Mazin B. Qumsiyeh, *Sharing the Land of Canaan*, London: Pluto Books, 2004, p. 36.

67. Interview with Benny Morris, *Ha'aretz*, 9 January 2004.

68. Morris, *The Birth of the Palestinian Refugee Problem*, pp. 237–8.

69. Pappe, *The Ethnic Cleansing of Palestine*, p. 57.

70. Rosemary Sayigh, *The Palestinians: From Peasants to Revolutionaries*, London: Zed Books, 2007, p. 96.

71. Morris, *The Birth of the Palestinian Refugee Problem*, p. 469.

72. *Ibid.*, p. 428.

73. *Ibid.*, p. 429; Pappe, *The Ethnic Cleansing of Palestine*, p. 169.

74. 'The fall of an Arab town in 1948', *Al Jazeera English* website, 20 July 2008, http://english.aljazeera.net/focus/60yearsofdivision/2008/07/20087116188515832.html (last accessed 4 September 2013).

75. Pappe, *The Ethnic Cleansing of Palestine*, p. 169; Morris, *The Birth of the Palestinian Refugee Problem*, p. 433.

76. Gideon Levy, *Ha'aretz*, 2 June 2004.

77. Morris, *The Birth of the Palestinian Refugee Problem*, p. 222; *ibid.* p. 225.

78. Khalidi, 'The Palestinians and 1948: the underlying causes of failure', p. 13; Qumsiyeh, *Sharing the Land of Canaan*, p. 36.

79. Pappe, *The Ethnic Cleansing of Palestine*, p. 104.

80. Morris, *The Birth of the Palestinian Refugee Problem*, p. 138.

81. *Ibid.*, p. 265.

82. Smith, *Palestine and the Arab-Israeli Conflict*, p. 200.

83. Pappe, *The Ethnic Cleansing of Palestine*, p. 54.

84. Morris, 'Revisiting the Palestinian exodus of 1948', p. 38.

85. Morris, *The Birth of the Palestinian Refugee Problem*, p. 514.

86. *Ibid.*, p. 515.

87. *Ibid.*, p. 532; p. 527.

88. *Ibid.*, p. 517.

89. *Ibid.*, p. 528.

90. *Ibid.*, p. 529.

91. *Ibid.*, p. 513.

92. Shlaim, *The Iron Wall*, p. 82.

93. Benny Morris, *Israel's Border Wars, 1949–1956: Arab Infiltration, Israeli Retaliation, and the Countdown to the Suez War*, Oxford: Oxford University Press, 1993, p. 432.

94. Shlaim, *The Iron Wall*, p. 82.

95. John Quigley, *The Case for Palestine: An International Law Perspective*, Durham, NC: Duke University Press, 2005, p. 232.

96. Morris, *The Birth of the Palestinian Refugee Problem*, p. 589.

97. *Ibid.*, p. 313.

98. Abu Hussein and McKay, *Access Denied*, p. 5.

99. Qumsiyeh, *Sharing the Land of Canaan*, p. 34.

100. Smith, *Palestine and the Arab-Israeli Conflict*, p. 200; Sayigh, *The Palestinians: From Peasants to Revolutionaries*, p. 99.

101. Abu Hussein and McKay, *Access Denied*, p. 4.

102. Morris, *The Birth of the Palestinian Refugee Problem*, p. 369.

103. Mike Marqusee, 'The great catastrophe', *The Hindu*, 9 March 2008.

104. Benvenisti, *Sacred Landscape*, p. 164.

105. Morris, *The Birth of the Palestinian Refugee Problem*, p. 390.

106. *Ibid.*, p. 393.

107. Benvenisti, *Sacred Landscape*, p. 14.

108. *Ibid.*, p. 34.

109. 'Report of the Commissioner-General of the United Nations Relief and Works Agency for Palestine refugees in the Near East', General Assembly 22nd session, 30 June 1967.

110. Nur Masalha, 'The historical roots of the Palestinian refugee question', in Naseer Aruri (ed.), *Palestinian Refugees: The Right of Return*, London: Pluto Press, 2001, pp. 36–67 (61).

111. Smith, *Palestine and the Arab-Israeli Conflict*, p. 279.

112. 'Report of the Secretary-General under General Assembly Resolution 2252 (ES-V) and Security Council Resolution 237 (1967)', released September 1967.

113. Thomas, *How Israel Was Won*, p. 183.

114. 'Report of the Commissioner-General of the United Nations Relief and Works Agency for Palestine refugees in the Near East'.

115. Nur Masalha, *The Bible and Zionism*, London: Zed Books, 2007, p. 84.

116. Tom Segev, *1967: Israel, the War, and the Year that Transformed the Middle East*, London: Little, Brown, 2007, p. 407.

117. Uri Avnery, 'Crying wolf?', 15 March 2003, www.jnul.huji. ac.il/ia/archivedsites/gushshalom010204/www.gush-shalom. org/archives/article236.html (last accessed 4 September 2013).

118. Human Rights Watch, 'Razing Rafah: mass home demolitions in the Gaza Strip', 2004, http://www.hrw.org/reports/2004/ rafah1004/5.htm (last accessed 4 September 2013).

119. 'Report of the Secretary-General under General Assembly Resolution 2252 (ES-V) and Security Council Resolution 237 (1967)'.

120. Thomas, *How Israel Was Won*, p. 183.

121. 'Report of the Secretary-General under General Assembly Resolution 2252 (ES-V) and Security Council Resolution 237 (1967)'.

122. 'The ghost city of 1967', UNRWA website, www.un.org/ unrwa/67commem/stories/GhostCity.html (last accessed 6 November 2008).

123. Avnery, 'Crying wolf?'

124. *Human Rights Watch*, 'Razing Rafah: mass home demolitions in the Gaza Strip'.

PART II: ISRAELI APARTHEID

1. Eliezer Schweid, 'Israel as a Zionist state', in *Zionism: Israel – Vision and Realization*, New York: Americn Zionist Youth Foundation, 1970.

2. Mazim B. Qumsiyeh, *Sharing the Land of Canaan*, London: Pluto Books, 2004, p. 96.
3. *New York Times*, 14 July 1992.
4. Virginia Tilley, *The One-State Solution*, Michigan, MI: University of Michigan Press, 2005, p. 147; 'Nationality status in Israel is not linked to origin from, or residence in a territory, as is the norm in international law', UN Commission on Human Rights, 59th session, 15 June 2002.
5. 'So this Jew, Arab, Georgian and Samaritan go to court ...', *Ha'aretz*, 28 December 2003.
6. 'I am Israeli', Prof. Uzzi Ornan, Ynetnews, 9 August 2008.
7. www.knesset.gov.il/laws/special/eng/basic2_eng.htm   (last accessed 7 September 2013).
8. 'Knesset speaker disqualifies Tibi bill on Nakba denial', *Jerusalem Post*, 4 July 2011.
9. 'PMO to Balad: We will thwart anti-Israel activity even if legal', *Ha'aretz*, 16 March 2007.
10. 'Shin Bet: Citizens subverting Israel key values to be probed', *Ha'aretz*, 20 March 2007.
11. 'Israel subverts human rights for a key critic', *Liberal Conspiracy*, 29 May 2010.
12. 'Equality and destruction', *Jerusalem Post*, 3 March 2007.
13. *Adalah* Newsletter, Vol. 43, December 2007, www.adalah.org/newsletter/eng/dec07/dec07.html (last accessed 6 September 2013).
14. Cited in Uri Davis, *Apartheid Israel*, London: Zed Books, 2003, p. 226, n. 51.
15. *Ibid.*, p. 70.
16. 'Analysis: what kind of aliya is best to ensure the survival of the Jewish people?' *Jerusalem Post*, 1 January 2007.
17. Jewish Agency (JA) website, www.jewishagency.org/JewishAgency/English/Aliyah/Aliyah+Info/The+Law+of+Return (last accessed 6 September 2013); Davis, *Apartheid Israel*, p. 203.
18. JA website.
19. Charles D. Smith, *Palestine and the Arab-Israeli Conflict*, 5th edn, Boston, MA: Bedford/St Martin's, p. 220.

20. *Ibid.*, p. 221.

21. Hussein Abu Hussein and Fiona McKay, *Access Denied*, London: Zed Books, p. 73.

22. John Quigley, *Palestine and Israel: A Challenge to Justice*, Durham, NC: Duke University Press, 1990, p. 108.

23. *Ibid.*, p. 106.

24. Nur Masalha, 'Present absentees and indigenous resistance', in Nur Masalha (ed.), *Catastrophe Remembered: Palestine, Israel and the Internal Refugees*, London: Zed Books, 2005, pp. 23–55 (32).

25. Abu Hussein and McKay, *Access Denied*, p. 88.

26. Ian Lustick, *Arabs in the Jewish State*, Austin, TX: University of Texas Press, 1980, p. 276 n. 26; Quigley, *Palestine and Israel*, p. 109.

24. Lustick, *Arabs in the Jewish State*, p. 57.

27. *Ibid.*, p. 58.

29. Roselle Tekiner, 'The "Who is a Jew" controversy in Israel: a product of political Zionism', in Roselle Tekiner, Samir Abed-Rabbo and Norton Mezvinsky (eds), *Anti-Zionism: Analytical Reflections*, Bratteleboro, VT: Amana Books, 1988, p. 71.

30. Davis, *Apartheid Israel*, p. 36.

31. *Ibid.*, p. 39.

32. *Ibid.*, p. 40.

33. Quigley, *Palestine and Israel*, p. 118.

34. Benvenisti, *Sacred Landscape*, pp. 176–7.

35. Abu Hussein and McKay, *Access Denied*, pp. 151–3.

36. 'After years of planning, PM announces wide land reforms', *Jerusalem Post*, 19 May 2011; Amotz Asa-El, 'Netanyahu's other crisis', *MarketWatch*, 20 May 2011; 'New Discriminatory Laws and Bills in Israel', Adalah.

37. Statement submitted by Habitat International Coalition and Adalah, UNCHR, 62nd session, 13 March–21 April 2006, www.adalah.org/eng/intl06/un-i6-jnf.pdf (last accessed 7 September 2013).

38. 'JNF's strange place in the sun', *Globes*, 28 March 2010; 'The new Israeli land reform', *Adalah* Newsletter, Vol. 63

(August 2009); JNF website, www.jnf.org/about-jnf/news/ understanding_land_swap.html (last accessed 6 September 2013).

39. Abu Hussein and McKay, *Access Denied*, p. 148.

40. Cited in *ibid.*, p. 146.

41. Quigley, *Palestine and Israel*, p. 124.

42. Tekiner, 'The "Who is a Jew?" controversy in Israel', pp. 62–89 (70–1).

43. Davis, *Apartheid Israel*, p. 40; Abu Hussein and McKay, *Access Denied*, p. 154.

44. Abu Hussein and McKay, *Access Denied*, p. 191, *Adalah Newsletter*, Vol. 42 (November 2007), www.adalah.org/ newsletter/eng/nov07/8.php (last accessed 6 September 2013); Human Rights Watch, 'Off the map: land and housing rights violations in Israel's unrecognized Bedouin villages', March 2008, www.hrw.org/reports/2008/iopt0308/4.htm#_ Toc193705071 (last accessed 6 September 2013).

45. 'Land, citizenship and exclusion in Israel', *openDemocracy*, 30 March 2011.

46. 'Israel: new laws marginalize Palestinian Arab citizens', Human Rights Watch, 30 March 2011, www.hrw.org/ news/2011/03/30/israel-new-laws-marginalize-palestinian-arab-citizens (last accessed 9 August 2013); 'In the wake of the Knesset Constitution, Law and Justice Committee's approval of the Admissions Committees Law: Adalah: there are now 695 communities in Israel where Arab citizens of the state are forbidden to live', Adalah, 4 November 2010, http:// adalah.org/eng/Articles/1086/In-the-wake-of-the-Knesset-Constitution,-Law-and-of (last accessed 9 August 2013).

47. Tom Segev, *1949: The First Israelis*, New York: Henry Holt and Company, 1998, p. 67.

48. Lustick, *Arabs in the Jewish State*, p. 68.

49. Sandy Sufian and Mark LeVine (eds), *Reapproaching Borders: New Perspectives on the Study of Israel-Palestine*, Lanham, MD: Rowman & Littlefield Publishers Inc., 2007, p. 82.

50. *Ibid.*

51. *Ibid.*, p. 83.

52. Abu Hussein and McKay, *Access Denied*, p. 165.
53. 'The view from the hilltops', *Ha'aretz*, 14 October 2010.
54. 'Jewish Agency readies plan to foster a "Zionist majority"', *Ha'aretz*, 28 October 2002.
55. 'Jewish communities planned to "block Bedouin expansion"', *Ha'aretz*, 5 June 2004.
56. 'Battling against Israeli "apartheid"', BBC news online, 23 December 2004, http://news.bbc.co.uk/2/hi/middle_east/4111915.stm (last accessed 6 September 2013); 'For Israel's Arab citizens, isolation and exclusion', *Washington Post*, 20 December 2007.
57. Lustick, *Arabs in the Jewish State*, p. 192.
58. 'Only 4% of development budget allocated for Arab sector', Ynetnews.com, 17 December 2007.
59. Jonathan Cook, *Blood and Religion*, London: Pluto Books, 2006, p. 123.
60. Gideon Levy, 'The threat of the "demographic threat"', *Ha'aretz*, 22 July 2007.
61. 'Arab birthrate drops for first time in years', *Ha'aretz*, 24 January 2005.
62. 'An alternative to child allowances', *Ha'aretz*, 2 March 2005.
63. 'Netanyahu: Israel's Arabs are the real demographic threat', *Ha'aretz*, 18 December 2003; 'Israel must remain Jewish', Ynetnews.com, 4 April 2005.
64. For example, see 'Boim: is Palestinian terror caused by a genetic defect?', *Ha'aretz*, 24 February 2004; 'The enemy within', *Ha'aretz*, 30 August 2002; 'A "lite" plan for the enlightened voter', *Ha'aretz*, 21 March 2006; Oren Yiftachel, 'The shrinking space of citizenship: ethnocratic politics in Israel', *Middle East Report*, Vol. 223 (Summer 2002).
65. See Adalah website, www.adalah.org/eng/Israeli-Discriminatory-Law-Database (last accessed 9 August 2013).
66. 'US State Department: Israel practices "institutional discrimination"', *The Electronic Intifada*, 22 April 2013.
67. 'Looking beyond the loyalty oath: the rising tide of Jewish nationalism and the Palestinian factor', *Muftah*, 5 November 2010.

68. 'What is behind the Israeli mistreatment of African migrants?' *New Statesman*, 28 May 2012.

69. Adalah website, www.adalah.org/eng/?mod=cat&ID=75 (last accessed 6 September 2013).

70. 'Forced displacement continues', Internal Displacement Monitoring Centre (IDMC), www.refworld.org/docid/48c7cf3c2.html (last accessed 6 September 2013).

71. www.adalah.org/newsletter/eng/jul08/3.php (last accessed 6 September 2013).

72. 'Human rights equated with national suicide', *Al Jazeera English*, 12 January 2012.

73. Abu Hussein and McKay, *Access Denied*, pp. 258–9.

74. 'Stop creating forests that are destroying Bedouin lives', *Amnesty International*, 11 April 2011.

75. Abu Hussein and McKay, *Access Denied*, p. 255; *Amnesty International*, 11 April 2011.

76. See Adalah website, www.adalah.org/eng/?mod=articles&ID=1589 (last accessed 9 August 2013).

77. 'Israel: ethnic cleansing in the Negev', *Al Jazeera English*, 22 October 2012.

78. Lustick, *Arabs in the Jewish State*, p. 51.

79. www.internal-displacement.org/idmc/website/countries.nsf/%28httpEnvelopes%29/A54D31AB54FF958FC1257677005CF147?OpenDocument (last accessed 7 September 2013).

80. The story of Kafr Bir'im and Iqrit is told in Nur Masalha's essay, 'Present absentees and indigenous resistance', in Masalha, *Catastrophe Remembered*, pp. 23–55 (36–41).

81. Abu Hussein and McKay, *Access Denied*, pp. 289–91.

82. Jeff Halper, 'The key to peace: dismantling the matrix of control', ICAHD UK website, http://uk.icahd.org/articles.asp?menu=6&submenu=3 (last accessed 7 September 2013).

83. Michael Ben-Yair, 'The war's seventh day', *Ha'aretz*, 3 March 2002.

84. Jad Isaac and Owen Powell, 'The transformation of the Palestinian environment', in Jamil Hilal (ed.), *Where Now for Palestine?* London: Zed Books, 2007, pp. 144–66 (152).

85. Quigley, *Palestine and Israel*, p. 174.

86. Eyal Weizman, *Hollow Land*, London: Verso, 2007, p. 116.

87. Amnesty International, 'Israel and the occupied territories, demolition and dispossession: the destruction of Palestinian homes', 1999.

88. Sara Roy, 'Decline and disfigurement: the Palestinian economy after Oslo', in Roane Carey (ed.), *The New Intifada*, London: Verso, 2001, pp. 91–109 (95).

89. Amnesty International, 1999.

90. Weizman, *Hollow Land*, p. 120.

91. 'Report on the situation of human rights in the Palestinian territories occupied since 1967', Mr Giorgio Giacomelli, Special Rapporteur, UN Commission on Human Rights, 56th session, 15 March 2000.

92. 'Just 0.7% of state land in the West Bank has been allocated to Palestinians, Israel admits', *Ha'aretz*, 28 March 2013, www.haaretz.com/news/diplomacy-defense/just-0-7-of-state-land-in-the-west-bank-has-been-allocated-to-palestinians-israel-admits.premium-1.512126 (last accessed 9 August 2013).

93. Amnesty International, 1999.

94. Weizman, *Hollow Land*, p. 81.

95. B'Tselem website, www.btselem.org/English/Settlements (last accessed 7 September 2013).

96. 'Population of Jewish settlements in West Bank up 15,000 in a year', *Guardian*, 26 July 2012, www.theguardian.com/world/2012/jul/26/jewish-population-west-bank-up (last accessed 9 August 2013); 'The humanitarian impact of Israeli settlement policies', OCHA, December 2012, www.ochaopt.org/documents/ocha_opt_settlements_FactSheet_December_2012_english.pdf (last accessed 9 August 2013).

97. Gershon Gorenburg, *The Accidental Empire*, New York: Henry Holt and Co., 2006, pp. 99, 101.

98. Quigley, *Palestine and Israel*, p. 174.

99. Weizman, *Hollow Land*, p. 46.

100. *Ibid.*, p. 92.

101. Marwan Bishara, *Palestine/Israel: Peace or Apartheid?*, London: Zed Books, 2004, p. 135.

102. B'Tselem, 'Forbidden roads: the discriminatory West Bank road regime', August 2004.

103. Qumsiyeh, *Sharing the Land of Canaan*, p. 136.

104. Jeff Halper, *Obstacles to Peace*, Bethlehem: PalMap of GSE, 2004, p. 14.

105. B'Tselem, 'Forbidden roads: the discriminatory West Bank road regime'.

106. 'Israel's new road plans condemned as "apartheid"', *Observer*, 5 December 2004; 'Israel plans West Bank roads just for Palestinians', Reuters, 23 February 2006.

107. 'Israel accused of "road apartheid" in West Bank', *Guardian* citing *Maariv* newspaper, 20 October 2005.

108. 'High Court closes off use of major highway to Palestinians', *Ha'aretz*, 19 March 2008.

109. 'Palestinians fear two-tier road system', *New York Times*, 28 March 2008.

110. *Ha'aretz*, 2 December 2004.

111. *Ha'aretz*, 7 March 2002.

112. 'West Bank access restrictions', OCHA, December 2012, www.ochaopt.org/documents/ocha_opt_west_bank_access_restrictions_dec_2012.pdf (last accessed 9 August 2013).

113. OCHA closure update, May 2008, http://reliefweb.int/report/occupied-palestinian-territory/opt-ocha-closure-update-may-2008 (last accessed 7 September 2013).

114. *Ha'aretz*, 8 January 2001.

115. Anne Le More, 'Are "realities on the ground" compatible with the international state-building and development agenda?' in Michael Keating, Anne Le More and Robert Lowe (eds), *Aid, Diplomacy and Facts on the Ground*, London: Royal Institute of International Affairs, 2005, pp. 27–40 (30).

116. *Ibid.*, p. 32.

117. Weizman, *Hollow Land*, p. 143; Roy, 'Decline and disfigurement: the Palestinian economy after Oslo', p. 100.

118. *Ha'aretz,* 24 September 2004.

119. IMEU Background briefing 4.13, 'What is Israel's separation wall or barrier?' http://imeu.net/news/article0080.shtml (last accessed 7 September 2013).

120. 'The Humanitarian Impact of the Barrier', OCHA, July 2013, www.ochaopt.org/documents/ocha_opt_barrier_factsheet_july_2013_english.pdf (last accessed 9 August 2013).

121. *Ibid.*

122. 'Three Years later: the humanitarian impact of the barrier since the International Court of Justice opinion', *OCHA Special Focus*, July 2007.

123. 'West Bank barrier ruling: key points', BBC news online, 9 July 2004.

124. 'Red Cross slams Israel barrier', BBC news online, 18 February 2004.

125. Amnesty International, 'Israel/OT: Israel must immediately stop the construction of wall', 7 November 2003.

126. 'One thousand, two hundred and seventy-six people per week', *Lawrence of Cyberia*, 29 September 2007, http://lawrence ofcyberia.blogs.com/news/2007/09/one-thousand-tw.html (last accessed 7 September 2013).

127. 'Shin Bet: Palestinian truce main cause for reduced terror', *Ha'aretz*, 2 January 2006.

128. 'Address by Prime Minister Ariel Sharon to the Foreign Press Corps in Israel', Israel Ministry of Foreign Affairs, 11 January 2004.

129. 'Most settlements lie east of fence, most settlers west', *Ha'aretz*, 16 August 2007.

130. 'Touring Israel's barrier with its main designer', *Washington Post*, 7 August 2007.

131. Anita Vitullo, 'The long economic shadow of the wall', in Michael Sorkin (ed.), *Against the Wall*, New York: The New Press, 2005, pp. 100–21 (109).

132. *Ibid.*, p. 112.

133. 'Letter from Jayyous', *The Nation*, 18 February 2004.

134. 'The barrier gate and permit regime four years on: humanitarian impact in the Northern West Bank', OCHA, 13 November 2007.

135. 'The Wall, 10 years on/part 5: A new way of resistance', *972*, 5 May 2012, http://972mag.com/the-wall-10-years-on-part-

5-a-new-way-of-resistance/44656/ (last accessed 7 September 2013).

136. 'Israel's plans for cutting up Jerusalem', *The Economist*, 12 April 2006.

137. 'Settlers vie for East Jerusalem', *Christian Science Monitor*, 12 December 2003.

138. Colin Chapman, *Whose Holy City?*, Oxford: Lion Hudson, 2004, p. 148.

139. *Ibid.*, p. 156.

140. B'Tselem website, www.btselem.org/english/Jerusalem/ Discriminating_Policy.asp (last accessed 7 September 2013).

141. B'Tselem website, www.btselem.org/English/Jerusalem (last accessed 7 September 2013).

142. *Ibid.*

143. Amir Cheshin, Bill Hutman and Avi Melamed, *Separate and Unequal: The Inside Story of Israeli Rule in East Jerusalem*, Cambridge, MA: Harvard University Press, 2001, p. 38.

144. 'Israel remembers war, and its spoils', *New York Times*, 1 June 1992; also see 'A policy of discrimination: land expropriation, planning and building in East Jerusalem', B'Tselem, Extracts from a summary, May 1995; 'Committee approves construction of three new Jewish neighborhoods in East Jerusalem', *Ha'aretz*, 10 May 2007; 'PMO: "nothing decided" on new E. J'lem Jewish neighborhood', *Ha'aretz*, 20 December 2007.

145. Chapman, *Whose Holy City?*, p. 156.

146. B'Tselem website, www.btselem.org/english/Jerusalem/ Revocation_Statistics.asp (last accessed 7 September 2013).

147. *The Economist*, 10 May 2007.

148. Chapman, *Whose Holy City?*, p. 162.

149. B'Tselem website, www.btselem.org/planning_and_building/ east_jerusalem_statistics (last accessed 9 August 2013).

150. Isaac and Powell, 'The transformation of the Palestinian environment', p. 149; Weizman, *Hollow Land*, p. 19.

151. *New Scientist*, 27 May 2004; Weizman, *Hollow Land*, p. 19.

152. FMEP website, www.fmep.org/settlement_info/settlement-info-and-tables/stats-data/comparison-of-water-allocation (last accessed 7 September 2013).

153. FMEP website, www.fmep.org/reports/archive/vol.-11/no.-3/ sharon-speaks (last accessed 7 September 2013).

154. Bishara, *Palestine/Israel: Peace or Apartheid?*, p. 138.

155. 'Israel rations Palestinians to trickle of water', Amnesty International, 27 October 2009, www.amnesty.org/en/ news-and-updates/report/israel-rations-palestinians-trickle-water-20091027 (last accessed 11 August 2013).

156. 'Thirsting for justice: Palestinian access to water restricted', Amnesty International, 27 October 2009, www.amnesty.org/ en/library/asset/MDE15/028/2009/en/634f6762-d603-4efb-98ba-42a02acd3f46/mde150282009en.pdf (last accessed 11 August 2013).

157. Amnesty International, 'Israel and the Occupied Territories: mass detention in cruel, inhuman and degrading conditions', 23 May 2002.

158. B'Tselem website, www.btselem.org/english/Administrative_ Detention/Occupied_Territories.asp (last accessed 7 September 2013).

159. www.ochaopt.org/annual/c1/7.html (last accessed 7 September 2013).

160. Halper, *Obstacle to Peace*, p. 13.

161. Addameer website, http://addameer.org/einside.php?id=9 (last accessed 12 August 2013). For more, see Abeer Baker and Anat Matar (eds), *Threat: Palestinian Political Prisoners in Israel*, London: Pluto Press, 2011.

162. Defence for Children International-Palestine, www. dci-palestine.org/sites/default/files/june_2013_detention_ bulletin_final_25jul2013.pdf (last accessed 12 August 2013).

163. 'Israel subjecting Palestinian children to "spiral of injustice"', *Guardian*, 26 June 2012, www.theguardian.com/world/2012/ jun/26/israel-palestinian-children-injustice (last accessed 12 August 2013); 'Palestinian children tortured, used as shields by Israel: UN', Reuters, 20 June 2013, www.reuters. com/article/2013/06/20/us-palestinian-israel-children-idUSBRE95J0FR20130620 (last accessed 11 August 2013).

164. B'Tselem website, www.btselem.org/english/Administrative_ Detention/Index.asp (last accessed 7 September 2013).

165. B'Tselem website, www.btselem.org/english/Administrative_ Detention/Israeli_Law.asp (last accessed 7 September 2013).

166. Addameer website, www.addameer.org/einside.php?id=9 (last accessed 7 September 2013).

167. B'Tselem website, www.btselem.org/English/Torture/Index. asp (last accessed 7 September 2013).

168. *Ibid*.

169. Human Rights Watch, 'Torture worldwide', 27 April 2005, www.hrw.org/legacy/english/docs/2005/04/27/china10549. htm#ISRAEL (last accessed 7 September 2013).

170. 'Absolute prohibition: the torture and ill-treatment of Palestinian detainees', May 2007, Joint report with Hamoked, Center for the Defence of the Individual, www.btselem.org/ publications/summaries/200705_utterly_forbidden (last accessed 7 September 2013).

171. Amnesty International, 1999.

172. Halper, *Obstacles to Peace*, p. 31.

173. ICAHD website, www.icahd.org/node/458 (last accessed 7 September 2013).

174. UN figures, http://unispal.un.org/unispal.nsf/85255db80 0470aa485255d8b004e349a/a18a8d06071986f385256ee7 005dbac8/$FILE/Executive_Summary.pdf (last accessed 7 September 2013).

175. David Shearer and Anuschka Meyer, 'The dilemma of aid under occupation', in Michael Keating et al. (eds), *Aid, Diplomacy and Facts on the Ground*, pp. 165–76 (174).

176. ICAHD-USA website, http://icahdusa.org/facts/faq/ (last accessed 7 September 2013).

177. 'UN: 94% of W. Bank construction denied', Associated Press, 27 May 2008.

178. B'Tselem website, www.btselem.org/planning_and_building/ statistics (last accessed 9 August 2013).

179. 'Area C of the West Bank: Key humanitarian concerns',OCHA, January 2013, www.ochaopt.org/documents/ocha_opt_ area_c_factsheet_January_2013_english.pdf (last accessed 9 August 2013).

180. Amnesty International, 'Under the rubble: house demolition and destruction of land and property', 18 May 2004.

181. Benny Morris, *Righteous Victims*, New York: Vintage Books, 2001, p. 341.

182. B'Tselem website, www.btselem.org/english/statistics/first_Intifada_Tables.asp (last accessed 7 September 2013).

183. Rosemary Radford Ruether and Herman J. Ruether, *The Wrath of Jonah*, Minneapolis, MN: Fortress Press, 2002, p. 115.

184. *Ha'aretz*, 30 June 2004; 'Diary', *London Review of Books*, 3 October 2002.

185. Derek Gregory, *The Colonial Present*, Oxford: Blackwell Publishing, 2004, p. 104.

186. Middle East Policy Council, www.mepc.org/resources/mrates.asp (last accessed 6 November 2008).

187. 'UN report details West Bank wreckage', *Guardian*, 2 August 2002.

188. See 'Jenin: IDF military operations', Human Rights Watch, 2 May 2002; 'Shielded from scrutiny: IDF violations in Jenin and Nablus', Amnesty International, 4 November 2002; Rema Hammami, 'Interregnum: Palestine after Operation Defensive Shield', *Middle East Report*, Vol. 223 (Summer 2002).

189. 'UNRWA: 45 homes razed in Rafah during Operation Rainbow', *Ha'aretz*, 26 May 2004; 'Operation Rainbow', *The Electronic Intifada*, http://electronicintifada.net/search/site/operation%20rainbow (last accessed 7 September 2013).

190. Gideon Levy, 'Killing children is no longer a big deal', *Ha'aretz*, 19 October 2004.

191. 'Palestinian death toll reaches 202 as "Operation Summer Rains" extends into its tenth week', OCHA report, 24 August 2006.

192. 'Israel's fabricated rocket crisis', *The Electronic Intifada*, 6 January 2009, http://electronicintifada.net/content/israels-fabricated-rocket-crisis/7927 (last accessed 7 September 2013).

193. 'Gaza: 1.5 million people trapped in despair', *ICRC*, 29 June 2009, www.icrc.org/eng/resources/documents/report/palestine-report-260609.htm (last accessed 7 September 2013).

194. 'Israel's targets in Gaza', *New Statesman*, 6 January 2009, www. newstatesman.com/middle-east/2009/01/israel-targets-gaza-hamas (last accessed 7 September 2013).

195. 'War crimes against children', Palestinian Centre for Human Rights, May 2009, www.pchrgaza.org/files/Reports/English/ pdf_spec/War%20Crimes%20Against%20Children%20Book. pdf (last accessed 7 September 2013).

196. 'Targeted civilians', Palestinian Centre for Human Rights, www.pchrgaza.org/files/Reports/English/pdf_spec/gaza%20 war%20report.pdf (last accessed 7 September 2013); "Operation Cast Lead': A Statistical Analysis', *Al-Haq*, August 2009, http://www.alhaq.org/attachments/article/252/gaza-operation-cast-Lead-statistical-analysis%20.pdf (last accessed 7 September 2013).

197. United Nations Office for the Coordination of Humanitarian Affairs occupied Palestinian territory (OCHA), http://unispal. un.org/UNISPAL.NSF/0/79636D6503391C25852575F400 695B31 (last accessed 7 September 2013).

198. Report of the United Nations Fact-Finding Mission on the Gaza Conflict, www2.ohchr.org/english/bodies/hrcouncil/ docs/12session/A-HRC-12-48.pdf (last accessed 7 September 2013).

199. Amnesty International country report 2010, www.amnesty. org/en/region/israel-occupied-palestinian-territories/ report-2010 (last accessed 7 September 2013).

200. 'Israel: white phosphorus use evidence of war crimes', Human Rights Watch, 25 March 2009, www.hrw.org/en/ news/2009/03/25/israel-white-phosphorus-use-evidence-war-crimes (last accessed 7 September 2013).

201. Amnesty International Annual Report 2013, www.amnesty. org/en/region/israel-and-occupied-palestinian-territories/ report-2013 (last accessed 7 September 2013); 'Palestinian families under fire in the Gaza Strip', *Al-Haq*, 22 November 2012, www.alhaq.org/documentation/weekly-focuses/642-palestinian-families-under-fire-in-the-gaza-strip- (last accessed 7 September 2013); 'Initial health assessment report: Gaza Strip', World Health Organization, December 2012,

www.emro.who.int/images/stories/palestine/documents/ WHO_Initial_Health_Assessment_Report_Gaza_Strip_-_ December_2012.pdf (last accessed 7 September 2013); Occupied Palestinian Territory: Escalation in hostilities Gaza and southern Israel, UN OCHA, 5 December 2012, www. ochaopt.org/documents/ochaopt_gaza_sitrep_05_12_2012_ english.pdf (last accessed 7 September 2013).

202. *Al-Haq*, 22 November 2012; 'Israel's shame: children, the true victims', 25 November 2012, www.independent.co.uk/ news/world/middle-east/israels-shame-children-the-true-victims-8348398.html (last accessed 7 September 2013).

203. OCHA, 5 December 2012; 'Remarks of the UN Resident and Humanitarian Coordinator in the Occupied Palestinian Territory, Mr James W. Rawley', 25 November 2012, http:// reliefweb.int/report/occupied-palestinian-territory/remarks-un-resident-and-humanitarian-coordinator-occupied (last accessed 7 September 2013).

204. Amnesty International Annual Report 2004, http://unispal. un.org/UNISPAL.NSF/0/DDBCC0A854ABDFB085256 EA000685E96 (last accessed 12 August 2013).

205. Defence for Children International-Palestine website, www. dci-palestine.org/sites/default/files/june_2013_violations_ bulletin_final_30jul2013.pdf (last accessed 12 August 2013).

206. 'CNN negates Palestinian victims and international law', *The Electronic Intifada*, 24 June 2002, http://electronicintifada.net/ content/cnn-negates-palestinian-victims-and-international-law/4031 (last accessed 9 August 2013).

207. 'Palestinian doctors despair at rising toll of children shot dead by army snipers', *Guardian*, 20 May 2004.

208. 'Israel army fails Palestinian complainants: NGO', AFP, 7 December 2011.

209. *Guardian*, 6 September 2005.

210. 'Gaza girl death officer cleared', BBC news online, 15 October 2004; 'Israeli army under fire after killing girl', *Christian Science Monitor*, 26 November 2004.

211. 'Gaza girl death officer cleared', BBC news online.

212. *Ha'aretz*, 14 December 2006.

213. Hammami, 'Interregnum: Palestine after Operation Defensive Shield', p. 223.

214. Gideon Levy, 'Mohammed al-Dura lives on', *Ha'aretz*, 7 October 2007.

215. 'Israel planned to keep Gaza's economy "on the brink of collapse," leaked cable says', *New York Times*, 'The Lede' blog, 5 January 2011, http://thelede.blogs.nytimes.com/2011/01/05/israel-planned-to-keep-gazas-economy-on-the-brink-of-collapse-leaked-cable-says/?_r=0 (last accessed 7 September 2013).

216. '"Israel aimed to keep Gaza economy on brink of collapse"', *Jerusalem Post*, 5 January 2011.

217. 'PM: Gazans can't expect normal lives while rockets hit Israel', *Ha'aretz*, 23 January 2008.

218. 'Commitments yet unfulfilled', *Gaza Gateway*, 24 June 2010, www.gazagateway.org/2010/06/commitments-yet-unfulfilled/ (last accessed 7 September 2013).

219. 'It's time to focus on Israel's separation policy, not just the siege', *Middle East Monitor*, 13 August 2012, www.middleeastmonitor.com/articles/debate/4146-its-time-to-focus-on-israels-separation-policy-not-just-the-siege (last accessed 7 September 2013).

220. 'The Gaza cheat sheet', *Gisha*, 9 July 2013, www.gisha.org/UserFiles/File/publications/Info_Gaza_Eng.pdf (last accessed 7 September 2013).

221. 'Five years of blockade: the humanitarian situation in the Gaza Strip', OCHA, June 2012, www.ochaopt.org/documents/ocha_opt_gaza_blockade_factsheet_june_2012_english.pdf (last accessed 7 September 2013).

222. *Gisha*, 9 July 2013.

223. 'The top 10 reasons why the opening of Rafah Crossing just doesn't cut it', *Gaza Gateway*, 16 June 2011, www.gazagateway.org/2011/06/the-top-10-reasons-why-the-opening-of-rafah-crossing-just-doesnt-cut-it/ (last accessed 7 September 2013).

224. OCHA, 5 September 2013, www.ochaopt.org/documents/ocha_opt_protection_of_civilians_weekly_report_2013_09_05_english.pdf (last accessed 7 September 2013).

225. OCHA, June 2012.

226. 'Is Gaza still occupied and why does it matter?' *Jadaliyya*, 5 December 2012.

227. 'Urgent appeal – children of the gravel', Defence for Children International Palestine, 17 January 2012, www.dci-palestine. org/documents/urgent-appeal-ua-410-children-gravel-0 (last accessed 7 September 2013).

228. 'What a "period of calm" looks like in the Occupied Territories', *Al Jazeera English*, 22 February 2013.

229. Tanya Reinhart, *The Road Map to Nowhere*, London: Verso, 2006, p. 157.

230. 'Address to the Knesset by Prime Minister Rabin on the Israel-Palestinian Interim Agreement', 5 October 1995, Israel Ministry of Foreign Affairs website.

231. Roy, 'Decline and disfigurement', p. 91; *ibid.*, p. 92.

232. 'Appendix II', in Keating et al., *Aid, Diplomacy and Facts on the Ground*, p. 219.

233. 'The Humanitarian Monitor', OCHA, No. 24, April 2008, www.ochaopt.org/documents/HM_Apr_2008.pdf (last accessed 8 September 2013).

234. Weizman, *Hollow Land*, p. 179.

235. Roy, 'Decline and disfigurement', p. 94.

236. Halper, *Obstacles to Peace*, p. 26.

PART III: TOWARDS INCLUSION AND PEACE –

RESISTING ISRAELI APARTHEID

1. Adalah Annual Report 2012, http://adalah.org/Public/files/ English/Publications/Annual%20Report/Annual-Report-Adalah-2012.pdf (last accessed 8 September 2013).

2. Adalah website, www.adalah.org/eng/category/95/About/1/ 0/0/ (last accessed 8 September 2013).

3. Adalah website, www.adalah.org/eng/?mod=cat&ID=16 (last accessed 8 September 2013).

4. Adalah website, adalah.org/eng/Israeli-Discriminatory-Law-Database (last accessed 8 September 2013).

5. Adalah website, adalah.org/eng/Articles/1483/The-Democratic-Constitution (last accessed 8 September 2013).

6. Nur Masalha, 'Present absentees and indigenous resistance', in Nur Masalha (ed.), *Catastrophe Remembered: Palestine, Israel and the Internal Refugees*, London: Zed Books, 2005, pp. 23–55 (42).

7. *Ibid.*, p. 43.

8. *Ibid.*, p. 42.

9. *Ibid.*, p. 45.

10. 'The Body Shop 2002 Human Rights Award focuses attention on internally displaced Palestinians', *Al-Majdal*, Winter 2002–Spring 2003, www.badil.org/it/al-majdal/item/987-the-body-shop-2002-human-rights-award-focuses-attention-on-internally-displaced-palestinians (last accessed 8 September 2013).

11. Masalha, 'Present absentees and indigenous resistance', p. 45.

12. Ben White, 'Israel's alternative independence day', *New Statesman* online, 9 May 2008, www.newstatesman.com/middle-east/2008/05/israel-palestinian-march-arab (last accessed 8 September 2013).

13. http://badil.org/en/about-badil (last accessed 8 September 2013).

14. www.ongoingnakba.org/en/ (last accessed 8 September 2013).

15. *Al-Majdal* Quarterly Magazine, http://badil.org/al-majdal/ (last accessed 8 September 2013); 'BADIL Proudly Announces the Release of its Report on Palestinian National Identity', *Jadaliyya*, 23 January 2013.

16. ICAHD website, www.icahd.org (last accessed 8 September 2013).

17. Jeff Halper, 'The key to peace: dismantling the matrix of control', http://uk.icahd.org/articles.asp?menu=6&submenu=3 (last accessed 8 September 2013).

18. American Friends Service Committee website, https://afsc.org/story/jeff-halper (last accessed 8 September 2013).

19. 'European Union drops ICAHD funding', *European Tribune*, 8 September 2008, www.eurotrib.com/?op=displaystory;sid=2008/9/8/155932/5994 (last accessed 8 September 2013).

20. 'Letter from Budrus', *The Nation*, 28 May 2004, www.thenation. com/article/letter-budrus#axzz2eHC851Pz (last accessed 8 September 2013).

21. Also see, for example, Aboud village, where the Committee was formed in 2005, www.leicester-holyland.org.uk/18th%20 %20November%202005.htm (last accessed 8 September 2013).

22. Bil'in website, www.bilin-village.org/english/discover-bilin/ (last accessed 8 September 2013).

23. See www.bilin-village.org/english/conferences (last accessed 8 September2013).

24. 'Help us stop Israel's wall peacefully', Mohammed Khatib, *International Herald Tribune*, 12 July 2005; 'Israel told to halt barrier work', BBC news online, 29 February 2004, http:// news.bbc.co.uk/2/hi/middle_east/3520115.stm (last accessed 8 September 2013); for example, 'Crackdown on non violent resistance', 17 June 2005, www.kibush.co.il/show_file. asp?num=4650 (last accessed 8 September 2013).

25. 'Defying occupier, Palestinians establish "Bab Al Shams" village on land seized for Jewish settlement', *The Electronic Intifada*, 11 January 2013.

26. 'Fighting new Nakba in the Negev', *Al Jazeera English*, 17 July 2013.

27. 'Norma Musih, Zochrot and the Nakba', *Washington Report on Middle East Affairs*, May–June 2007, www.wrmea.com/ archives/May-June_2007/0705025.html (last accessed 8 September 2013).

28. Zochrot website, www.zochrot.org/en (last accessed 8 September 2013).

29. 'Norma Musih, Zochrot and the Nakba', *Washington Report on Middle East Affairs*.

30. Jacob Pace, 'Ethnic cleansing 101: the case of Lifta Village', *The Electronic Intifada*, 2 March 2005, http://electronicintifada. net/content/ethnic-cleansing-101-case-lifta-village/5493 (last accessed 8 September 2013).

31. See, for example, 'This is Palestine: social media and Palestinian activism', Abir Kopty's blog, 7 February 2012, http://abirkopty.

wordpress.com/2012/02/07/this-is-palestine-social-media-and-palestinian-activism/ (last accessed 8 September 2013).

32. 'Palestinians forge new strategies of resistance', *Al Jazeera English*, 29 March 2012.

33. See, for example, 'Why Palestinians will protest on 15 March', *The Electronic Intifada*, 14 March 2011, http://electronicintifada.net/content/why-palestinians-will-protest-15-march/9823 (last accessed 8 September 2013).

34. 'Civic registration for direct elections to the PNC', *The Electronic Intifada*, 11 November 2011, http://electronicintifada.net/blogs/jalal-abukhater/civic-registration-direct-elections-pnc (last accessed 8 September 2013).

35. See online FAQs, http://palestiniansregister.org/?p=577 (last accessed 8 September 2013).

36. Al-Shabaka website, http://al-shabaka.org/ (last accessed 8 September 2013); Visualizing Palestine website, www.visualizingpalestine.org (last accessed 8 September 2013).

37. For a decent overview, see BADIL's *Al-Majdal*, No. 38 (Summer 2008).

38. The Boycott Divestment Sanctions website is a great resource: http://bdsmovement.net (last accessed 8 September 2013).

39. 'Palestinian civil society call for BDS', 9 July 2005, www.bdsmovement.net/call (last accessed 8 September 2013).

40. See, for example, 'BDS victories', www.bdsmovement.net/victories (last accessed 8 September 2013).

41. See www.bdsmovement.net/BNC (last accessed 8 September 2013).

42. 'Beyond Brooklyn College: how and why Israel advocates are fighting BDS', *Middle East Monitor*,7 February 2013, www.middleeastmonitor.com/articles/debate/5180-beyond-brooklyn-college-how-and-why-israel-advocates-are-fighting-bds (last accessed 8 September 2013).

43. Mada al-Carmel, 'The Haifa Declaration, 2007', http://mada-research.org/en/files/2007/09/haifaenglish.pdf (last accessed 8 September 2013).

44. 'On questioning the Jewish State', *New York Times*, 9 March 2013, http://opinionator.blogs.nytimes.com/2013/03/09/

on-questioning-the-jewish-state/?_r=0 (last accessed 8 September 2013); 'Israel needs a new map', *Los Angeles Times*, 21 March 2013, http://articles.latimes.com/2013/mar/21/opinion/la-oe-lustick-zionism-obama-israel-20130321 (last accessed 8 September 2013); 'Rethinking Israel-Palestine: beyond Bantustans, beyond Reservations', *The Nation*, 21 March 2013, www.thenation.com/article/173466/rethinking-israel-palestine-beyond-bantustans-beyond-reservations#axzz2eHC851Pz (last accessed 8 September 2013).

FREQUENTLY ASKED QUESTIONS

1. 'Eggs fail to recognize omelette's right to exist', *Lawrence of Cyberia*, 6 March 2007, http://lawrenceofcyberia.blogs.com/news/2007/03/eggs_fail_to_re.html (last accessed 8 September 2013).
2. *New York Review of Books*, Vol. 50, No. 19 (4 December 2003).
3. Sharif Elmusa, 'Searching for a solution', in Jamil Hilal (ed.), *Where Now for Palestine?* London: Zed Books, 2007, pp. 211–32 (223).
4. 'Memories of a promised land', *New Humanist*, Vol. 123, Issue 3 (May/June 2008).
5. 'The end of Zionism', *Guardian*, 15 September 2003.
6. *Ha'aretz*, 10 November 2005.
7. *Ha'aretz*, 6 September 2005.
8. 'Prime Minister Ariel Sharon's speech at the Knesset', 22 April 2004, http://mfa.gov.il/MFA/PressRoom/2004/Pages/PM%20Sharon%20Knesset%20speech%2022-Apr-20-4.aspx (last accessed 8 September 2013).
9. 'Israel will strengthen strategic bases after Gaza pullout: PM', AFP, 16 June 2005.
10. 'Prime Minister Ariel Sharon's speech at the Jewish Agency Assembly', 28 June 2005, www.jewishfederations.org/page.aspx?id=110030 (last accessed 8 September 2013).
11. B'Tselem website, www.btselem.org/english/Gaza_Strip/Israels_obligations.asp (last accessed 8 September 2013).

12. B'Tselem website, www.btselem.org/english/Gaza_Strip/ Gaza_Status.asp (last accessed 8 September 2013).

13. 'Israeli-Palestinian fatalities since 2000', *OCHA Special Focus*, 31 August 2007.

14. 'Almost half the fatalities in the Gaza Strip in July were civilians not taking part in the hostilities', B'Tselem, 3 August 2006.

15. Khaled Hroub, *Hamas: A Beginner's Guide*, London: Pluto Press, 2006, pp. 20–1.

16. *Ha'aretz*, 15 August 2003.

17. *Ibid.*

18. Dr Philip Mendes, 'The forgotten refugees: the causes of the post-1948 Jewish exodus from Arab countries', Australian Association of Jewish Studies 14th Annual Conference, March 2002.

19. *The Magnes Zionist*, 6 November 2007, http://themagneszionist. blogspot.com/2007/11/forgotten-refugees-jewish-refugees-from.html (last accessed 8 September 2013).

20. *Ha'aretz*, 15 August 2003.

21. 'House equates Jewish, Palestinian refugees', *The Jewish Week*, 2 April 2008.

22. *The Economist*, 10 April 2008.

23. Tom Segev, *One Palestine, Complete*, London: Abacus, 2002, p. 403.

24. Nur Masalha, *Expulsion of the Palestinians*, Washington, DC: The Institute for Palestine Studies, 2001, p. 107.

25. Benny Morris, *Righteous Victims*, New York: Vintage Books, 2001, p. 37.

26. Charles D. Smith, *Palestine and the Arab-Israeli Conflict*, Boston, MA: Bedford/St Martin's, 2004, pp. 498–500.

27. *Ibid.*, p. 494.

Select Bibliography

Abu Hussein, Hussein and Fiona McKay (2003) *Access Denied* (London: Zed Books).

Abunimah, Ali (2006) *One Country* (New York: Henry Holt).

Adalah (2003) UN CESCR Information Sheet No. 3: *Land and Housing Rights – Palestinian Citizens of Israel*.

—— (2010a) 'New discriminatory laws and bills in Israel'.

—— (2011) 'The Inequality Report: the Palestinian Arab minority in Israel'.

Amnesty International (1999) 'Israel and the Occupied Territories, demolition and dispossession: the destruction of Palestinian homes'.

—— (2001) 'Racism and the administration of justice'.

—— (2002a) 'Israel and the Occupied Territories: mass detention in cruel, inhuman and degrading conditions'.

—— (2002b) 'Shielded from scrutiny: IDF violations in Jenin and Nablus'.

—— (2003) 'Israel/OT: Israel must immediately stop the construction of wall'.

—— (2004a) 'Under the rubble: house demolition and destruction of land and property'.

—— (2004b) 'Israel/Occupied Territories: killing of children must be investigated'.

Baroud, Ramzy (2006) *The Second Palestinian Intifada* (London: Pluto Press).

Benvenisti, Meron (2002) *Sacred Landscape* (Berkeley, CA: University of California Press).

Bishara, Marwan (2004) *Palestine/Israel: Peace or Apartheid?* (London: Zed Books).

B'Tselem and Hamoked (2007) 'Absolute prohibition: the torture and ill-treatment of Palestinian detainees'.

Bremner, Lindsay (2005) 'Border/Skin', in Michael Sorkin (ed.), *Against the Wall* (New York: The New Press) pp. 122–37.

Chapman, Colin (2004) *Whose Holy City?* (Oxford: Lion Hudson).

Cheshin, Amir, Bill Hutman and Avi Melamed (2001) *Separate and Unequal: The Inside Story of Israeli Rule in East Jerusalem* (Cambridge, MA: Harvard University Press).

Christison, Kathleen (2001) *Perceptions of Palestine* (Berkeley, CA: University of California Press).

Cook, Jonathan (2006) *Blood and Religion* (London: Pluto Books).

Davis, Uri (2003) *Apartheid Israel* (London: Zed Books).

Elmusa, Sharif (2007) 'Searching for a solution', in Jamil Hilal (ed.), *Where Now for Palestine?* (London: Zed Books) pp. 211–32.

Farsoun, Samih K. and Naseer H. Aruri (2006) *Palestine and the Palestinians* (Boulder, CO: Westview Press).

Finkelstein, Norman G. (1995) *Image and Reality of the Israel-Palestine Conflict* (London: Verso).

Friedman, Isaiah (1992) *The Question of Palestine: British-Jewish-Arab Relations, 1914–1918* (London: Transaction Publishers).

Glaser, Daryl (2003) 'Zionism and apartheid: a moral comparison', *Ethnic and Racial Studies*, Vol. 26, Issue 3, pp. 403–21.

Gorenburg, Gershon (2006) *The Accidental Empire* (New York: Times Books/Henry Holt and Co.).

Gregory, Derek (2004) *The Colonial Present* (Malden, MA: Blackwell Publishing).

Halper, Jeff (2004) *Obstacles to Peace* (Bethlehem: PalMap of GSE).

Hammami, Rema (2002) 'Interregnum: Palestine after Operation Defensive Shield', *Middle East Report*, No. 223, pp. 18–27.

Hertzberg, Arthur (ed.) (1997) *The Zionist Idea* (Philadelphia, PA: The Jewish Publication Society).

Hirst, David (2002) *The Gun and the Olive Branch* (London: Faber and Faber).

Hroub, Khaled (2006) *Hamas: A Beginner's Guide* (London: Pluto Press).

Human Rights Watch (2002) 'Jenin: IDF military operations'.

—— (2004) 'Razing Rafah: mass home demolitions in the Gaza Strip'.

—— (2005) 'Torture worldwide'.

—— (2008) 'Off the map'.

Hunter, Jane (1987) *Israeli Foreign Policy: South Africa and Central America* (Boston, MA: South End Press).

Isaac, Jad and Owen Powell (2007) 'The transformation of the Palestinian environment', in Jamil Hilal (ed.), *Where Now for Palestine?* (London: Zed Books) pp. 144–66.

Joseph, Benjamin M. (1988) 'Separatism at the wrong time in history', in Roselle Tekiner, Samir Abed-Rabbo and Norton Mezvinsky (eds), *Anti-Zionism: Analytical Reflections* (Brattleboro, VT: Amana Books) pp. 136–52.

Khalidi, Rashid (2007) 'The Palestinians and 1948: the underlying causes of failure', in Eugene L. Rogan and Avi Shlaim (eds), *The War for Palestine* (Cambridge: Cambridge University Press) pp. 12–36.

Khalidi, Walid (2007) 'Revisiting the UNGA Partition Resolution', in Ilan Pappe (ed.), *The Israel/Palestine Question: A Reader* (Abingdon: Routledge) pp. 97–114.

Kovel, Joel (2007) *Overcoming Zionism* (London: Pluto Press).

Kimmerling, Baruch (2006) *Politicide* (London: Verso).

La Guardia, Anton (2002) *Holy Land Unholy War* (London: John Murray Publishers).

Le More, Anne (2005) 'Are "realities on the ground" compatible with the international state-building and development agenda?' in Michael Keating, Anne Le More and Robert Lowe (eds), *Aid, Diplomacy and Facts on the Ground* (London: Royal Institute of International Affairs) pp. 27–40.

Lentin, Ronit (ed.) (2008) *Thinking Palestine* (London: Zed Books).

Lustick, Ian (1980) *Arabs in the Jewish State* (Austin, TX: University of Texas Press).

Makdisi, Saree (2008) *Palestine Inside Out: An Everyday Occupation* (New York: W.W. Norton).

Masalha, Nur (2001a) *Expulsion of the Palestinians* (Washington, DC: Institute for Palestine Studies).

—— (2001b) 'The historical roots of the Palestinian refugee question', in Naseer Aruri (ed.), *Palestinian Refugees: The Right of Return* (London: Pluto Press) pp. 36–67.

—— (ed.) (2005) *Catastrophe Remembered: Palestine, Israel and the Internal Refugees* (London: Zed Books).

—— (2007) *The Bible and Zionism* (London: Zed Books).

Massad, Joseph A. (2006) *The Persistence of the Palestinian Question* (Oxon: Routledge) pp. 154–65.

McCarthy, Justin (1990) *The Population of Palestine: Population History and Statistics of the Late Ottoman Period and the Mandate* (New York: Columbia University Press).

Morris, Benny (1993) *Israel's Border Wars, 1949–1956: Arab Infiltration, Israeli Retaliation, and the Countdown to the Suez War* (Oxford: Oxford University Press).

—— (2001) *Righteous Victims* (New York: Vintage Books).

—— (2004) *The Birth of the Palestinian Refugee Problem Revisited* (Cambridge: Cambridge University Press).

—— (2007) 'Revisiting the Palestinian exodus of 1948', in Eugene L. Rogan and Avi Shlaim (eds), *The War for Palestine* (Cambridge: Cambridge University Press) pp. 37–59.

Nathan, Susan (2005) *The Other Side of Israel* (London: HarperCollins).

Nazzal, Nafez (1974) 'The Zionist Occupation of Western Galilee, 1948', *Journal of Palestine Studies*, Vol. 3, No. 3, pp. 58–76.

Neslen, Arthur (2006) *Occupied Minds* (London: Pluto Press).

Pappe, Ilan (2007) *The Ethnic Cleansing of Palestine* (Oxford: Oneworld Publications).

—— (2011) *The Forgotten Palestinians: A History of the Palestinians in Israel* (New Haven, CT: Yale University Press).

Peretz, Don (1958) *Israel and the Palestine Arabs* (Washington, DC: The Middle East Institute).

Peters, Joel (1992) *Israel and Africa: The Problematic Friendship* (London: British Academic Press).

Piterberg, Gabriel (2008) *The Returns of Zionism: Myths, Politics and Scholarship in Israel* (London: Verso).

Quigley, John (1990) *Palestine and Israel: A Challenge to Justice* (Durham, NC: Duke University Press).

—— (2005) *The Case for Palestine: An International Law Perspective* (Durham, NC: Duke University Press).

Qumsiyeh, Mazin B. (2004) *Sharing the Land of Canaan* (London: Pluto Books).

Rabkin, Yakov M. (2006) *A Threat From Within: A Century of Jewish Opposition to Zionism* (London: Zed Books).

Reinhart, Tanya (2006) *The Road Map to Nowhere* (London: Verso).

Rodinson, Maxime (2001) *Israel: A Colonial-Settler State?* (New York: Pathfinder Press).

Rose, N.A. (1973) *The Gentile Zionists: A Study in Anglo-Zionist Diplomacy, 1929–1939* (London: Routledge).

Roy, Sara (2001) 'Decline and disfigurement: the Palestinian economy after Oslo', in Roane Carey (ed.), *The New Intifada* (London: Verso) pp. 91–109.

Ruether, Rosemary Radford and Herman J. Ruether (2002) *The Wrath of Jonah* (Minneapolis, MN: Fortress Press).

Said, Edward W. (2000) *The End of the Peace Process* (London: Granta Books).

Sayigh, Rosemary (2007) *The Palestinians: From Peasants to Revolutionaries* (London: Zed Books).

Segev, Tom (1998) *1949: The First Israelis* (New York: Henry Holt and Company).

—— (2002) *One Palestine, Complete* (London: Abacus).

—— (2007) *1967: Israel, the War, and the Year that Transformed the Middle East* (London: Little, Brown).

Shafir, Gershon (2007) 'Zionism and colonialism', in Ilan Pappe (ed.), *The Israel/Palestine Question: A Reader* (Abingdon: Routledge) pp. 78–93.

Shearer, David and Anuschka Meyer (2005) 'The dilemma of aid under occupation', in Michael Keating, Anne Le More and Robert Lowe (eds), *Aid, Diplomacy and Facts on the Ground* (London: Royal Institute of International Affairs) pp. 165–76.

Shlaim, Avi (2000) *The Iron Wall* (New York: W.W. Norton).

—— (2007) 'The debate about 1948', in Ilan Pappe (ed.), *The Israel/Palestine Question: A Reader* (Abingdon: Routledge) pp. 139–60.

Smith, Charles D. (2004) *Palestine and the Arab-Israeli Conflict*, Fifth edn (Boston, MA: Bedford/St Martin's).

Stevens, Richard P. (1973) 'Smuts and Weizmann', *Journal of Palestine Studies*, Vol. 3, No. 1, pp. 35–59.

Sufian, Sandy and Mark LeVine (eds) (2007) *Reapproaching Borders: New Perspectives on the Study of Israel-Palestine* (Lanham, MD: Rowman & Littlefield Publishers Inc.).

Tekiner, Roselle (1988) 'The "Who is a Jew?" controversy in Israel: a product of political Zionism', in Roselle Tekiner, Samir Abed-Rabbo and Norton Mezvinsky (eds), *Anti-Zionism: Analytical Reflections* (Brattleboro, VT: Amana Books) pp. 62–89.

Thomas, Baylis (1999) *How Israel was Won: A Concise History of the Arab-Israeli Conflict* (Lanham, MD: Lexington Books).

Tilley, Virginia (2005) *The One-State Solution* (Michigan, MI: University of Michigan Press).

Tutu, Desmond (1984) *Hope and Suffering* (London: Fount Paperbacks).

Veracini, Lorenzo (2006) *Israel and Settler Society* (London: Pluto Press).

Vitullo, Anita (2005) 'The long economic shadow of the wall', in Michael Sorkin (ed.), *Against the Wall* (New York: The New Press) pp. 100–21.

Weizman, Eyal (2007) *Hollow Land* (London: Verso).

White, Ben (2012) *Palestinians in Israel: Segregation, Discrimination and Democracy* (London: Pluto Press).

Will, Donald and Sheila Ryan (1990) *Israel and South Africa* (Trenton, NJ: Africa World Press).

Yiftachel, Oren (2002) 'The shrinking space of citizenship: ethnocratic politics in Israel', *Middle East Report*, No. 223, pp. 38–45.

Younis, Mona (2000) *Liberation and Democratization* (Minneapolis, MN: Minnesota University Press).

Zureik, Elia (1979) *The Palestinians in Israel: A Study in Internal Colonialism* (London: Routledge and Kegan Paul).

Index